THE CBC GUIDE TO THE SUMMER OLYMPICS*

Published by CBC Enterprises/Les Entreprises Radio-Canada, a division of the
Canadian Broadcasting Corporation, P.O. Box 500, Station A, Toronto (Ontario),
Canada M5W 1E6.

Publié par CBC Enterprises/Les Entreprises Radio-Canada, une division de la
Société Radio-Canada, C.P. 500, Succursale «A», Toronto (Ontario), Canada M5W 1E6.

This project was created and produced for CBC by Clarke MCC Inc. who retain all
rights and responsibility for content.

Although every reasonable effort has been made to ensure the information herein
is as accurate as possible and as complete as the limited space allows, and to ensure
permissions for all material were obtained, apology is made for any inadvertent
errors or omissions.

Canadian Cataloguing in Publication Data

Golla, Jim, 1932–
The CBC guide to the 1984 Summer Olympics

ISBN 0-88794-138-9

1. Olympic Games (23rd: 1984: Los Angeles, Calif.).   2. Sports – Rules. I. CBC
Enterprises. II. Title

GV722 1984. G64 1984   796.4'8   C84-098513-4

General Manager/Directeur général: Guy R. Mazzeo
Publisher/Éditeur: Glenn Edward Witmer
Managing Editor/Direction de la rédaction: Robert Daley
Editor/Révision: Geri Savits-Fine
Production Supervisor/Chef de fabrication: Gaynor Fitzpatrick
Designer/Conception graphique: Ron Richards
Typesetter/Composition: Gandalf Typographers Inc.
Printer/Impression: The Bryant Press Limited

Printed and bound in Canada

ACKNOWLEDGEMENTS

Clarke MCC Inc. and CBC Enterprises/Les Entreprises Radio-Canada, publisher of The CBC Guide To The Summer Olympics, wish to express appreciation to the following organizations and individuals for their respective contributions to the production of this reference book. Readers particularly enjoying or identifying with one or more sports who wish to learn how they can assist the athletes involved or to obtain further information can write to the representative organization(s).

Federation of Canadian Archers, Inc.
333 River Road, Vanier, Ontario K1L 8H9

Canadian Federation of Amateur Baseball
333 River Road, Vanier, Ontario K1L 8H9

Basketball Canada
333 River Road, Vanier, Ontario K1L 8H9

Canadian Amateur Boxing Association
333 River Road, Vanier, Ontario K1L 8H9

Canadian Canoe Association
333 River Road, Vanier, Ontario K1L 8H9

Canadian Cycling Association
333 River Road, Vanier, Ontario K1L 8H9

Canadian Amateur Diving Association
333 River Road, Vanier, Ontario K1L 8H9

Canadian Equestrian Federation
333 River Road, Vanier, Ontario K1L 8H9

Canadian Fencing Association
333 River Road, Vanier, Ontario K1L 8H9

Canadian Field Hockey Council
333 River Road, Vanier, Ontario K1L 8H9

Canadian Gymnastics Federation
333 River Road, Vanier, Ontario K1L 8H9

Canadian Rhythmic Sportive Gymnastics Federation
333 River Road, Vanier, Ontario K1L 8H9

Canadian Team Handball Federation
333 River Road, Vanier, Ontario K1L 8H9

Judo Canada
333 River Road, Vanier, Ontario K1L 8H9

Canadian Modern Pentathlon Association
25 Cr. Chevrier (Duvernay), Ville de Laval,
Quebec, H7E 3Z7

Canadian Amateur Rowing Association
333 River Road, Vanier, Ontario K1L 8H9

Shooting Federation of Canada
333 River Road, Vanier, Ontario K1L 8H9

Canadian Soccer Association
333 River Road, Vanier, Ontario K1L 8H9

Canadian Amateur Swimming Association
333 River Road, Vanier, Ontario K1L 8H9

Canadian Amateur Synchronized Swimming Association
333 River Road, Vanier, Ontario K1L 8H9

Tennis Canada
25 Imperial Street, Toronto, Ontario M5P 1B9

Ontario Track and Field Association
1220 Sheppard Avenue East, Willowdale, Ontario M2K 2X1

Canadian Volleyball Association
333 River Road, Vanier, Ontario K1L 8H9

Canadian Water Polo Association
333 River Road, Vanier, Ontario K1L 8H9

Canadian Weightlifting Federation
333 River Road, Vanier, Ontario K1L 8H9

Canadian Amateur Wrestling Association
333 River Road, Vanier, Ontario K1L 8H9

Canadian Yachting Association
333 River Road, Vanier, Ontario K1L 8H9

Athlete Information Bureau
333 River Road, Vanier, Ontario K1L 8H9
(for multi-sport photos)

National Sport and Recreation Centre
333 River Road, Vanier, Ontario K1L 8H9
(for logistical assistance)

Claus Andersen Photography Ltd.
425 First Street, Ste. G., London, Ontario N5W 5K5
(for track and field photos)

Pam Gollish, Tennis Canada
25 Imperial Street, Toronto, Ontario M5P 1B9
(for Carling Bassett tennis photo)

Ontario Team Handball Federation
1220 Sheppard Avenue East, Willowdale, Ontario M2K 2X1
(for team handball photos)

Royal Studios
Regina, Saskatchewan
(for synchronized swimming photo)

PAST OLYMPIADS

CONTENTS

GAMES HISTORY

ST. LOUIS — 1904, LOS ANGELES — 1932, 1984

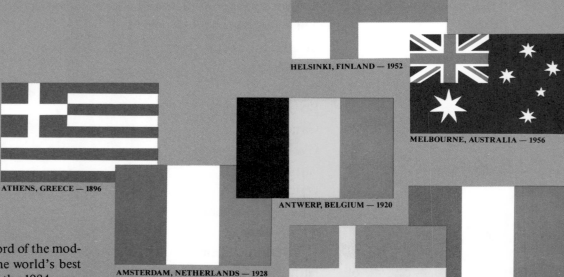

HELSINKI, FINLAND — 1952

MELBOURNE, AUSTRALIA — 1956

ATHENS, GREECE — 1896

ANTWERP, BELGIUM — 1920

AMSTERDAM, NETHERLANDS — 1928

ROME, ITALY — 1960

STOCKHOLM, SWEDEN — 1912

LONDON, ENGLAND — 1908, 1948

TOKYO, JAPAN — 1964

GAMES CANCELLED — 1916, 1940, 1944

MEXICO CITY, MEXICO — 1968

Boycott has become a byword of the modern Olympic Games. As the world's best athletes were preparing for the 1984 competitions, Iran became the first country to declare a Los Angeles Games boycott. The Iranian Prime Minister, Hussein Musavi, said the United States was not qualified to play host to the Games because it had committed "crimes upon the masses" in the Middle East, Latin America, Lebanon, El Salvador, Nicaragua and Grenada. This pronouncement comes at a time when the memory of the 1980 boycott is still fresh in the minds of the world's sports fans.

The 1980 Games were awarded to the city of Moscow, the crown jewel of the Soviet Union. Since entering the Olympic Games in 1952, the Soviets had steadily honed their athletic skills and had become one of the world's top sports powers. They were anxious to showcase their athletic prowess in front of their countrymen in the 100,000-seat Lenin Stadium. But in 1979, the Soviet army invaded Afghanistan. The reaction from many international sport organizations was one of boycott.

The United States said it would pass up the Games in Moscow. Canada and some 45 other nations, including Iran, also declared themselves out. Yet, the 1980 Games went on even though stripped of some of the world's top competitors from the countries outside the Iron Curtain bloc.

The boycott tactic had been used before. In the 1976 Games in Montreal, some two dozen Third World countries did not participate in order to protest the presence of New Zealand. The African nations in particular were angry at New Zealand for having played a soccer exhibition against South Africa. The countries supporting the Montreal boycott felt it was not right for New Zealand to have sports relations with apartheid practising South Africa.

The word boycott, or even the possibility of it, probably never entered the mind of Baron de Coubertin back in 1892 when the Frenchman started to preach the modern revival of the ancient Olympic Games. The Baron was a good salesman, and by 1893, had gained the support of 34 countries. He suggested that the first modern Games be held in France. Sentimentalists among that first organizing committee, however, could not turn down a Greek request for Athens to hold the first Games in 1896. After all, the last of the ancient

Games in Greece ended in 393 A.D.

Plagued by transportation and communication problems, the 1896 Games opened in Athens. Missing were representatives of 21 nations. Many of the countries stated that transportation costs were too expensive while others said they were uncertain of schedules.

The Greeks loved the Games. They were especially thrilled when one of their own, a shepherd named Spyridon Louis, won the marathon long-distance run. The Games were deemed a success and the sports world looked forward to the 1900 Games in Paris.

The Paris Games had to battle the World Exhibition for attention, and the Olympic officials came away satisfied that their production was not second-rate. A few world records helped to attract attention to the Games and its future success appeared guaranteed.

After the 1904 Games in St. Louis and the 1906 version in Athens (to mark the 10th anniversary of the rebirth of the Games), the Games went to London (1908) and to Stockholm (1912). Athletic performances were getting better and an increasing number of sports fans around the world believed the Olympics had truly become a world event.

MONTREAL, CANADA — 1976

BERLIN, MUNICH — 1936, 1972

PARIS, FRANCE — 1900, 1924

MOSCOW, RUSSIA — 1980

World War One forced the cancellation of the 1916 Games awarded to Berlin. A couple of years after hostility ended, the Olympic Games were back, bigger and better than ever in 1920 in Antwerp, Belgium. When the 1924 Paris Games began, more than 3,000 competitors representing 44 nations took part.

The Germans, who had prudently stayed out of the Games, were back in the Olympic programme in 1928 at Amsterdam and in 1932 the Olympic Games were presented in Los Angeles for the first time. Again the performances of the athletes were greatly upgraded and the Games' future looked bright.

But Olympians found themselves in a new situation in the 1936 Berlin Games. The Nazi government attempted to use the Games as a promotional vehicle to glorify their ideals. Several countries, including the United States, talked of boycott but relented. The black American, Jesse Owens, dominated the sprint events much to the chagrin of the Nazi officials.

World War Two forced cancellation of the 1940 and 1944 Games scheduled for Tokyo, yet the Olympic movement lived on. In 1948, Great Britain held the Games when the financial burden proved too much for Helsinki. Finland was trying to recover from the effect of the war.

The 1948 Games in London attracted more than 4,000 athletes from 59 countries. And once again, the athletes ran faster, jumped higher and showed greater strength than ever before. The Games sparked the imagination of a war-weary world.

The success of the Olympics continued through Helsinki (1952) and in Melbourne (1956). In Helsinki, the Soviet Union indicated it was determined to be a world power in athletics. The Soviet team picked up 71 medals, topped only by the United States, which earned 76. At Melbourne, the Soviets topped the medal list with 98, the United States earning 74.

When the Olympians showed up in Rome in 1960, the team concept was once again being emphasized. The Soviets finished on top earning 103 medals, including 43 golds. The United States was second with 71 medals, 34 of them golds.

In the 1964 Games in Tokyo, the United States regained its team supremacy. The Americans led with 36 golds out of 90 medals. The Soviets had more medals, 96, with 31 of them golds. The United States was determined to remain No. 1 in world athletics.

The Americans stepped up their programme and became a powerhouse when the 1968 Games were held in Mexico City. They earned a whopping 107 medals, including 45 gold. The Soviets were second with 91 and only 29 gold medals. Boycott had been talked about before the Games. Some 40 black nations did not want South Africa competing in the Olympics. The IOC barred South Africa and the Games went on.

By the time the 1972 Games in Munich rolled around, a scientific approach to training was in vogue. Athletes were getting bigger and stronger. The Soviets topped the team list with 99 medals, with more than half (50) being gold. The United States had 94, including 31 golds.

Seven of the U.S. gold medals were won by swimmer Mark Spitz who put on a devastating display in the pool. Only 11 hours after he won his seventh medal, tragedy struck the Olympics. A terrorist group from the Palestine Liberation Organization (PLO) massacred 11 members of the Israeli team. It was the blackest hour in Olympic history.

By 1976 the high cost of staging the Olympic Games was a major topic. The overrun costs at Montreal were staggering and are still being paid for through lotteries. The Olympic Stadium became known as the Big Owe and plans to cover it remain doubtful to this day. The cost factor became secondary news in the media after the Third World countries instituted their boycott.

THE LOS ANGELES OLYMPICS

After 52 years, the Summer Olympics return to Los Angeles in 1984 on a historic note. For the first time, a host city is not responsible for Olympic-related costs. They will be paid from the Olympic Trust Fund which was established to bring the Games to Los Angeles.

The International Olympic Committee was at first reluctant to accept the idea of a private organizing committee guaranteeing the finances. The IOC initially balked because it was unsure of the ability of the private group to stage the Games. Ultimately, the IOC relented and the rule that requires a host city to be responsible for financing and organizing the Olympics was declared not applicable to Los Angeles.

The revenues for organizing and administering the Games come from three primary sources: the sale of television rights (about $283 million), tickets (about $92 million) and a limit of 35 corporate sponsors. The sponsors agreed to support the Games by providing money, material goods and services as needed. McDonald's, for instance, built the new swimming and diving facilities, and the Southland Corporation constructed the new velodrome for cycling.

The Los Angeles Olympic Organization Committee estimated an operating budget of between $450 and $500 million and plans to realize a surplus from what is expected to be the biggest of all Olympic Games. They expect about 10,000 athletes, 4,000 officials and 8,000 media.

Yet, the amount of people involved, including spectators, will only be a small percentage of those touched by the Olympics. It is estimated that 2.3 billion people, about half the world's population, will see the Games on television. In addition, there will be written reports on the 16 days of competition filed by newsmen from 150 nations.

The excitement, glamour and timeliness of the Olympics is best captured on television. The American Broadcasting Corporation paid a record $225 million for the American rights, easily topping the previous record high of $85 million anted by the National Broadcasting Company for U.S. rights at the 1980 Games in Moscow. ABC plans an unprecedented 207 hours of coverage, most of it live, for the United States. The European audiences will have a staggering 450 hours of coverage.

The Canadian Broadcasting Corporation, which paid $3 million for Canadian television rights, also plans extensive coverage in both English and French.

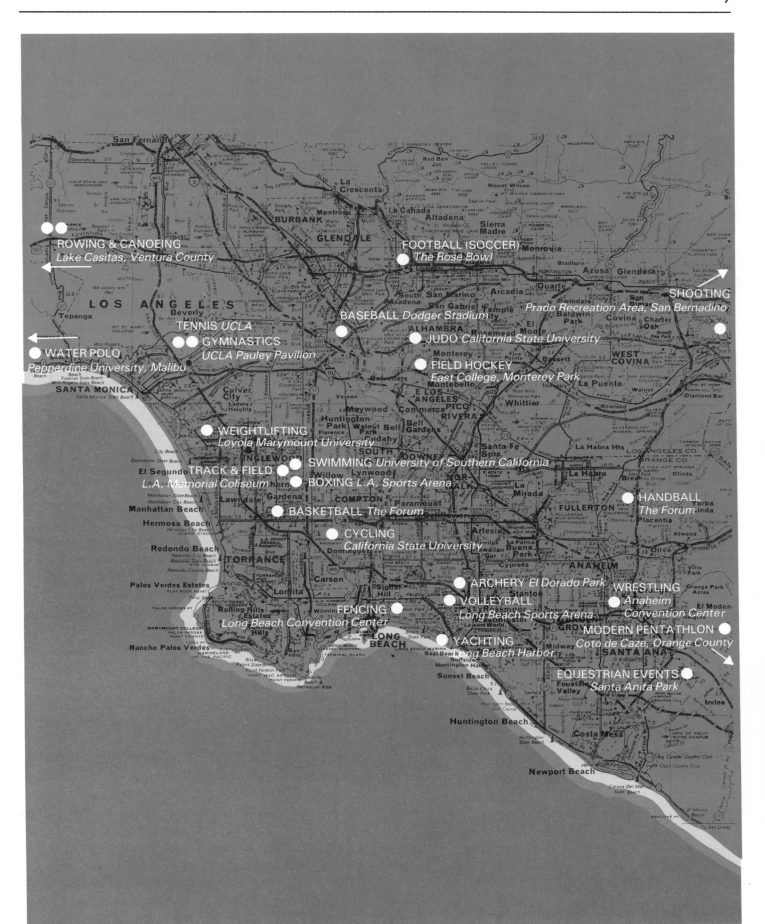

Some 220 reporters, analysts and technicians will be in Los Angeles complete with their own electronic news gathering units to highlight the performances of the athletes. In total, CBC is scheduling more than 180 hours of coverage — 12 hours a day with live prime-time coverage of many of the major events.

If an operating budget of close to $500 million seems overwhelming, the Games organizers point out the tremendous economic benefits generated by the Games. About $3.3 billion in benefits will come from the Games, according to a study by an independent Los Angeles-based research and consulting firm. The report says the Games will create tens of thousands of jobs.

The $3.3-billion figure reflects two levels of expenditure in constant 1982 dollars: primary expenditures and induced spending. Primary impact refers to first-round spending associated with the Games; induced impact — also called the multiplier effect — results from subsequent respending of the primary impact income.

Total primary economic impact is estimated at $945 million with payroll earnings of $425 million for 22,700-person work years. Induced economic impact is projected at $2.37 billion with payroll earnings of $1.2 billion for 79,870-person work years. The report estimates that other positive benefits from staging the Games will be $231 million in taxes to the federal government; $179 million in state and local taxes along with a host of new facilities and $10 million in improvements for the Coliseum where track and field events will be held along with opening and closing ceremonies. Incidentally, tickets for the opening and closing ceremonies range up to $200.

Aside from the approximately 22,000 athletes, officials and media people at the Games, the report estimates that some 625,000 visitors will spend at least five days each in Los Angeles for the Games. Visitors and residents will spend an estimated $455 million on commercial accommodations, food and beverage, transportation and parking, souvenirs, tickets and miscellaneous items.

The vast number of athletes and officials will be housed in two villages, one on the campus of the University of California at Los Angeles (UCLA) and the other at the University of Southern California (USC). In addition, the rowing and canoeing contestants will be housed at the University of California, Santa Barbara, close to their Lake Casitas competition sites. The Los Angeles Olympic Organizing

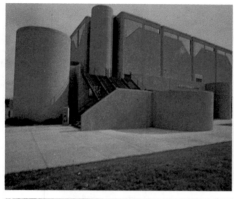  

Committee points out that the Olympic Village concept was introduced at Los Angeles back in 1932.

With such a large number of athletes, security has been given a high priority by Games organizers. The memory of the slaughter of 11 members of the Israeli team by a Palestinian Liberation Organization assassination squad which infiltrated security measures at the 1972 Olympic Games in Munich is still fresh. Los Angeles officials are utilizing a plan integrating federal, state and local police agencies.

Along with facing tight security measures, the athletes are once again facing drug controls. The laboratory facility at the University of California at Los Angeles is one of the few of its kind in the world. Others are in Montreal, Cologne, West Germany, London, Leningrad and Moscow in the Soviet Union and Kreische in East Germany. Drug controls were first introduced in the 1968 Winter Olympic Games in Grenoble, France. Femininity controls (checks for the presence of male hormones in women) were also introduced at Grenoble.

A total of 1,667 athletes underwent drug tests in the 1980 Games in Moscow, with no disqualifications. At Montreal in 1976, eight persons were disqualified after 2,001 athletes were tested. There were seven disqualifications in Munich in 1972 after 2,078 athletes were tested.

The Los Angeles Games will also reflect the changes and advances women have made in the world of sport. Altogether, women will compete in 15 sports and 75 events. New Olympic events for women are the individual road race for cyclists; the air rifle, standard rifle and pistol match in shooting; the 200-metre medley and synchronized duet in swimming, the marathon, 3,000-metre race, the 400-metre hurdles and the heptathlon (changed from pentathlon) in track and field; the kayak fours (500 metres) in canoeing; and sportive rhythmic gymnastics.

When Los Angeles held its first Olympic Games in 1932, a total of 127 women competed in three sports totalling 14 events. The participation of women has grown steadily, reaching a high of 1,251 competitors at the 1976 Games in Montreal. The number fell to 1,088 women at Moscow in 1980, the decline attributed to the fact that many countries, including Canada and the United States, boycotted the Moscow Games because of the Soviet Union invasion of Afghanistan.

A new event at Los Angeles, boardsailing, will provide mixed competition. Other events added to the Games programme for men are the superheavyweight category in boxing, individual points race in cycling, the 200-metre medley and the 4 x 100 metre freestyle relay in swimming.

COUNTRIES AFFILIATED WITH THE INTERNATIONAL OLYMPIC COMMITTEE

NAME	ABBREVIATION I.O.C.	ZONE
AFGHANISTAN	AFG	ASIA
ALBANIA	ALB	EUROPE
ALGERIA	ALG	AFRICA
ANDORA	AND	AFRICA
ANGOLA	ANG	AFRICA
ANTIGUA	ANT	NORTH AMERICA
ARGENTINA	ARG	SOUTH AMERICA
AUSTRALIA	AUS	OCEANIA
AUSTRIA	AUT	EUROPE
BAHAMAS	BAH	NORTH AMERICA
BAHRAIN	BRN	ASIA
BARBADOS	BAR	NORTH AMERICA
BELGIUM	BEL	EUROPE
BELIZE	BEL	NORTH AMERICA
BENIN	BEN	AFRICA
BERMUDA	BER	NORTH AMERICA
BOLIVIA	BOL	SOUTH AMERICA
BOTSWANA	BOT	AFRICA
BRAZIL	BRA	SOUTH AMERICA
BRITISH HONDURAS	HBR	NORTH AMERICA
BULGARIA	BUL	EUROPE
BURMA	BIR	ASIA
CAMBODIA	KHM	ASIA
CAMEROON	CMR	AFRICA
CANADA	CAN	NORTH AMERICA
CAYMAN ISLANDS	CAY	NORTH AMERICA
CENTRAL AFRICA	CAF	AFRICA
CEYLON	CEY	ASIA
CHAD	CHA	AFRICA
CHILE	CHI	SOUTH AMERICA
CHINA R.O.	ROC	ASIA
COLOMBIA	COL	SOUTH AMERICA
CONGO	CGO	AFRICA
CONGO KINSHASA	COK	AFRICA
COSTA RICA	CRC	NORTH AMERICA
CUBA	CUB	NORTH AMERICA
CYPRUS	CYP	ASIA
CZECHOSLOVAKIA	TCH	EUROPE
DAHOMEY	DAH	AFRICA
DENMARK	DEN	EUROPE
DOMINICAN REPUBLIC	DOM	NORTH AMERICA
ECUADOR	ECU	SOUTH AMERICA
EGYPT	EGY	UNITED ARAB REP.
EL SALVADOR	SAL	NORTH AMERICA
ETHIOPIA	ETI	AFRICA
FIJI (ISLANDS)	FIJ	OCEANIA
FINLAND	FIN	EUROPE
FRANCE	FRA	EUROPE
GABON	GAB	AFRICA
GERMANY *	FRG	EUROPE
GERMAN DEMOCRATIC REP. **	GDR	EUROPE
GHANA	GHA	AFRICA
GREAT BRITAIN	GBR	EUROPE
GREECE	GRE	EUROPE
GUATEMALA	GUA	NORTH AMERICA
GUYANA	GUY	AFRICA
GUINEA	GUI	AFRICA
HAITI	HAI	NORTH AMERICA
HONDURAS	HON	NORTH AMERICA
HONG KONG	HKG	ASIA
HUNGARY	HUN	EUROPE
ICELAND	ISL	EUROPE
INDIA	IND	ASIA
INDONESIA	INA	ASIA
IRAN	IRN	ASIA
IRAQ	IRQ	ASIA
IRELAND	IRL	EUROPE
ISRAEL	ISR	ASIA
ITALY	ITA	EUROPE
IVORY COAST	CIV	AFRICA
JAMAICA	JAM	NORTH AMERICA
JAPAN	JPN	ASIA

* hereafter referred to as Germany or West Germany
** hereafter referred to as East Germany

NAME	ABBREVIATION I.O.C.	ZONE
JORDAN	JOR	ASIA
KENYA	KEN	AFRICA
KOREA	KOR	ASIA
D.PR. KOREA	PRK	ASIA
KUWAIT	KUW	ASIA
LAOS	LAO	ASIA
LEBANON	LIB	ASIA
LESOTHO	LES	AFRICA
LIBERIA	LBR	AFRICA
LIECHTENSTEIN	LIE	EUROPE
LUXEMBOURG	LUX	EUROPE
LYBIA	LBA	AFRICA
MADAGASCAR	MAD	AFRICA
MALAWI	MAW	AFRICA
MALAYSIA	MAL	ASIA
MALI	MLI	AFRICA
MALTA	MLT	EUROPE
MAURITANIA	MTN	AFRICA
MAURITIUS	MRI	AFRICA
MEXICO	MEX	NORTH AMERICA
MONACO	MON	EUROPE
MONGOLIA	MGL	ASIA
MOROCCO	MAR	AFRICA
MOZAMBIQUE	MOZ	AFRICA
NEPAL	NEP	ASIA
NETHERLANDS	HOL	EUROPE
NETHERLAND ANTILLES	AHO	NORTH AMERICA
NEW ZEALAND	NZL	OCEANIA
NICARAGUA	NCA	NORTH AMERICA
NIGER	NIG	AFRICA
NIGERIA	NGR	AFRICA
NORWAY	NOR	EUROPE
PAKISTAN	PAK	ASIA
PANAMA	PAN	NORTH AMERICA
PAPUA NEW GUINEA	NGU	ASIA
PARAGUAY	PAR	SOUTH AMERICA
PERU	PER	SOUTH AMERICA
PHILIPPINES	PHI	ASIA
POLAND	POL	EUROPE

NAME	ABBREVIATION I.O.C.	ZONE
PORTUGAL	POR	EUROPE
PUERTO RICO	PUR	NORTH AMERICA
RHODESIA	RHO	AFRICA
RUMANIA	ROM	EUROPE
SAN MARINO	SMR	EUROPE
SAUDI ARABIA	ARS	ASIA
SENEGAL	SEN	AFRICA
SEYCHELLES	SEY	AFRICA
SIERRA LEONE	SLE	AFRICA
SINGAPORE	SIN	ASIA
SOMALI REPUBLIC	SOM	AFRICA
SPAIN	ESP	EUROPE
SUDAN	SUD	AFRICA
SURINAM	SUR	SOUTH AMERICA
SWAZILAND	SWZ	AFRICA
SWEDEN	SWE	EUROPE
SWITZERLAND	SUI	EUROPE
SYRIA	SYR	ASIA
TAIWAN	TPE	ASIA
TANZANIA	TAN	AFRICA
THAILAND	THA	ASIA
TOGO	TOG	AFRICA
TRINIDAD AND TOBAGO	TRI	NORTH AMERICA
TUNISIA	TUN	AFRICA
TURKEY	TUR	ASIA
UGANDA	UGA	AFRICA
UNITED ARAB EMIRATES	UAE	ASIA
UNITED STATES OF AMERICA	USA	NORTH AMERICA
UPPER VOLTA	VOL	AFRICA
URUGUAY	URU	SOUTH AMERICA
U.S.S.R.	URS	EUROPE
VENEZUELA	VEN	SOUTH AMERICA
VIET-NAM	VNM	ASIA
VIRGIN ISLANDS	ISV	NORTH AMERICA
YUGOSLAVIA	YUG	EUROPE
ZAIRE	ZAI	AFRICA
ZAMBIA	ZAM	AFRICA
ZIMBABWE	ZIM	AFRICA

THE CANADIAN OLYMPIC ASSOCIATION

*

The Canadian Olympic Association (COA) has overseen Canada's participation in the Olympic Games since 1904. It is part of the international structure of Olympic sports that culminates every four years with colour and pageantry.

The International Olympic Committee (IOC) is the "heart" of the Olympic Movement, but the "beat" is generated by the more than 145 national Olympic associations of which the COA is one. The national organizations in turn draw their strength from their own national sports federations.

The IOC is headquartered in the Chateau de Vidy in Lausanne, Switzerland, and is run by an executive board of nine directors. It has the power to award Games to cities who have submitted bids. Only one bid per country can be endorsed for this purpose by the country's national Olympic committee.

The IOC membership is comprised of individuals — not national Olympic committees. Members are nominated by the executive board, and once inducted, they become ambassadors of the IOC and the Olympic Movement in their respective countries. Canada currently has two members, James Worrall and Richard Pound.

Both Worrall and Pound have served as presidents of the COA, which like other national organizations, was originally established as a territorial agent for the IOC responsible for the participation of Canada in the Olympic Games every four years. The COA duties go beyond the basic responsibilities of selecting, managing and providing for national teams, by focusing on sport and sport issues while resisting political interference and all religious and racial discrimination.

The COA had its roots in the Amateur Athletic Union (AAU) of Canada. In 1904, the AAU formed a special Olympic committee within its own ranks to pick a team for the 1904 Games in St. Louis. But it wasn't until 1907 that the IOC granted official recognition to this committee. Canada became the tenth nation so recognized by the IOC.

In 1946 the organization took its present name. It was not freed of its ties to the AAU until 1952. A federal charter made the Canadian Olympic Association a corporation, a separate entity that grew dramatically.

Motivated by the prospect of Montreal obtaining the 1976 Olympic Games, the COA went through a "revitalization" in the 1960s. It acquired a "home." The construction of Olympic House was started in 1966 and completed the following year in time to be featured as a pavilion at Expo '67 in Montreal. A couple of years after Expo, the COA adopted a new constitution to expand its horizons and to foster development of sport in Canada.

The COA was quick to realize that with its new image it had entered the world of "big business." Expenses were growing into the millions of dollars. Concern led to the establishment of Olympic Trust in 1970 where COA officials work together with some of the country's top business leaders. Olympic Trust assumed sole responsibility for raising and administering the funds required to fulfil the objectives of the COA.

Olympic Trust found four basic sources for its revenues. Sponsorship programmes and special promotions bring in about 60 per cent of revenues annually. Public donations account for 22 per cent, federal government grants bring in 11 per cent with interest and other sources adding seven per cent. Although the government role in financial affairs over the years has been significant, the COA is not an agency of the government.

COA membership is about 250 people. Each national sports federation can have up to five members, one of which is designated as a COA director. This group recruits members from the general public, usually selecting industry and community leaders with an interest in amateur sport. The membership is filled out with the two IOC members (Worrall and Pound) and with honorary members who do not have the right to vote. All must be Canadian citizens.

As varied as their lifestyles may be, the Canadian Olympic Association members all have one common belief: that given proper inspiration, encouragement and support, Canada's youth will be as good competitively as any in the world and better than most.

ARCHERY

The tightly grouped arrows on the target face have been shot about the length of a football field.

HISTORY

Until the gun came into being, the bow and arrow was an instrument of war; a weapon of power for its earliest masters. It was the well-trained bowman who enabled the English to vanquish the French in the historic fourteenth-century battle of Agincourt. Genghis Khan rode to power behind his hordes of expert bowmen, capturing China and Turkestan in the early thirteenth century. When explorers and settlers moved into North America they faced the bow, for the Indians had discovered that this hunting tool was also a weapon of war.

It is believed the bow's importance as a weapon was first recognized by the ancient Egyptians. Many artifacts from the golden days of the Pharoahs portray bowmen in action, either hunting or at war. But while it was known as an instrument of war, the bow had its periods of romanticism. What child hasn't heard of William Tell shooting an apple off his son's head with a crossbow or of the heroic deeds of Robin Hood, the ever popular rogue of Sherwood Forest?

With the invention of gunpowder, the bow and arrow was relegated to the position of a sportsman's tool, and this led to the development of archery as a sport. In England, archers formed the Royal Toxopholite Society in 1781. The Society, which is still in existence today, established the York round in which competitive distances were 100, 80 and 60 yards. In 1879, the National Archery Association in the United States was formed, and just before the First World War, the first international competition took place in France. In Canada, the Federation of Canadian Archers was formed in 1927.

The sport's ruling body, the Federation internationale de Tir a L'arc (FITA) was established in 1931 with the aim of holding annual international competitions. During its early competitions, FITA used long and short metric rounds. For men the distances were: 90 metres, 70 metres, 50 metres and 50 metres, 35 metres, 25 metres. For women the two rounds had shorter distances: 70 metres, 60 metres, 50 metres and 50 metres, 35 metres, 25 metres respectively.

Supporters of archery laboured tenaciously to have the sport included in the Olympics and succeeded in having the sport seen at the 1900, 1904, 1908 and 1920 Games. Attendance was sporadic and the International Olympic Committee (IOC) dropped archery from its programme. FITA worked on improvements and in 1955 the official round's point system was standardized.

That didn't appear to suit the IOC, which turned down further requests for inclusion. Finally, due to the efforts of FITA President Inger Frith, archery was given official recognition for the 1972 Games in Munich.

PROCEDURE

Olympic competitors must participate in qualifying events held by their respective countries. The FITA minimums are 1,100 points for men and 1,050 for women (both out of 1,440), but most countries, including Canada, set their standards higher than that for both men and women, using the same format as in the Olympics.

In the Olympics, competition is spread over four days, and is made up of two FITA rounds. A FITA round comprises four series of 36 arrows shot at 90, 70, 50 and 30 metres for men and at 70, 60, 50 and 30 metres for women. A round is completed by each archer in two days.

At the beginning of each day, every competitor is allowed a maximum of six practice shots. Once the competition has begun, each archer must shoot three ar-

rows in a 2½-minute time period with a 20-second interval between competitors.

The target is 122 centimetres in diameter for the 90-, 70-, and 60-metre events and 80 centimetres in diameter for the 50- and 30-metre distances.

The target is divided into five concentric circles, each further divided in two for a total of 10 scoring areas. The scoring zones progress from one to 10 points. The best score totalled over four days wins.

Each country is entitled to enter three female and three male competitors. Only recurve bows are permitted. Viewfinders with lenses or prisms may not be used, however, spotting scopes and binoculars may be used to tell exactly where the arrows hit the target face.

Eldorado Park in Long Beach, California, is the site of the 1984 archery competition.

VIEWING TIPS

For the television viewer, archery may be a difficult sport to follow. Archers appear to simply walk to the line, stand there and wait for the starting signal to shoot their arrows. However, depending upon the camera angle, you may take note of the following:

Each archer has an individual shooting style. Notice the way the fingers come off the string. Notice the body alignment. Does the archer's body look long and stretched out during the drawing of the bow? The good shooter's does. If you are able to see arrow flight or if the television has a "split screen" presentation, you will notice that sometimes the "nicest" looking shooters do not hit the very centre of the target face.

Finally, observe how tightly the arrows group together on the target face. If you stop to think that the men are shooting the length of a football field and the women slightly short of that, you will realize that the level of skill required for an Olympic medal is very high.

Weather can play havoc with performance. Wind and rain affect arrow flight and, of course, the score. It is expected that the television commentators will update the viewers on the weather conditions.

EQUIPMENT

Advanced archers generally use composite bows with handles made of magnesium, and limbs made of wood, with fibreglass lamination. Any form of recurve bow is permitted except the crossbow, which is not manually drawn.

There is no specific length for a bow but it is common knowledge that longer bows are steadier in the hand while shorter bows shoot a faster arrow less affected by the wind.

Archers aim at the target with sights fitted to the bow in order to estimate distance efficiently and to compensate for lateral drift.

Attachments such as lenses, prisms, rearsights and mechanical releases are forbidden. Compound bows are also forbidden.

The arrows are made of tubular aluminum alloy. The length, weight and stiffness vary to suit the individual archer. They are lightweight and chosen to produce the best arrow grouping. Each is marked to identify the archer.

The target is divided into five concentric circles, each further divided in two for a total of 10 scoring rows. The target face has five colours to help determine the score with the range going from 10 points for centre to one point for the white outer ring. The rings are gold, red, blue, black and white.

The archer's equipment:

1. Lower limb
2. Compensator (optional)
3. Stabilizers
4. Counter weight (optional)
5. Arrow rest
6. Sight aperture
7. Sight bar
8. Upper limb
9. Draw check indicator
10. Grip
11. Riser
12. Serving
13. Working limb tip
14. Nocking point indicator
15. Tip or arrow point
16. Arrow shaft
17. String
18. Arrow nock
19. Vanes or fletch
20. Arm guard
21. Finger tab

TECHNICAL TERMS

Anchor point — a spot on the shooter's face to where the string hand draws back, giving consistency to shooting.

Arm guard — protects the arm from the bowstring, usually leather and worn on the inside of the forearm.

Arrow rest — an extraneous device on the bow to provide a resting point, or shelf to support the arrow.

Bow arm — the arm that holds the bow out toward the target.

Bowstring — the string of the bow usually made of kevlar.

Butt — a backstop behind the target for holding arrows shot past the target.

Cast — the distance a bow can shoot an arrow; the degree of efficiency of the bow.

Cock feather — the feather at right angles to the nock slot; often a different colour than the other fletch.

Draw — to pull the bowstring and the arrow back into the anchor position.

Drift — natural deflection of an arrow from its normal path due to outside factors such as wind.

End — a number of arrows shot at one time, as required by the round being shot.

Finger tab — leather worn on the drawing hand to protect the fingers and

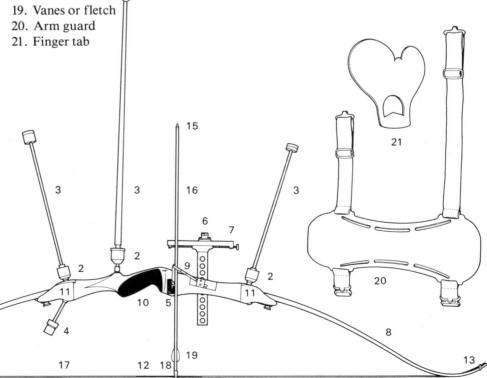

give a smoother release of the bowstring.

Fletch — the feathers or plastic vanes on an arrow. To fletch is to glue the fletching on an arrow shaft.

Freestyle — shooting with the aid of a bowsight and stabilizers.

Grip — the part of the bow handle held by the shooter.

Handle riser — the reinforced centre part of the bow, usually made of magnesium or aluminum.

Laminate — a bow limb having two or more kinds of wood or fibreglass.

Left-hand archer — one who holds the bow in the right hand and draws with the left hand.

Limbs — the two ends of a bow, from the handle riser out. The limbs bend and give the arrow the stored energy that propels it.

Nock — the groove in the end of an arrow in which the bowstring fits; also the grooves at both ends of the bow that hold the bowstring loops.

Nocking point — the marked place on the bowstring where the arrow nock is placed before drawing and releasing.

Point — the tip on the end of the arrow.

Quiver — something to hold arrows; can be ground, belt, back or pocket types.

Recurve — a bow curved at the tip ends.

Release — to let the bowstring slip off the fingertips releasing the arrow.

Right-hand archer — one who holds the bow with the left hand and draws with the right hand.

Stabilizers — these are aluminum rods attached to the bow to improve the efficiency of the arrow flight and bow reaction.

Stance — the physical alignment of the body in relation to the target in preparation for shooting.

Weight — the amount of effort (in pounds) required to pull the bow to full draw (usually measured at 71 centimetres) and computed for longer or shorter draws.

TOP COMPETITORS

Darrell Pace of the United States was the 1976 Olympic champion with a record 2,571 score out of a possible 2,880 points. He sat out the 1980 Olympics as part of the U.S. boycott, and Finland's Tomi Poikolinen emerged as champion

Archers aim with sights that help estimate distance and compensate for lateral drift.

with a 2,455 total.

Other very talented U.S. archers are Richard McKinney, (the current world champion), Larry Smith and Edwin Eliason. Kyosti Laasonen and Paivi Meriuloto give Finland some depth.

Among the women, the current world champion, Jin-ho Kim, and Mi-yong Kim have been shooting well for South Korea while the Soviet Union has a trio of sharpshooters in Butuzova, Arshankova and Rustamova. Luann Ryon heads the U.S. list, having won the Olympic gold in 1976. She sat out in 1980.

CANADA'S BEST

Linda Kazienko, Lisa Buscomb and Lucille Lemay were ranked eighth women's team during the 1983 World Championships. Linda Kazienko finished fourth, only four points out of second place. In doing so, she broke six Canadian records and won the bronze distance medal at 60 metres. This was Canada's best showing since 1969.

Top contenders in the men's division include Eric Amos of Terra Cotta, Ontario, Roger Lemay, Boisbriand, Quebec, Daniel Desnoyers of Loretteville, Quebec and Ted Gamble, Calgary.

MEDAL WINNERS

ARCHERY (double F.I.T.A. round) Men

YEAR	PLACE	NAME	COUNTRY
1972	1	**John C. Williams**	U.S.A.
	2	Gunnar Jarvil	Sweden
	3	Kyoesti Laasonen	Finland
1976	1	**Darrell Place**	U.S.A.
	2	Hiroshi Michinaga	Japan
	3	Giancarlo Ferrari	Italy
1980	1	**Tomi Polkolainen**	Finland
	2	Boris Isachenko	URS
	3	Giancarlo Ferrari	Italy

ARCHERY (double F.I.T.A. round) Women

YEAR	PLACE	NAME	COUNTRY
1972	1	**Doreen Wilbur**	U.S.A.
	2	Irena Szydlwska	Poland
	3	Emma Gapchenko	URS
1976	1	**Luann Ryon**	U.S.A.
	2	Valentina Kovpan	URS
	3	Zebiniso Rustamova	URS
1980	1	**Keto Losaberidze**	URS
	2	Natalya Butuzova	URS
	3	Paivi Meriluoto	Finland

(Archery was included in the Games of 1900, 1904, 1908 and 1920. But none of the events in those celebrations compare with the championship events of 1972-80.)

BASKETBALL

EVENT DATE			THE FORUM, INGLEWOOD		
JULY	29	6 games—preliminaries, men	AUGUST	5	3 games—round robin, women 2 games—semi-finals, men's consolation
	30	3 games—round robin, women 3 games—preliminaries, men		6	4 games—quarterfinals, men
	31	3 games—round robin, women 3 games—preliminaries, men		7	2 games—finals (1-4 places), women
AUGUST	1	6 games—preliminaries, men		8	4 games—semifinals, men
	2	3 games—round robin, women 3 games—preliminaries, men		9	2 games—finals (9-12 places), men 1 game—final (3-4 places), men
	3	3 games—round robin, women 3 games—preliminaries, men		10	2 games—finals (5-8 places), men 1 game—final (1-2 places), men
	4	6 games—preliminaries, men			

Basketball demands speed, endurance and deft ball-handling ability.

HISTORY

Basketball had its beginning in a dull, dark gymnasium in Springfield Massachusetts back in 1891. At that time a Canadian clergyman, Dr. James Naismith, who was an instructor at the Young Men's Christian Association (YMCA), was looking for an indoor game that would give exercise and enjoyment during the bleak winter.

Dr. Naismith had a gymnasium, a ball and a concept. He needed a target for the ball and a "score" to give meaning to its purposeful movement. He decided on a couple of mounted boxes for the target and dispatched a YMCA worker to seek them out. The man assigned to the task could only find peach baskets and hung them from a gym balcony. The game of basketball was born.

Dr. Naismith set up 13 rules prohibiting holding, pushing and tripping, and placed emphasis on passing and teamwork. The ball he chose was the soccer ball. The imaginative clergyman declared a "goal" would be scored by putting the ball through the 3-metre high basket with one or both hands. He stated that the number of players on a team would be determined by the floor space, envisioning teams of three to 40. He felt that the game would be more fun with more players.

Very quickly the game settled into a fixed pattern of five players on a team: two guards, two forwards and a centre. The peach baskets gave way to metal hoops with a rope mesh, which sped up the game as no time was wasted plucking the ball from the wooden basket.

With refinement came steady growth, and now basketball is played worldwide in more than 140 countries. Although the game spread rapidly throughout the high schools and colleges of North America, it didn't gain a foothold in Europe, where growth of the sport was slow, until after the First World War.

For reasons best forgotten, basketball, in the 1936 Olympics, was scheduled for the infield of the large Berlin stadium rather than indoors. Only 24 hours before Canada was to meet the United States for the gold medal, the rains came and stayed all night. When the players showed up, the "court" was covered with about three centimetres of water. Beneath the water was mud. For players accustomed to indoor courts, conditions were, to say the least, terrible. But they played. Canada took a quick 3-0 lead, but then the Americans came on to win 19-8.

The 1972 final is remembered for the stunning upset victory by the Soviet Union over the United States. With the Soviets leading by one point late in the game, Doug Collins of the U.S. team stole the ball and drove for the basket only to be fouled. He was awarded two free throws and sank them both to put the Americans in front 50-49 with three seconds left on the clock.

The Soviet Union called a time out. The notification from the timer to the referee was late, or not heard, and the referee chose to stop the clock with one second remaining. After considerable confusion and protests by both teams, the decision was made to reset the clock to show three seconds. Ivan Edeshko

The Los Angeles Forum, site of the 1984 Summer Olympics basketball competition.

made the throw-in to a teammate and when the buzzer sounded the Americans started to celebrate another gold medal. It was then realized that the throw-in had been made before the timer had reset the clock to show three seconds.

The clock was reset, giving the Soviets another chance. This time Edeshko's pass was caught by Alexander Belov who put the ball through the net as the game ended, giving the Soviets a 51-50 victory. It was the kind of game Dr. Naismith had in mind when he sent the YMCA worker to find a couple of boxes for a new indoor game.

GENERAL DESCRIPTION

There are five men on a team (two guards, two forwards and a centre) on a court that is 26-metres long and 14-metres wide.

The object is to deposit the ball in the basket for a field goal worth two points. In the case of a free throw, where a player shoots undisturbed from the free-throw line after a foul, the "goal" is worth one point. The team with the most points wins. The ball may be passed, dribbled or rolled but may not be carried or kicked.

Over the years, the rules that predominate in U.S. colleges have grown closer to those for international competition, but there are still some distinct differences. In the Olympics, there is a 30-second shot clock requiring the offensive team to attempt a shot within 30 seconds of attaining possession of the ball. Since there is no time limit in college games, the 30-second shot helps to eliminate the stall or delay that has become so irritating to U.S. college fans.

Under international rules when a player is fouled while shooting, he or she is awarded three attempts to make two free baskets from the foul line, as compared to two attempts in college play. If the player scores a field goal during the foul, he or she is allowed only one shot.

The defence counters the offence.

Common (nonshooting) fouls carry a two shot penalty after the offending team has accumulated eight team fouls in each half.

The most interesting difference is the right of option used in the Olympics. If a team is fouled and awarded two shots, the floor captain has the option of either allowing the fouled player to attempt the free throws or of retaining possession of the ball by taking it out of bounds. U.S. college players must take the shots.

In international games, a jump ball is used if possession of the ball is in doubt. The referee tosses the ball between two players, who try to tip it to their sides. There is an alternating possession rule in the North American version.

PROCEDURE

For men, there are five qualifying tournaments in five world zones to determine qualifiers who will build a dozen teams for the 1984 Olympic Games. The two best teams of the last Olympics qualify. This year they are Yugoslavia and Italy.

The host nation (the United States) gains an automatic berth.

Three teams, including Canada's, qualify through a tournament reserved for the countries of the Americas.

Three teams qualify through a tournament reserved for the countries of Europe.

One team qualifies through an African tournament, another through a tournament for Asian countries and another qualifies through a tournament reserved for the countries of Oceania. (Australia, New Zealand, Melanesia, Micronesia, and Polynesia).

For women, the host country (the United States) and the last Olympic winner (the Soviet Union) gain automatic berths in the six-team tournament. The other four teams qualify through a pre-Olympic world qualifying tournament involving approximately 25 countries at least nine weeks before the Games. The Canadian women compete in this tournament.

VIEWING TIPS

The tendency of the viewer is to follow the movement of the ball, thus missing a lot of the court action taking place away from the ball. As the ball wriggles through the mesh, the player's skill is relegated to a secondary role. Since the basketball player you will see in the 1984 Olympics is a wonderful athlete with great skill and acrobatic ability, try to take note of his or her performance. The athlete is also well disciplined, for as a team game, basketball requires discipline for victory. Individual performances may provide the viewing impact, but team play usually determines the winner.

The teams will use a variety of patterns on offence. Some prefer precise patterns, others enjoy the impromptu play that is fostered by individuality when players are turned loose at the proper time. While the offensive players are moving the ball around, they are trying to "read" the defence, looking for openings and a chance for a basket.

The defences fall into two categories, the zone and man-to-man. In the latter, each player is responsible for one player. In the zone, the player protects a specific area.

The slam dunk, the rebound, the fastbreak and the playmaking make basketball one of the finest spectator sports in the world. Sit back and enjoy.

TECHNICAL TERMS

Backcourt — the half of the court where a team's defensive basket is located.

Forecourt — the half of the court where the offensive basket is located.

Baseline/end — the out-of-bounds line at the end of the court.

Basket/bucket/hoop — common usage for goal when the ball goes through the hoop.

Backboard/glass — the rebound surface on which the basket is mounted.

Key — the area where teams line up to shoot foul shots, formerly shaped like a key.

Ten-second line — the centre line of the court. Teams must advance the ball over it within 10 seconds of gaining possession after a basket.

Technical foul — the penalty for unsportsmanlike conduct.

Violation — giving up the ball to the opponents because of minor infractions such as travelling (running with the ball), double dribble (catching the ball between dribbles), three-seconds (staying three seconds or longer in the key area without the ball), 10 seconds (taking more than 10 seconds to move the ball from backcourt to forecourt).

Screen/pick — the act of a player setting a stationary block for a teammate who attempts to get free of a defensive player.

Fastbreak — when the offensive team moves the ball quickly from its backcourt to the forecourt before the defensive team has a chance to set up its defensive patterns.

Free throw/foul shot — an unguarded shot from the foul line awarded a player who is fouled by his or her opponent. Players fouled in the act of shooting are awarded three attempts to make two shots. Common (nonshooting) fouls carry a two shot penalty after the offending team is in the penalty situation (accumulated eight fouls in each half).

EQUIPMENT

Ball — must be spherical and must have a leather, rubber or synthetic base with a rubber bladder. Its circumference is 75 to 80 centimetres and it must weigh 600 to 650 grams.

Baskets — Orange-painted iron rings with cord nets. They are three metres off the ground and are attached to backboards from which the ball may be played. The basket has an inside diameter of 45 centimetres.

Dress — players wear rubber-soled shoes and shirts and jerseys. Players cannot wear any object that may injure another player.

Court — is 26-metres long and 14-metres wide.

TOP TEAMS

Although European teams have shown steady improvement in past decades, the team to beat is the United States which has a wealth of college talent to draw from. The U.S. won seven consecutive gold medals before losing to the Soviet Union in the controversial 1972 final. It won again in 1976, but boycotted the 1980 Games.

Yugoslavia and the Soviet Union will be tough and Canada, based on the most recent performances, has an excellent chance for a medal.

In women's play, the Soviet Union has won the gold medal in the past two Olympics and it is the team to beat again. The United States has a tall team and has home court advantage. The Canadian women have consistently ranked in the top six teams in the world since 1977.

CANADA

Men: — With the highly reputable coach, Jack Donohue, at the helm, the team can never be sold short. Jay Triano of Niagara Falls, Eli Pasquale of Sudbury, Gerald Kazanowski of Nanaimo, B.C. and Danny Meagher of St. Catharines, Ontario.

Women: — Coach Don McCrae leads a team that features veteran players Bev Smith of Salmon Arm, B.C., Sylvia Sweeney of Montreal, Debbie Huband of Ottawa and Candy Lohr of Guelph, Ontario.

Both the men's and women's teams are quite short by international standards, which may hurt them when playing against the good, taller teams.

Their fortunes lie with the ability of their tall players to neutralize their opponents' dominating centres. Seven foot Bill Wennington of Montreal and 6'11" Greg Wiltjer of Victoria will help the men, while 6'7" Charlotte Lusschen of London, Ontario, will contribute to the women's cause.

MEDAL WINNERS

BASKETBALL—Men

YEAR	PLACE	COUNTRY
1936	1	**U.S.A.**
	2	Canada
	3	Mexico
1948	1	**U.S.A.**
	2	France
	3	Brazil
1952	1	**U.S.A.**
	2	U.S.S.R.
	3	Uruguay
1956	1	**U.S.A.**
	2	U.S.S.R.
	3	Uruguay
1960	1	**U.S.A.**
	2	U.S.S.R.
	3	Brazil
1964	1	**U.S.A.**
	2	U.S.S.R.
	3	Brazil
1968	1	**U.S.A.**
	2	Yugoslavia
	3	U.S.S.R.
1972	1	**U.S.S.R.**
	2	U.S.A.
	3	Cuba
1976	1	**U.S.A.**
	2	Yugoslavia
	3	U.S.S.R.
1980	1	**Yugoslavia**
	2	Italy
	3	U.S.S.R.

BASKETBALL—Women/New Olympic event—1976

YEAR	PLACE	NAME	COUNTRY
1976	1		**U.S.S.R.**
	2		U.S.A.
	3		Bulgaria
1980	1		**U.S.S.R.**
	2		Bulgaria
	3		Yugoslavia

BOXING

EVENT DATE			LOS ANGELES SPORTS ARENA		
JULY	29	Preliminary bouts	**AUGUST**	5	Preliminary bouts
	30	Preliminary bouts		6	Preliminary bouts
	31	Preliminary bouts		7	Quarterfinal bouts
AUGUST	1	Preliminary bouts		8	Quarterfinal bouts
	2	Preliminary bouts		9	Semifinal bouts
	3	Preliminary bouts		11	Final bouts
	4	Preliminary bouts			

Boxing in the Olympics dates back to the early Greek Games.

HISTORY

When the first punch was thrown is anyone's guess, but historians have traced the sport of boxing back to the ancient Greeks who included it in their Olympic Games.

The ancient Romans thought boxing was great entertainment and after conquering the Greeks, they encouraged its development. The Romans, however, permitted the use of leather wrapped tightly around the hands for the competitors who fought to the finish. The later inclusion of metal studs and spikes embedded in the leather straps made this early sport a brutal one.

Eventually, the public tired of the brutality, and a few decades after the birth of Christ, boxing went in remission for almost 1,600 years. It surfaced once again in the form of bare-knuckle bouts,

however, the more controls were being sought. Surprisingly, a suggestion for the use of gloves was turned down. "Leave the gloves for training," argued the bare-knuckle advocates. And so the use of gloves remained in training quarters.

One of bare-knuckle fighting's drawbacks was the long bout. There were no time-limits. The fault was with the rules, which stated that a round ended when a boxer was knocked down, and that there was to be a 30-second wait between rounds. The tired, but wise boxer simply slipped to the canvas to end the round and get his 30-second break. Bouts often lasted 60 rounds or more.

The sport got a boost and some legitimacy in 1866 when the Marquis of Queensbury, affectionately known as the father of modern boxing, developed

Tunney and Joe Louis, and in recent years with such heavy hitters as Rocky Marciano, Muhammad Ali and Larry Holmes.

Unlike professional boxing, amateur boxing heavily emphasizes defensive skills. These are extremely important in Olympic bouts where there are only three rounds of three-minute duration each. Professional championship bouts have a 12- or 15-round limit, and judges tend to favour the offensive boxer.

Amateur boxing has been a stepping stone for some into the professional ranks and many Olympic champions have gone on to win world professional championships. Muhammad Ali was known as Cassius Clay when he won the Olympic light-heavyweight title in 1960 before becoming world heavyweight champion. Others who took that successful route include Italy's Nino Benvenuti, Mate Parlov of Yugoslavia, Pascual Perez of Argentina and Americans, George Foreman, Joe Frazier, Sugar Ray Leonard and the Spinks brothers, Leon and Michael.

Despite the large financial rewards that are offered Olympic champions to turn professional, not all of them are eager to move into the fight-for-pay ranks. Most notable is the Cuban Teofilo Stevenson who won the Olympic heavyweight title three times, in 1972, 1976 and 1980 and has refused to turn professional.

The only other boxer to win three gold medals in the Olympics is Hungarian Laszlo Papp. He won the light-middleweight title (up to 71 kilograms) in the 1952 and 1956 Games after capturing the gold medal in the middleweight division (up to 75 kilograms) in 1948.

Former world heavyweight champion Ingemar Johansson of Sweden describes his only Olympic appearance as one of frustration. He was disqualified for "inactivity" during the final of the heavyweight event in the 1952 Games. Johansson got a second shock, when Olympic officials decided to withhold his silver medal. Almost 30 years elapsed before they relented and gave it to him.

And if you think Johansson had his problems, how about Santiago Lovell of Argentina? Lovell won the Olympic heavyweight championship in the 1932 Games in Los Angeles and was expect-

The Los Angeles Coliseum and Sports Arena is the site of 1984 Olympic boxing.

which were nurtured in England during the seventeenth, eighteenth and nineteenth centuries.

At first, bare-knuckle bouts permitted some wrestling and pushing, but the style dramatically changed after students learned how to clench their fists and punch expertly.

The bouts attracted gamblers. They were quick to realize that people were prepared to bet on their favourites. Gamblers stimulated the betting action by offering prize money to both attract and inspire boxers. Professional boxing was born and became entrenched in society. The more attention the sport got,

a set of rules. They were widely applauded and accepted. The rules made the use of gloves mandatory and called for three-minute rounds with a minute rest period between them. Queensbury, standardized the fighting area to a 7.3-metre square ring. Perhaps the most significant new rule was the one that said if a knocked-down boxer did not get to his feet at the end of a 10-second count, he would lose the bout.

Professional boxing became one of the major sporting events in North America, built on the talents of great heavyweight fighters such as John L. Sullivan, James Corbett, Jack Dempsey, Gene

ing a hero's welcome on his return to Buenos Aires. He was greeted all right — by the police. They promptly marched him off to jail. Lovell's crime? Well, it appeared he didn't quite agree with the philosophies of the Argentine government and was outspoken about it during the Games.

GENERAL DESCRIPTION

A new weight category has been included for the 1984 Olympic Games in Los Angeles. It is the super-heavyweight class for boxers weighing more than 91 kilograms (200.6 pounds).

Weight Limits

1. Up to 48 kilograms (105.8 pounds).
2. Up to 51 kilograms (112.4 pounds).
3. Up to 54 kilograms (119 pounds).
4. Up to 57 kilograms (125.7 pounds).
5. Up to 60 kilograms (132.3 pounds).
6. Up to 63.5 kilograms (140 pounds).
7. Up to 67 kilograms (147.7 pounds).
8. Up to 71 kilograms (156.5 pounds).
9. Up to 75 kilograms (165.4 pounds).
10. Up to 81 kilograms (178.6 pounds).
11. Up to 91 kilograms (200.6 pounds).
12. Over 91 kilograms.

The weight categories have changed dramatically over the years in an effort to have the opponents as equal as possible. Competitors must be at least 17 years old and face a maximum of three rounds of three-minutes each. The five judges seated around the ring score the bout to determine a winner if there is no knockout. The referee does not have a ballot in amateur and Olympic boxing.

The judges rate the fighters after each round, awarding points for clean hits (with the knuckle part of the clenched fist) on the target areas (front of the head and body to the belt of the trunks). The judges award 20 points to the winner of each round with the loser given proportionately less. The aggregate points total determines the winner. In the case of a tie, judges give the decision to the boxer who had the better defensive skills, style or who was being the aggressor.

Unlike rowing and a few other events, there is no second chance for boxers. It is one loss and disqualification, with the winners progressing through to the final. The two finalists meet for the gold and silver medals. The two losers in the semi-finals are each awarded bronze medals.

VIEWING TIPS

Skill is as important as power in boxing. Watch for the boxers who try to land a "hit." The "hit" or blow to the target area helps the boxer build up points which are used to determine the winner.

Most Olympic boxers will be skilled defensively as well as offensively. Thus it is important to watch how a boxer handles an aggressive opponent. He may rely on blocking punches with his arms or hands or resort to counterpunching, that is to take, block or evade a punch and retaliate with a "hit."

A boxer with a longer arm reach will tend to keep well away from his opponent so that his longer reach can be effective. Boxers of short, stocky build and short punching range tend to "tie up" opponents by forcing them on the ropes or into corners and staying in close quarters so that there is little opportunity for the rival with the longer reach to lash out.

Boxers are quick and agile and there is usually constant movement in the ring. If a boxer has to stay alert to avoid being hit by a knockout punch, a television viewer must stay alert not to miss one.

EQUIPMENT

Gloves — weigh 224 grams (8 ounces). Before putting on the gloves, a boxer wraps his hands with a gauze bandage. The use of the bandage helps cut down hand fractures. It does not give any punching strength.

Ring — in the Olympics, the boxers will compete in a ring that is 6.1 metres by 6.1 metres with the measurement taken inside the three ropes. There must be 39.4 centimetres of floor space between the lower rope and mat. The corner posts must be padded to afford protection in case a boxer is knocked into one. The floor covering is canvas over an underlay of felt or rubber up to 3.8 centimetres in thickness.

Dress — competitors wear shorts, shirts and light boxing boots. They also wear an athletic support with a cup protector and mouthguards. For the first time, headgear is optional at the 1984 Olympic Games in Los Angeles.

TOP COMPETITORS

Traditionally, the United States is a powerhouse in Olympic boxing and has won the most medals, 74 including 33 golds. The Soviet Union has come on strongly in the past 30 years and has won 46 Olympic medals, including 13 gold. They should once again have a strong team in Los Angeles. In the European championships last spring in Bulgaria, the Soviets won eight of 12 gold medals.

The country making the greatest strides in recent years, however, is Cuba which won six gold medals in the 1980 Games in Moscow. It should be pointed out that the United States boycotted the Moscow Games to protest the Soviet invasion of Afghanistan.

One of the gold medals in Moscow was taken by Cuban heavyweight Teofilo Stevenson. It was his third Olympic gold medal in that division and he will be looking for his fourth in Los Angeles.

TOP CANADIANS

Shawn O'Sullivan — the Toronto boxer is one of the premier amateurs in the 71-kilogram class. He won the World Cup in 1981 and the North American championship in 1983. He is rated among the favourites for an Olympic medal.

Willie deWit — from Grande Prairie, Alberta, deWit competes in the up to 91-kilogram class, which is commonly called the heavyweight class. Like O'Sullivan, he is highly rated and an Olympic medal favourite. He has won the North American title the past two years. Last September, he defeated world champion Aleksandr Iagubkin of the Soviet Union in Reno, Nevada. An injury kept deWit out of the World Cup competitions last fall.

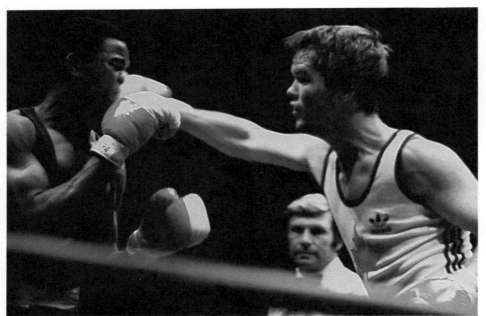

Fighters are awarded points for clean hits to the target areas.

MEDAL WINNERS

BOXING (light flyweight) Men

YEAR	PLACE	NAME	COUNTRY
1968	1	F. Rodriguez	Venezuela
	2	Yong-Ju Jee	Korea
	3	H. Marbley/	U.S.A./
		H. Skrzypczak	Poland
1972	1	G. Gedo	Hungary
	2	U. Gil Kim	North Korea
	3	R. Evans/	Great Britain/
		E. Rodriguez	Spain
1976	1	Jorge Hernandez	Cuba
	2	Byong Uk Li	Dem. People's Rep. of Korea
	3	Payao Pooltarat	Thailand
1980	1	Shamil Sabyrov	U.S.S.R.
	2	Hipolito Ramos	Cuba
	3	Byong Uk Li/	Dem. People's Rep. of Korea/
		Ismail Moustafov	Bulgaria

BOXING (flyweight) Men

YEAR	PLACE	NAME	COUNTRY
1904	1	G. Finnegan	U.S.A.
	2	M. Burke	U.S.A.
1920	1	F. de Genaro	U.S.A.
	2	A. Petersen	Denmark
	3	W. Cuthbertson	Great Britain
1924	1	F. LaBarba	U.S.A.
	2	J. McKenzie	Great Britain
	3	R. Fee	U.S.A.
1928	1	A. Kocsis	Hungary
	2	A. Appel	France
	3	C. Cavagnoli	Italy
1932	1	I. Enekes	Hungary
	2	F Cabanas	Mexico
	3	L. Salica	U.S.A.
1936	1	W. Kaiser	Germany
	2	G. Matta	Italy
	3	L. Lauria	U.S.A.
1948	1	P. Perez	Argentina
	2	S. Bandinelli	Italy
	3	S.A. Han	Korea
1952	1	N. Brooks	U.S.A.
	2	E. Basel	Germany
	3	A. Bulakov/	U.S.S.R./
		W. Toweel	South Africa
1956	1	T. Spinks	Great Britain
	2	M. Dobrescu	Rumania
	3	J. Caldwell/	Eire/
		R. Libeer	France
1960	1	G. Török	Hungary
	2	S. Sivko	U.S.S.R.
	3	K. Tanabe/	Japan/
		A. Elguindi	U.A.R.
1964	1	F. Atzori	Italy
	2	A. Olech	Poland
	3	R. Carmody/	U.S.A./
		S. Sorokin	U.S.S.R.
1968	1	R. Delgado	Mexico
	2	A. Olech	Poland
	3	S. de Oliveira/	Brazil/
		L. Rwabwogo	Uganda
1972	1	G. Kostadinov	Bulgaria
	2	L. Rwabwogo	Uganda
	3	L. Blazynski/	Poland/
		D. Rodriguez	Cuba
1976	1	Leo Randolph	U.S.A.
	2	Ramon Duvalon	Cuba
	3	Leszek Blazynski/	Poland/
		David Torosyan	U.S.S.R.
1980	1	Petar Lessov	Bulgaria
	2	Victor Miroshnickenko	U.S.S.R.
	3	Hugh Russell/	Ireland/
		Jnos Varadt	Hungary

BOXING (bantamweight) Men

YEAR	PLACE	NAME	COUNTRY
1904	1	O.L. Kirk	U.S.A.
	2	G. Finnegan	U.S.A.
1908	1	A. Thomas	Great Britain
	2	J. Condon	Great Britain
	3	W. Webb	Great Britain
1920	1	C. Walker	South Africa
	2	C. Graham	Canada
	3	J. McKenzie	Great Britain
1924	1	W. Smith	South Africa
	2	S. Tripoli	U.S.A.
	3	J. Ces	France
1928	1	V. Tamagnini	Italy
	2	J. Daley	U.S.A.
	3	H. Isaacs	South Africa
1932	1	H. Gwynne	Canada
	2	H. Ziglarski	Germany
	3	J. Villanueva	Philippines
1936	1	U. Sergo	Italy
	2	J. Wilson	U.S.A.
	3	F. Ortiz	Mexico
1948	1	T. Csik	Hungary
	2	G. Zuddas	Italy
	3	J. Venegas	Puerto Rico
1952	1	P. Hämäläinen	Finland
	2	J. McNally	Eire
	3	G. Garbuzov/	U.S.S.R./
		J. Kang	Korea

BOXING (featherweight) Men

YEAR	PLACE	NAME	COUNTRY
1956	1	W. Behrendt	Germany
	2	S.C. Song	Korea
	3	F. Gilroy/	Eire/
		C. Barrientos	Chile
1960	1	O. Grigoryev	U.S.S.R.
	2	P Zamparini	Italy
	3	B. Bendig/	Poland/
		O. Taylor	Australia
1964	1	T. Sakurai	Japan
	2	S.C. Chung	Korea
	3	J. Mendoza/	Mexico/
		W. Rodriguez	Uruguay
1968	1	V. Sokolov	U.S.S.R.
	2	E. Mukwanga	Uganda
	3	E. Morioka/	Japan/
		K.C. Chang	Korea
1972	1	O. Martinez	Cuba
	2	A. Zamora	Mexico
	3	R. Carreras/	U.S.A./
		G. Turpin	Great Britain
1976	1	Yong Jo Gu	Dem. People's Rep. of Korea
	2	Charles Mooney	U.S.A.
	3	Patrick Cowdell/	Great Britain/
		Chul Soon Hwang	Korea
1980	1	Juan Hurnandez	Cuba
	2	Bernardo Finango	Venezuela
	3	Michael Anthony/	Guyana/
		Dumitru Cipere	Rumania

BOXING (featherweight) Men

YEAR	PLACE	NAME	COUNTRY
1904	1	O.L. Kirk	U.S.A.
	2	F. Haller	U.S.A.
1908	1	R.K. Gunn	Great Britain
	2	C. Morris	Great Britain
	3	H. Roddin	Great Britain
1920	1	P. Fritsch	France
	2	J. Gachet	France
	3	E. Garzena	Italy
1924	1	J. Fields	U.S.A.
	2	J. Salas	U.S.A.
	3	P. Quartucci	Argentina
1928	1	L. van Klaveren	Netherlands
	2	V. Peralta	Argentina
	3	H. Devine	U.S.A.
1932	1	C. Robledo	Argentina
	2	J. Schleinkofer	Germany
	3	C. Carlsson	Sweden
1936	1	O. Casanovas	Argentina
	2	C. Catterall	South Africa
	3	J. Miner	Germany
1948	1	E. Formenti	Italy
	2	D. Shepperd	South Africa
	3	A. Antkiewicz	Poland
1952	1	J. Zachara	Czechoslovakia
	2	S. Caprari	Italy
	3	J. Ventaja/	France/
		L. Leisching	South Africa
1956	1	V. Safronov	U.S.S.R.
	2	T. Nicholls	Great Britain
	3	H. Niedzwiedzki/	Poland/
		P. Härnäläinen	Finland
1960	1	F. Musso	Italy
	2	J. Adamski	Poland
	3	W. Meyers/	South Africa/
		J. Limmonen	Finland
1964	1	S. Stepaschkin	U.S.S.R.
	2	A. Villanueva	Philippines
	3	C. Brown/	U.S.A./
		H. Schulz	Germany
1968	1	A. Roldan	Mexico
	2	A. Robinson	U.S.A.
	3	P. Waruingi/	Kenya/
		I. Mikhailov	Bulgaria
1972	1	B. Kousnetsov	U.S.S.R.
	2	P. Waruingi	Kenya
	3	C. Rojas/	Colombia/
		A. Botos	Hungary
1976	1	Angel Herrera	Cuba
	2	Richard Nowakowski	German Dem. Rep.
	3	Leszek Kosedowski/	Poland/
		Juan Paredes	Mexico
1980	1	Rudi Fink	German Dem. Rep.
	2	Adolfo Horta	Cuba
	3	Viktor Rybakov/	U.S.S.R./
		Krzysztof Kosedowski	Poland

BOXING (lightweight) Men

YEAR	PLACE	NAME	COUNTRY
1904	1	**H.J. Spanger**	**U.S.A.**
	2	J. Eagan	U.S.A.
	3	R. Van Horn	U.S.A.
1908	1	**F. Grace**	**Great Britain**
	2	F. Spiller	Great Britain
	3	H. Johnson	Great Britain
1920	1	**S. Mosberg**	**U.S.A.**
	2	G. Johanssen	Denmark
	3	C. Newton	Canada
1924	1	**H. Nielsen**	**Denmark**
	2	A. Copello	Argentina
	3	F. Boylstein	U.S.A.
1928	1	**C. Orlandi**	**Italy**
	2	S. Halaiko	U.S.A.
	3	G. Berggren	Sweden
1932	1	**L. Stevens**	**South Africa**
	2	T. Ahlqvist	Sweden
	3	N. Bor	U.S.A.
1936	1	**I. Harangi**	**Hungary**
	2	N. Stepulov	Estonia
	3	E. Agren	Sweden
1948	1	**G. Dreyer**	**South Africa**
	2	J. Vissers	Belgium
	3	S. Wad	Denmark
1952	1	**A. Bolognesi**	**Italy**
	2	A. Antkiewicz	Poland
	3	G. Fiat/	Rumania/
		E. Pakkanen	Finland
1956	1	**R. McTaggart**	**Great Britain**
	2	H. Kurschat	Germany
	3	A. Byrne/	Eire/
		A. Lagetko	U.S.S.R.
1960	1	**K. Pazdzior**	**Poland**
	2	S. Lopopolo	Italy
	3	R. McTaggart/	Great Britain/
		A. Laudonio	Argentina
1964	1	**J. Grudzien**	**Poland**
	2	V. Barannikov	U.S.S.R.
	3	R. Harris/	U.S.A./
		J. McCourt	Eire
1968	1	**R. Harris**	**U.S.A.**
	2	J. Grudzien	Poland
	3	C. Cutov/	Rumania/
		Z. Vujin	Yugoslavia
1972	1	**J. Szczepanski**	**Poland**
	2	L. Orban	Hungary
	3	A. Perez/	Colombia
		S. Mbuga	Kenya
1976	1	**Howard Davis**	**U.S.A.**
	2	Simion Cutov	Rumania
	2	Ace Ruseuski/	Yugoslavia/
		Vasiliy Solomin	U.S.S.R.
1980	2	**Angel Herrera**	**Cuba**
	2	Viktor Demianenko	U.S.S.R.
	3	Kazimierz Adach/	Poland/
		Richard Nowakowski	German Dem. Rep.

BOXING (light welterweight) Men

YEAR	PLACE	NAME	COUNTRY
1952	1	**C. Adkins**	**U.S.A.**
	2	V. Mednov	U.S.S.R.
	3	E. Mallenius/	Finland/
		B. Visintin	Italy
1956	1	**V. Yengibaryan**	**U.S.S.R.**
	2	F. Nenci	Italy
	3	H. Loubscher/	South Africa/
		C. Dumitrescu	Rumania
1960	1	**B. Nemecek**	**Czechoslovakia**
	2	C. Quartey	Ghana
	3	Q. Daniels/	U.S.A./
		M. Kasprzyk	Poland
1964	1	**J. Kulej**	**Poland**
	2	Y. Frolov	U.S.S.R.
	3	E. Blay/	Ghana/
		H. Galhia	Tunisia
1968	1	**J. Kulej**	**Poland**
	2	E. Regueiferos	Cuba
	3	A. Nilsson/	Finland/
		J. Wallington	U.S.A.
1972	1	**R. Seales**	**U.S.A.**
	2	A. Anghelov	Bulgaria
	3	I. Daborg/	Nigeria/
		Z. Vujin	Yugoslavia

BOXING (welterweight) Men

YEAR	PLACE	NAME	COUNTRY
1976	1	**Ray Leonard**	**U.S.A.** ✕
	2	Andres Aldama	Cuba
	3	Vladimir Kolev/	Bulgaria/
		Kazimier Szczerba	Poland
1980	1	**Patrizio Oliva**	**Italy**
	2	Serik Konakbaev	U.S.S.R.
	3	Anthony Willis/	United Kingdom/
		Jose Aguilar	Cuba

YEAR	PLACE	NAME	COUNTRY
1904	1	**A. Young**	**U.S.A.**
	2	H. Spanger	U.S.A.
	3	J. Lydon	U.S.A.
1920	1	**A. Schneider**	**Canada**
	2	A. Ireland	Great Britain
	3	F. Colberg	U.S.A.
1924	1	**J. Delarge**	**Belgium**
	2	H. Mendez	Argentina
	3	D. Lewis	Canada
1928	1	**E. Morgan**	**New Zealand**
	2	R. Landini	Argentina
	3	R. Smillie	Canada
1932	1	**E. Flynn**	**U.S.A.**
	2	E. Campe	Germany
	3	B. Ahlberg	Finland
1936	1	**S. Suvio**	**Finland**
	2	M. Murach	Germany
	3	G. Petersen	Denmark
1948	1	**J. Torma**	**Czechoslovakia**
	2	H. Herring	U.S.A.
	3	A. d'Ottavio	Italy
1952	1	**Z. Chychla**	**Poland**
	2	S. Schtscherbakov	U.S.S.R.
	3	V. Jörgensen/	Denmark/
		G. Heidemann	Germany
1956	1	**N. Linca**	**Rumania**
	2	F. Tiedt	Eire
	3	K. Hogarth/	Australia/
		N. Gargano	Great Britain
1960	1	**G. Benvenuti**	**Italy**
	2	Y. Radonyak	U.S.S.R.
	3	L. Drogosz/	Poland/
		J. Lloyd	Great Britain
1964	1	**M. Kasprzyk**	**Poland**
	2	R. Tarnulis	U.S.S.R.
	3	P. Purhonen/	Finland/
		S. Bertini	Italy
1968	1	**M. Wolke**	**East Germany**
	2	J. Bessala	Cameroons
	3	V. Mussalimov/	U.S.S.R./
		M. Guilloti	Argentina
1972	1	**E. Correa**	**Cuba**
	2	J. Kajda	Hungary
	3	J. Valdez/	U.S.A./
		D. Murunga	Kenya
1976	1	**Jochen Bachfeld**	**German Dem. Rep.**
	2	Padro J. Gamarro	Venezuela
	3	Reinhard Skricek/	Germany/
		Victor Zilberman	Rumania
1980	1	**Andres Aldama**	**Cuba**
	2	John Mugabi	Uganda
	3	Karl-Heinz Kiuger	German Dem. Rep./
		Kazimierz Szcezerba	Poland

BOXING (light middleweight) Men

YEAR	PLACE	NAME	COUNTRY
1952	1	**L. Papp**	**Hungary**
	2	T. Van Schalkwyk	South Africa
	3	B. Tischin/	U.S.S.R./
		E. Herrera	Argentina
1956	1	**L. Papp**	**Hungary**
	2	J. Torres	U.S.A.
	3	J. McCormack/	Great Britain/
		Z. Pietrzykowski	Poland
1960	1	**W. McClure**	**U.S.A.**
	2	C. Bossi	Italy
	3	B. Lagutin/	U.S.S.R./
		W. Fisher	Great Britain
1964	1	**B. Lagutin**	**U.S.S.R.**
	2	J. Gonzales	France
	3	N. Maiyegun/	Nigeria/
		J. Grzesiak	Poland
1968	1	**B. Lagutin**	**U.S.S.R.**
	2	R. Garbey	Cuba
	3	J. Baldwin/	U.S.A./
		G. Meier	West Germany

BOXING (middleweight) Men

YEAR	PLACE	NAME	COUNTRY
1972	1	**D. Kottysch**	**West Germany**
	2	W. Rudkowski	Poland
	3	A. Minter/	Great Britain/
		P. Tiepold	East Germany
1976	1	**Jerzy Rybicki**	**Poland**
	2	Tadija Kacar	Yugoslavia
	3	Rolando Garbey/	Cuba/
		Victor Savchenko	U.S.S.R.
1980	1	**Armando Martinez**	**Cuba**
	2	Alexsandr Koshkin	U.S.S.R.
	3	Zan Farnek/	Czechoslovakia/
		Detlef Kastner	German Dem. Rep.

YEAR	PLACE	NAME	COUNTRY
1904	1	**C. Mayer**	**U.S.A.**
	2	B. Spradley	U.S.A.
1908	1	**J. Douglas**	**Great Britain**
	2	R. Baker	Australia
	3	W. Philo	Great Britain
1920	1	**H. Mallin**	**Great Britain**
	2	G. Prudhomme	Canada
	3	M. Herscovitch	Canada
1924	1	**H. Mallin**	**Great Britain**
	2	J. Elliott	Great Britain
	3	J. Beecken	Belgium
1928	1	**P. Toscani**	**Italy**
	2	J. Hermanek	Czechoslovakia
	3	L. Steyaert	Belgium
1932	1	**C. Barth**	**U.S.A.**
	2	A. Azar	Argentina
	3	E. Pierce	South Africa
1936	1	**J. Despeaux**	**France**
	2	H. Tiller	Norway
	3	R. Villareal	Argentina
1948	1	**L. Papp**	**Hungary**
	2	J. Wright	Great Britain
	3	I. Fontana	Italy
1952	1	**F. Patterson**	**U.S.A.**
	2	V. Tita	Rumania
	3	B. Nikolov/	Bulgaria/
		S. Sjölin	Sweden
1956	1	**G. Schatkov**	**U.S.S.R.**
	2	R. Tapia	Chile
	3	G. Chapron/	France/
		V. Zalazar	Argentina
1960	1	**E. Crook**	**U.S.A.**
	2	T. Walasek	Poland
	3	I. Monea/	Rumania/
		E. Feofanov	U.S.S.R.
1964	1	**V. Popentschenko**	**U.S.S.R.**
	2	E. Schulz	Germany
	3	F. Valle/	Italy/
		T. Walasek	Poland
1968	1	**C. Finnegan**	**Great Britain**
	2	A. Kisselyov	U.S.S.R.
	3	A. Zaragoza/	Mexico/
		A. Jones	U.S.A.
1972	1	**V. Lemechev**	**U.S.S.R.**
	2	R. Virtanen	Finland
	3	P. Amartey/	Ghana/
		M. Johnson	U.S.A.
1976	1	**Michael Spinks**	**U.S.A.** ✕
	2	Lufat Riskiev	U.S.S.R.
	3	Alec Nastac/	Rumania/
		Luis Martinez	Cuba
1980	1	**Jose Gomez**	**Cuba**
	2	Viktor Savchenko	U.S.S.R.
	3	Valentin Silaghi/	Rumania/
		Jerzy Rybicki	Poland

BOXING (light heavyweight) Men

YEAR	PLACE	NAME	COUNTRY
1920	1	**E. Eagan**	**U.S.A.**
	2	S. Sörsdal	Norway
	3	H. Franks	Great Britain
1924	1	**H. Mitchell**	**Great Britain**
	2	T. Petersen	Denmark
	3	S. Sörsdal	Norway
1928	1	**V. Avendano**	**Argentina**
	2	E. Pistulla	Germany
	3	K. Miljon	Netherlands
1932	1	**D. Carstens**	**South Africa**
	2	G. Rossi	Italy
	3	P. Jörgensen	Denmark

Skill and power are used to overcome the opponent.

YEAR	PLACE	NAME	COUNTRY
1936	1	R. Michelot	France
	2	R. Vogt	Germany
	3	F. Risiglione	Argentina
1948	1	G. Hunter	South Africa
	2	D. Scott	Great Britain
	3	M. Cia	Argentina
1952	1	N. Lee	U.S.A.
	2	A. Pacenza	Argentina
	3	A. Perov/	U.S.S.R./
		H. Siljander	Finland
1956	1	J. Boyd	U.S.A.
	2	G. Negrea	Rumania
	3	C. Lucas/	Chile/
		R. Murauskas	U.S.S.R.
1960	1	C. Clay	U.S.A.
	2	Z. Pietrzykowski	Poland
	3	A. Madigan/	Australia/
		G. Saraudi	Italy
1964	1	C. Pinto	Italy
	2	A. Kisselyov	U.S.S.R.
	3	A. Nikolov/	Bulgaria/
		Z. Pietrzykowski	Poland
1968	1	D. Pozdnyak	U.S.S.R.
	2	I. Monea	Rumania
	3	G. Stankov/	Bulgaria/
		S. Dragan	Poland
1972	1	M. Parlov	Yugoslavia
	2	G. Carrillo	Cuba
	3	I. Ikhouria/	Nigeria/
		J. Gortat	Poland
1976	1	Leon Spinks	U.S.A.
	2	Sisto Soria	Cuba
	3	Kostica Dafinoiu/	Rumania/
		Janusz Gortat	Poland
1980	1	Slobodan Kacar	Yugoslavia
	2	Panew Skrzecz	Poland
	3	Herbert Bauch/	German Dem. Rep.
		Ricardo Rojas	Cuba

BOXING (heavyweight) Men

YEAR	PLACE	NAME	COUNTRY
1904	1	S. Berger	U.S.A.
	2	C. Mayer	U.S.A.
1908	1	A.L. Oldham	Great Britain
	2	S. Evans	Great Britain
	3	F. Parks	Great Britain
1920	1	R. Rawson	Great Britain
	2	S. Petersen	Denmark
	3	X. Eluère	France
1924	1	O. von Porat	Norway
	2	S. Petersen	Denmark
	3	A. Porzio	Argentina
1928	1	A.R. Jurado	Argentina
	2	N. Ramm	Sweden
	3	M. Michaelsen	Denmark
1932	1	S. Lovell	Argentina
	2	L. Rovati	Italy
	3	F. Feary	U.S.A.
1936	1	H. Runge	Germany
	2	G. Lovell	Argentina
	3	E. Nilsen	Norway
1948	1	R. Iglesias	Argentina
	2	G. Nilsson	Sweden
	3	J. Arthur	South Africa
1952	1	E. Sanders	U.S.A.
	2	disqualified	
	3	A. Nieman/	South Africa/
		I. Koski	Finland
1956	1	P. Rademacher	U.S.A.
	2	L. Mukhin	U.S.S.R.
	3	D. Bekker/	South Africa/
		G. Bozzano	Italy

YEAR	PLACE	NAME	COUNTRY
1960	1	F. de Piccoli	Italy
	2	D. Bekker	South Africa
	3	J. Nemec/	Czechoslovakia/
		G. Siegmund	Germany
1964	1	J. Frazier	U.S.A.
	2	H. Huber	Germany
	3	G. Ros/	Italy/
		V. Yemelyanov	U.S.S.R.
1968	1	G. Foreman	U.S.A.
	2	I. Tschepulis	U.S.S.R.
	3	G. Bambini/	Italy/
		J. Rocha	Mexico
1972	1	T. Stevenson	Cuba
	2	I. Alexe	Rumania
	3	P. Hussing/	West Germany/
		H. Thomsen	Sweden
1976	1	Teofilo Stevenson	Cuba
	2	Mircea Simon	Rumania
	3	Johnny Tate/	U.S.A.
		Clarence Hill	Bermuda
1980	1	Teofilo Stevenson	Cuba
	2	Pyotr Zaev	U.S.S.R.
	3	Istvan Levai/	Hungary
		Jurgen Fanghanel	German Dem. Rep.

CANOEING

EVENT DATE			LAKE CASITAS, VENTURA COUNTY

AUGUST	6	500m heats, men & women
		500m repechage, men & women
	7	1,000m heats, men/500m heats, women
		1,000m repechage, men/500m repechage, women
	8	500m semifinals, men & women
	9	1,000m semifinals, men/500m semifinals, women

AUGUST	10	500m finals, men & women
	11	1,000m finals, men

Canoeing became an official Olympic event in 1936.

HISTORY

Along with the raft, the canoe was one of man's earliest modes of transportation on water, with some examples dating back to the Stone Age. But unlike the awkward raft, the canoe was a sleek, swift craft powered by the rhythmic strokes of its occupants.

The early "open" canoes generally were carved out of wood, which offered natural flotation. When shaped and properly balanced by its occupants, the canoe was indeed a sturdy craft. Farther north, the "closed" kayak came into existence, pioneered by the Eskimo who stretched a waterproof sealskin across the frame of his boat.

The Polynesians used large canoes with outriggers to explore the South Pacific, while the North American Indian used his large, bark canoes to haul goods and warriors. Today, canoes are used for outings by high school and university students during their summer vacations to explore the many lakes that abound in North America, and for racing.

It was inevitable that competitive racing was taken up by both the canoe and the kayak enthusiast, since self-propelled speed, delicate balance and strength are natural ingredients for competition. The kayak has proved to be ideal for "white water" events in which the boats are raced through the churning waters of fast-flowing streams and rapids.

Competitive canoeing can be traced back to London's Royal Canoe Club. By 1874, the first trophy for canoe racing was awarded.

In North America, and in particular Canada, canoe racing made solid inroads and by the 1920s, the sport enjoyed a great deal of respectability. By 1924, international events were being held and the International Canoeing Federation was established to foster canoe racing's growth. The group managed to have canoeing demonstrated in the 1924 Olympics, but it did not become part of the official Olympic programme until 1936. Since then the growth has been steady if not spectacular. There are now just over 40 countries affiliated with the International Canoeing Federation.

Women made their Olympic debut in 1948 with the kayak singles event. In 1960, the women's doubles event was added, and in 1984 the fours, where four women are in one kayak, will be included.

GENERAL DESCRIPTION

Lots are drawn for starting positions. Boats line up with their bows on the starting line. The aligner raises a white flag when all boats are stationary and level.

The starter then takes over. He says, "ready" and then fires a shot or says, "go" to get the race under way. It is a false start if a competitor starts paddling before the "go." A crew can be disqualified for two false starts, whether it is caused by them or not. If a competitor breaks a paddle within 15 metres of the start, there is a recall and a new start.

For the entire race, the boats must be kept in their respective lanes and cannot come closer than five metres to another craft.

The still-water course is marked by buoys and flags. The 500- and 1,000-metre races are straight and marked with lane markers if possible.

The race is deemed over when the first boat's bow passes between the red finishing flags. When all boats have finished, the umpire shows a white flag if no rule has been infringed, or a red flag if there has been an infringement.

Boats qualifying for the next round (semifinal or repechage), or the first four boats in a final, are then re-measured and weighed.

There may be heats (qualifying rounds) held for some events. They must be held, along with the final, on the same stretch of water and none may include more than nine canoes. Allocation to heats and lanes is decided by lot. The heat system allows three canoes to proceed to the next stage and finishing positions (not times) are the deciding factor.

Intervals between semifinals and finals should not be less than one hour for 500-metre events or one-and-a-half hours for 1,000-metre events.

For Olympic events, the water depth over the whole course should be at least three metres. If that is impossible, a uniform depth of at least two metres is acceptable. The lanes must be 9-metres wide.

PROCEDURE

Entries for the Olympic Games are limited to one per nation for each of the nine events for men and three for women.

Substitutes are permitted in all events but a crew may not be changed after it has begun to compete in an event.

The events for men:
Canadian canoe singles at 500 and 1,000 metres.
Canadian canoe pairs at 500 and 1,000 metres.
Kayak singles at 500 and 1,000 metres.

Secured in for the kayak race

Kayak pairs at 500 and 1,000 metres.
Kayak fours at 1,000 metres.

The events for women:
Kayak singles, pairs and fours at 500 metres.

VIEWING TIPS

Racing kayaks and canoes have almost no lateral stability. Along with the need to maintain direction, the competitor must also fight the battle of balance. These problems are easily hidden from the uninitiated viewer, who is often more impressed with the energetic efforts of the paddlers and their rising and falling paddles.

Because of the need to propel and steer the boat with only one blade, the canoe racer has difficulty in maintaining forward direction, especially if there is a crosswind. Maintaining direction is much easier for kayak racers who have foot-controlled rudders and double-bladed paddles. Balance, however, is still a problem for kayak racers and you should not be deceived by the apparent ease in which the kayak glides through the water.

The whirlwind motion of the kayak paddlers is basically a stroke in three phases. The first is a rotation of the upper body to reach forward with the paddle, allowing a strong catch as the paddle is speared into the water. Second, the body counterrotates pulling the paddle through the water. The last phase occurs when the paddle is exited when the blade or hand reaches the hip. The paddle is lifted up and the paddler sets up the stroke on the other side.

You should also watch the precision in which the athletes stay in stroke with each other in the pairs and fours events. The paddler in the front position sets the stroke and the others follow, trying to have their paddles enter and exit the water at exactly the same time. If they remain synchronized, the paddlers will have a smooth ride. But there are plenty of chances for error. Remember, there will be about 120 strokes per minute in the kayak fours (K-4), a race that lasts over three minutes.

The canoe events are commonly referred to as the Canadian singles or pairs (C-1 or C-2). The kayak events are called singles, pairs or fours (K-1, K-2 or K-4).

TECHNICAL TERMS

K-1, kayak singles — kayak for one man or woman, the K standing for kayak and the 1 for one person.

K-2, kayak pairs — the two-person kayak for men or women.

K-4, kayak fours — the four-person kayak for men or women.

C-1, Canadian singles or canoe singles — the one-man canoe. Raced by men only. Named after Canada because of its Indian tradition and effort to introduce the event to the Olympics.

C-2, Canadian pairs or canoe tandem — the two-man canoe. Raced only by men.

Stroke rate — the number of strokes taken per minute by a competitor or crew. Varies with different body size and race length.

Heat, repechage, semifinal and final — all competitors start in the preliminary round called a heat. Depending on the number of entries, and the finishing place, a competitor may advance directly to the semifinal or have a second chance through a repechage. After the semifinals, nine entries qualify for the final and the medals.

EQUIPMENT

Boats — there are minimum dimensions laid down for each class. For all canoes, the sectional and longitudinal lines of the hull must be convex and uninterrupted. The canoe must be built symmetrically upon the axis. Rudders or any similar apparatus for directing the course of the canoe are forbidden. Steering rudders, however, are allowed for kayaks. See graphics.

Paddles — usually made of wood and designed for speed and lightness. The blade is slightly spoon-shaped to give clean entry into the water.

Number plates — these must have black numbers on a yellow background and measure 18 centimetres x 20 centimetres. They are carried on the afterdeck of the kayaks and the foredecks of the Canadian canoes.

Dress — racing shirts bear national colours or insignia. All athletes wear black competitor numbers on a white background.

TOP CANADIANS

Larry Cain of Oakville, Ontario was seventh in the world championships at Tampere, Finland, 1983, in both the 500- and 1,000-metre events for Canadian canoe singles. He won a C-1 500-metre event in an international meet in Bulgaria and a C-1 1,000-metre event in East Germany. Cain was the 500- and 1,000-metre champion in the C-1 events in the 1981 world junior championships.

Hugh Fisher of Coquitlam, B.C. and Alwyn Morris of Caughnawaga, Quebec, were second in the 1,000-metre kayak (K-2) events in 1983 in Moscow and East Germany. They were third in the K-2 500-metre test in the world championships last summer.

Sue Holloway of Ottawa and Alexandra Barré of Jonquiere, Quebec, were seventh in the women's K-2 event at the 1983 world championships. Holloway was a member of the eighth-place crew in the event in the 1976 Olympic Games in Montreal.

MEDAL WINNERS

CANOEING (kayak singles — 500 metres) Men

New Olympic Event — 1976

YEAR	PLACE	NAME	COUNTRY
1976	1	V. Diba	Rumania
	2	Z. Szytanity	Hungary
	3	R. Helm	East Germany
1980	1	V. Parfenovich	U.S.S.R.
	2	J. Sumegi	Austria
	3	V. Diba	Rumania

CANOEING (kayak singles — 1,000 metres) Men

YEAR	PLACE	NAME	COUNTRY
1936	1	G. Hradetzky	Austria
	2	H. Cämmerer	Germany
	3	J. Kraaier	Netherlands
1948	1	G. Fredriksson	Sweden
	2	J. Kobberup	Denmark
	3	H. Eberhardt	France
1952	1	G. Fredriksson	Sweden
	2	T. Strömberg	Finland
	3	L. Gantois	France
1956	1	G. Fredriksson	Sweden
	2	I. Pissaryev	U.S.S.R.
	3	L. Kiss	Hungary
1960	1	E. Hansen	Denmark
	2	I. Szöllösi	Hungary
	3	G. Fredriksson	Sweden
1964	1	R. Peterson	Sweden
	2	M. Hesz	Hungary
	3	A. Vernescu	Rumania
1968	1	M. Hesz	Hungary
	2	A. Schaparenko	U.S.S.R.
	3	E. Hansen	Denmark
1972	1	A. Schaparenko	U.S.S.R.
	2	R. Peterson	Sweden
	3	G. Czapo	Hungary
1976	1	R. Helm	German Dem. Rep.
	2	G. Csapo	Hungary
	3	V. Diba	Rumania
1980	1	R. Helm	German Dem. Rep.
	2	A. Lebas	France
	3	I. Birladeanu	Rumania

C-1
Length 5.20m (17') max.
Beam 75cm (2'6") min.
Weight 16kg (35 lb) min.

C-2
Length 6.50m (21'4") max.
Beam 75cm (2'6") min.
Weight 20kg (44 lb) min.

K-1
Length 5.20m (17') max.
Beam 51cm (1'9") min.
Weight 12kg(27 lb) min.

K-2
Length 6.50m (21'4") max.
Beam 55cm (1'10") min.
Weight 18kg (40 lb) min.

K-4
Length 11m (36') max.
Beam 60cm (1'11½") min.
Weight 30kg (66 lb) min.

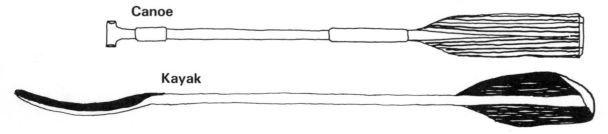

Canoe

Kayak

CANOEING (kayak pairs — 500 metres) Men

New Olympic Event — 1976			
YEAR	PLACE	NAME	COUNTRY
1976	1	**J. Mattern** **B. Olbricht**	**East Germany**
	2	S. Nagorny V. Romanovski	U.S.S.R.
	3	L. Serghei P. Malihin	Rumania
1980	1	**V. Parfenovich** **S. Chukhrai**	**U.S.S.R.**
	2	H. Menendez G. Del Riego	Spain
	3	B. Olbricht R. Helm	East Germany

CANOEING (kayak pairs — 1,000 metres) Men

YEAR	PLACE	NAME	COUNTRY
1936	1	**A. Kainz/** **A. Dorfner**	**Austria**
	2	E. Tilker/ F. Bondroit	Germany
	3	N. Tates/ W. Vander-Kroft	Netherlands
1948	1	**H. Berglund/** **L. Kligström**	**Sweden**
	2	E. Hansen/ B. Jensen	Denmark
	3	T. Axelsson/ N. Björklöf	Finland
1952	1	**K. Wires/** **Y. Hietanen**	**Finland**
	2	L. Glasser/ I. Hedberg	Sweden
	3	M. Raub/ H. Wiedermann	Austria
1956	1	**M. Scheuer/** **M. Miltenberger**	**Germany**
	2	M. Kaaleste/ A. Demitkov	U.S.S.R.
	3	M. Raub/ H. Wiedermann	Austria
1960	1	**G. Fredriksson/** **S. Sjödelius**	**Sweden**
	2	A. Szente/ G. Mészáros	Hungary
	3	S. Kalaniak/ W. Zielinki	Poland
1964	1	**S. Sjödelius/** **N. Utterberg**	**Sweden**
	2	A. Geurts/ P. Hoekstra	Netherlands
	3	H. Büker/ H. Zander	Germany
1968	1	**A. Schaparenko/** **V. Morozov**	**U.S.S.R.**
	2	C. Giczi/ I. Timár	Hungary
	3	G. Siebold/ G. Pfaff	Austria

YEAR	PLACE	NAME	COUNTRY
1972	1	N. Gorbachev/ V. Karatassyuk	U.S.S.R.
	2	J. Deme/ Ratkai	Hungary
	3	W. Szuszkiewicz/ R. Piszcz	Poland
1976	1	S. Nagorny/ V. Romanovski	U.S.S.R.
	2	J. Mattern/ B. Olbricht	East Germany
	3	Z. Bako/ I. Szabo	Hungary
1980	1	V. Parfenovich/ S. Chukhrai	U.S.S.R.
	2	I. Szabo/ I. Joos	Hungary
	3	L. Ramos/ H.H. Menendez	Spain

CANOEING (kayak fours — 1,000 metres) Men

YEAR	PLACE	COUNTRY
1964	1	U.S.S.R.
	2	Germany
	3	Rumania
1968	1	Norway
	2	Rumania
	3	Hungary
1972	1	U.S.S.R.
	2	Rumania
	3	Norway
1976	1	U.S.S.R.
	2	Hungary
	3	East Germany
1980	1	East Germany
	2	U.S.S.R.
	3	Hungary

CANOEING (Canadian singles — 500 metres) Men

New Olympic Event — 1976

YEAR	PLACE	NAME	COUNTRY
1976	1	A. Rogov	U.S.S.R.
	2	J. Wood	Canada
	3	M. Ljubek	Yugoslavia
1980	1	S. Postrekhin	U.S.S.R.
	2	L. Lubenov	Bulgaria
	3	O. Heukrodt	East Germany

CANOEING (Canadian singles — 1,000 metres) Men

YEAR	PLACE	NAME	COUNTRY
1936	1	F. Amyot	Canada
	2	B. Karlik	Czechoslovakia
	3	E. Koschik	Germany
1948	1	J. Holecek	Czechoslovakia
	2	D. Bennett	Canada
	3	R. Boutigny	France
1952	1	J. Holecek	Czechoslovakia
	2	J. Parti	Hungary
	3	O. Ojanperä	Finland
1956	1	L. Rotman	Rumania
	2	I. Hernek	Hungary
	3	G. Bukharin	U.S.S.R.
1960	1	J. Parti	Hungary
	2	A. Silayev	U.S.S.R.
	3	L. Rotman	Rumania
1964	1	J. Eschert	Germany
	2	A. Igorov	Rumania
	3	E. Penyayev	U.S.S.R.
1968	1	T. Tatai	Hungary
	2	D. Lewe	Germany
	3	V. Galkov	U.S.S.R.
1972	1	I. Patzaichin	Rumania
	2	T. Wichmann	Hungary
	3	D. Lewe	Germany
1976	1	M. Ljubek	Yugoslavia
	2	V. Urchenko	U.S.S.R.
	3	T. Wichman	Hungary
1980	1	L. Lubenov	Bulgaria
	2	S. Postrekhin	U.S.S.R.
	3	E. Leve	East Germany

CANOEING (Canadian pairs — 500 metres) Men

YEAR	PLACE	NAME	COUNTRY
1976	1	S. Petrenko/ A. Vinogradov	U.S.S.R.
	2	Jerzy Opara/ A. Gronowicz	Poland
	3	T. Buday/ Oszkar Frey	Hungary
1980	1	L. Foltan/ I. Vaskut	Hungary
	2	I. Patzaichin/ I. Capusta	Rumania
	3	B. Ananiev/ N. Ikov	Bulgaria

CANOEING (Canadian pairs — 1,000 metres) Men

YEAR	PLACE	NAME	COUNTRY
1936	1	V. Syrovátka/ J. Brzák	Czechoslovakia
	2	R. Weinstabl/ K. Proisl	Austria
	3	F. Saker/ H. Charters	Canada
1948	1	J. Brzák/ B. Kudrna	Czechoslovakia
	2	S. Lysak/ S. Macknowski	U.S.A.
	3	G. Dransart/ G. Gandil	France
1952	1	B. Rasch/ F. Haunstoft	Denmark
	2	J. Brzák/ B. Kudrna	Czechoslovakia
	3	E. Drews/ W. Soltau	Germany
1956	1	A. Dumitru/ S. Ismailciuc	Rumania
	2	P. Kharin/ G. Botev	U.S.S.R.
	3	K. Wieland/ F. Mohacsi	Hungary
1960	1	L. Geischtor/ S. Makarenko	U.S.S.R.
	2	A. Dezi/ F. LaMacchia	Italy
	3	I. Farkas/ A. Toro	Hungary
1964	1	A. Khimitsch/ S. Oschtschepkov	U.S.S.R.
	2	J. Boudehen/ M. Chapuis	France
	3	P. Nielsen/ J. Sörensen	Denmark
1968	1	I. Patzaichin/ S. Covaliov	Rumania
	2	T. Wichmann/ G. Petrikovics	Hungary
	3	N. Prokupets/ M. Zamotin	U.S.S.R.
1972	1	V. Chessyunas/ Y. Lobanov	U.S.S.R.
	2	I. Patzaichin/ S. Kovaliov	Rumania
	3	F. Damianov/ I. Bourtschine	Bulgaria
1976	1	S. Petrenko/ A. Vinogradov	U.S.S.R.
	2	G. Danielov/ G. Simionov	Rumania
	3	T. Buday/ O. Frey	Hungary
1980	1	I. Patzaichin/ I. Simionov	Rumania
	2	O. Heukrodt/ U. Madeja	East Germany
	3	Y. Yurchenko/ Y. Lobanov	U.S.S.R.

CANOEING (kayak singles — 500 metres) Women

YEAR	PLACE	NAME	COUNTRY
1948	1	K. Hoff	Denmark
	2	A.V. Anker-Doedans	Netherlands
	3	F. Schwingl	Austria
1952	1	S. Saimo	Finland
	2	G. Liebhart	Austria
	3	N. Savina	U.S.S.R.
1956	1	Y. Dementyeva	U.S.S.R.
	2	T. Zenz	Germany
	3	T. Söby	Denmark
1960	1	A. Seredina	U.S.S.R.
	2	T. Zenz	Germany
	3	D. Walkowiak	Poland
1964	1	L. Khvedosyuk	U.S.S.R.
	2	H. Lauer	Rumania
	3	M. Jones	U.S.A.
1968	1	L. Pinayeva-Khvedosyuk	U.S.S.R.
	2	R. Breuer	Germany
	3	V. Dumitru	Rumania
1972	1	Y. Ryabchinskaya	U.S.S.R.
	2	M. Jaapies	Holland
	3	A. Pfeffer	Hungary
1976	1	C. Zirzow	East Germany
	2	T. Korshunova	U.S.S.R.
	3	K. Rajnai	Hungary
1980	1	B. Fischer	East Germany
	2	V. Checheva	Bulgaria
	3	A. Melnikova	

CANOEING (kayak pairs — 500 metres) Women

YEAR	PLACE	NAME	COUNTRY
1960	1	M. Schubina/ A. Seredina	U.S.S.R.
	2	T. Zenz/ I. Hartmann	Germany
	3	V. Egresi/ K. Fried-Bánfalvi	Hungary
1964	1	R. Esser/ A. Zimmermann	Germany
	2	F. Fox/ G. Perrier	U.S.A.
	3	H. Lauer/ C. Sideri	Rumania
1968	1	R. Esser/ A. Zimmermann	Germany
	2	A. Pfeffer/ K. Rozsnyoi	Hungary
	3	L. Pinayeva/ A. Seredina	U.S.S.R.
1972	1	L. Pinayeva/ E. Duryshka	U.S.S.R.
	2	I. Kaschube/ P. Grabowski	East Germany
	3	M. Michiforov/ V. Dumitru	Rumania
1976	1	N. Gopova/ G. Kreft	U.S.S.R.
	2	A. Pfeffer/ K. Rojnai	Hungary
	3	B. Koster/ C. Zirzow	East Germany
1980	1	C. Genauss/ M. Bischof	East Germany
	2	G. Alexeyeva/ N. Trofimova	U.S.S.R.
	3	E. Rakusz/ M. Zakarias	Hungary

CYCLING

EVENT DATE

CALIFORNIA STATE UNIVERSITY, DOMINGUEZ HILLS

JULY	**29**	70 km individual road race, women 190 km individual road race, men
	30	Individual pursuit—qualification 1 km time trial—final
	31	Individual pursuit—quarterfinals/Sprint repechage Points race—qualification
AUGUST	**1**	Individual pursuit—semifinals & finals Sprint—quarterfinals/Points race—qualification

AUGUST	**2**	Sprint—semifinals Team pursuit—qualification & quarterfinals
	3	Sprint—finals Team pursuit—semifinals & finals/Points race—final
	5	100 km road race team time trial (Held on Artesia Freeway, Route 91)

Cycling down the long and winding route

HISTORY

Even though the wheel has been around since the days of prehistoric man, the bicycle did not come into being until about 150 years ago. The early bicycles were crude and as rough looking as the roads they had to face. Yet, these new fangled inventions grew in popularity in pockets of France and England.

The earliest pedal driven bicycles were aptly nicknamed "boneshakers" and appeared in the early 1800's. They had wood or steel wheels. The "ordinary," or "penny farthing" appeared in 1869, incorporating the same pedal mechanism as the boneshaker (pedals on the front wheel axle) but with a larger front wheel to increase the speed of the machine.

Then came the revolutionary chain-driven bicycle with front and rear wheels of the same size. It was an instant success and the bicycle became an important mode of transportation and sport.

Further major developments followed quickly. In 1888, the Scot John Dunlop, developed the first air-filled tire and started a family business that became renowned throughout the world. A couple of years after Dunlop made his breakthrough, the Michelin brothers of France produced a removable tire. Then came the coaster brake (operating off the pedals). Once these essential parts were invented, all that remained to be produced were bicycle variations.

Racing gripped the fitness-minded. Bicycle manufacturers were turning out swifter and lighter models, which whetted the appetite of those hungry for speed and competition. In 1896, bicycle racing was introduced to the Olympic Games, and a special concrete racing course was constructed in Athens to hold the 100-kilometre event. By the turn of the century, the bicycle was at its height of popularity. The automobile had yet to make its mark.

As the automobile started taking over the roads, the bicycle became less appealing as a means of transportation. It did, however, retain its appeal for exercise and as a toy for children.

Like most Olympic events, cycling has undergone several changes in format. Cyclists now compete on the track and road. The indoor events are held in velodromes with tracks that are 333.3-metres long and 7-metres wide, with a banked racing surface of 33 degrees.

The velodromes proved popular. Along with providing uniform racing conditions for competitors, the velodromes provided plenty of seating for spectators to watch all the action.

The inauguration of such popular sporting events as the Tour de France, which was started in 1903, has helped sustain the interest in bicycle racing between Olympic Games. The Tour de France is one of the most publicized events in Europe, making France a hotbed for cycle racing. The sport is as satisfying to Frenchmen as a fine wine.

French spectators attending the 100-kilometre road race in Berlin in 1936 had a lot to cheer about. In the final metres, Frenchmen Robert Charpentier and Guy Lapébie were racing side by side toward the finish line and the gold medal. Charpentier won by a very slim margin, but he had pulled a fast one. As the two riders neared the finish line, Charpentier had reached out and grabbed Lapébie by the shirt, pulling him backwards. That illegal move wasn't spotted by the officials and escaped immediate detection. It didn't, however, escape being exposed by a photograph taken near the finish line by a spectator.

Over the years, cyclists have shown considerable sportsmanship. It is not uncommon for a cyclist to stop and wait for a rival having a broken bicycle repaired.

GENERAL DESCRIPTION

Racing bicycles are light in weight — 7 kilograms for track bikes; 9 kilograms for road bikes — and must conform to specified dimensions so that all competitors use virtually the same equipment. Of course, the only power to move the bicycle must be provided by the rider.

It is mandatory for the bicycles used in road racing to be equipped with a working brake for each wheel. In track events the bicycles are free of brakes because officials want to avoid sudden stops which can cause crashes.

In the team time-trial road event, the racers cover 100 kilometres and the four-man team races against the clock. The time of the top three finishers is used to determine the team's total time.

In the individual road race, the winner is the first across the finish line. This is a tactical as well as an endurance event, in which teammates and even rivals exchange the lead (to break the wind) or open a gap to gain an advantage over the rest of the field.

The track, or velodrome, events generally provide more excitement for the spectators because all the action takes place on the track which is 333.3-metres

The Olympic Velodrome is the site of the cycling competition.

Looking out for the competition

The four man team pursuit

long, 7-metres wide and is banked 33 degrees so that the riders can handle high speeds around the turns. In most cases, the track is surrounded by up to 10,000 seats.

Speed is not the only requisite for track racing as spectators discover when watching the 1,000-metre sprint. This very tactical race of head-to-head competition is a sprint over the last 200 to 300 metres only. In the beginning of the race the two competitors pedal slowly, carefully watching one another, somewhat like boxers waiting for an opening to strike. They circle the track eyeing each other until shortly before the 200-metre mark when the disadvantage of high speed is outweighed by the advantage of having the lead position in a sprint to the finish line. The only time recorded is the final 200 metres. Gold medal winner Daniel Morelon of France won the 1968 Games final at Mexico City in 10.68 seconds, meaning he was travelling about 67.5 kilometres an hour during the last 200 metres.

In the 1,000-metre sprint, racers must progress through a heat or qualifying system. The winners advance while the losers in the qualifying rounds go into the repechage or second-chance heats, which enable them to qualify for the higher rounds. The greatest speed is seen in the final 200 metres. Time is not the deciding factor. The first man across the finish line wins the race.

The individual pursuit is a very demanding test of more than 4,000 metres. It calls for a quick start and then sustained speed before a final burst of extreme speed at the finish. The riders race in pairs, starting on opposite sides of the track, ''pursuing'' one another (hence the name) until one is caught, or until this distance has been completed. In case one cyclist does not overtake, or catch, the other rider, the cyclist with the fastest time is declared the winner.

The team pursuit is similar to the individual pursuit. A team of four riders races against another team of four over 4,000 metres. Victory is decided by the third rider's time across the line in each team. During the event, the teammates share the work of breaking the wind, then swing up the banking of the track before dropping down behind the last rider to rest before taking another turn at breaking the wind.

PROCEDURE

Each country may enter up to 15 competitors, none of which may be younger than 17 years of age. Each nation is limited to one starter in the three individual events and four starters in each of the team events. There is an allowance, however, for all riders to act as substitutes in all races other than the ones they have been specifically entered in.

There is no luck of the draw for the individual road race. It simply calls for a mass start.

Canadian road and track cyclists compete in a series of competitions designated as selection or assessment events before being selected by the racing committee of the Canadian Cycling Association, which then nominates its choices for the Olympic Games to the Canadian Olympic Association. In their bids to earn an Olympic spot, many Canadian cyclists have travelled extensively in the United States and Europe in search of both good training weather and competition.

Readers will also be interested to note that 1984 marks the first Olympics to include women in the cycling events.

VIEWING TIPS

The track events are ideal for viewing for they give the spectators an opportunity to closely watch the competitors racing tactics and to easily follow the high-speed action. Your television set gives you the best seat in the house.

In the 1,000-metre time-trial, the cyclists leave from a standing start and then speed around the oval three times. The race is strictly against the clock. In the 1,000-metre sprint, watch the riders jockeying for position as they speed up and reduce speed in the early part of the race. It is a cat-and-mouse game that ends in the final 200 metres when the riders go all-out to the finish.

Competitors in the individual and team pursuit line up at opposite ends of the track. It is particularly interesting to watch the skill involved when the lead rider of the four-man team rapidly changes position. As he tires, he swings up the banking of the track and then goes down to the tail of the team for a brief rest. This positioning is practised throughout the race. Team effort is a must for success.

Leading the pack

Fighting off the competition

To calculate the performances, officials use the time of each team's third rider who finishes in the race. The third-man timing theme is also used in the 100-kilometre team road time-trial.

Watching a road race is best done by sitting in front of the television set. Several camera locations can pick up the action at critical points.

EQUIPMENT

Bicycles — must conform to specified dimensions and can be propelled only by human force. For road races, the bicycles must have one working brake on each wheel.

Dress — Cyclists must wear protective helmets (usually strips of dense foam or a rigid moulded material). They must wear a racing jersey that covers the shoulders and close-fitting spandex shorts that reach midthigh to prevent bunching at the point of contact with the saddle.

TOP CANADIANS

Alex Stieda of Vancouver won a bronze medal last summer at the World University Games in the 4,000-metres individual pursuit.

Karen Strong, thirty—two time Canadian champion and bronze and silver medalist at the World Championships is Canada's best hope among the women.

MEDAL WINNERS

CYCLING—1,000 metres Sprint

YEAR	PLACE	NAME	COUNTRY
1896	1	P. Masson	France
	2	S. Nikolopoulos	Greece
	3	L. Flameng	France
1900	1	G. Taillandier	France
	2	Sanz	France
	3	Lake	U.S.A.
1908		Race declared void, time limit exceeded.	
1920	1	M. Peeters	Netherlands
	2	H.T. Johnson	Great Britain
	3	H. Ryan	Great Britain
1924	1	L. Michard	France
	2	J. Meijer	Netherlands
	3	J. Cugnot	France
1928	1	R. Beaufrand	France
	2	A. Mazairac	Netherlands
	3	W. Falck-Hansen	Denmark
1932	1	J. van Egmond	Netherlands
	2	L. Chaillot	France
	3	B. Pellizzari	Italy
1936	1	T. Merkens	Germany
	2	A. van Vliet	Netherlands
	3	L. Chaillot	France
1948	1	M. Ghella	Italy
	2	R. Harris	Great Britain
	3	A. Schandorff	Denmark
1952	1	E. Sacchi	Italy
	2	L. Cox	Australia
	3	W. Potzernheim	Germany
1956	1	M. Rousseau	France
	2	G. Pesenti	Italy
	3	R. Ploog	Australia
1960	1	S. Gaiardoni	Italy
	2	L. Sterckx	Belgium
	3	V. Gasparella	Italy
1964	1	G. Pettenella	Italy
	2	S. Bianchetto	Italy
	3	D. Morelon	France
1968	1	D. Morelon	France
	2	G. Turrini	Italy
	3	P. Trentin	France
1972	1	D. Morelon	France
	2	J. Nicholson	Australia
	3	O. Phakadze	U.S.S.R.
1976	1	A. Tkac	Czechoslovakia
	2	D. Morelon	France
	3	H. Geschke	German Dem. Rep.
1980	1	L. Hesslich	German Dem. Rep.
	2	Y. Cahard	France
	3	S. Kopylov	U.S.S.R.

CYCLING—1,000 metres Time Trial

YEAR	PLACE	NAME	COUNTRY
1928	1	W. Falck-Hansen	Denmark
	2	G. van Drakestein	Netherlands
	3	E. Gray	Australia
1932	1	E. Gray	Australia
	2	J. van Egmond	Netherlands
	3	C. Rampelberg	France
1936	1	A. Van Vliet	Netherlands
	2	P. Georget	France
	3	R. Karsch	Germany
1948	1	J. Dupont	France
	2	P. Nihant	Belgium
	3	T. Godwin	Great Britain
1952	1	R. Mockridge	Australia
	2	M. Morettini	Italy
	3	R. Robinson	South Africa
1956	1	L. Faggin	Italy
	2	L. Foucek	Czechoslovakia
	3	A. Swift	South Africa
1960	1	S. Gaiardoni	Italy
	2	D. Gieseler	Germany
	3	R. Vargaschkin	U.S.S.R.
1964	1	P. Sercu	Belgium
	2	G. Pettenella	Italy
	3	P. Trentin	France

YEAR	PLACE	NAME	COUNTRY
1968	1	P. Trentin	France
	2	N. Fredborg	Denmark
	3	J. Kierzkowski	Poland
1972	1	N. Fredborg	Denmark
	2	D. Clark	Australia
	3	J. Schutze	East Germany
1976	1	K. Grunke	German Dem. Rep.
	2	M. Vaarten	Belgium
	3	N. Fredborg	Denmark
1980	1	L. Thoms	German Dem. Rep.
	2	A. Panfilov	U.S.S.R.
	3	D. Weller	Jamaica

CYCLING—4,000 metres Individual Pursuit

YEAR	PLACE	NAME	COUNTRY
1964	1	J. Daler	Czechoslovakia
	2	G. Ursi	Italy
	3	P. Isaksson	Denmark
1968	1	D. Rebillard	France
	2	M. Frey	Denmark
	3	X. Kurmann	Switzerland
1972	1	K. Knudson	Norway
	2	X. Kurmann	Switzerland
	3	H. Lutz	West Germany
1976	1	G. Braun	German Dem. Rep.
	2	H. Ponsteen	Holland
	3	T. Huschke	German Dem. Rep.
1980	1	R. Dill-Bundi	Switzerland
	2	A. Bondue	France
	3	H. Orsted	Denmark

CYCLING—4,000 metres Team Pursuit

YEAR	PLACE	COUNTRY
1908	1	Great Britain
	2	Germany
	3	Canada
1920	1	Italy
	2	Great Britain
	3	South Africa
1924	1	Italy
	2	Poland
	3	Belgium
1928	1	Italy
	2	Netherlands
	3	Great Britain
1932	1	Italy
	2	France
	3	Great Britain
1936	1	France
	2	Italy
	3	Great Britain
1948	1	France
	2	Italy
	3	Great Britain
1952	1	Italy
	2	South Africa
	3	Great Britain
1956	1	Italy
	2	France
	3	Great Britain
1960	1	Italy
	2	Germany
	3	U.S.S.R.
1964	1	Germany
	2	Italy
	3	Netherlands
1968	1	Denmark
	2	Germany
	3	Italy
1972	1	Germany
	2	East Germany
	3	Great Britain
1976	1	W. Germany
	2	U.S.S.R.
	3	Great Britain
1980	1	U.S.S.R.
	2	E. Germany
	3	Czechoslovakia

CYCLING—Road Race

YEAR	PLACE	NAME	COUNTRY
1896	1	A. Konstantinidis	Greece
	2	A. Goedrich	Germany
	3	F. Battel	Great Britain
1912	1	R. Lewis	South Africa
	2	F. Grubb	Great Britain
	3	S. Schutte	U.S.A.
1920	1	H. Stenqvist	Sweden
	2	H. Kaltenbrun	South Africa
	3	F. Canteloube	France
1924	1	A. Blanchonnet	France
	2	H. Hoevenaers	Belgium
	3	R. Hamel	France
1928	1	H. Hansen	Denmark
	2	F. Southall	Great Britain
	3	G. Carlsson	Sweden
1932	1	A. Pavesi	Italy
	2	G. Segato	Italy
	3	B. Britz	Sweden
1936	1	R. Charpentier	France
	2	G. Lapébie	France
	3	E. Nievergelt	Switzerland
1948	1	J. Beyaert	France
	2	G. Voorting	Netherlands
	3	L. Wouters	Belgium
1952	1	A. Noyelle	Belgium
	2	R. Grondelaers	Belgium
	3	E. Ziegler	Germany
1956	1	E. Baldini	Italy
	2	A. Geyre	France
	3	A. Jackson	Great Britain
1960	1	V. Kapitonov	U.S.S.R.
	2	L. Trapè	Italy
	3	W. van den Berghen	Belgium
1964	1	M. Zanin	Italy
	2	K. Rodian	Denmark
	3	W. Godefroot	Belgium
1968	1	P. Vianelli	Italy
	2	L. Mortensen	Denmark
	3	G. Pettersson	Sweden
1972	1	H. Kuiper	Holland
	2	K. Sefton	Australia
	3	J. Huelarno	Spain
1976	1	B. Johansson	Sweden
	2	G. Martinelli	Italy
	3	M. Nowicki	Poland
1980	1	S. Sukhoruchenkov	U.S.S.R.
	2	C. Lang	Poland
	3	Y. Barinov	U.S.S.R.

CYCLING—100 Km Team Time Trial

YEAR	PLACE	COUNTRY
1960	1	Italy
	2	Germany
	3	U.S.S.R.
1964	1	Netherlands
	2	Italy
	3	Sweden
1968	1	Netherlands
	2	Sweden
	3	Italy
1972	1	U.S.S.R.
	2	Poland
	3	Netherlands
1976	1	U.S.S.R.
	2	Poland
	3	Denmark
1980	1	U.S.S.R.
	2	East Germany
	3	Czechoslovakia

EQUESTRIAN

JULY	**29**	Three-day event—dressage test		**AUGUST**	**7**	Team jumping competition
	30	Three-day event—dressage test			**8**	Team dressage competition
AUGUST	**1**	Three-day event—endurance test (Held at Fairbanks Country Club—San Diego)			**9**	Team dressage competition
	3	Three-day event—jumping test			**10**	Individual dressage competition
		All three-day event tests			**12**	Individual jumping competition
	4	Jumping training competition				

Canadian Hugh Graham at the Pan American Games, 1983

HISTORY

It was inevitable that once man tamed the horse it would be used for more than domestic chores. This swift and intelligent animal became an instrument of war and sport. By the late nineteenth century, it was playing a prominent role with the military. Centuries earlier, the horse had an important part in the ancient Greeks' first Olympic Games, where chariot races were a regular feature.

Sporting life was short-lived and the horse was relegated to its transportation and war roles until, in 1900, the Olympic Games introduced a Grand Prix jumping event. Aime Haegeman, a Belgian, won the competition.

Equestrians did not return to Olympic competition until 1912, when jumping, dressage and three-day events became part of the programme. The events had all the ingredients of a military operation (see General Description). Only men participated and medals were awarded for individual and team performances. Team dressage was included in 1928.

When the horse became less important to the military because of the advancement of motorized vehicles, the task of finding riders and maintaining competitive horses fell to the wealthy. Equestrian events reached a class status that put them beyond most people and some governments. But love of the horse is not easy to dispense with and the sport's development continued.

In 1956, there was a dramatic breakthrough in the Olympic sport. Women were not only included in competition, they were allowed to compete against men. Since then, women have been an important part of the international equestrian scene.

One problem for the equestrians in recent years has been the absence of good horses, particularly in the jumping events. Top performing Olympic horses are rare and costly — price can run as high as one million dollars — making competition all the more frustrating for international teams. The cost factor is particularly disturbing to Canadian patrons, who are allowed merely a minimal tax deduction for donating a horse to the team. Full-tax writeoffs are given to U.S. patrons of the sport, while, in France, the horses are government-

Santa Anita, the site of the 1984 Olympic equestrian competition

owned and given to the national equestrian team.

Canada made its Olympic debut in 1952, and in 1956, Jim Elder, Brian Herbinson and John Rumble earned a bronze medal in the three-day event team competition. In 1968, Canada won a gold medal in the team jumping competition. Elder, Jim Day and Tom Gayford were on that team. Gayford, currently team manager, directs the fortunes of the jumping team.

GENERAL DESCRIPTION

There are three disciplines of competition and we'll deal with them separately.

The Dressage was the first equestrian event admitted to the Olympic Games. The art of dressage is geared toward the harmonious development of the horse's physique and ability.

For the Olympic Team Competition, each country is permitted to enter three riders and three horses. Each rider executes the Grand Prix which is a series of 39 movements to be performed from memory. The rider must take the horse through the movements with invisible hand and leg movements and without use of voice.

The horse must remain calm, obedient and alert while achieving perfect understanding with its rider. There must be freedom and regularity of the paces and the balance, and lightness and ease of the movements. The horse must remain straight in any movement on a straight

line and bend accordingly when moving on a curved line. Overall, the horse gives an impression of handling itself; confident and heedful, it fully surrenders to the rider's control.

The performances are rated from 0 to 10 for each movement by the five judges placed around a 60-metre by 20-metre arena. The scores are totalled and the team with the highest total wins. For individual medals, the top 12 placed competitors in the Team Competition ride the Grand Prix Special test to determine the winners.

The Three-Day Event begins with a dressage test, but since there are usually a large number of competitors this test is held over two days, thus making it a four-day event.

The second part is the four-phase endurance test. Phases A and C are on roads and tracks over distances of 16 to 21 kilometres. They must be completed within specified times.

Phase B is a 4-kilometre steeplechase course with 10 to 12 fences to be cleared. The rider must average about 690 metres per minute.

Phase C starts immediately after the steeplechase. There is a compulsory veterinary check at the end of Phase C to ensure the horses are fit to tackle Phase D, the demanding cross-country course of about eight kilometres and 33 fixed obstacles.

Before the start of Stadium Jumping, the final test of the three-day event, the horses once again are given compulsory checks by the veterinarians. Any horse declared unfit is eliminated. In the jumping, the course consists of a dozen obstacles over a distance of 984 metres and must be completed within a specified time. In this discipline a team is comprised of four riders and horses with the best three to count. Individual medals are awarded to the top three competitors.

In the **Team Jumping**, a team is comprised of four riders and four horses. They compete over a two-round course with the best three to count in each round. The team with the least number of total faults is the winner. In the event of a tie for first, second or third place, there will be a jump-off over a shortened course against the clock with the fences heightened and widened.

All entries compete in the first round. Participation in the second round is restricted to the 12 best placed teams after the first round, including those who tie for 12th place. The course must be between 700 and 900 metres in length and has 12 to 15 obstacles (combinations count as one obstacle), including a water jump of 4.75 metres. Maximum height and width of the other obstacles are not to exceed 1.60 metres and 2.20 metres respectively.

For individual medals, only three members of each team are permitted to compete. Fences in this competition are somewhat larger than in the team event. This is also a two-round competition, which must be carried out in one day as follows:

A first course (A) is judged under Table A within the time allowed for a speed of 400 metres per minute; but not against the clock.

A second course (B) in which the 25 best placed competitors in the first course (A) may take part (including those who tie for 25th place). Course (B) is judged under Table A within the time allowed for a speed of 400 metres per minute; but not against the clock.

The order of starting in course (B) will follow the reverse order of penalties incurred in course (A), i.e. the competitor with the highest total of penalties will start first, the last competitor to start being the one with the lowest total of penalties.

The final result will be obtained by adding the penalties incurred in the two courses (A) and (B). If there is a tie for the first, second and/or third places, there will be jump-off against the clock for a speed of 400 metres per minute over six obstacles used in course B which may be raised and/or enlarged.

TECHNICAL TERMS

Refusal — committed when a horse halts in front of an obstacle to be jumped; whether or not the horse knocks it down or displaces it.

Resistance — when a horse halts, rears or turns around.

Run-out — when the horse escapes the rider's control and avoids an obstacle that has to be jumped.

Water-jump fault — one or more hooves in the water or on the white line defining the jump's limits.

Disobedience — a refusal, run-out or resistance.

Fall of rider — a competitor is considered to have fallen when he is separated from his horse, which has not fallen, in such a way that he touches the ground or finds it necessary, in order to get back into the saddle, to use some form of support or outside assistance.

Fall of horse — a horse is considered to have fallen when the shoulder and quarters have touched the ground or the obstacle and the ground.

Walk — a marching pace in which the footfalls of the horse's hooves follow one another in "four time."

Trot — the trot is a pace of "two time" on alternate diagonal legs (near left fore and right hind leg and vice versa) separated by a moment of suspension.

Canter — a pace of "three time," where at canter to the right, for instance, the footfalls follow one another in this sequence; left hind, left diagonal (simultaneously left fore and right hind), right fore, followed by a moment of suspension with all four feet in the air before the next stride begins.

Passage — a measured, very collected, very elevated and very cadenced trot.

Piaffer — a high-stepping, majestic trot on the spot. Each diagonal pair of legs is raised and returned to the ground alternately with an even cadence and a slightly prolonged suspension.

Travers — performed along the wall or centre line, it demands that the horse is slightly bent around the inside leg of the rider. Its outside legs pass and cross in front of its inside legs, while the horse looks in the direction it is going.

Fault — a refusal to take a jump or any infraction of the competition where points are lost.

Volte — a circle with a diameter of about six metres.

Figure eight — made up of two voltes or circles joined at the centre of the eight.

Serpentine — a series of loops across the arena.

Combinations — a series of two, three or more obstacles to be jumped separately and consecutively.

Time limit — the time limit is twice the time allowed. Elimination is the penalty for exceeding time limits.

TOP TEAMS

With a combination of fine riders and good horses, the United States has an excellent chance for a jumping gold. Switzerland and France along with the Soviet Union, Great Britain, Canada and West Germany have experienced teams.

West Germany has been dominant in the dressage events in recent Olympics, although the Soviet Union won the team title in 1980 in Moscow when nearly all western countries boycotted the Games. The Soviet Union also won the three-day event in Moscow. The United States, the 1976 champions, sat out.

TOP CANADIANS JUMPING

Veteran Jim Elder is still around but there is a solid group of riders in Mario Deslauriers, Ian Millar, Terrence Millar, Hugh Graham, Michel Vaillancourt and Mark Laskin.

Canadian Jo Tudor riding Ossian in the dressage event   Photo by Terry Bramham

MEDAL WINNERS

EQUESTRIAN (team) Grand Prix Jumping

YEAR	PLACE	COUNTRY
1912	1	**Sweden**
	2	France
	3	Germany
1920	1	**Sweden**
	2	Belgium
	3	Italy
1924	1	**Sweden**
	2	Switzerland
	3	Portugal
1928	1	**Spain**
	2	Poland
	3	Sweden
1932	1	no nation com-
	2	pleted the course
	3	with three riders
1936	1	**Germany**
	2	Netherlands
	3	Portugal
1948	1	**Mexico**
	2	Spain
	3	Great Britain
1952	1	**Great Britain**
	2	Chile
	3	U.S.A.
1956	1	**Germany**
	2	Italy
	3	Great Britain
1960	1	**Germany**
	2	U.S.A.
	3	Italy
1964	1	**Germany**
	2	France
	3	Italy
1968	1	**Canada**
	2	France
	3	West Germany
1972	1	**West Germany**
	2	U.S.A.
	3	Italy
1976	1	**France**
	2	West Germany
	3	Belgium
1980	1	**USSR**
	2	Poland
	3	Mexico

EQUESTRIAN (individual) Grand Prix Jumping

YEAR	PLACE	NAME	COUNTRY
1900	1	**A. Haegeman**	**Belgium**
	2	G. van de Poele	Belgium
	3	de Champsavin	France
1912	1	**J. Cariou**	**France**
	2	R. von Kröcher	Germany
	3	E. Blommaert	Belgium
		de Soye	
1920	1	**T. Lequio**	**Italy**
	2	A. Valerio	Italy
	3	G. Lewenhaupt	Sweden
1924	1	**A. Gemuseus**	**Switzerland**
	2	T. Lequio	Italy
	3	A. Krolikiewicz	Poland
1928	1	**F. Ventura**	**Czechoslovakia**
	2	P. de Balanda	France
	3	C. Kuhn	Switzerland
1932	1	**T. Nishi**	**Japan**
	2	H. Chamberlin	U.S.A.
	3	C. von Rosen	Sweden
1936	1	**K. Hasse**	**Germany**
	2	H. Rang	Rumania
	3	J. Platthy	Hungary
1948	1	**H. Mariles Cortés**	**Mexico**
	2	R. Uriza	Mexico
	3	J. d'Orgeix	France
1952	1	**P.J. d'Oriola**	**France**
	2	O. Cristi	Chile
	3	F. Thiedemann	Germany

YEAR	PLACE	NAME	COUNTRY
1956	1	H. Winkler	Germany
	2	R. d'Inzeo	Italy
	3	P. d'Inzeo	Italy
1960	1	R. d'Inzeo	Italy
	2	P. d'Inzeo	Italy
	3	D. Broome	Great Britain
1964	1	P.J. d'Oriola	France
	2	H. Schridde	Germany
	3	P. Robeson	Great Britain
1968	1	W. Steinkraus	U.S.A.
	2	M. Coakes	Great Britain
	3	D. Broome	Great Britain
1972	1	G. Mancinelli	Italy
	2	A. Moore	Great Britain
	3	N. Shapiro	U.S.A.
1976	1	A. Schockemöhle	Germany
	2	M. Vailliancourt	Canada
	3	F. Mathy	Belgium
1980	1	J. Kowalczyk	Poland
	2	N. Korolkov	URS
	3	J. Perez Heras*	Mexico

* Won Jump off

EQUESTRIAN (individual) Grand Prix Dressage

YEAR	PLACE	NAME	COUNTRY
1912	1	C. Bonde	Sweden
	2	G. Boltenstern	Sweden
	3	H. von Blixen-Finecke	Sweden
1920	1	J. Lundblad	Sweden
	2	B. Sandström	Sweden
	3	H. von Rosen	Sweden
1924	1	E. Linder	Sweden
	2	B. Sandström	Sweden
	3	X. Lesage	France
1928	1	C. von Langen	Germany
	2	C. Marion	France
	3	R. Olsson	Sweden
1932	1	X. Lesage	France
	2	C. Marion	France
	3	H. Tuttle	U.S.A.
1936	1	H. Pollay	Germany
	2	F. Gerhard	Germany
	3	A. Podhajsky	Austria
1948	1	H. Moser	Switzerland
	2	A. Jousseaume	France
	3	G. Boltenstern	Sweden
1952	1	H. St. Cyr	Sweden
	2	L. Hartel	Denmark
	3	A. Jousseaume	France
1956	1	H. St. Cyr	Sweden
	2	L. Hartel	Denmark
	3	L. Linsenhoff	Germany
1960	1	S. Filatov	U.S.S.R.
	2	G. Fischer	Switzerland
	3	J. Neckermann	Germany
1964	1	H. Chammartin	Switzerland
	2	H. Boldt	Germany
	3	S. Filatov	U.S.S.R.
1968	1	I. Kizimov	U.S.S.R.
	2	J. Neckermann	West Germany
	3	R. Klimke	West Germany
1972	1	L. Lisenhoff	West Germany
	2	E. Petushkova	U.S.S.R.
	3	J. Neckermann	West Germany
1976	1	C. Stueckelberger	Switzerland
	2	H. Boldt	Germany
	3	R. Klimke	Germany
1980	1	E. Theurer	Austria
	2	Y. Kovshov	U.S.S.R.
	3	V. Ugryumov	U.S.S.R.

EQUESTRIAN (team) Grand Prix Dressage

YEAR	PLACE	COUNTRY
1928	1	Germany
	2	Sweden
	3	Netherlands
1932	1	France
	2	Sweden
	3	U.S.A.
1936	1	Germany
	2	France
	3	Sweden
1948	1	France
	2	U.S.A.
	3	Portugal
1952	1	Sweden
	2	Switzerland
	3	Germany
1956	1	Sweden
	2	Germany
	3	Switzerland
1964	1	Germany
	2	Switzerland
	3	U.S.S.R.
1968	1	West Germany
	2	U.S.S.R.
	3	Switzerland
1972	1	U.S.S.R
	2	West Germany
	3	Sweden
1976	1	Germany
	2	Switzerland
	3	U.S.A.
1980	1	U.S.S.R.
	2	Bulgaria
	3	Rumania

EQUESTRIAN (individual) Three Day Event

YEAR	PLACE	NAME	COUNTRY
1912	1	A. Norlander	Sweden
	2	F. von Rochow	Germany
	3	J. Cariou	France
1920	1	H. Mörner	Sweden
	2	A. Lundström	Sweden
	3	E. Caffaratti	Italy
1924	1	A. van Zijp	Netherlands
	2	F. Kirkebjerg	Denmark
	3	S. Doak	U.S.A.
1928	1	C.F. de Mortanges	Netherlands
	2	G.P. de Krujiff	Netherlands
	3	B. Neumann	Germany
1932	1	C.F. de Mortanges	Netherlands
	2	E. Thomson	U.S.A.
	3	C. von Rosen	Sweden
1936	1	L. Stubbendorf	Germany
	2	E. Thomson	U.S.A.
	3	H. Lunding	Denmark
1948	1	B. Chevallier	France
	2	F. Henry	U.S.A.
	3	J.R. Selfelt	Sweden
1952	1	H. von Blixen-Finecke	Sweden
	2	G. Lefrant	France
	3	W. Büsing	Germany
1956	1	P. Kastenman	Sweden
	2	A. Lütke-Westhues	Germany
	3	F. Weldon	Great Britain
1960	1	L. Morgan	Australia
	2	N. Lavis	Australia
	3	A. Bühler	Switzerland
1964	1	M. Checcoli	Italy
	2	C. Moratorio	Argentina
	3	F. Ligges	Germany
1968	1	J.J. Guyon	France
	2	D. Allhusen	Great Britain
	3	M. Page	U.S.A.
1972	1	R. Meade	Great Britain
	2	A. Argenton	Italy
	3	J. Jonsson	Sweden

YEAR	PLACE	COUNTRY
1976	1	France
	2	West Germany
	3	Belgium
1980	1	USSR
	2	Poland
	3	Mexico

EQUESTRIAN (team) Three Day Event

YEAR	PLACE	COUNTRY
1912	1	Sweden
	2	Germany
	3	U.S.A.
1920	1	Sweden
	2	Italy
	3	Belgium
1924	1	Netherlands
	2	Sweden
	3	Italy
1928	1	Netherlands
	2	Norway
	3	Poland
1932	1	U.S.A.
	2	Netherlands
	3*	
1936	1	Germany
	2	Poland
	3	Great Britain
1948	1	U.S.A.
	2	Sweden
	3	Mexico
1952	1	Sweden
	2	Germany
	3	U.S.A.
1956	1	Great Britain
	2	Germany
	3	Canada
1960	1	Australia
	2	Switzerland
	3	France
1964	1	Italy
	2	U.S.A.
	3	Germany
1968	1	Great Britain
	2	U.S.A.
	3	Australia
1972	1	Great Britain
	2	U.S.A.
	3	West Germany
1976	1	U.S.A.
	2	Germany
	3	Australia
1980	1	U.S.S.R.
	2	Italy
	3	Mexico

* 1932 — only four teams competed. Two were eliminated.

FENCING

AUGUST	1	Foil—individual preliminaries, men
	2	Foil—individual preliminaries, men & women Foil—individual finals, men
	3	Foil—individual preliminaries, women/Sabre—individual preliminaries, men/Foil—individual finals, women
	4	Foil—team preliminaries, men/Sabre—individual preliminaries, men/Sabre—individual finals, men
	5	Foil—team preliminaries, men & women Foil—team finals, men
	7	Foil—team preliminaries, women/Epee—individual preliminaries, men/Foil—team finals, women

AUGUST	8	Sabre—team preliminaries, men/Epee—individual preliminaries, men/Epee—individual finals, men
	9	Sabre—team preliminaries, men Sabre—team finals, men
	10	Epee—team preliminaries, men
	11	Epee—team preliminaries, men Epee—team finals, men

Experience, timing and quick reactions are essential to a fencer's success.

HISTORY

Swords have been around for more than 5,000 years. The most treasured sword, believed to be the oldest in the world, was found in Japan. Museums are filled with swords of the past. They include the large, two-handed swords so popular with the Knights of the Crusade; the curved blades of the deadly short sword used by the Saracens; the cutlas used by pirates; and the sabres used by the cavalry in both Europe and North America.

The sword has earned a niche in history as both a weapon of war and a weapon for duellists, who sought to defend their honour in matters of love or general argument. The need to develop fighting skills in order to survive on the battlefield produced the first Academie d'Armes during the late fifteenth century. When duelling was outlawed fencing salles, or clubs as they are known today, grew in popularity all over Europe as swordplay earned a certain amount of legitimacy as a sport.

When the modern Olympic Games were revived in 1896 in Athens, the Europeans considered fencing as important as any other event. Two of the three men's events were represented: foil and sabre. Épée was introduced later. The women's foil competition was not officially included in the Olympic programme until 1924. By this time, fencing was also being established in North America, and in the early 1900s national championships were held in Canada.

For two decades, the Soviet Union has entered formidable teams in Olympic fencing events, but in the 1980 Olympics in Moscow, France captured the team title in both the foil and the épée. The Soviets won the sabre team title for the fourth time in the past five Olympics.

GENERAL DESCRIPTION

Though fencing over the centuries has changed from deadly combat to a sport, the speed of movement and intricate tactics remain important qualities for world-class fencers. Experience, mental poise, maturity and quick reactions, along with delicate timing are other tools for success. Therefore, competitors at the Olympics will probably be in the 20- to 30-year-old age bracket; much older than the teenagers who predominate in swimming and gymnastics.

Long Beach is the site of the Olympic fencing competition.

Competitions are held in three weapons — the foil, the épée and the sabre in both individual and team events. Women usually compete in foil only. Although it is customary to specialize in one weapon, some fencers have become proficient in two or three.

Because the sport has a premium on speed rather than brute strength, scoring was a visual problem until the electrical scoring system to register "touchés" (hits) for épée was adopted in 1936. The system was also adopted for the foil in 1956 and a similar one is in the works for the sabre.

Competitions are staged, using a combination of round-robin pools and direct elimination, progressively eliminating entrants until the winners are determined.

Within a pool, ranking of competitors is determined by the number of victories obtained and, in case of a tie, by a calculation based on the number of hits scored and received.

In the foil, points are scored by hitting the opponent's target area, which is restricted by convention to the trunk of the body, with the point of the foil. An electrical scoring machine is used to determine the hits and a buzzer sounds simultaneously with the hit. Because of this, a fencer must wear an electrically conductive jacket over the target area. The field of play (called a piste) is 12-metres long and 2-metres wide.

In épée, the electrical scoring machine is also used. The whole body is the épée's target area, including the arms, head and legs. A hit must be made by the point of the épée.

In sabre, most hits are scored with cutting actions using either the front or back edges of the blade. Touchés may also be scored with the point. The target comprises all portions of the body, including head and arms, above an imaginary horizontal line drawn across the tops of the thighs.

PROCEDURE

For team events in the Olympics, each country may enter up to 20 competitors (four fencers per event) plus one reserve and one woman reserve in the women's foil. For individual events, each country may enter three competitors.

Competitors fence at their own risk and injuries have been known to happen.

At the start of individual events, the president de jury calls the two fencers to their respective guardlines. He shouts "en garde" and after checking for readiness he orders "play." The president can stop proceedings by shouting "halt" and he can reposition fencers before restarting the bout by again shouting "play."

After a valid hit, fencers return to their respective guardlines, but if a hit is invalid, they will continue from the spot play was halted. In sabre, the fencers switch ends after half the number of hits has been reached.

VIEWING TIPS

The speed of the action makes fencing very difficult to follow. Here are a few keys for watching this fascinating sport.

Do not try to watch both fencers. Concentrate on one, preferably the attacker. If the attacker's move is parried, watch him or her go on the defensive to prepare for the opponent's riposte — the quick thrust after the parry — before he or she again takes the offensive.

Watch the footwork. Notice how the fencers maintain safe distance from each other and how one or the other will try suddenly to break the distance to gain an advantage for an attack. Try to recognize the split-second in which the fencer you are watching attacks or in which he or she launches a false attack, and try to determine the opponent's reaction.

As you become accustomed to the speed, you will begin to follow the tactics and countertactics of the fencers; you will begin to sense their strategy; and you will learn to enjoy the sport.

Note that the scoring lights record the hits *against* the fencer on that side, not *for* the fencer. The winner of a bout is the fencer with the *least* hits against. In épée, if both fencers have five hits against at the end of the time limit, both lose.

SCORING

Foil — the electrical scoring machine is used to determine hits in the target area — the trunk of the body — with the point of the foil.

Foil fencing is governed by the conventional right-of-way concept. The fencer initiating the attack has right-of-way. The fencer who is attacked must defend himself by deflecting the attacker's blade, that is by parrying, before launching a return attack (riposte). The parry gives the right-of-way to the defender whose riposte in turn can be parried and followed by a counter-riposte. A point is scored when one of these offensive actions hits the target. It is awarded to the first such hit in the sequence of rights-of-way. Nonvalid hits are not awarded and stop the action. Simultaneous attacks are annulled even though they may arrive on target.

Épée — as in foil, hits are scored with the tip of the blade and determined by an electric machine. Unlike foil, there is no right-of-way concept. Épée hits are scored solely on the basis of which fencer makes the hit first. The whole body is the target, including head, arms and legs.

Since there are no off-target areas in épée, the electric scoring circuitry differs from foil. A hit by one fencer automatically shuts off the opponent's electrical circuit if the hits are separated by a 25th of a second. If two fencers hit simultaneously, both touchés will register and be scored. In such a case if the score is 5-5, the bout is continued until a decision is reached within the maximum time limit.

Sabre — although most hits are scored with cutting actions using either the front or back edges of the blade, touchés can also be scored with the point. The valid target area comprises all portions of the body, including head and arms, above an imaginary horizontal line drawn across the tops of the thighs. Sabre is governed by the same convention of right-of-way as the foil. Since electrical scoring machines have not yet been perfected for sabre, hits are determined by a jury composed of a president and four corner judges.

To win a bout in any of the three weapons, a fencer must score five hits on his opponent within six minutes of actual fencing time. If time expires, the fencer with the least hits against him or her wins. If tied, the fencers continue until a deciding hit is made. The scoring lights, coloured for a hit on target and white for an off-target hit, record the hit *against* the fencer on that side. In the direct elimination, each bout is fought for a maximum of 10 hits (eight for women).

The hits are awarded by a president de jury who is in sole control of the match, aided either by an electrical scoring machine or four corner judges. His duty is to observe the sequences of fencing actions and when a hit is seen, to analyse the actions leading to the hit. He awards the point in light of the conventions and regulations applying to that weapon. The judges, when used, are limited to giving an opinion on whether or not a hit landed on target. They may voice no opinion whatsoever on the analysis of the action.

TECHNICAL TERMS

Absence of blade — a position when the blades are not in contact (i.e. not engaged).

Advance — step forward.

Aids — the last three fingers of the swordhand.

Attack — the initial offensive movement made with an extended arm.

Change of engagement — the engagement of the opponent's blade in the opposite line.

Compound attack/riposte — an offensive movement which includes two or more simple fencing actions. Also called a composed attack/riposte.

Corps a corps — when two fencers are in contact so that they cannot wield their weapons correctly.

Counter-disengagement — the action of faking a circular motion in order to score a point.

Counter-riposte — the offensive action which follows the parry of a riposte of another counter riposte, without delay.

Covered — the position of a weapon that blocks off a direct thrust.

Cut-over (coupe) — a simple attack made by passing the point over the opponent's point.

Development — the extension of the arm and the lunge.

Direct attack/riposte — an attack or riposte made in the line of engagement.

Disengagement — moving from the line of engagement to another line by moving around the opponent's blade.

Engagement — The act of contact with the opponent's blade, or the position of contact.

En garde — a basic position of readiness of the arms, body and legs adopted by a fencer.

Feint (attack) — a continuous offensive movement made to resemble an attack in order to draw a reaction from the opponent.

Fencing line — the imaginary line on the piste drawn through the four heels of two fencers, or, more exactly, the line drawn between the leading feet of two fencers.

Fencing measure — the distance from which the fencer can reach his opponent by a full lunge.

Fencing positions — the positions in which the swordarm and weapon may be placed to cover one of the lines of the target.

Fencing time — the time (relative) required to perform one simple fencing

The fencer attacks and then hits his opponent.

action.

Field of play — the piste and its extensions on which fencing takes place.

Foible — the half of the blade nearest the point; the weaker half of the blade.

Forte — the half of the blade nearest the guard; the stronger half of the blade.

Grip — the manner in which the weapon is held.

Guard — the bell-shaped part of the weapon between the handle and the blade which protects the hand.

High lines — the relative position of the blade when the point is above the opponent's guard.

Hit — the offensive action that lands with the point on the target.

Indirect attack/riposte — a simple attack or riposte made in another line.

Invitation — the opening of a line to offer the opponent a chance for an offensive movement.

Low lines — the relative position of the blade when the point is below the opponent's guard.

Lunge — the extension of the arm and legs used to reach an opponent.

Manipulators — the thumb and index finger of the swordhand.

Parry — a defensive action which deflects the attacker's blade.

Phrase — a sequence of fencing movements exchanged between two fencers.

Piste — the regulation area within which fencing takes place.

Principle of defence — the opposition of the forte of the blade to the foible of the opponent's blade to deflect it.

Pronation — the position of the swordhand with the fingernails downwards.

Recovery — the return to the en garde position after a lunge.

Retreat — retire, step back.

Salute — the acknowledgement with the weapon accorded to the president de jury and the opponent at the commencement and conclusion of a bout.

Simple attack/riposte — an offensive movement made with one direct or indirect movement.

Simultaneous actions — when both fencers conceive and execute a movement at the same time.

Stance — the position of the feet and legs in the en garde position.

Straight thrust — a simple and direct offensive action.

Supination — the position of the swordhand with the fingernails upwards.

Target — the area of the body within which a hit is counted as valid.

Valid hits/touchés — hits that arrive on the target.

EQUIPMENT

Foil — a light, flexible weapon that cannot weigh more than 500 grams. It cannot be more than 110 centimetres in length. Its blade is quadrangular and must be pliable. The point must be covered if a nonelectric blade is used.

Épée — heavier than the foil, the point on its triangular blade must be covered (also if nonelectric). It cannot be more than 110 centimetres in length (90 centimetres for the blade) and must weigh less than 770 grams.

Sabre — the blade is triangular, the top being flat. It is often referred to as a light version of the cavalry sword. It must weigh less than 500 grams and its length must not exceed 105 centimetres.

Electric judging equipment — used in foil and épée events. Positioned opposite the centre line, a scoring box registers hits by means of lights and buzzers. A valid hit is signalled by a coloured light and a white light indicates a hit in a nonvalid area. A wire, connected to the scoring box, is attached to the fencer via a spring-load drum at each end of the piste.

The Piste — is the fencing area and must be flat and evenly lit. It is made of various substances such as plastic, wood and linoleum. It is 14-metres long and 1.8- to 2-metres wide.

Clothing — must be white, of strong material. The mask must conform to safety regulations.

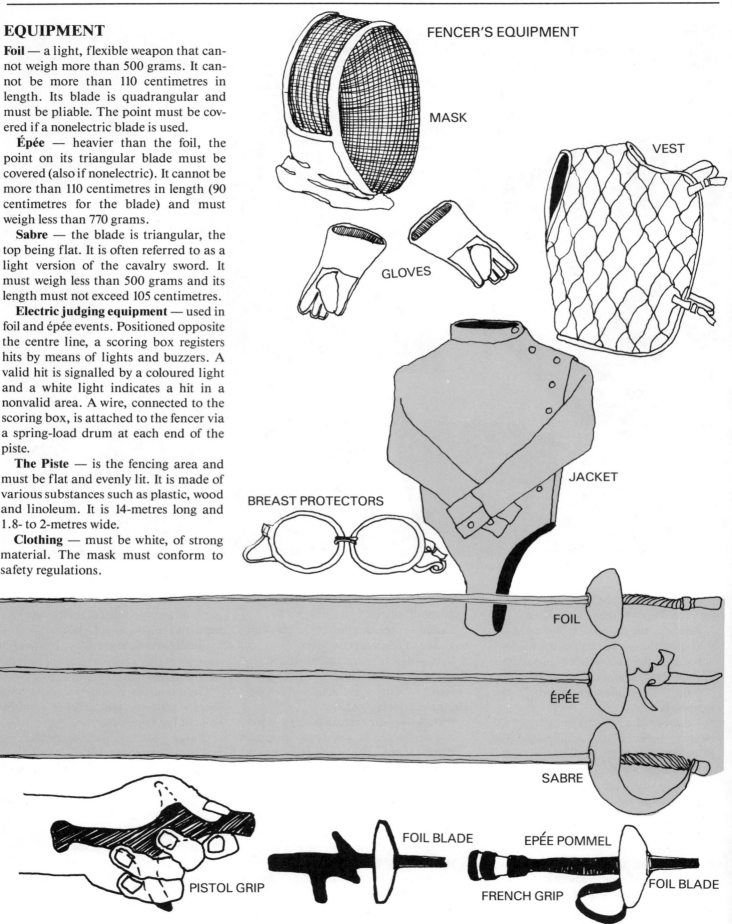

FENCER'S EQUIPMENT

MASK

VEST

GLOVES

JACKET

BREAST PROTECTORS

FOIL

ÉPÉE

SABRE

PISTOL GRIP

FOIL BLADE

EPÉE POMMEL

FRENCH GRIP

FOIL BLADE

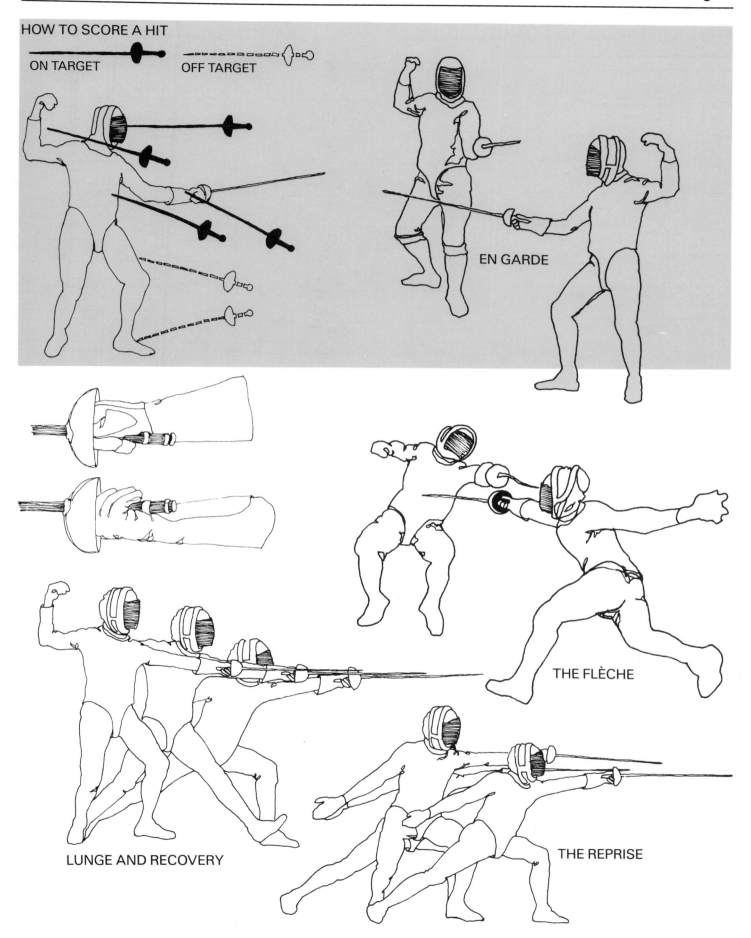

HOW TO SCORE A HIT

ON TARGET   OFF TARGET

EN GARDE

THE FLÈCHE

LUNGE AND RECOVERY

THE REPRISE

MEDAL WINNERS

FENCING (individual foil) Men

YEAR	PLACE	NAME	COUNTRY
1896	1	E. Gravelotte	France
	2	H. Callot	France
	3	P. Pierrakos	Greece
1900	1	E. Coste	France
	2	H. Masson	France
	3	J. Boulanger	France
1904	1	R. Fonst	Cuba
	2	A. Post	Cuba
	3	C. Tatham	Cuba
1912	1	N. Nadi	Italy
	2	P. Speciale	Italy
	3	R. Verderber	Austria
1920	1	N. Nadi	Italy
	2	P. Cattiau	France
	3	R. Ducret	France
1924	1	R. Ducret	France
	2	P. Cattiau	France
	3	M. van Damme	Belgium
1928	1	L. Gaudin	France
	2	E. Casmir	Germany
	3	G. Gaudini	Italy
1932	1	G. Marzi	Italy
	2	J. Levis	U.S.A.
	3	G. Gaudini	Italy
1936	1	G. Gaudini	Italy
	2	E. Gardère	France
	3	G. Bocchino	Italy
1948	1	J. Buhan	France
	2	C. d'Oriola	France
	3	L. Maszlay	Hungary
1952	1	C. d'Oriola	France
	2	E. Mangiarotti	Italy
	3	M. di Rosa	Italy
1956	1	C. d'Oriola	France
	2	G. Bergamini	Italy
	3	A. Spallino	Italy
1960	1	V. Schdanovitsch	U.S.S.R.
	2	Y. Sissikin	U.S.S.R.
	3	A. Axelrod	U.S.A.
1964	1	E. Franke	Poland
	2	J. Magnan	France
	3	D. Revenu	France
1968	1	I. Drimba	Rumania
	2	J. Kamuti	Hungary
	3	D. Revenu	France
1972	1	W. Woyda	Poland
	2	J. Kamuti	Hungary
	3	C. Noel	France
1976	1	F. Dal Zotto	Italy
	2	A. Romankov	U.S.S.R.
	3	B. Talvard	France
1980	1	V. Smirnov	U.S.S.R.
	2	P. Jolyot	France
	3	A. Romankov	U.S.S.R.

FENCING (team foil) Men

YEAR	PLACE	COUNTRY
1904	1	Cuba
	2	U.S.A.
	3*	
1920	1	Italy
	2	France
	3	U.S.A.
1924	1	France
	2	Belgium
	3	Hungary
1928	1	Italy
	2	France
	3	Argentina
1932	1	France
	2	Italy
	3	U.S.A.
1936	1	Italy
	2	France
	3	Germany
1948	1	France
	2	Italy
	3	Belgium
1952	1	France
	2	Italy
	3	Hungary
1956	1	Italy
	2	France
	3	Hungary
1960	1	U.S.S.R.
	2	Italy
	3	Germany
1964	1	U.S.S.R.
	2	Poland
	3	France
1968	1	France
	2	U.S.S.R.
	3	Poland
1972	1	Poland
	2	U.S.S.R.
	3	France
1976	1	West Germany
	2	Italy
	3	France
1980	1	France
	2	U.S.S.R.
	3	Poland

* 1904—Only two teams were entered, although the American team was made up of several nationalities

FENCING (individual foil) Women

YEAR	PLACE	NAME	COUNTRY
1924	1	E. Osiier	Denmark
	2	G. Davis	Great Britain
	3	G. Heckscher	Denmark
1928	1	H. Mayer	Germany
	2	M. Freeman	Great Britain
	3	O. Oelkers	Germany
1932	1	E. Preis	Austria
	2	H. Guinness	Great Britain
	3	E. Bogen	Hungary
1936	1	I. Schacherer-Elek	Hungary
	2	H. Meyer	Germany
	3	E. Preis	Austria
1948	1	I. Schacherer-Elek	Hungary
	2	K. Lachmann	Denmark
	3	E. Muller-Preis	Austria
1952	1	I Camber	Italy
	2	I. Schacherer-Elek	Hungary
	3	K. Lachmann	Denmark
1956	1	G. Sheen	Great Britain
	2	O. Orban	Rumania
	3	R. Garilhe	France
1960	1	H. Schmid	Germany
	2	V. Rastvorova	U.S.S.R.
	3	M. Vicol	Rumania
1964	1	I. Ujlaki-Rejtö	Hungary
	2	H. Mees	Germany
	3	A. Ragno	Italy
1968	1	E. Novikova	U.S.S.R.
	2	P. Roldan	Mexico
	3	I. Ujlaki-Rejtö	Hungary
1972	1	A. Ragno	Italy
	2	I. Bobis	Hungary
	3	G. Gorokhova	U.S.S.R.
1976	1	I. Schwarczenberger	Hungary
	2	Maria C. Collino	Italy
	3	E. Novikova-Belova	U.S.S.R.
1980	1	P. Trinquet	France
	2	M. Maros	Hungary
	3	B. Wysoczanska	Poland

FENCING (team foil) Women

YEAR	PLACE	COUNTRY
1960	1	U.S.S.R.
	2	Hungary
	3	Italy
1964	1	Hungary
	2	U.S.S.R.
	3	Germany
1968	1	U.S.S.R.
	2	Hungary
	3	Rumania
1972	1	U.S.S.R.
	2	Hungary
	3	Rumania
1976	1	U.S.S.R.
	2	France
	3	Hungary
1980	1	France
	2	U.S.S.R.
	3	Hungary

FENCING (individual Sabre) Men

YEAR	PLACE	NAME	COUNTRY
1896	1	**J. Georgiadis**	**Greece**
	2	T. Karakalos	Greece
	3	H. Nielsen	Denmark
1900	1	**G. de la Falaise**	**France**
	2	L. Thiébaut	France
	3	S. Flesch	Austria
1904	1	**M. Diaz**	**Cuba**
	2	W. Grebe	U.S.A.
	3	A. Post	Cuba
1908	1	**J. Fuchs**	**Hungary**
	2	B. Zulavszky	Hungary
	3	V.G. von Lobsdorf	Bohemia
1912	1	**J. Fuchs**	**Hungary**
	2	B. Bekessy	Hungary
	3	E. Meszaros	Hungary
1920	1	**N. Nadi**	**Italy**
	2	A. Nadi	Italy
	3	A.E. W. de Jong	Netherlands
1924	1	**S. Posta**	**Hungary**
	2	R. Ducret	France
	3	J. Garay	Hungary
1928	1	**O. Tersztyanszky**	**Hungary**
	2	A. Petschauer	Hungary
	3	B. Bini	Italy
1932	1	**G. Piller**	**Hungary**
	2	G. Gaudini	Italy
	3	E. Kabos	Hungary
1936	1	**E. Kabos**	**Hungary**
	2	G. Marzi	Italy
	3	A. Gerevich	Hungary
1948	1	**A. Gerevich**	**Hungary**
	2	V. Pinton	Italy
	3	P. Kovacs	Hungary
1952	1	**P. Kovacs**	**Hungary**
	2	A. Gerevich	Hungary
	3	T. Berczelly	Hungary
1956	1	**R. Karpati**	**Hungary**
	2	J. Pawlowski	Poland
	3	L. Kuznyetsov	U.S.S.R.
1960	1	**R. Karpati**	**Hungary**
	2	Z. Horvath	Hungary
	3	W. Calarese	Italy
1964	1	**T. Pézsa**	**Hungary**
	2	C. Arabo	France
	3	U. Mavlikhanov	U.S.S.R.
1968	1	**J. Pawlowski**	**Poland**
	2	M. Rakita	U.S.S.R.
	3	T. Pézsa	Hungary
1972	1	**V. Sidiak**	**U.S.S.R.**
	2	P. Maroth	Hungary
	3	V. Nazloymov	U.S.S.R.
1976	1	**V. Krovopouskov**	**U.S.S.R.**
	2	V. Nazlimov	U.S.S.R.
	3	V. Sidiak	U.S.S.R.
1980	1	**V. Krovopouskov**	**U.S.S.R.**
	2	M. Burtsev	U.S.S.R.
	3	I. Gedovari	Hungary

FENCING (team sabre) Men

YEAR	PLACE	COUNTRY
1908	1	**Hungary**
	2	Italy
	3	Bohemia
1912	1	**Hungary**
	2	Austria
	3	Netherlands
1920	1	**Italy**
	2	France
	3	Netherlands
1924	1	**Italy**
	2	Hungary
	3	Netherlands
1928	1	**Hungary**
	2	Italy
	3	Poland

(team sabre continued)

YEAR	PLACE	COUNTRY
1932	1	**Hungary**
	2	Italy
	3	Poland
1936	1	**Hungary**
	2	Italy
	3	Germany
1948	1	**Hungary**
	2	Italy
	3	U.S.A.
1952	1	**Hungary**
	2	Italy
	3	France
1956	1	**Hungary**
	2	Poland
	3	U.S.S.R.
1960	1	**Hungary**
	2	Poland
	3	Italy
1964	1	**U.S.S.R.**
	2	Italy
	3	Poland
1968	1	**U.S.S.R.**
	2	Italy
	3	Hungary
1972	1	**Italy**
	2	U.S.S.R.
	3	Hungary
1976	1	**U.S.S.R.**
	2	Italy
	3	Rumania
1980	1	**U.S.S.R.**
	2	Italy
	3	Hungary

FENCING (individual épée) Men

YEAR	PLACE	NAME	COUNTRY
1900	1	**R. Fonst**	**Cuba**
	2	L. Perrée	France
	3	L. Sée	France
1904	1	**R. Fonst**	**Cuba**
	2	C. Tatham	Cuba
	3	A. Post	Cuba
1908	1	**G. Alibert**	**France**
	2	A. Lippmann	France
	3	E. Olivier	France
1912	1	**P. Anspach**	**Belgium**
	2	I. Osiier	Denmark
	3	P de Beaulieu	Belgium
1920	1	**A. Massard**	**France**
	2	A. Lippmann	France
	3	G. Buchard	France
1924	1	**C. Delporte**	**Belgium**
	2	R. Ducret	France
	3	N. Hellsten	Sweden
1928	1	**L. Gaudin**	**France**
	2	G. Buchard	France
	3	G. Calnan	U.S.A.
1932	1	**G. Cornaggia-Medici**	**Italy**
	2	G. Buchard	France
	3	C. Agostoni	Italy
1936	1	**F. Riccardi**	**Italy**
	2	S. Ragno	Italy
	3	G. Cornaggia-Medici	Italy
1948	1	**L. Cantone**	**Italy**
	2	O. Zappelli	Switzerland
	3	E. Mangiarotti	Italy
1952	1	**E. Mangiarotti**	**Italy**
	2	D. Mangiarotti	Italy
	3	O. Zappelli	Switzerland
1956	1	**C. Pavesi**	**Italy**
	2	G. Delfino	Italy
	3	E. Mangiarotti	Italy
1960	1	**G. Delfino**	**Italy**
	2	A. Jay	Great Britain
	3	B. Khabarov	U.S.S.R.

(individual épée continued)

YEAR	PLACE	NAME	COUNTRY
1964	1	**G. Kriss**	**U.S.S.R.**
	2	H. Hoskyns	Great Britain
	3	G. Kostava	U.S.S.R.
1968	1	**G. Kulcsar**	**Hungary**
	2	G. Kriss	U.S.S.R.
	3	G. Saccaro	Italy
1972	1	**C. Fenyvesi**	**Hungary**
	2	J. la Degaillerie	France
	3	G. Kulcsar	Hungary
1976	1	**A. Pusch**	**West Germany**
	2	J. Hehn	West Germany
	3	G. Kulcsár	Hungary
1980	1	**J. Harmenberg**	**Sweden**
	2	E. Kolczonay	Hungary
	3	P. Riboud	France

FENCING (team épée) Men

YEAR	PLACE	COUNTRY
1908	1	**France**
	2	Great Britain
	3	Belgium
1912	1	**Belgium**
	2	Great Britain
	3	Netherlands
1920	1	**Italy**
	2	Belgium
	3	France
1924	1	**France**
	2	Belgium
	3	Italy
1928	1	**Italy**
	2	France
	3	Portugal
1932	1	**France**
	2	Italy
	3	U.S.A.
1936	1	**Italy**
	2	Sweden
	3	France
1948	1	**France**
	2	Italy
	3	Sweden
1952	1	**Italy**
	2	Sweden
	3	Switzerland
1956	1	**Italy**
	2	Hungary
	3	France
1960	1	**Italy**
	2	Great Britain
	3	U.S.S.R.
1964	1	**Hungary**
	2	Italy
	3	France
1968	1	**Hungary**
	2	U.S.S.R.
	3	Poland
1972	1	**Hungary**
	2	Switzerland
	3	U.S.S.R.
1976	1	**Sweden**
	2	West Germany
	3	Switzerland
1980	1	**France**
	2	Poland
	3	U.S.S.R.

FOOTBALL SOCCER

The Rose Bowl, site of the 1984 Olympic soccer competition.

EVENT DATE   ROSE BOWL PASADENA, CALIFORNIA

JULY	29	Preliminary match	AUGUST	5	Quarterfinal match
	30	Preliminary match		6	Quarterfinal match
	31	Preliminary match		8	Semifinal match
AUGUST	1	Preliminary match		10	Final match (3-4 places)
	2	Preliminary match		11	Final match (1-2 places)
	3	Preliminary match			

HARVARD UNIVERSITY CAMBRIDGE, MASSACHUSETTS

JULY	29	Preliminary match	AUGUST	2	Preliminary match
	30	Preliminary match		3	Preliminary match
	31	Preliminary match			
AUGUST	1	Preliminary match			

U.S. NAVAL ACADEMY ANNAPOLIS, MARYLAND

JULY	29	Preliminary match	AUGUST	1	Preliminary match
	30	Preliminary match		2	Preliminary match
	31	Preliminary match		3	Preliminary match

STANFORD UNIVERSITY PALO ALTO, CALIFORNIA

JULY	29	Preliminary match	AUGUST	3	Preliminary match
	30	Preliminary match		5	Quarterfinal match
	31	Preliminary match		6	Quarterfinal match
AUGUST	1	Preliminary match		8	Semifinal match
	2	Preliminary match			

HISTORY

Historians argue soccer's origins, citing games of "football" in ancient China and Rome, or pointing to the wild savages of South America, who got their kicks by playing with the skulls of their victims. Whatever folklore you wish to accept (and it seems every country has a story relating to the origin of soccer), popular consensus is that modern soccer was born in nineteenth-century Great Britain.

The English Football Association took control of the sport in 1863. It brought the standard to 11 players on each side and also tried to make clear that the sport was indeed different from rugby, from which North American football evolved. Once this idea was accepted the word soccer came into being, meaning a no-hands, kicking game. But because of its association with the English Football Association, soccer became known as "football" in the United Kingdom.

Indeed, visitors and immigrants from Great Britain appear, at first, puzzled to find another sport called football in the United States and Canada. They argue that the North American game only occasionally calls upon its players to use their feet to kick the ball.

The popularity of soccer has grown world-wide. Simple and easy to follow, the game does not force limitations on physical size, but the player must be agile with his feet and head. And unlike the high cost of North American football, soccer is a relatively inexpensive game to learn. Shoes, shorts, a ball and a field are all the equipment players need. And if a field isn't available, any roadway will do.

From the dirt and dust of corner lots to the lush fields of private schools and city-operated parks, soccer has created many international stars, the most popular being Pelé from Brazil. His skills have become legendary; his followers enormous and in every corner of the world.

Soccer is known as the "world's sport" to its fans, with an estimated 25-million club players in 150 countries. Crowds of 100,000 for soccer matches have become common throughout the world, and a remarkable record was set back in 1950 when 199,854 fans turned out at the Maracana Stadium in Rio de Janiero to see Brazil play Uruguay in the World Cup final. South Americans have taken to the game like skiers to fresh powder snow. They love it, nurture it and have found success.

Soccer was introduced to the Olympics as a demonstration sport back in 1900, and to no one's suprise, Great Britain emerged the winner. In 1904, in the Games at St. Louis, Missouri, a club team from Galt, Ontario won.

In 1908, soccer formally became part of the Olympic programme. Great Britain won the gold medal and repeated its success four years later. But the sport made deep inroads in other countries and Great Britain has not won a soccer gold medal since and has formally withdrawn from Olympic competition.

Hungary managed back-to-back triumphs in 1964 and 1968 after having won a gold previously in 1952. Uruguay won golds in 1924 and 1928. Czechoslovakia was the 1980 champion and will be granted a berth in the 1984 qualifying rounds in the United States.

PROCEDURE

As defending champion, Czechoslovakia obtains a bye into the 16-team playdown which will be held at four sites: Harvard University in Cambridge, Massachusetts, U.S. Naval Academy in Annapolis, Maryland, Stanford University in Palo Alto, California and at the Rose Bowl in Pasadena, California. The other bye goes to the United States as host nation.

The final 16 teams are three countries from Africa, two from South America, three from Asia and Oceania, five countries from Europe and three from CONCACAF, made up of countries from North America, Central America and the Caribbean.

Aside from Czechoslovakia and the United States which have byes, countries must play preliminary, qualifying games to reach the Olympics. At the Olympics, each country will play at least three games and will be seeded for purposes of establishing a balanced draw for each of the four groups from which quarter-finalists will emerge.

VIEWING TIPS

A team consists of 10 players plus a goalie. Included are rear defenders (often four), mid-fielders (two, three or four) and forwards (two, three or four). The goalie is the only player allowed to touch the ball with his hands. The goalie's use of hands, however, is restricted to the penalty area, 40.04 metres by 16.38 metres, and he is not allowed to take more than four steps when holding the ball.

Unlike the goalie, other players can only advance the ball on the field which is 105-metres long and 68-metres wide, by dribbling, kicking or hitting the ball with the head, in effect using any part of the body except the hands and arms.

There will be numerous throw-ins when the ball leaves the area of play. The ball is returned to play with a two-handed overhead throw by the team that had not touched the ball prior to leaving the field of play. If the ball goes off the field at either end, it is put back in play by a goal-kick, if touched last by the attacking team, or by a corner-kick if touched last by the defending team.

The game is divided into a pair of 45-minute halves. A free-kick or penalty kick is awarded for infringements such as charging, kicking, holding and kneeling, if the offence happened in the penalty area.

One delightful aspect of the game is watching a player move up the field with the ball, his deft footwork and change of pace frustrating defenders. And, of course, keep an eye out for the "headers" from high jumping players in goal-area action.

TECHNICAL TERMS

Offside — a player is offside if he's in the opponent's half of the field with one or no opponents between him and the goal at the moment the ball is passed forward. For each case of offside, an indirect free-kick is awarded at the point of infraction.

Free-kicks — are taken when the ball is stationary and at the point of the infringement. All opposing players must be at least 9.25 metres from the ball, until it is in play, unless they are standing on their own goal line between the goal posts.

Penalty kick — awarded for the most serious infringement by a defensive player on a defensive player. The penalty kick is taken from a point located within the penalty area, 11 metres in front of the goal.

Throw-In — consists of throwing in the ball, overhead, once it has gone over the touchline (outside the boundary marker). This is the only time players can

FOOTBALL (soccer) Men

YEAR	PLACE	COUNTRY
1900	1	**Great Britain**
	2	France
	3	Belgium
1904	1	**Canada**
	2	U.S.A.
	3	U.S.A.
1908	1	**Great Britain**
	2	Denmark
	3	Netherlands
1912	1	**Great Britain**
	2	Denmark
	3	Netherlands
1920	1	**Belgium**
	2	Spain
	3	Netherlands
1924	1	**Uruguay**
	2	Switzerland
	3	Sweden
1928	1	**Uruguay**
	2	Argentina
	3	Italy
1936	1	**Italy**
	2	Austria
	3	Norway
1948	1	**Sweden**
	2	Yugoslavia
	3	Denmark
1952	1	**Hungary**
	2	Yugoslavia
	3	Sweden
1956	1	**U.S.S.R.**
	2	Yugoslavia
	3	Bulgaria
1960	1	**Yugoslavia**
	2	Denmark
	3	Hungary
1964	1	**Hungary**
	2	Czechoslovakia
	3	Germany
1968	1	**Hungary**
	2	Bulgaria
	3	Japan
1972	1	**Poland**
	2	Hungary
	3	East Germany/ U.S.S.R.
1976	1	**East Germany**
	2	Poland
	3	U.S.S.R.
1980	1	**Czechoslovakia**
	2	East Germany
	3	U.S.S.R.

handle the ball. No goals can be scored directly from a throw-in.

Corner-kick — when a ball last played by a defender passes over the goal line (not including between the goal posts), a member of the attacking team takes a corner-kick from the quarter circle at the corner-flag post nearest to the point where the ball passes over the line.

Goal-kick — when the ball passes over the goal line, excluding the goal, and was last played by an attacker. It is put directly into play by a goal-kick which is taken from a point within the half of the goal area nearest to where the ball crossed the line by a player of the defending team.

EQUIPMENT

Field — must be grass and 105-metres long and 68-metres wide. The goal is 2.44-metres high, 7.32-metres in width and 3.50-metres deep. The penalty spot is 11-metres from tie goal and the penalty area is 40.04 metres by 16.38 metres.

Ball — must be spherical with a circumference of 68 to 71 centimetres and a weight of 396 to 453 grams.

Clothing — a player must not wear anything that may be dangerous to another player. The usual attire is jersey, shorts, socks and footwear.

GYMNASTICS

EVENT DATE			UNIVERSITY OF CALIFORNIA, LOS ANGELES		
JULY	29	Compulsory exercises, men	AUGUST	4	Apparatus finals, men
	30	Compulsory exercises, women		5	Apparatus finals, women
	31	Optional exercises, men Optional exercises—team finals, men		9	Rhythmic preliminaries, women
AUGUST	1	Optional exercises, women Optional exercises—team finals, women		10	Rhythmic preliminaries, women
	2	All-around finals, men		11	Rhythmic finals, women
	3	All around finals, women			

HISTORY

There was little to excite the world about gymnastics, until the bubbly, effervescent Olga Korbut burst upon the Olympic scene in the 1972 Games in Munich. This diminutive and highly talented Soviet was a sensation. Her entertaining, and at times daring, style captivated audiences. Suddenly, gymnastics had a "star" for the first time.

Korbut was a film and television natural, with her charm, grace and showmanship. She became a worldwide celebrity when her Olympic performances were relayed around the world via television. But she had more than showmanship; she had talent, winning the gold medal in beam and floor exercise. Her compatriot Ludmilla Tourischeva was better technically and won the all-

She won the balance beam and uneven bars and placed third in the floor exercise. She won the all-round championship. Her performance was overpowering, even for the judges. They gave her perfect scores of 10 for six routines.

Comaneci was the first gymnast in the history of the sport to be honoured with a perfect score. She received tremendous media coverage. Almost no one noticed that Korbut had been runnerup to Comaneci in the balance beam. The spotlight had shifted. Also lightly appreciated was that Nellie Kim of the Soviet Union had been given perfect scores of 10 twice during her routines.

Until Korbut and Comaneci came along, the top gymnasts performed virtually in seclusion, their efforts recognized only by the sport's officials, family

but she shook them off to retain the all-round championship.

Caslavska's remarkable performances in two Olympics earned her seven gold and four silver medals. The most prolific gymnast in Olympic history, however, was Larissa Latynina of the Soviet Union. Latynina picked up a total of 18 medals, half of them gold, during the 1956, 1960, and 1964 Games.

Sawao Kato of Japan has mined more gold than any male gymnast. He earned eight gold medals in three Olympics (1968, 1972 and 1976). The Soviet Union's Nikolai Andrianov has earned a total of 15 medals, including seven gold and five silver during the past three Olympics.

The Soviets and the Japanese have dominated Olympic gymnastics and the United States holds down third-place in the medals race. Canada has yet to win a medal in Olympic gymnastics.

The beginnings of gymnastics are traced to the ancient Greeks, who felt that outdoor exercise would be helpful in developing the body. A series of exercises were designed and youths performed in outdoor gymnasiums. Eventually, the sport found its way indoors and free of inclement weather. Yet, there was little done to promote its values and gymnastics virtually stagnated until Friedrich Ludwig Jahn of Germany came along in the nineteenth century. Jahn felt that with a few changes there was a future for gymnastics. By the time he died in 1852, he had pioneered the use of the horizontal bar, the parallel bars and the rings.

Despite its new apparatus, gymnastics remained static, confined mostly to European gymnasiums and occasionally practised in Canada and the United States by immigrants. When Olga Korbut smiled at the judges and spectators a new era was launched for gymnastics. Friedrich Ludwig Jahn would have loved it.

The Pauley Pavilion, the site of the gymnastics competition

round championship, but when people spoke of gymnastics, they spoke of Korbut.

Tours to North America brought Korbut more fame. Spectators, who never before showed an interest in gymnastics packed arenas. Gymnastic officials were basking in this newly found exposure. The highly skilled Korbut was able to sustain interest into the 1976 Olympics in Montreal, but insiders were already touting a new "star," unsmiling Nadia Comaneci of Rumania. Comaneci was to prove an outstanding technician.

With mechanically perfect precision, Comaneci performed almost flawlessly.

and friends. Little was said or written about Vera Caslavska, when the Czechoslovak arrived in Mexico City in 1968 to defend the all-round title she had won four years previously in Tokyo. The media focused on the rarefied air and the potential of many world records in track and field due to fighting against less air pressure in the high altitude. Few bothered with Caslvaska and the internal pressure she felt. Two Soviet girls were rated by the experts ahead of her. And just two months before, the Soviet army moved into her country to quell an uprising by freedom-seeking people. These thoughts weighed heavily on her mind

A young gymnast performing the floor exercises

On the balance beam

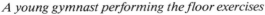

GENERAL DESCRIPTION

The men's and women's events are held separately. Each gymnast exudes strength and grace. The men compete on six apparatus and women compete on four.

For both men and women, the Olympic competition is a three-part procedure. Firstly, the gymnast competes in the team programme. Secondly, the gymnast advances into the individual all-round competition. And thirdly, the gymnast competes in individual events in specific disciplines (apparatus). Each gymnast is scored from 0 to 10 in each discipline.

In the team competition, six gymnasts from each country perform a series of compulsory and optional routines in each discipline. The men compete on the rings, parallel bars, horizontal bar, side horse, long horse vault and in the floor exercise. The women compete on the asymmetrical (uneven) bars, balance beam and horse vault as well as in the floor exercise. The team score is tabu-

lated by adding the best five out of six gymnast's scores on each event. The team with the most points after these competitions wins the gold medal.

The scores in the team competition are also used to declare the competitors for the individual all-round championship. The top 36 competitors from the team event (maximum three per country) advance to the individual all-round competition. The competitors in this event must then complete a further optional exercise for each event and new marks are awarded. These marks are added to the average of their previous total team competition marks and medals and placings are awarded according to standing.

Based on the team competition scores, the officials then pick the top eight competitors in each event for the individual final. A further optional exercise must be performed and the marks for that are added to the average of the gymnast's previous marks to determine the winner and runnersup in each of the

A gymnast's agility is the greatest demand in performing on the horse vault

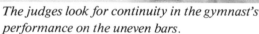
The judges look for continuity in the gymnast's performance on the uneven bars.

Performing on the men's long horse vault

events.

Let's take a look at the various events:

Women's floor exercises — full of cartwheels, pivots, handsprings, backward and forward walkovers. This event entails compulsory exercises. The programme, from 70-to-90 seconds long is performed to the accompaniment of music. The judges look for grace, suppleness, and coordination. The judges also rate the degree of difficulty of optional exercises. Competitors may be penalized for leaving the mat area.

Women's balance beam — although the beam is only 10-centimetres wide, the gymnasts run, jump, turn, somersault and dance on this narrow platform. It takes a high degree of balance for the gymnast who must include some balancing moves in her routine while using the entire length of the 5-metre long beam. Judges also look for constant motion by the gymnast in her 70-to-90-second routines.

Women's asymmetrical (uneven) bars — a quick moving event with the women rotating from the upper bar which is 2.3-metres high to the lower bar which is 1.5-metres high. The judges watch for continuity and keep a sharp eye on the gymnasts who change hand grasps on each bar and occasionally use the bars, which are 350-centimetres long, for support. In case of a fall, the gymnast has 30 seconds to resume the routine.

Women's horse vault — demands a great amount of agility for the gymnast. She runs at the apparatus at a high speed, bounces off the springboard, touches the horse which is 1.20-metres high and vaults across it before landing on her feet. All this without losing balance. The compulsory and optional exercises feature three types of vaults — horizontal, vaults with turns and handstands. All vaults must be performed with both hands on the horse. Judges rate competitors on first flight (takeoff), hand support, second flight (when the hands leave horse) and landing.

Men's floor exercises — the stress is on technique in all elementary move-ments of the body. Movements should display strength and balance as well as the required skill. The gymnast must use as much of the mat area as possible, creating constant change of direction. This event is great for self expression and optional exercises often convey the character of the gymnast. Routines run about a minute with competitors given an audible warning at the 50-second mark. Routines running longer than 70 seconds or shorter than 50 seconds are penalized by the judges.

Men's long horse vault — at 1.35-metres high, it is slightly higher than the one used by women. The direction of the vault must follow the length of the horse and all competitors must use the support of one or two hands. The men are scored for preflight (takeoff from springboard), second flight and landing.

Men's side horse (pommel horse) — appears similar to the horse vault but with two handles and 1.1-metres high. The gymnast performs a series of exercises that utilize all upper parts of the

The gymnast must perform a series of compulsory and optional exercises on the pommel horse.

horse as divided by the handles. The exercises must be continuous with mostly double leg circles and upper body and hand movement.

Men's rings — there are three key points; the swing, strength and hold, for gymnasts who grasp two rings, 2.5- to 2.8-metres high. The gymnast must go through his compulsory and optional exercises without swinging the rings. There must be two handstands by the gymnast, one executed with strength, the other with a swing. Handstand holds must last two seconds.

Men's parallel bars — the bars are 350-centimetres long, 1.75 metres above the floor, with 42 to 52 centimetres of space between them, according to the gymnast's size. Judges watch for swing and flight movements and swinging and hold moves. The gymnast will include exercises of strength and holds such as the handstand, which must last at least two seconds.

Men's horizontal bar — located 2.55 to 2.75 metres above the floor, the bar places a premium on swinging without stops. There should be at least one combination in which the gymnast lets the grip of both hands go, and then simultaneously regrabs the bar with both hands.

PROCEDURE

The top dozen women's and men's teams at the world championships last year qualified for the Olympic Games in Los Angeles.

The women's ranking is: (1) Soviet Union; (2) Rumania; (3) East Germany; (4) Bulgaria; (5) China; (6) Czechoslovakia; (7) United States; (8) West Germany; (9) Hungary; (10) Canada; (11) North Korea; and (12) Japan.

Spain, Switzerland and Italy will each be allowed to send three gymnasts to Los Angeles while Great Britain, France and Cuba can each send two. In addition, nine others will be named, bringing the total to 96 individuals and 16 teams.

The men's top dozen at the world championship were: (1) China; (2) Soviet Union; (3) Japan; (4) United States; (5) East Germany; (6) Hungary; (7) Bulgaria; (8) West Germany; (9) France; (10) Switzerland; (11) Rumania; and (12) Cuba.

Canada, North Korea and Czechoslovakia are entitled to send three gymnasts while Italy, Great Britain and South Korea can each send two. In addition, nine other individuals will be named, bringing the total to 96.

The three Canadian representatives will be named after the national championships scheduled for the spring of 1984. Among those attempting to qualify for the Olympic trip are Dan Gaudet, the 1983 Canadian champion, Philippe Chartrand, Warren Long and Brad Peters.

Strength, balance and skill are required for all movements.

The men's horizontal bar

SCORING

Team — each gymnast performs compulsory and optional exercises on each of the apparatus (six for men, four for women). The top five scores per event from each team of six gymnasts are added together to determine the team winners. There are separate championships for men and women.

Individual all-round — the top 36 gymnasts from each of the team competitions advance to this event. There is a maximum, however, of three gymnasts in each of the men's and women's sections for each country. The score given for the optional routine performed is then added to the halved score the gymnast compiled in two days of team competition. The new aggregate score determines final placings for the all-round championship.

Individual event — the top eight gymnasts in each event during the team competition qualify for the individual event competition. There is a limit of two gym-

The gymnast performs exercises of strength, such as a handstand on the parallel bars.

nasts from each country for each of the men's and women's events. The score the gymnast earned during the team competition is halved and is added to the score the gymnast earned for an optional routine in the individual event finals. Final scores determine the placings and medal winners.

In all cases, the scoring of a gymnast's performance is done by judges who rate the competitor on a basis of 0 to 10. Gymnasts may be penalized for obvious faults such as lack of rhythm, lack of confidence or basic faults in the exercise. Of the scores awarded by the four panel judges, the high and low scores are dropped and the middle two are averaged. If there is a wide difference in the scoring, the head judge confers with the other judges in a bid to reduce the differences. In women's events, the head judge may add her score to the two middle ones and find a base score.

EQUIPMENT

Floor — is 12-metres square; a double flex spring floor covered by an ethafoam carpet.

Side horse — is 110-centimetres high and 160-centimetres long. There are two handles in the centre of the apparatus which the gymnast grabs. Because of the excess movement by the gymnast, the side horse must be firmly anchored.

Horse vault — is 120-centimetres high and 163-centimetres long for women. The men's horse is 135-centimetres high and the same length.

Parallel bars — the two, 350-centimetre-long bars are 42-52 centimetres apart and are 175 centimetres high.

Asymmetrical (uneven) bars — two horizontal bars 350-centimetres long positioned parallel to each other. The lower bar is 150-centimetres off the ground, the higher bar 230-centimetres. They are adjustable.

Beam — only 10-centimetres wide, the 5-metre long beam must be firmly anchored. It is 120-centimetres high.

Rings — are suspended 255-centimetres from the floor. The rings themselves have a diameter of 18-centimetres.

Horizontal bar — a 240-centimetre long bar is supported 255-centimetres above the floor on uprights. It is held firmly in place by support wires.

Dress — men must always wear a jersey. They can opt for shorts for the floor exercise and vault competitions but long, white pants are mandatory for the other events. Footwear is optional for the vault and floor exercise. Women wear leotards. The use of gymnastic slippers is optional.

TOP COMPETITORS

Men

Dmitri Belozerchev of the Soviet Union was the all-round champion in the 1983 world championships in Budapest last October. The youngster won individual titles in the horizontal bar and side horse, was co-winner in the rings, and was runnerup to China's Tong Fei in the floor exercise. Belozerchev is considered the best gymnast in the world.

Japanese veteran Koji Gushiken was runnerup in the all-round competition and tied Belozerchev for first place in the rings. The Japanese, like the Russians, traditionally have strong teams.

China also will be tough. Lou Yun won the parallel bars event at the world championship and Li Ning was second in the long horse vault and third in the floor exercise.

Arthur Akopian, Vladimir Artemov and Alexandr Pogorelov are other standout performers for the Soviet Union.

Women

Natalia Yourchenko of the Soviet Union won the women's all-round title in the world championships with compatriot Olga Mostepanova second and Ecaterina Szabo of Hungary third. Szabo won the floor exercise and also picked up a second in the asymmetric bars and a third in the horse vault. Maxie Knauck of East Germany is a veteran who won the asymmetric bars.

TOP CANADIANS

Anita Botnen of Vancouver, Elfi Schlegel of Toronto, Janice Kerr of Toronto and Leanne Gallant of Toronto helped Canada to a 10th-place finish in the world championships. Helping Canada earn 10th-place were Bonnie Wittmeier of Winnipeg and Andrea Thomas of Toronto, who also advanced to the all-round competition after the team competition.

MEDAL WINNERS

GYMNASTICS—Men—Combined Exercises Individual

YEAR	PLACE	NAME	COUNTRY
1900	1	S. Sandras	France
	2	N. Bas	France
	3	L. Démanet	France
1904	1	J. Lenhart	Austria
	2	W. Weber	Germany
	3	A. Spinnier	Switzerland
1908	1	A. Braglia	Italy
	2	S.W. Tysal	Great Britain
	3	J. Ségura	France
1912	1	A. Braglia	Italy
	2	L. Ségura	France
	3	A. Tunesi	Italy
1920	1	G. Zampori	Italy
	2	M. Torrès	France
	3	J. Gounot	France
1924	1	L. Stukelj	Yugoslavia
	2	R. Prazak	Czechoslovakia
	3	B. Supcik	Czechoslovakia
1928	1	G. Miez	Switzerland
	2	H. Hänggi	Switzerland
	3	L. Stukelj	Yugoslavia
1932	1	R. Neri	Italy
	2	I. Pelle	Hungary
	3	H. Savolainen	Finland
1936	1	A. Schwarzmann	Germany
	2	E. Mack	Switzerland
	3	K. Frey	Germany
1948	1	V. Huhtanen	Finland
	2	W. Lehmann	Switzerland
	3	P. Aaltonen	Finland
1952	1	V. Tschukarin	U.S.S.R.
	2	G. Schaginyan	U.S.S.R.
	3	J. Stalder	Switzerland
1956	1	V. Tschukarin	U.S.S.R.
	2	T. Ono	Japan
	3	Y. Titov	U.S.S.R.
1960	1	B. Schakhlin	U.S.S.R.
	2	T. Ono	Japan
	3	Y. Titov	U.S.S.R.
1964	1	Y. Endo	Japan
	2	S. Tsurumi/ B. Schakhlin/ V. Lisitsky	Japan/ U.S.S.R./ U.S.S.R.
1968	1	S. Kato	Japan
	2	M. Voronin	U.S.S.R.
	3	A. Nakayama	Japan
1972	1	S. Kato	Japan
	2	E. Kenmotsu	Japan
	3	A. Nakayama	Japan
1976	1	Nikolai Andrianov	U.S.S.R.
	2	Sawao Kato	Japan
	3	Mitsuo Tsukahara	Japan
1980	1	Alexandr Ditiatin	U.S.S.R.
	2	Nikolai Andrianov	U.S.S.R.
	3	Stoyan Deltchev	Bulgaria

GYMNASTICS—Men—Combined Exercises Team

YEAR	PLACE	COUNTRY
1904*	1	U.S.A.
1908	1	Sweden
	2	Norway
	3	Finland
1912	1	Italy
	2	Hungary
	3	Great Britain
1920	1	Italy
	2	Belgium
	3	France
1924	1	Italy
	2	France
	3	Switzerland
1928	1	Switzerland
	2	Czechoslovakia
	3	Yugoslavia

Year	Place		Country
1932	1		Italy
	2		U.S.A.
	3		Finland
1936	1		Germany
	2		Switzerland
	3		Finland
1948	1		Finland
	2		Switzerland
	3		Hungary
1952	1		U.S.S.R.
	2		Switzerland
	3		Finland
1956	1		U.S.S.R.
	2		Japan
	3		Finland
1960	1		Japan
	2		U.S.S.R.
	3		Italy
1964	1		Japan
	2		U.S.S.R.
	3		Germany
1968	1		Japan
	2		U.S.S.R.
	3		East Germany
1972	1		Japan
	2		U.S.S.R.
	3		East Germany
1976	1		Japan
	2		U.S.S.R.
	3		East Germany
1980	1		U.S.S.R.
	2		East Germany
	3		Hungary

* The first five places went to teams from American clubs

GYMNASTICS—Men—Floor Exercises

YEAR	PLACE	NAME	COUNTRY
1932	1	I. Pelle	Hungary
	2	G. Miez	Switzerland
	3	M. Lertora	Italy
1936	1	G. Miez	Switzerland
	2	J. Walter	Switzerland
	3	K. Frey/	Germany/
		E. Mack	Switzerland
1948	1	F. Pataki	Hungary
	2	J. Mogyorosi-Klencs	Hungary
	3	Z. Ruzicka	Czechoslovakia
1952	1	K. Thoresson	Sweden
	2	T. Uesako	Japan
	3	J. Jokiel	Poland
1956	1	V. Muratov	U.S.S.R.
	2	N. Aihara/	Japan/
		W. Thoresson/	Sweden/
		V. Tschukarin	U.S.S.R.
1960	1	N. Aihara	Japan
	2	Y. Titov	U.S.S.R.
	3	F. Menichelli	Italy
1964	1	F. Menichelli	Italy
	2	V. Lisitsky	U.S.S.R.
	3	Y. Endo	Japan
1968	1	S. Kato	Japan
	2	A. Nakayama	Japan
	3	T. Kato	Japan
1972	1	N. Andrianov	U.S.S.R.
	2	A. Nakayama	Japan
	3	S. Kasamatsu	Japan
1976	1	Nikolai Andrianov	U.S.S.R.
	2	Vladimir Marchenko	U.S.S.R.
	3	Peter Kormann	U.S.A.
1980	1	Ronald Bruckner	German Dem. Rep.
	2	Nikolai Andrianov	U.S.S.R.
	3	Alexandr Ditiatin	U.S.S.R.

GYMNASTICS—Men—Rings

YEAR	PLACE	NAME	COUNTRY
1896	1	I. Miltropoulos	Greece
	2	H. Weingärtner	Germany
	3	P. Persakis	Greece
1904	1	H. Glass	U.S.A.
	2	W.A. Merz	U.S.A.
	3	E. Voigt	U.S.A.

1924	1	F. Martino	Italy
	2	R. Prazak	Czechoslovakia
	3	L. Vacha	Czechoslovakia
1928	1	L. Stukelj	Yugoslavia
	2	L. Vacha	Czechoslovakia
	3	E. Löffler	Czechoslovakia
1932	1	G. Gulack	U.S.A.
	2	W. Denton	U.S.A.
	3	G. Lattuada	Italy
1936	1	A. Hudec	Czechoslovakia
	2	L. Stukelj	Yugoslavia
	3	M. Volz	Germany
1948	1	K. Frei	Switzerland
	2	M. Reusch	Switzerland
	3	Z. Ruzicka	Czechoslovakia
1952	1	G. Schaginyan	U.S.S.R.
	2	V. Tschukarin	U.S.S.R.
	3	H. Eugster/	Switzerland/
		D. Leonkin	U.S.S.R.
1956	1	A. Azaryan	U.S.S.R.
	2	V. Muratov	U.S.S.R.
	3	M. Takemoto/	Japan/
		M. Kubota	Japan
1960	1	A. Azaryan	U.S.S.R.
	2	B. Schakhlin	U.S.S.R.
	3	V. Kapsazov/	Bulgaria/
		T. Ono	Japan
1964	1	T. Hayata	Japan
	2	F Menichelli	Italy
	3	B. Schakhlin	U.S.S.R.
1968	1	A. Nakayama	Japan
	2	M. Voronin	U.S.S.R.
	3	S. Kato	Japan
1972	1	A. Nakayama	Japan
	2	M. Voronin	U.S.S.R.
	3	M. Tsukahara	Japan
1976	1	Nikolai Andrianov	U.S.S.R.
	2	Aleksandr Ditiatin	U.S.S.R.
	3	Danut Grecu	Rumania
1980	1	Alexandr Ditiatin	U.S.S.R.
	2	Alexandr Tkachyov	U.S.S.R.
	3	Jiri Tabak	Czechoslovakia

GYMNASTICS—Men—Horse Vault

YEAR	PLACE	NAME	COUNTRY
1896	1	K. Schuhmann	Germany
	2	J. Zutter	Switzerland
1904	1	A. Heida/	U.S.A./
		G. Eyser	U.S.A.
	3	W.A. Merz	U.S.A.
1924	1	F. Kriz	U.S.A.
	2	J. Koutny	Czechoslovakia
	3	B. Morkovsky	Czechoslovakia
1928	1	E. Mack	Switzerland
	2	E. Löffler	Czechoslovakia
	3	S. Derganc	Yugoslavia
1932	1	S. Guglielmetti	Italy
	2	A. Jochim	U.S.A.
	3	E. Carmichael	U.S.A.
1936	1	K. Schwarzmann	Germany
	2	E. Mack	Switzerland
	3	M. Volz	Germany
1948	1	P. Aaltonen	Finland
	2	O. Rove	Finland
	3	J. Mogyorosi-Klencs/	Hungary/
		F. Pataki/	Hungary/
		L. Sotornik	Czechoslovakia
1952	1	V. Tschukarin	U.S.S.R.
	2	M. Takemoto	Japan
	3	T. Uesako/	Japan/
		T. Ono	Japan
1956	1	H. Bantz/	West Germany/
		V. Muratov	U.S.S.R.
	3	Y. Titov	U.S.S.R.
1960	1	T. Ono/	Japan/
		B. Schakhlin	U.S.S.R.
	3	V. Portnoi	U.S.S.R.
1964	1	H. Yamashita	Japan
	2	V. Lisitsky	U.S.S.R.
	3	H. Rantakari	Finland
1968	1	M. Voronin	U.S.S.R.
	2	Y. Endo	Japan
	3	S. Diomidov	U.S.S.R.

1972	1	K. Köste	East Germany
	2	Y. Klimenko	U.S.S.R.
	3	N. Andrianov	U.S.S.R.
1976	1	Nikolai Andrianov	U.S.S.R.
	2	Mitsuo Tsukahara	Japan
	3	Hiroshi Kajiyama	Japan
1980	1	Nikolai Andrianov	U.S.S.R.
	2	Alexandr Ditiatin	U.S.S.R.
	3	Roland Bruckner	German Dem. Rep.

GYMNASTICS—Men—Side Horse (Pommel)

YEAR	PLACE	NAME	COUNTRY
1896	1	J. Zutter	Switzerland
	2	H. Weingärtner	Germany
1900	1	Event not held	
1904	1	A. Heida	U.S.A.
	2	G. Eyser	U.S.A.
	3	W.A. Merz	U.S.A.
1924	1	J. Wilhelm	Switzerland
	2	J. Gutweniger	Switzerland
	3	A. Rebetez	Switzerland
1928	1	H. Hänggi	Switzerland
	2	G. Miez	Switzerland
	3	H. Savolainen	Finland
1932	1	I. Pelle	Hungary
	2	O. Bonoli	Italy
	3	F. Haubold	U.S.A.
1936	1	K. Frey	Germany
	2	E. Mack	Switzerland
	3	A. Bachmann	Switzerland
1948	1	P. Aaltonen/	Finland/
		V. Huhtanen/	Finland/
		H. Savolainen	Finland
	2	L. Zanetti	Italy
	3	G. Fogone	Italy
1952	1	V. Tschukarin	U.S.S.R.
	2	Y. Korolkov/	U.S.S.R./
		G. Schaginyan	U.S.S.R.
	3*		
1956	1	B. Schakhlin	U.S.S.R.
	2	T. Ono	Japan
	3	V. Tschukarin	U.S.S.R.
1960	1	B. Schakhlin/	U.S.S.R./
		E. Ekman	Finland
	3	S. Tsurumi	Japan
1964	1	M. Cerar	Yugoslavia
	2	S. Tsurumi	Japan
	3	Y. Tsapenko	U.S.S.R.
1968	1	M. Cerar	Yugoslavia
	2	O. Laiho	Finland
	3	M. Voronin	U.S.S.R.
1972	1	Y. Klimenko	U.S.S.R.
	2	S. Kato	Japan
	3	E. Kenmotsu	Japan
1976	1	Zoltan Magyar	Hungary
	2	Eizo Kenmotzu	Japan
	3	Nikolai Andrianov	U.S.S.R.
1980	1	Zoltan Magyar	Hungary
	2	Alexandr Ditiatin	U.S.S.R.
	3	Michael Nikolay	German Dem. Rep.

* No Bronze medal was awarded

GYMNASTICS—Men—Parallel Bars

YEAR	PLACE	NAME	COUNTRY
1896	1	A. Flatow	Germany
	2	J. Zutter	Switzerland
	3	H. Weingärtner	Germany
1900		Event not held	
1904	1	G. Eyser	U.S.A.
	2	A. Heida	U.S.A.
	3	J. Duha	U.S.A.
1924	1	A. Güttinger	Switzerland
	2	R. Prazak	Czechoslovakia
	3	G. Zampori	Italy
1928	1	L. Vacha	Czechoslovakia
	2	J. Primozic	Yugoslavia
	3	H. Hänggi	Switzerland

YEAR	PLACE	NAME	COUNTRY
1932	1	**R. Neri**	**Italy**
	2	I. Pelle	Hungary
	3	H. Savolainen	Finland
1936	1	**K. Frey**	**Germany**
	2	M. Reusch	Switzerland
	3	A. Schwarzmann	Germany
1948	1	**M. Reusch**	**Switzerland**
	2	V. Huhtanen	Finland
	3	C. Kipfer/	Switzerland
		J. Stalder	Switzerland
1952	1	**H. Eugster**	**Switzerland**
	2	V. Tschukarin	U.S.S.R.
	3	J. Stalder	Switzerland
1956	1	**V. Tschukarin**	**U.S.S.R.**
	2	M. Kubota	Japan
	3	T. Ono/	Japan/
		M. Takemoto	Japan
1960	1	**B. Schakhlin**	**U.S.S.R.**
	2	G. Carminucci	Italy
	3	T. Ono	Japan
1964	1	**Y. Endo**	**Japan**
	2	S. Tsurumi	Japan
	3	F. Menichelli	Italy
1968	1	**A. Nakayama**	**Japan**
	2	M. Voronin	U.S.S.R.
	3	V. Klimenko	U.S.S.R.
1972	1	**S. Kato**	**Japan**
	2	S. Kasamatsu	Japan
	3	E. Kenmotsu	Japan
1976	1	**Sawao Kato**	**Japan**
	2	Nikolai Andrianov	U.S.S.R.
	3	Mitsuo Tsukahara	Japan
1980	1	**Alexandr Tkachyov**	**U.S.S.R.**
	2	Alexandr Ditiatin	U.S.S.R.
	3	Roland Bruckner	German Dem. Rep.

GYMNASTICS—Men—Horizontal Bar

YEAR	PLACE	NAME	COUNTRY
1896	1	**H. Weingärtner**	**Germany**
	2	A. Flatow	Germany
1900		**Event not held**	
1904	1	**A. Heida/**	**U.S.A./**
		E. Hennig	**U.S.A.**
	3	G. Eyser	U.S.A.
1924	1	**L. Stukelj**	**Yugoslavia**
	2	J. Gutweniger	Switzerland
	3	A. Higelin	France
1928	1	**G. Miez**	**Switzerland**
	2	R. Neri	Italy
	3	E. Mack	Switzerland
1932	1	**D. Bixler**	**U.S.A.**
	2	H. Savolainen	Finland
	3	E. Terasvirta	Finland
1936	1	**A. Saarvala**	**Finland**
	2	K. Frey	Germany
	3	A. Schwarzmann	Germany
1948	1	**J. Stalder**	**Switzerland**
	2	W. Lehmann	Switzerland
	3	V. Huhtanen	Finland
1952	1	**J. Günthard**	**Switzerland**
	2	J. Stalder/	Switzerland/
		A. Schwarzmann	Germany
1956	1	**T. Ono**	**Japan**
	2	Y. Titov	U.S.S.R.
	3	M. Takemoto	Japan
1960	1	**T. Ono**	**Japan**
	2	M. Takemoto	Japan
	3	B. Schakhlin	U.S.S.R.
1964	1	**B. Schakhlin**	**U.S.S.R.**
	2	Y. Titov	U.S.S.R.
	3	M. Cerar	Yugoslavia
1968	1	**A. Nakayama/**	**Japan/**
		M. Voronin	**U.S.S.R.**
	3	E. Kenmotsu	Japan
1972	1	**M. Tsukahara**	**Japan**
	2	S. Kato	Japan
	3	S. Kasamatsu	Japan
1976	1	**Mitsuo Tsukahara**	**Japan**
	2	Eizo Kenmotsu	Japan
	3	Eberhard Gienger	Germany
1980	1	**Stoyan Deltchev**	**Bulgaria**
	2	Alexandr Ditiatin	U.S.S.R.
	3	Nikolai Andrianov	U.S.S.R.

GYMNASTICS—Women—Combined Exercises Individual

YEAR	PLACE	NAME	COUNTRY
1952	1	**M. Gorokhovskaya**	**U.S.S.R.**
	2	N. Botscharova	U.S.S.R.
	3	M. Korondi	Hungary
1956	1	**L. Latynina**	**U.S.S.R.**
	2	A. Keleti	Hungary
	3	S. Muratova	U.S.S.R.
1960	1	**L. Latynina**	**U.S.S.R.**
	2	S. Muratova	U.S.S.R.
	3	P. Astakhova	U.S.S.R.
1964	1	**V. Caslavska**	**Czechoslovakia**
	2	L. Latynina	U.S.S.R.
	3	P. Astakhova	U.S.S.R.
1968	1	**V. Caslavska**	**Czechoslovakia**
	2	Z. Voronina	U.S.S.R.
	3	N. Kutschinskaya	U.S.S.R.
1972	1	**L. Tourischeva**	**U.S.S.R.**
	2	K. Janz	East Germany
	3	T. Lazakovitsch	U.S.S.R.
1976	1	**Nadia Comaneci**	**Rumania**
	2	Nelli Kim	U.S.S.R.
	3	Lyudmila Tourischeva	U.S.S.R.
1980	1	**Yelena Davydova**	**U.S.S.R.**
	2	Maxi Gnauck/	German Dem. Rep./
	3	Nadia Comaneci	Rumania

GYMNASTICS—Women—Combined Exercises Team

YEAR	PLACE	COUNTRY
1928	1	**Netherlands**
	2	Italy
	3	Great Britain
1936	1	**Germany**
	2	Czechoslovakia
	3	Hungary
1948	1	**Czechoslovakia**
	2	Hungary
	3	U.S.A.
1952	1	**U.S.S.R.**
	2	Hungary
	3	Czechoslovakia
1956	1	**U.S.S.R.**
	2	Hungary
	3	Rumania
1960	1	**U.S.S.R.**
	2	Czechoslovakia
	3	Rumania
1964	1	**U.S.S.R.**
	2	Czechoslovakia
	3	Japan
1968	1	**U.S.S.R.**
	2	Czechoslovakia
	3	East Germany
1972	1	**U.S.S.R.**
	2	East Germany
	3	Hungary
1976	1	**U.S.S.R.**
	2	Rumania
	3	East Germany
1980	1	**U.S.S.R.**
	2	Rumania
	3	East Germany

GYMNASTICS—Women—Floor Exercises

YEAR	PLACE	NAME	COUNTRY
1952	1	**A. Keleti**	**Hungary**
	2	M. Gorokhovskaya	U.S.S.R.
	3	M. Korondi	Hungary
1956	1	**A. Keleti/**	**Hungary/**
		L. Latynina	**U.S.S.R.**
	3	E. Leustean	Rumania
1960	1	**L. Latynina**	**U.S.S.R.**
	2	P. Astakhova	U.S.S.R.
	3	T. Lyukhina	U.S.S.R.
1964	1	**L. Latynina**	**U.S.S.R.**
	2	P. Astakhova	U.S.S.R.
	3	A. Jánosi	Hungary
1968	1	**V. Cáslavská/**	**Czechoslovakia/**
		L. Petrik	**U.S.S.R.**
	3	N. Kutschinskaya	U.S.S.R.

GYMNASTICS—Women—Horse Vault

YEAR	PLACE	NAME	COUNTRY
1972	1	**O. Korbut**	**U.S.S.R.**
	2	L. Tourischeva	U.S.S.R.
	3	T. Lazakovitsch	U.S.S.R.
1976	1	**Nelli Kim**	**U.S.S.R.**
	2	Lyudmila Tourischeva	U.S.S.R.
	3	Nadia Comaneci	Rumania
1980	1	**Nelli Kim**	**U.S.S.R./**
		Nadia Comaneci	**Rumania**
	3	Maxi Gnauck	U.S.S.R./ German Dem. Rep.

(above listed under GYMNASTICS—Women—Combined Exercises... the following is Horse Vault)

GYMNASTICS—Women—Horse Vault

YEAR	PLACE	NAME	COUNTRY
1952	1	**Y. Kalintschuk**	**U.S.S.R.**
	2	M. Gorokhovskaya	U.S.S.R.
	3	G. Minaitscheva	U.S.S.R.
1956	1	**L. Latynina**	**U.S.S.R.**
	2	T. Manina	U.S.S.R.
	3	A. Colling/	Sweden/
		O. Tass	Hungary
1960	1	**M. Nikolayeva**	**U.S.S.R.**
	2	S. Muratova	U.S.S.R.
	3	L. Latynina	U.S.S.R.
1964	1	**V. Cáslavská**	**Czechoslovakia**
	2	L. Latynina/	U.S.S.R./
		B. Radochla	Germany
1968	1	**V. Cáslavská**	**Czechoslovakia**
	2	E. Zuchold	East Germany
	3	Z. Voronina	U.S.S.R.
1972	1	**K. Janz**	**East Germany**
	2	E. Zuchold	East Germany
	3	L. Tourischeva	U.S.S.R.
1976	1	**Nelli Kim**	**U.S.S.R.**
	2	Lyudmila Tourischeva	U.S.S.R./
		Carola Dornbeck	German Dem. Rep.
1980	1	**Natalia Shaposhnikova**	**U.S.S.R.**
	2	Steffi Kraker	German Dem. Rep.
	3	Melita Ruhn	Rumania

GYMNASTICS—Women—Beam

YEAR	PLACE	NAME	COUNTRY
1952	1	**N. Botscharova**	**U.S.S.R.**
	2	M. Gorokhovskaya	U.S.S.R.
	3	M. Korondi	Hungary
1956	1	**A. Keleti**	**Hungary**
	2	E. Bosakova/	Czechoslovakia/
		T. Manina	U.S.S.R.
1960	1	**E. Bosáková**	**Czechoslovakia**
	2	L. Latynina	U.S.S.R.
	3	S. Muratova	U.S.S.R.
1964	1	**V. Cáslavská**	**Czechoslovakia**
	2	T. Manina	U.S.S.R.
	3	L. Latynina	U.S.S.R.
1968	1	**N. Kutschinskaya**	**U.S.S.R.**
	2	V. Cáslavská	Czechoslovakia
	3	L. Petrik	U.S.S.R.
1972	1	**O. Korbut**	**U.S.S.R.**
	2	T. Lazakovitsch	U.S.S.R.
	3	K. Janz	East Germany
1976	1	**Nadia Comaneci**	**Rumania**
	2	Olga Korbut	U.S.S.R.
	3	Teodora Ungureanu	Rumania
1980	1	**Nadia Comaneci**	**Rumania**
	2	Yelena Davydova	U.S.S.R.
	3	Natalia Shaposhnikova	U.S.S.R.

GYMNASTICS—Women—Uneven Bars

YEAR	PLACE	NAME	COUNTRY
1952	1	**M. Korondi**	**Hungary**
	2	M. Gorokhovskaya	U.S.S.R.
	3	A. Keleti	Hungary
1956	1	**A. Keleti**	**Hungary**
	2	L. Latynina	U.S.S.R.
	3	S. Muratova	U.S.S.R.
1960	1	**P. Astakhova**	**U.S.S.R.**
	2	L. Latynina	U.S.S.R.
	3	T. Lyukhina	U.S.S.R.
1964	1	**P. Astakhova**	**U.S.S.R.**
	2	K. Makray	Hungary
	3	L. Latynina	U.S.S.R.
1968	1	**V. Caslavska**	**Czechoslovakia**
	2	K. Janz	East Germany
	3	Z. Voronina	U.S.S.R.
1972	1	**K. Janz**	**East Germany**
	2	O. Korbut	U.S.S.R.
	3	E. Zuchold	East Germany
1976	1	**Nadia Comaneci**	**Rumania**
	2	Teodora Ungureanu	Rumania
	3	Marta Egervari	Hungary
1980	1	**Maxi Gnauck**	**German Dem. Rep.**
	2	Emilia Eberle	Rumania
	3	Steffi Kraker/	German Dem. Rep./
		Melita Ruhn/	Rumania
		Maria Filatova	U.S.S.R.

RHYTHMIC SPORTIVE GYMNASTICS

Lori Fung, reigning Canadian champion, demonstrates the fluid, graceful movements of rhythmic sportive gymnastics.

HISTORY

Rhythmic sportive gymnastics (RSG), an internationally recognized sport since the 1950's, has been influenced in its evolution by many individuals and schools of thought. With its origins dau (known for his work with balls, hoops and clubs), Isadora Duncan and Rudolph Laban (dance experts), and the impetus given to it as a sporting discipline by the Soviets and Eastern Europeans, RSG has evolved into the in the championships in Cuba in 1971. In 1976, Ontario hosted the Maple Leaf Meet, the first international RSG competition to be held in Canada. This year marks the debut of RSG in the Olympic Games; a milestone in the evolution of the sport. It is believed that its inclusion in the Olympics will provide the impetus for the "coming of age" of rhythmic sportive gymnastics in Canada.

A perfect example of the high degree of flexibilty required in rhythmic sportive gymnastics.

stretching back to ancient Greece, the concepts of natural flowing movement, harmonious mind/body development and total physical exercise have remained central to RSG. From the eighteenth century, natural gymnastics of Jean Jacques Rousseau, through Johann Guts Muths (the grandfather of gymnastics), Jacques Dalcroze (the originator of eurhythmics), Rudolph Bode (a pioneer of rhythmic gymnastics), Hinrich Me-

"sport/art" it is today.

Previously known as "Modern Rhythmic Gymnastics," rhythmic sportive gymnastics became an internationally recognized sport by the Federation of International Gymnastics (FIG) in June 1962. The first world championships were held in 1963 in Budapest, Hungary, and have since been held every two years in various locations throughout the world. Canada first participated

GENERAL DESCRIPTION

Rhythmic sportive gymnastics is a beautiful and challenging sport, offering total physical exercise, graceful, expressive movement and challenging physical skills. This athletic-aesthetic sport emphasizes speed, flexibility, strength and excellent apparatus control. The rhythmics apparatus include the rope, hoop, ball, clubs and ribbon, and all apparatus manipulations must be performed in close harmony with flowing, expressive body movement.

Each routine, performed to music, incorporates the hand-held apparatus (one pair, in the case of the clubs) in a specified time of one minute to one minute, thirty seconds. Each routine must demonstrate fundamental prescribed elements, at least two superior and six medium difficulty movements, equal sidedness (i.e., use of both left and right sides of body and equal use of both left and right hands in handling apparatus), good floor coverage and technical exactness, as prescribed in the governing technical document of the sport, the FIG Code of Points. As well, the elements of creativity, musical interpretation and expression must be present to ensure the aestheticism of the sport. Acrobatic elements (such as cartwheels and handstands) are disallowed, as are static positions of the apparatus.

The apparatus must be in constant motion, never used as a decorative ornament, and must gracefully and "playfully" interact with the gymnast's movements. Acrobatic elements are disallowed because the intent of the routine is to project grace, flexibility, strength and coordination in harmony with the apparatus, and no movements should detract from, or supersede this harmony.

PROCEDURE

The RSG representation at the 1984 Olympic Games will be the top 50 gymnasts in the world (from the 1983 world championships in Strasbourg, France), with a maximum of two gymnasts per country. It was through the performances of our Canadian champion, Lori Fung, of Vancouver, B.C., who was coached by Mall Vesik, and national silver medalist Adrianne Dunnett of Weston, Ontario, who was coached by Liliana Dimitrova, that Canada earned two berths to the Olympic Games: a superior accomplishment.

At the Games, each gymnast will perform four routines: hoop, ball, clubs, and ribbon. Unlike the usual competitive format (in which a general competition determines the overall champions over four apparatus events, and finals determine the champion in each apparatus), the Olympics format will entail a general competition involving all 50 gymnasts, the top 20 of whom will advance to finals and, from their combined results, an overall Olympic champion and medalists will be declared.

It is hoped that by the 1988 Games in Seoul, South Korea, the group event, an event in which Canada has consistently fielded a strong team, will be included in the roster. The group competition involves a two minute, thirty second to three minute routine performed by six gymnasts, each with identical apparatus or in a combination of three plus three (i.e., three gymnasts with one type of apparatus, the remaining three with a different type). The group competition is a spectacular event, in which the gymnasts must interact among themselves and the apparatus with dynamism, apparatus exchanges and exciting floor patterns and combinations.

VIEWING TIPS

Watch for magnificent control and speed of execution, breathtaking apparatus manipulations teamed with equally spectacular body movements, and unique styles and interpretations among gymnasts and nations. A top performer will make even the most difficult moves look deceptively simple: That's the key to watch for — flawless execution in a performance that takes your breath away.

EQUIPMENT

The equipment may be of any colour except gold, silver or bronze, and must be in constant motion throughout the routine.

Hoop — wood or plastic, minimum weight 300 grams, interior diameter 80 to 90 centimetres. Used in demonstration at the ceremonies of the 1936 Olympic Games, a good hoop routine today must include the elements of rolling, rotation, throws, swings, circles, figures of eight, turning and passing through and over the hoop.

Ball — rubber or synthetic, minimum weight 400 grams, diameter 18 to 20 centimetres. Elements such as throws, bounces, rolls and swings are integral to the ball routine.

Clubs — wood, plastic or synthetic, minimum weight 150 grams each, 40 to 50 centimetres in length. Believed to be the oldest hand apparatus, clubs evolved from a heavy "bowling pin" version to the lighter, streamlined clubs of today. Requiring great dexterity and coordination, the clubs must describe mills, swings, circles, taps and throws throughout the routine.

Ribbon — satin or similar material, 6-metres long, 4- to 6-centimetres wide, minimum weight of 35 grams (without the stick or attachment), attached to a wood, plastic or fibreglass stick, 50 to 60 centimetres in length, including attachment. A spectacular crowd pleaser, the ribbon routine incorporates spirals, snakes, throws, swings, circles, and figures of eight in a swirl of activity and colour.

Rope — hemp or synthetic, proportionate in length to the gymnast, knotted at the ends. A "universal" apparatus, the rope develops cardiovascular endurance, agility, speed, coordination and rhythm, and routines should include such elements as leaps, skips, swings, circles and throws. (To be reintroduced into the FIG apparatus cycle in 1985-86, when the programme will be rope, ball, clubs and ribbon).

Floor Area — 12 × 12 metres. When two floor areas are provided, one should be carpeted in a neutral colour, the other uncarpeted (e.g., hardwood floor).

Ceiling Height — minimum height 8 metres for official FIG Championships. Good ceiling height is essential to optimal performance of apparatus manipulations/throws.

SCORING

Each routine is judged by four judges and a head judge, who independently give a mark between zero and 10 points, by tenths of a point. Scoring is based on the guidelines and point value deductions outlined in the FIG Code of Points (examples of deductions: loss of balance, drop of apparatus, absence of left-hand difficulties). The head judge drops the highest and lowest scores, and averages the middle two to obtain the final score. Though this score is not counted, (it is used as a "yardstick" only) the average must be in line with the head judge's score.

TOP COMPETITORS

Bulgaria continues to dominate the world in RSG. At the 1983 world championships, Bulgaria swept both the group and individual events, with Diliana Gueorguiva capturing the gold, and teammates Lilia Ignatova and Anelia Ralenkova tying with the Soviet Union's Galina Beloglazova for the silver. A strong fifth place showing was made by Dalia Kutkaite of the Soviet Union. After the sensational showing at the worlds, one can only marvel at what the first Olympic Games for RSG holds in store.

TOP CANADIAN

Lori Fung of Vancouver is the reigning Canadian champion, and top qualifier for the Olympic Games. This diminutive gymnast combines fast paced performances with a crowd-pleasing style uniquely her own. With a 23 placing out of 92 gymnasts at the 1983 world championships, (and 13th and 12th placings in clubs and ribbon respectively), Lori has proven she is a force to be reckoned with.

Kaarina Dillabough, President
Canadian Rhythmic Sportive
Gymnastics Federation

HANDBALL TEAM

EVENT DATE			CALIFORNIA STATE UNIVERSITY, FULLERTON		
JULY	31	6 games—preliminaries, men	AUGUST	7	3 games—round robin, women
AUGUST	1	3 games—round robin, women		8	6 games—preliminaries, men
	2	6 games—preliminaries, men		9	3 games—round robin, women
	3	3 games—round robin, women		10	2 games—finals (5-8 places), men 2 games—finals (9-12 places), men
	4	6 games—preliminaries, men		11	**The Forum, Inglewood** 2 games—finals (1-4 places), men
	5	3 games—round robin, women			
	6	6 games—preliminaries, men			

HISTORY

Team handball, as an indoor sport, is a relatively new arrival to the Games. The men's event was added in 1972 and the women's event was included in 1976.

The origin of the game is vague, but the general consensus is that it started as an outdoor game back in the 1880s as something to keep gymnasts tuned up during the summer.

Team handball was very much confined to Europe at the time of the first international match, between Denmark and Sweden, in the mid-1930s. Because of its popularity in Germany, the game was added to the 1936 Berlin Olympic Games programme. Playing outdoors, the 11-man German team easily won the gold medal.

But changes were on the way. When the team was cut down to seven players (including a goalie), and moved indoors, team handball started to catch on. It was swift, at times rough, and featured a lot of scoring. Just what North Americans love.

The post-war flood of immigrants to North America helped to popularize the game here, while at the same time it was taking a foothold in about 50 other countries. Standardization of rules in 1952 gave the sport stability and a foundation on which to grow.

When the Olympic Games returned to Germany (Munich, 1972), team handball was on the Olympic programme as an indoor event and the crowds flooded in. Yugoslavia took the gold medal. The Soviet Union won the gold medal in the 1976 Montreal Olympics and East Germany won top honours in the 1980 Games in Moscow. The Soviet women won the first women's gold in 1976 and repeated their success in 1980.

GENERAL DESCRIPTION

For the first-time viewer, team handball appears to be a combination of several games, notably basketball and soccer.

Played indoors on a 40-metre by 20-metre area, this fast-paced game has the team's six players and goalie doing wonderful things with the ball. They pass it. They dribble it. And they shoot it. All for the purpose of scoring goals. The team with the most goals comes up a winner.

The task of scoring goals is compli-

cated by the presence of a goalkeeper, who has quick reflexes, great anticipation and a disposition that enables him or her to rationalize the fact that he or she must protect a net that is 3-metres wide and 2-metres high.

A player may play the ball with one or both hands, the leg above the knee or the head. The ball cannot be kicked as in soccer.

The rules give the players considerable leeway in developing individual styles, and so weird, off-balance shots are presented. There's the jump shot, the diving shot and an assortment of others to foil defender or goalie.

The offensive players are restricted in that they are prohibited from taking a shot on the net from within the goal-area line which extends like a semicircle some six metres in front and out from both sides of the net. They may, however, jump into the 6-metre zone provided the ball is released prior to making contact with the floor.

They are also prohibited from taking more than three steps with the ball. This ensures plenty of passing rather than a lot of one-on-one moves so common is basketball. In addition, the rules are designed to eliminate stalling tactics. A player may not keep the ball in team possession if there is no attempt to penetrate the defensive formation for a shot on goal.

On defence, the player may try to use his or her hands to gain possession of the ball or use his or her torso to block an opponent. But the defensive player may not use arms, legs or hands to obstruct an opponent or hold, push or jump into an opponent.

Body contact is inevitable in this game and severe rule infractions can be costly. Penalty shots are awarded from the penalty line seven metres from the goal.

The game of two, 30-minute periods gets underway with a throw-off, which is taken from the centre of the court. Team captains toss a coin to determine which ends they will protect and for the right to the throw-off. After the interval between periods, the throw-off changes to the other team for the second period.

PROCEDURE

There are a dozen men's teams with the host nation (the United States) automatically gaining one berth.

The other berths will be filled by the three champions of the Americas, Asia and Africa and eight European teams named after qualifying tournaments. The Soviet Union, Yugoslavia, Poland, Denmark and Rumania have qualified. Three countries have yet to be named.

There will be only six teams in the women's competition. The host nation (the United States) has an automatic berth with four others going to the top four teams in the 1983 world championships. One berth will go to the winning team of a qualifying tournament for countries in the Americas, Asia and Africa.

In the Olympics, the men's teams will be divided into two groups. Each group of six teams will play each other once in the preliminary round. Points will be awarded (two for a win, one for a draw) in games made up of two 30-minute sessions. If there is a tie for team placings after the preliminary round of play, goals for and against will determine final standing.

With the group standings set, the top teams in each group will meet for the gold and silver medals. The two second-place teams in each group will meet to determine the bronze medal.

The women play a round-robin series and when that is concluded, the top two teams meet for the gold and silver medals with the third and fourth teams battling for the bronze medal.

TECHNICAL TERMS

Penalty-throw — awarded for an infraction such as grabbing or tripping a player. Taken from the penalty-throw line, the player may not cross or touch the line before the ball has left his or her hand. The goalie is free to move as he or she likes but may not come within three metres of the thrower.

Corner-throw — awarded to the attacking team if the ball, having last been touched by a defender, passes over the goal line outside the goal either in the air or on the ground. While taking the corner throw, an attacker must keep one of his or her feet stationary where the goal line and touchline meet, until the ball has been thrown. A goal may be scored directly from the corner throw.

Referee's throw — taken by a referee after two opposing players tie up the ball. The referee tosses the ball vertically at the point of interruption with the players at least three metres away. The players then move for the loose ball.

Free throw — given for a minor infraction, generally at the point where the foul took place. Defending players must remain outside the 9-metre free-throw line.

Goal throw — taken by the goalie who must throw the ball from the goal area out over the goal-area line into the playing area. Usually awarded when the ball crosses the goal line outside the goal after last being touched by the goalkeeper.

Throw-off — taken from centre court to open each half and after each goal.

EQUIPMENT

Ball — for men, the ball must have a circumference of not less than 58 centimetres or more than 60 centimetres and weigh not more than 475 grams and not less than 425 grams. For women, the ball must be 54 to 56 centimetres and 325 to 400 grams.

Goals — are 3-metres wide and 2-metres high and are centred on the goal lines. Netting must be loose enough so that a ball will not rebound quickly after a shot.

Dress — sport shoes are worn. Any items that may cause damage (necklaces, watches, etc.) are forbidden.

Court — is 40-metres long and 20-metres wide.

MEDAL WINNERS

HANDBALL (team) Men

YEAR	PLACE	COUNTRY
1936	1	**Germany**
	2	Austria
	3	Switzerland
1972	1	**Yugoslavia**
	2	Czechoslovakia
	3	Rumania
1976	1	**USSR**
	2	Rumania
	3	Poland
1980	1	**East Germany**
	2	USSR
	3	Rumania

HANDBALL (team) Women / New Olympic Event — 1976

YEAR	PLACE	COUNTRY
1976	1	**USSR**
	2	East Germany
	3	Hungary
1980	1	**USSR**
	2	Yugoslavia
	3	East Germany

HOCKEY FIELD

EVENT DATE			EAST LOS ANGELES COLLEGE MONTEREY PARK		
JULY	29	3 games—preliminaries, men	**AUGUST**	6	3 games—preliminaries, men 1 game—round robin, women
	30	3 games—preliminaries, men		7	2 games—round robin, women 3 games—preliminaries, men
	31	3 games—preliminaries, men 1 game—round robin, women		8	2 games—semifinals, men
AUGUST	1	3 games—preliminaries, men 2 games—round robin, women		9	4 games—semifinals, men 1 game—round robin, women
	2	3 games—preliminaries, men 1 game—round robin, women		10	1 game—final (11-12 places), men/2 games— finals (7-10 places), men/2 games—round robin, women
	3	3 games—preliminaries, men 2 games—round robin, women		11	3 games—finals (1-6 places), men
	4	3 games—preliminaries, men 1 game—round robin, women			
	5	3 games—preliminaries, men 2 games—round robin, women			

East Los Angeles College, the site of the 1984 Summer Olympics field hockey games.

HISTORY

Many countries lay claim to the origin of field hockey. Some point to ancient relics and insist that "pictures" depict men with curved sticks playing with a ball, while other countries contend that it was an ancestral game played in the wide-open fields to pass idle time. Egypt, Greece, Italy and Spain all claim origin of the sport. Similarily, England, Ireland and Scotland present ancestral debates.

In any case, field hockey, as it is known today, took shape in the 1800s and continued to develop and grow, so that now it is played in more that 100 countries. Known as "hockey" throughout the world, Canada and the United States call the game "field hockey" to distinguish it from "ice hockey."

Its proponents proudly point out that it is the second largest outdoor team sport in the world, even though there is very little promotion of the game in North America.

Field hockey made its Olympic debut in 1908 with England winning and Ireland coming in second. The event was bypassed in the 1912 Games and when the sport was resumed in the 1920 Olympics, England successfully returned to defend its title.

Four years later, field hockey once again was excluded. When it was included in the 1928 programme, the gold medal was won by India; a new "power"

was starting to make its mark. India went on to win six consecutive gold medals before finishing second to Pakistan in 1960. India won golds again in 1964 and 1980.

Ironically, for Great Britain, India's and Pakistan's success in field hockey can be attributed to the British who introduced the game to them. Since its gold medal triumphs of 1908 and 1920, Great Britain has only managed a silver medal (1948) and a bronze (1952).

In the 1980 Games, the Olympic committee opened the door to women. The gold was carried off by Zimbabwe with Czechoslovakia taking the silver and the Soviet Union taking the bronze medal.

GENERAL DESCRIPTION

Field hockey is affectionately referred to as "soccer with sticks." Understandably so. Some of the rules, such as offside, and the number of players (11), are similar to soccer. Like soccer, field hockey is played on a large outdoor area, traditionally grass, although the game is played increasingly on artificial surfaces.

The 11 players, include a goalkeeper, a centre forward, a centre half, left and right halves, left and right inside forwards, left and right wing forwards and two fullbacks.

The field is 9.5 metres by 54.9 metres and the centre of attention is a little white leather or plastic-covered ball usually

made of cork and twine. The object of the game is to score goals, by hitting the ball with the curved stick. The stick has a flat and rounded side, but only the flat side is used to stop or play the ball.

Unlike ice hockey, goals in field hockey cannot be scored from anywhere on the playing surface. Field hockey goals are restricted to the "striking circle," which is an area marked by a semicircle in front of the goal. At its furthest distance, the semicircle is 14.6 metres from the goal which is 2.13-metres high and 3.66-metres wide.

The goalkeeper, who may use any part of his or her body in play, is the only player allowed to use his or her feet to kick or stop the ball. This can only be done within the "striking circle."

The teams play two 35-minute halves, changing sides after a five-minute to 10-minute interval between halves. Each team is allowed two substitutions during the game but once a player leaves the field, he or she may only return for penalty stroke competition.

Naturally, the team with the most goals wins. The game is supervised by two umpires.

PROCEDURE

Men

A dozen countries are named to the Olympic tournament by the International Hockey Federation. They are divided into two pools (A and B) on a seeded basis.

In each pool, the teams play each other once in a round-robin series with two points awarded for a win and one for a tie. The top two teams in each pool qualify for interpool play in a four-team semifinal. The winning teams reach the final play for the gold and silver medals with the two semifinal losers playing for the bronze medal.

Canada qualified for men's play by winning the Pan-American Games gold medal in Venezuela last summer. The Canadian men will play in a group (pool) with the Netherlands, Pakistan, the Soviet Union, New Zealand and either Kenya or Egypt. The other pool consists of Australia, West Germany, India, Spain, Malaysia and the United States, which gains a berth by being the host country.

Women

The International Hockey Federation named six countries, including Canada, for the women's competition at Los Angeles. Others named were New Zealand, Australia, the Netherlands, West Germany and the United States, as host nation.

The addition of the Canadian women's team was based on its performance over the past four years. They were rated No. 10 by the Federation at the start of 1983 but finished second in the world championships last summer in Malaysia.

The women's teams will play a round-robin series to determine medal winners.

TECHNICAL TERMS

Goal — for a goal to be scored, the ball must be played by an attacker within 14.6 metres of the goal; this distance is marked by a semicircle which is known as the "striking circle."

Obstruction — a player cannot use his or her body or stick to prevent an opponent from playing the ball. Obstructing a player in this manner is a foul.

Offside — an attacking player is offside and loses possession of the ball unless there are at least two opponents (one of which may be the goalkeeper) nearer to their own goal line when the ball is hit or pushed. A player is not offside, however, when in his or her own half of the field, or if closer to his or her own goal line than the ball when the ball is played by the player's team.

Hit — if a player puts the ball over the sideline, a hit is awarded to the opposing team and is taken on the side line where the ball went out. It must be put in play along the ground with all players standing at least five yards away. Lifting the ball and swinging the stick above the shoulders is not permitted.

Free hit — if a foul is committed against one team, the opposing team is awarded a free hit. The free hit must be taken where the foul occurred and must be hit or pushed along the ground. Scooping or lifting the ball is not permitted. All players must be at least five yards away from the free hit.

16-yard hit — when the ball goes over the endline and was last touched in play by the attacking team, the defending team is awarded a free hit, 16 yards out from where the ball went over the endline.

Corner — when a defender unintentionally plays the ball over his own endline, the attacking team is awarded a "corner hit," which is a free hit from a spot on the goal line, five yards from the corner flag.

Penalty Corner — taken from a point on the endline 10 yards from either goal post, and is awarded for an offence by a defender within the "striking circle" or an intentional offence within the 25-yard line.

Penalty stroke — this is awarded for an intentional breach of the rules by a defender within the "striking circle" or where a defender stops a "sure" goal by committing a foul, such as a goalkeeper lying on the ball or another defender stopping the ball on the goal line with his foot. A push, scoop or flick shot from seven yards out is awarded to the attacking team with only the goalkeeper in the goal to defend.

EQUIPMENT

Ball — usually made of cork and twine. The cover is usually leather or plastic and is about 22.8 centimetres in circumference and weighs about .18 grams.

Stick — has a flat side and a round side. The flat side is used to stop or play the ball. The head of the stick is made of wood which should be rounded and free of any metal. The maximum weight is one gram.

Dress — the wearing of boots with metal studs, spikes or nails is forbidden as is the wearing of dangerous objects such as rings and watches. Players wear shorts or skirts and shirts.

Goal — is 3.7-metres wide and 2.1-metres high.

Field — is 91.5-metres long and 54.9-metres wide and is marked by a "striking circle", a 25-yard line and a centre line.

TOP TEAMS

Australia won a men's international tournament last summer in Kuala Lumpur with Pakistan and India finishing second and third.

The Canadian men's team earned considerable respect for winning the gold medal at the Pan-American Games while other respected teams have come from the Soviet Union, Holland, Spain and West Germany.

The top three women's teams are New Zealand, Australia and our own highly talented Canadians.

TOP CANADIANS

Bubli Chohan and Dave Bissett of Vancouver and Reg Plummer of Ottawa helped Canada win the gold medal in the Pan-American Games. All three have more than 100 international matches to their credit. Darlene Stoyka and Zöe MacKinnon of Toronto and Shelley Andrews of Victoria were all strong players on the 1983 World Cup team in Malaysia. Stoyka was one of the leading goal scorers and was a member of the 1983 world all-star team.

Duelling sticks

Rough and tumble action

Fancy stick handling

Time to tee-off

MEDAL WINNERS

FIELD HOCKEY—Men

YEAR	PLACE	COUNTRY
1908	1	**Great Britain**
	2	Ireland
	3	Scotland/
		Wales
1920	1	**Great Britain**
	2	Denmark
	3	Belgium
1928	1	**India**
	2	Netherlands
	3	Germany
1932	1	**India**
	2	Japan
	3	U.S.A.
1936	1	**India**
	2	Germany
	3	Netherlands
1948	1	**India**
	2	Great Britain
	3	Netherlands
1952	1	**India**
	2	Netherlands
	3	Great Britain
1956	1	**India**
	2	Pakistan
	3	Germany
1960	1	**Pakistan**
	2	India
	3	Spain
1964	1	**India**
	2	Pakistan
	3	Australia
1968	1	**Pakistan**
	2	Australia
	3	India
1972	1	**Germany**
	2	Pakistan
	3	India
1976	1	**New Zealand**
	2	Australia
	3	Pakistan
1980	1	**India**
	2	Spain
	3	U.S.S.R.

Women

YEAR	PLACE	COUNTRY
1980	1	**Zimbabwe**
	2	Czechoslovakia
	3	U.S.S.R.

JUDO

EVENT DATE   **CALIFORNIA STATE UNIVERSITY, LOS ANGELES**

AUGUST	4	Extra lightweight
	5	Half lightweight
	6	Lightweight
	7	Half middleweight
	8	Middleweight

AUGUST	9	Half heavyweight
	10	Heavyweight
	11	Open category

HISTORY

Judo is the only Olympic sport that originated in the Orient. Japan is judo's birthplace and its father is acknowledged to be Jigoro Kano, a slight man born in 1860, who took the ancient form of self-defence, jujitsu, and refined it.

Kano felt jujitsu offered nothing beyond its violence. It had been developed by commoners who were forbidden by Japanese law to carry weapons, and emphasized "kill" tactics. When Kano opened the Kodokan (judo school) in 1882, the Japanese took to judo quickly, as it was a moral as well as physical sport, emphasizing subduing an opponent rather than causing injury.

Judo gained great acceptance in Japan, and as the Japanese ventured out into the rest of the world, Kano's sport travelled with them. England's first view of the sport was as a novelty act on the Music Hall stage.

Because many of the judo practitioners in the sport's early days were men of slight stature, the myth grew that small men armed with the knowledge of judo could easily defeat much larger men. The myth faded when men of big physical stature took to the sport, and today it is seldom that a competitor from a low weight class enters the open category which is dominated by large men.

The degree of skill varied among competitors and Kano decided to rate them. He adopted the jujitsu method of having competitors wear "belts" to denote their skill factor. In the west, a beginner wears a white belt and progresses through a series of coloured belts. The much respected black belt is graded from one to 10. The eighth degree is the highest while the ninth and tenth (red in colour) are for the sport's masters.

The spread of competitive judo in the western world was slow. Only Canada, the United States and the United Kingdom had more than a handful of practitioners in the 1930s. After World War Two, judo spread so rapidly an international ruling body was established and the first world championships were organized in 1956.

As host nation for the 1964 Olympic Games in Tokyo, Japan was given permission by the International Olympic Committee to include judo in the Games programme. The Japanese quickly learned how seriously the rest of the world had taken to their sport.

In the open category (no weight limit), king-sized Anton Geesink from Holland used his 6-foot, 6-inch frame in expert fashion to defeat Japan's heavily favoured Akio Kaminaga. In the over 93-kilogram class, Japan's Isao Inokuma narrowly defeated Canadian Doug Rogers who had intensely studied judo in Japan for two years.

If the Japanese were stunned by the performance by Anton Geesink, they were doubly stunned by another Dutchman, Willem Ruska at the 1972 Munich Games. Ruska won both the open category and the over 93-kilogram class and is, and will remain, the only man to have won two gold medals in Olympic judo. A new Olympic rule forbids competitors to

Pinning the opposition.

enter the open category as well as their own weight division.

In recent years the sport of judo has attracted many women, and there is a strong lobby to have women participate in their own categories at the 1988 Olympic Games in South Korea. The International Olympic Committee insists that any new event in its programme must have had at least two world championships. That criterion has been met.

GENERAL DESCRIPTION

Following are the categories that will be competed in at the 1984 Olympic Games in Los Angeles:

Weight Limits

1. Open
2. 60 kilograms and under
3. Over 60 kilograms up to and including 65 kilograms
4. Over 65 kilograms up to and including 71 kilograms
5. Over 71 kilograms up to and including 78 kilograms
6. Over 78 kilograms up to and including 86 kilograms
7. Over 86 kilograms up to and including 95 kilograms
8. Over 95 kilograms

Judo still retains its Japanese terminology. Opponents are "judoka" and each wears a "judogi" or judo suit. They compete on a "tatami" or judo mat.

The combatants attempt to throw each other, but if a throw does not bring victory, groundwork or "ne-waza" may follow in which one opponent tries to hold the other to the mat for 30 seconds or gain a submission. Strangleholds and arm locks may be applied in the standing position, but this is rare.

PROCEDURE

Each country may enter a competitor in each weight class. A controversial rule by the International Olympic Committee has stopped a competitor from entering their weight class and the open category event. While the IOC believes a competitor should be in only one class (either his weight or open category), judo traditionalists are opposed.

Prior to the competition, a draw is held to determine the bouts in each weight class. Losers in the opening bouts are eliminated, except those defeated by the two finalists, who are drawn against each other. The winners of these two "second chance" or repechage pools are declared bronze medal winners. The two finalists, of course, meet to decide the gold and silver medals.

The matches in the preliminary and repechage events are limited to five minutes while the finals and bronze-medal matches are of seven-minute duration.

VIEWING TIPS

There are a variety of throwing techniques. The opponents begin in a standing position and may continue into the groundwork. Throws can be made with the hands, hips and feet or by a thrower dropping to the mat first to throw his opponent over the top.

The idea is to score a point or "ippon" and gain a clear win. Victories may also be posted by two half-points or "waza-aris." Smaller scores, used for deciding a match that goes to full time, are the "yuko" and "koka" (see Technical Terms).

A competitor can score an "ippon" with a good, hard throw or by pinning his opponent for 30 seconds. In addition, an "ippon" can be scored when a competitor is caught in a stranglehold or arm lock and submits.

If one opponent has earned a "waza-ari" or half-point, he can win the match by holding his opponent on the mat for 25 seconds.

If at the end of the time period allotted for the bout there is no clear decision, the winner is declared by the vote of two judges and a referee.

Setting up to throw an opponent

Caught in a hold

Pinning the opposition

TECHNICAL TERMS

Nage-waza — throwing technique.
Ne-waza — the groundwork.
Kansetsu-waza — arm lock.
Shime-waza — choke or strangle hold.
Ippon — point.
Waza-ari — half point.
Yuko — small score.
Koka — very small score.
Hansoku-make — disqualification.
Keikoku — warning from referee.
Chui — caution from referee.
Shido — a very slight infraction.
Osaekomi — hold down
Judogi — suit worn by competitors.
Judoka — the competitor.
Tatami — the mat.

EQUIPMENT

Judogi — must be white and the jacket must cover the hips. The lapels are strengthened to take the stress of pulling into a throw. The sleeves must be loose enough to allow the opponent to grip.

Tatami — the contest area is 10 metres by 10 metres with a two-metre safety zone. A one-metre red band within the contest area designates the danger zone. Penalties are assessed against a competitor who deliberately steps out of the contest area or who deliberately forces his opponent out.

TOP TEAMS

Japan and the Soviet Union have strong teams. Canada has been steadily upgrading its talent and has some good individual prospects.

TOP CANADIANS

Louis Jani of Montreal won the 86-kilogram title at the Pan-American Games last summer in Venezuela. Mark Berger of Winnipeg won a gold in the 95-kilogram plus division. Phil Takahashi of Ottawa was a bronze medal winner in the under 60-kilogram class in the 1981 world championships, and in the same competition, Kevin Doherty of Toronto won a bronze in the under 78-kilogram class. Brad Farrow of Toronto is highly rated in the under 65-kilogram class in Canada.

MEDAL WINNERS

JUDO (open) Men

YEAR	PLACE	NAME	COUNTRY
1964	1	**A. Geesink**	**Netherlands**
	2	A. Kaminaga	Japan
	3	T. Boronovskis/	Austria/
		K. Glahn	Germany
1972	1	**W. Ruska**	**Netherlands**
	2	W. Kusnjetsow	U.S.S.R.
	3	J. Brodani/	France/
		A. Parisi	Great Britain
1976	1	**H. Uemura**	**Japan**
	2	K. Remfry	United Kingdom
	3	S. Chochoshvili/	U.S.S.R./
		J. Cho	Korea
1980	1	**D. Lorenz**	**East Germany**
	2	A. Parisi	France
	3	A. Mapp/	United Kingdom/
		A. Ozsvar	Hungary

JUDO (lightweight) Men

YEAR	PLACE	NAME	COUNTRY
1964	1	**T. Nakatani**	**Japan**
	2	F. Hänni	Switzerland
	3	O. Stepanov/	U.S.S.R./
		A. Bogolyubov	U.S.S.R.
1972	1	**T. Kawaguchi**	**Japan**
	2	B. Buidaa*	Mongolia
	3	Y. Kim/	North Korea/
		J. Mounier	France
1976	1	**H. Rodriguez**	**Cuba**
	2	E. Kyung Chang	Korea
	3	E. Mariani/	Italy/
		J. Tuncsik	Hungary

*disqualified

JUDO (light heavyweight) Men

YEAR	PLACE	NAME	COUNTRY
1972	1	**S. Chochoshvili**	**U.S.S.R.**
	2	D. Starbrook	Great Britain
	3	C. Ishii/	Brazil/
		P. Barth	Germany
1976	1	**K. Ninomiya**	**Japan**
	2	R. Harshiladze	U.S.S.R.
	3	D.C. Starbrook/	United Kingdom/
		J. Roethlisberger	Switzerland

JUDO (middleweight) Men

YEAR	PLACE	NAME	COUNTRY
1964	1	**I. Okano**	**Japan**
	2	W. Hofmann	Germany
	3	J. Bregman/	U.S.A./
		U. Kim	South Korea
1972	1	**S. Sekine**	**Japan**
	2	S. Oh	South Korea
	3	B. Jacks/	Great Britain/
		J. Coche	France
1976	1	**A. Sonoda**	**Japan**
	2	V. Dvoinikov	U.S.S.R.
	3	S. Obadov/	Yugoslavia/
		Y. Chul Park	Korea

JUDO (welterweight) Men

YEAR	PLACE	NAME	COUNTRY
1972	1	**T. Nomura**	**Japan**
	2	A. Zajkowski	Poland
	3	D. Hötger/	East Germany/
		A. Novikov	U.S.S.R.
1976	1	**V. Nevzorov**	**U.S.S.R.**
	2	K. Kuramoto	Japan
	3	P. Vial/	France/
		M. Talaj	Poland

JUDO (heavyweight) Men

YEAR	PLACE	NAME	COUNTRY
1964	1	**I. Inokuma**	**Japan**
	2	A. Rogers	Canada
	3	P. Tschikviladze	U.S.S.R.
		A. Kiknadze	U.S.S.R.
1972	1	**W. Ruska**	**Netherlands**
	2	K. Glahn	Germany
	3	G. Onashvili/	U.S.S.R./
		M. Nishimura	Japan
1976	1	**S. Novikov**	**U.S.S.R.**
	2	G. Neureuther	West Germany
	3	S. Endo/	Japan/
		E. Coage	U.S.A.

JUDO (over 95 Kg – 209¼ lb) Men

YEAR	PLACE	NAME	COUNTRY
1980	1	**A. Parisi**	**France**
	2	D. Zaprianov	Bulgaria
	3	V. Kocman	Czechoslovakia
		R. Kovacevic	Yugoslavia

JUDO (up to 95 Kg – 209¼ lb) Men

YEAR	PLACE	NAME	COUNTRY
1980	1	**R. Van De Walle**	**Belgium**
	2	T. Khubuluri	U.S.S.R.
	3	D. Lorenz	East Germany
		H. Numan	Netherlands

JUDO (up to 86 Kg – 189½ lb) Men

YEAR	PLACE	NAME	COUNTRY
1980	1	**J. Roethlisberger**	**Switzerland**
	2	I. Azcuy	Cuba
	3	A. Iatskevich	U.S.S.R.
		D. Ultsch	East Germany

JUDO (up to 78 Kg – 171¾ lb) Men

YEAR	PLACE	NAME	COUNTRY
1980	1	**S. Khabareli**	**U.S.S.R.**
	2	J. Ferrer	Cuba
	3	B. Tchoullouyan	France
		H. Heinke	East Germany

JUDO (up to 71 Kg – 156½ lb) Men

YEAR	PLACE	NAME	COUNTRY
1980	1	**E. Gamba**	**Italy**
	2	N. Adams	United Kingdom
	3	K.H. Lehmann	East Germany
		R. Davaadalai	Mongolia

JUDO (up to 65 Kg – 143¼ lb) Men

YEAR	PLACE	NAME	COUNTRY
1980	1	**N. Solodukhin**	**U.S.S.R.**
	2	T. Damdin	Mongolia
	3	I. Nedkov	Bulgaria
		J. Pawlowski	Poland

JUDO (up to 60 Kg – 132¼ lb) Men

YEAR	PLACE	NAME	COUNTRY
1980	1	**T. Rey**	**France**
	2	J. Rodriguez	Cuba
	3	A. Emizh	U.S.S.R.
		T. Kinces	Hungary

MODERN PENTATHLON

EVENT DATE			**COTO DE CAZA, ORANGE COUNTY**		
JULY	**29**	Riding	**AUGUST**	**1**	Shooting/Running
	30	Fencing			
	31	Swimming			

HISTORY

When the ancient Greeks introduced the pentathlon event into their Olympic Games, they were looking for a versatile performer. He had to be an outstanding long jumper, an accurate and powerful javelin thrower, a sprinter, a discus thrower, and a wrestler. In short, the pentathlete was to be the model soldier, a person who could best handle the trials and tribulations of war.

Baron de Coubertin, the man who is called the father of the modern day Olympic movement, had those military thoughts in mind when he asked the organizing committee for the 1912 Games in Sweden to rekindle the search for a versatile performer. The Swedes obliged and the modern pentathlon competition was born.

Some historians say the event's origins are with the military dispatch rider who moved through enemy territory on horseback, fighting his way with pistol and sword, and then swimming and running to his destination. The pentathlon (from the Greek meaning five events) now consists of horseback riding, fencing, swimming, shooting and cross-country running. It is a superb test of strength and stamina for the individual. The modern pentathlon has been restricted to men, but is expected to have a woman's event in the 1988 Olympics.

If the old theory that "anything goes in love and war" holds true, then Boris Onischenko of the Soviet Union deserves a special award. He was disqualified for cheating at the 1976 Games in Montreal. Onischenko was among the favourites to win the gold medal. His credentials were impeccable and included an Olympic gold medal (pentathlon team in 1972) and two silver medals (team in 1968 and individual in 1972).

In Montreal, however, officials ruled that Onischenko was guilty of using an illegal épée weapon in the fencing part of the competition. They said he had tampered with the épée so that it registered an electrical "hit" even though no contact with an opponent had been made. It was a monumental scandal and a sharp contradiction to the Olympic ideal that emphasizes participation rather than winning. Onischenko was sent home in shame.

In the early years modern pentathlon was dominated by the Swedes who have won nine gold medals, including two by Lars Hall in 1952 and 1956. In the team competition, where each competitor is scored individually and the aggregate total determines team placing, the Soviet Union is the defending champion and has previously won the team title in 1956, 1964 and 1972.

GENERAL DESCRIPTION

There are five events — horseback riding, fencing, swimming, shooting and cross-country running.

Horseback riding — riding a horse drawn by lot, the athlete must cover a 600-metre course sprinkled with 15 obstacles, including one double, one triple and one water jump in 1 minute 43 seconds. The double and triple obstacles are two or three fences placed closely together. The riders are only permitted 20 minutes and six jumps in the warm-up. Since this is the opening-day event, it is crucial for competitors to get a good start of at least 980 points.

Fencing — the competitors use the épée (famed in the past as a duelling weapon) for this event. The competitors are hooked up to an electrical scoring system which registers "hits" in the target area — the whole body, including the arms and legs.

This event is particularly gruelling in that each entrant must face each of the other competitors in a three-minute bout. The first "hit" is the winner. With the great amount of Olympic entries, a competitor can expect to spend 10 to 13 hours fencing. A constant psychological pace is needed along with physical endurance for this second day of competition.

Swimming — this is a freestyle event of 300 metres for men. It is demanding in that 300 metres is considered an unnatural distance. The longest sprint race in swimming events is 200 metres and the shortest distance race is 400 metres.

The consensus is that if any swimmer covers the 300 metres (about the length of three football fields) in 3 minutes 20 seconds or less, he'll improve his standings. This is the lone event for the competitors on Day Three.

Shooting — this is the fourth of the five-event test. Competitors use a rapid-fire .22-calibre pistol and are stationed 25 metres from a turning, silhouette target. This is considered the "tense" phase of the pentathlon. Muscle control and mental stamina are required as the competitor must fire five sets of five shots at the target, the first five of which may be practice.

The athlete has three seconds in which to fire one shot at the target. He then has seven seconds in which he must lower his arm to a 45-degree angle and prepare for the next three-second interval. Consensus is that the athlete must score at least 192 out of 200 to remain in the medal hunt.

Cross-country running — the final event and the second of the last day. The course is 4,000-metres long. Whoever leads after the first four events leaves the starting gate first. All the other competitors' results are calculated on a rate of three points per second behind the leader. For example, if the leader (after four events) has 4,000 points, his starting time is designated as .00. If the second-place competitor has 3,997 points, he starts at .09 or nine seconds behind the leader. Competitors improve their positions by passing the runners in front of them on the course which is in the open country and free of roads and obstacles.

PROCEDURE

Organizers must provide one horse for two competitors. Each horse, therefore, jumps the course twice, once in the morning and once in the afternoon.

It is advantageous for a pentathlete to ride in the second round because he can spend the morning watching the horses jump and learn what to expect from his mount.

Each country must draw for the riding positions for three athletes from each country. The draw decides if the country will have one or two men in the afternoon events.

The riders are permitted only 20 minutes and six practice jumps in preparation for the events. Prior to the competition, a jury must determine if the horses are suitable.

In fencing, each competitor must face every opponent in a three-minute round (maximum) with the first hit a winner. Simultaneous hits do not count and if there is no "hit" after the time limit expires, each competitor is tagged with a defeat. All competitors are wired to the electrical scoring system.

In swimming, all competitors race against the standard in the 300-metre event. The key here is that the athlete must pace himself for the demanding distance.

In shooting, the competitors provide their own .22-calibre pistols. All pistols must be submitted for official examination and competitors are penalized two target points for each shot taken with an unexamined pistol.

Competitors may have five practice shots. In the competition they must fire four series of five shots each at a standard silhouette target from 25 metres. The targets are exposed for three seconds and hidden for seven seconds. Competitors may fire only one shot at each exposure; those who fire more than one shot are eliminated.

In cross-country running, the course must be clearly marked with tape on both sides and competitors must finish where they start. Competitors wear clearly marked clothing for identification.

SCORING

Scoring is not as complicated as people think. In each of the five events there is a standard performance equated to 1,000 pentathlon points. The only exception is riding where the maximum points available are 1,100. When the pentathlete acquires more than the standard 1,000 points, he is awarded extra points, and if the pentathlete fails to achieve this standard, he has points deducted. The winner, of course, is the athlete with the highest point total.

Here's the breakdown:

Riding — a clear round of 1 minute 43 seconds is worth 1,100 points. Point deductions are made for refusal (when the horse will not go over the obstacle), knockdown, fall or failing to complete the course in the specified time. There is a two-point penalty for each second beyond the time limit; a 30-point penalty for a knockdown; a 30-point penalty if the foot of the horse is in the water at the water jump; a 40-point penalty for disobedience (each time), and a 60-point penalty for the fall of the horse, the rider or both.

Fencing — a competitor who wins 70 per cent of his bouts scores 1,000 points.

Each victory above or below this average also gains or loses the athlete points equalled to 1,100 divided by the number of bouts.

Swimming — there are 1,000 points awarded for meeting the standard of 3 minutes 54 seconds for the 300 metres. Every second above or below is worth eight points; thus if the athlete is timed at 3:44 he earns 1,080 points.

Shooting — scoring 194 out of a possible 200 is worth 1,000 points. Every score above or below the standard is worth 22 points; thus if an athlete manages a 190 total he will earn 912 points.

Running — completing the 4,000-metre course in the standard time of 14 minutes 15 seconds is worth 1,000 points. Every second above or below is worth three points; thus if an athlete completes the course in 14 minutes even he will have earned 1,045 points.

It should be noted that scores are regarded as "bests" simply because there is no valid way of determining "records" due to the variance of the different courses. The "best" Olympic peformance was the 5,568 points earned by the Soviet Union's Anatoly Starostin in the 1980 Olympics in Moscow. The Soviet Union won the team title with 16,126 points for the three-man team.

TOP COMPETITORS

The Soviet Union is the defending team champion in the Olympics and is also the current world champion. Hungary is close behind with France, West Germany, Poland, the United States, and Sweden considered other powers.

Anatoly Starostin of the Soviet Union is the world champion and defending champion in the Olympics.

Compatriot Evgenis Zinkovski was third in the 1983 world championships while other top competitors are Thomas Szombatkely of Hungary, Richard Phelps or Great Britain, Janusz Peciak of Poland and the U.S. pair of Dean Glewesk and Bob Nieman.

CANADA'S BEST

Canada will hold its qualifying event in June, 1984. Top Canadian is Barry Kennedy of Edmonton who was 30th in the world championships. Other Canadians to watch are Lawrence Keyte and Luke O'Grady, both of Ottawa, who placed 20th and 27th respectively at the world junior championships earlier this year.

MEDAL WINNERS

MODERN PENTATHLON

YEAR	PLACE	NAME	COUNTRY
1912	1	G. Lilliehöök	Sweden
	2	K.G. Asbrink	Sweden
	3	G. de Laval	Sweden
1920	1	G. Dyrssen	Sweden
	2	E. de Laval	Sweden
	3	G. Runö	Sweden
1924	1	B. Lindman	Sweden
	2	G. Dyrssen	Sweden
	3	B. Uggla	Sweden
1928	1	S. Thofelt	Sweden
	2	B. Lindman	Sweden
	3	H. Kahl	Germany
1932	1	J. Oxenstierna	Sweden
	2	B. Lindman	Sweden
	3	R. Mayo	U.S.A.
1936	1	G. Handrick	Germany
	2	C.F Leonard	U.S.A.
	3	S. Abba	Italy
1948	1	W. Grut	Sweden
	2	G. Moore	U.S.A.
	3	G. Gärdin	Sweden
1952	1	L. Hall	Sweden
	2	G. Benedek	Hungary
	3	I. Szondy	Hungary
1956	1	L. Hall	Sweden
	2	O. Mannonen	Finland
	3	V. Korhonen	Finland
1960	1	F. Nemeth	Hungary
	2	I. Nagy	Hungary
	3	R. Beck	U.S.A.
1964	1	F. Török	Hungary
	2	I. Novikov	U.S.S.R.
	3	A. Mokeyev	U.S.S.R.
1968	1	B. Ferm	Sweden
	2	A. Balczo	Hungary
	3	P. Lednev	U.S.S.R.
1972	1	A. Balczo	Hungary
	2	B. Onischenko	U.S.S.R.
	3	P. Lednev	U.S.S.R.
1976	1	Janusz Pyciak-Peciak	Poland
	2	Pavel Lednev	U.S.S.R.
	3	Jan Bartu	Czechoslovakia
1980	1	Anatoly Starostin	U.S.S.R.
	2	Tamas Szmobathelyi	Hungary
	3	Pavel Ledney	U.S.S.R.

PENTATHLON (team)

YEAR	PLACE	COUNTRY
1952	1	Hungary
	2	Sweden
	3	Finland
1956	1	U.S.S.R.
	2	U.S.A.
	3	Finland
1960	1	Hungary
	2	U.S.S.R.
	3	U.S.A.
1964	1	U.S.S.R.
	2	U.S.A.
	3	Hungary
1968	1	Hungary
	2	U.S.S.R.
	3	France
1972	1	U.S.S.R.
	2	Hungary
	3	Finland
1976	1	Great Britain
	2	Czechoslovakia
	3	Hungary
1980	1	U.S.S.R.
	2	Hungary
	3	Sweden

ROWING

EVENT DATE

LAKE CASITAS, VENTURA COUNTY

JULY	**30**	Elimination heats, women
	31	Elimination heats, men
AUGUST	**1**	Repechage, men & women
	2	Semifinals, men & women

AUGUST	**3**	Finals (7-12 places), men & women
	4	Finals (1-6 places), women
	5	Finals (1-6 places), men

HISTORY

Long before the oar became an instrument of competitive rowing, it served a more useful purpose as the "power" to move boats for the ancient Egyptians and Greeks. Though the early ships had sails, the employment of rowers was effective when manoeuvring in battle or tight channels. Some men behind the oars were slaves, who had survival on their minds but occasionally found themselves in "friendly" competition. Captains were not adverse to having a challenge match while racing to a port.

If this was the impromptu beginning of competitive rowing, the sport's real foundation is in England. In olden days English life revolved around the water, in particular on the river Thames. Rowing races were the sport of the day in the early 1600s. Within a century, it became a national pastime and with the interest came the gambling. Spectators were not adverse to placing a wager or two on their favourite rowers.

Lake Castitas, the site of the Olympic rowing and canoeing competitions

As the years went by, new competitions sprung up. In 1829, Oxford and Cambridge, those venerable institutions of knowledge, started a match race that still draws thousands of fans annually. By this time, rowing had already been on the sports menu at another famed school, Eton, for more than two decades.

Enthusiasts started to organize clubs making training and facilities readily available. The famed Leander Club was established in 1815. Club interest popularized the regattas, those one-day out-ings with a picnic atmosphere on the banks and competitors battling on the water. In 1839, the most famous regatta was established at Henley-on-Thames.

As the English rowed full swing at home, they were also "selling" the sport abroad. English sailors and immigrants spread the gospel, especially in North America. Canadians took to rowing in the summer with the same zeal displayed for hockey in the winter. Rowing was the thing to do for bright, strong young men and the sport flourished with the help of champion oarsmen, Jack Guest, Joe Wright and Jake Gaudaur. A host of rowing clubs, such as the Toronto Argonauts, which went on to sponsor the Toronto Argonaut football team, also helped give the sport solid financial and promotional backing.

The Olympic committee allowed rowing as a demonstration sport in the 1896 Games, and in 1900, it was in the Games to stay.

Through the years, boats became more sophisticated, sleeker and faster. The attention centred on these swift, lightweight crafts and after the 1906 Games, the cumbersome 16-man naval boat event was dropped.

Although the greatest speed is naturally generated by the eights with its eight-man crew, the glamour event for oarsmen is the single sculls. The event demands a high state of physical and mental conditioning.

The Soviet Union's Vyacheslav Ivanov is the only man to win three gold medals in sculling in Olympic competi-tion. He won his first in 1956, the second in 1960 and the third in 1964. He had an unusual accident after his first victory. Ivanov was so happy over his triumph, he threw his medal in the air, and lost it as it fell into Australia's Lake Wendou-ree. Efforts to recover it failed, and Ivanov received a replacement from the Olympic committee.

Pertti Karppinen of Finland won the past two sculls. In the 1976 Games in Montreal he shared the sculls spotlight with Christine Scheiblich of East Germany. At long last, women had their own Olympic rowing events.

The East Germans and the Soviet Union have dominated the women's events, winning a dozen and 10 medals respectively. And they are expected to be strong again in Los Angeles.

The United States has been the leader in men's rowing, having won 52 medals including 26 golds, despite boycotting the 1980 Games in Moscow. West Germany and Great Britain have each won 34 medals.

Canada has won a total of 13 medals, including a pair of gold. It also has a special medal from the King of Sweden. When the eights rowing final was held in 1912, the Argonaut Club entry finished out of the medals, but it was learned that they had rowed a longer course than the other finalists due to improper measuring by Olympic officials. The Canadians did not protest and the King of Sweden gave them a special award for "good sportsmanship."

The first Canadian gold medal came in the 1956 Games when westerners Archie McKinnon, Lorne Loomer, Walter d'Hondt and Don Arnold captured the coxless fours events, upsetting a highly rated U.S. team. George Hungerford and Roger Jackson gave Canada another rowing gold in the coxless pairs in the 1964 Games.

GENERAL DESCRIPTION

Rowing events all have one classification, but there are two divisions — the rowing and sculling events. The art of sculling is to row with two oars, one in each hand. Rowing means to compete with one oar held in two hands.

It is a no no to refer to competitors as rowers. He or she is either a sculler or an oarsman. More than one person in a boat is called a crew (not a team). A "shell" is the boat built for racing.

There are eight events for the men and six for the women in the 1984 Games. Races are 2,000 metres for men, 1,000 metres for women.

Single sculls — considered the premier event in rowing because of the demand for outstanding physical conditioning, a dramatic sense of timing and a high sense of mental awareness for a race that is 2,000-metres long. Shells weigh about 13.6 kilograms and are 5.2-metres long.

Double sculls — two men in a boat. This event requires exact timing. The stroke should be of the same length and pressure to maintain the boat's glide through the water. Shells are 10.4-metres long and weigh about 29.5 kilograms.

Coxless pairs — two men in a boat, each with one oar. Exact timing is required in the use of the oars. There is almost no room for error, for the slightest breakdown can prove disastrous.

Coxed pairs — a third person, the "coxswain," joins the pairs and occupies a seat at the rear of the shell. He or she calls the beat to the oarsmen and details the race positions of other crews.

Note: The coxswain is regarded as a member of the crew and as such must be of the same sex. In men's events, the coxswain must have a minimum weight of 50 kilograms. In women's events the minimum weight is 45 kilograms.

Coxless fours — teamwork is of the essence as the four oarsmen work without the benefit of a coxswain. The key man in the bow (front) must keep the boat straight and provide the power to move it. The bowman will constantly be shouting out instructions to the crew to keep the boat in line. In fours, the boat is 13.4-metres long and weighs 72.6 kilograms.

Coxed fours — the coxswain is the fifth person in the boat. He calls the beat

A competitor in the sculling event

The double sculls event requires exact timing between the two men.

and shouts out the position of other boats as the crew tries to maintain a rhythmic stroke.

Quadruple sculls — came on the Olympic scene in Montreal in 1976 and is an event held without the help of a coxswain. The emphasis is on timing and a unified stroke of equal pressure. The bowman must keep the boat in line.

Eights with cox — provides the highlight of any rowing competition. The race demands outstanding physical conditioning and a highly tuned rhythm of oarsmanship. An exhausting event, it often leaves the oarsmen bent over and gasping for breath at the end of the race. The boats are 18.3-metres long and weigh about 118 kilograms.

Although rowing events have been held on an assortment of lakes, rivers and basins, the Olympic competition is held on a straight course with no current, enabling six crews to race side-by-side.

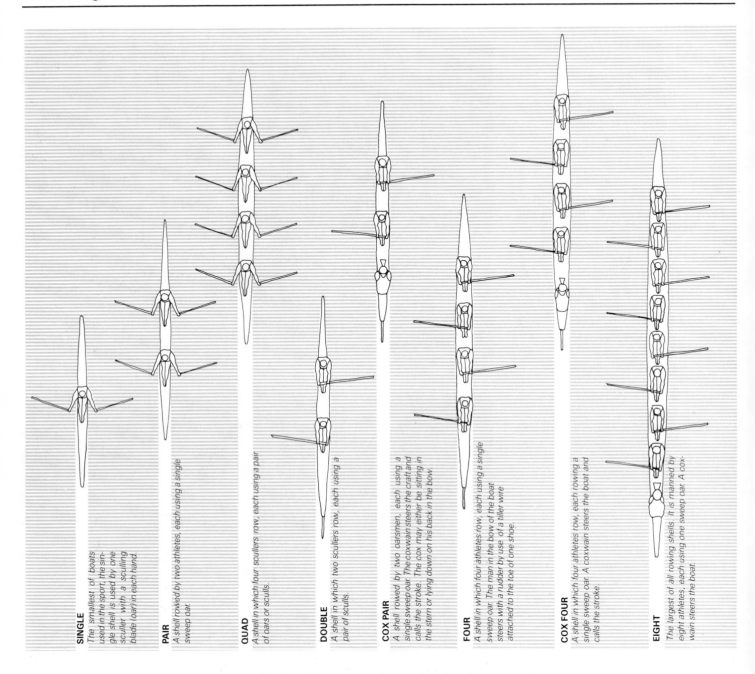

SINGLE
The smallest of boats used in the sport, the single shell is used by one sculler with a sculling blade (oar) in each hand.

PAIR
A shell rowed by two athletes, each using a single sweep oar.

QUAD
A shell in which four scullers row, each using a pair of oars or sculls.

DOUBLE
A shell in which two scullers row, each using a pair of sculls.

COX PAIR
A shell rowed by two oarsmen, each using a single sweep oar. The coxswain steers the craft and calls the stroke. The cox may either be sitting in the stern or lying down on his back in the bow.

FOUR
A shell in which four athletes row, each using a single sweep oar. The man in the bow of the boat steers with a rudder by use of a tiller wire attached to the toe of one shoe.

COX FOUR
A shell in which four athletes row, each rowing a single sweep oar. A coxswain steers the boat and calls the stroke.

EIGHT
The largest of all rowing shells. It is manned by eight athletes, each using one sweep oar. A coxswain steers the boat.

PROCEDURE

Boats must be at the start at least two minutes before the race. They are lined up, sometimes with the help of officials, and when they are in proper position, the aligner signals with a white flag. The starter then asks the crews, "are you ready?" If they are, he drops a red flag and says, "go."

If during a race one of the boats is off line and appears headed for a collision with another competitor, an umpire may warn the wayward boat. If a collision or interference occurs after a warning, the offending boat will be disqualified.

When all crews finish, a white flag is hoisted by the umpire to signal a clean race. If there is a protest, he will raise a red flag. As in horse racing, the judges may use photographs to determine placings of the crews. There can be no placings for a crew that loses its cox, but boats that have lost an oarsman can be placed.

VIEWING TIPS

It is important to watch the run of the boat. If the crew has its act together and is stroking as one, the boat will glide easily through the water. Experts look to see how far the boat is moved with each stroke.

EQUIPMENT

Oars — usually run from 3.7 metres to 3.86 metres in length and weigh about 3.6 kilograms. The oars used in sculling are slightly bigger, ranging from 2.9 metres to 3.1 metres in length, and are a little lighter than the other oars.

The oars generally have a short, wide blade and are painted in the colour of the crew's national association.

Shells — single sculls are about 8-metres long and weigh about 13.6 kilograms; coxless pairs and double sculls are about 10.4-metres long and weigh about 29.5 kilograms; coxless fours and quadruple sculls are about 13.4-metres long and weigh about 72.6 kilograms; coxed fours are about 13.7-metres long and weigh about 74.8 kilograms; eights are about 18.3-metres long and weigh about 117.9 kilograms.

Dress — oarsmen and scullers wear undershirts bearing national colours and shorts. The coxswain may wear other clothing.

TOP CREWS

West Germany, East Germany, the Soviet Union, New Zealand, Czechoslovakia, Norway and Italy are the top-ranked countries followed by Canada and the United States for men's events.

In the sculls, Peter Michael Kolbe of West Germany won the world championship last summer, beating an East German, Uwe Mund to the finish line. American Christopher Wood was third.

The West Germans won the quadruple sculls and coxless fours while the East Germans took the double sculls, coxless pairs and coxed pairs. New Zealand took the coxed fours and eights.

In women's events, the East Germans, the Soviet Union and Rumania are the powers followed closely by the United States and Canada. Juta Hampe of East Germany won the sculls in last summer's world championship.

TOP CANADIANS

The consensus is that Canada's rowing team had its best season in the past 20 years during 1983, with 21 high performance crews participating in the Pan-American Games and world championships. For the first time, Canada may have a full Olympic crew for Los Angeles after early summer trials.

Phil Haggerty and Robert Mills won the Pan-American gold in doubles while Greg Murphy, Mel LaForme, Phil Haggerty and Robert Mills captured the quad sculls gold in Venezuela.

In the world championships, Tim Storm and Peter MacGowan were fifth in the doubles; Bruce Ford, Phil Monckton, Mike Hughes and Doug Hamilton were fourth in the quad sculls; Mike and Mark Evans were fifth in the pairs and Andrea Schreiner was fifth in the women's sculls. Betty Craig and Trisa Smith won a bronze medal in the women's pairs. This was their third medal in three successive world championships.

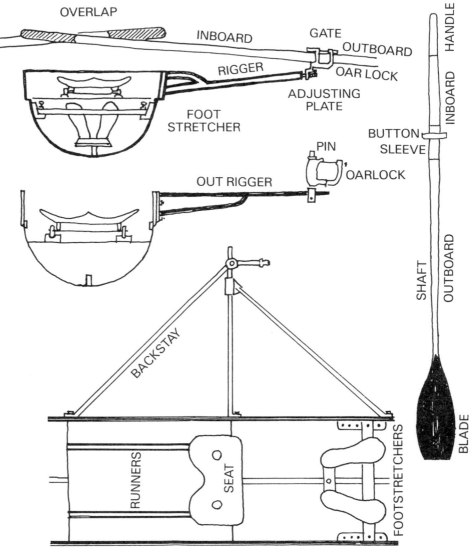

MEDAL WINNERS

ROWING (single sculls) Men

YEAR	PLACE	NAME	COUNTRY
1900	1	**H. Barrelet**	**France**
	2	A. Gaudin	France
	3	S-G. Ashe	Great Britain
1904	1	**F. Greer**	**U.S.A.**
	2*	J. Juvenal	U.S.A.
	3*	C. Titus	U.S.A.
1908	1	**H. Blackstaffe**	**Great Britain**
	2*	A. McCulloch	Great Britain
	3	B. von Gaza	Germany
1912	1	**W. Kinnear**	**Great Britain**
	2*	P. Veirman	Belgium
	3	E. Butler	Canada
1920	1	**J. Kelly**	**U.S.A.**
	2	J. Beresford	Great Britain
	3	D. d'Arcy	New Zealand
1924	1	**J. Beresford**	**Great Britain**
	2	W. Garrett-Gilmore	U.S.A.
	3	J. Schneider	Switzerland
1928	1	**H. Pearce**	**Australia**
	2	K. Myers	U.S.A.
	3	T.D. Collet	Great Britain
1932	1	**H. Pearce**	**Australia**
	2	W. Miller	U.S.A.
	3	G. Douglas	Uruguay
1936	1	**G. Schäfer**	**Germany**
	2	J. Hasenöhrl	Austria
	3	D. Barrow	U.S.A.
1948	1	**M. Wood**	**Australia**
	2	E. Risso	Uruguay
	3	R. Catasta	Italy
1952	1	**Y. Tyukalov**	**U.S.S.R.**
	2	M. Wood	Australia
	3	T. Kocerka	Poland
1956	1	**V. Ivanov**	**U.S.S.R.**
	2	S. Mackenzie	Australia
	3	J.B. Kelly	U.S.A.
1960	1	**V. Ivanov**	**U.S.S.R.**
	2	A. Hill	Germany
	3	T. Kocerka	Poland
1964	1	**V. Ivanov**	**U.S.S.R.**
	2	A. Hill	Germany
	3	G. Kottman	Switzerland
1968	1	**H. Wienese**	**Netherlands**
	2	J. Meissner	Germany
	3	A. Demiddi	Argentina
1972	1	**U. Malishev**	**U.S.S.R.**
	2	A. Demiddi	Argentina
	3	W. Güldenpfennig	East Germany
1976	1	**Pertti Karppinen**	**Finland**
	2	Peter Kolbe	Germany
	3	Joachim Dreifke	German Dem. Rep.
1980	1	**Pertti Karppinen**	**Finland**
	2	Vasily Yakusha	U.S.S.R.
	3	Peter Kersten	German Dem. Rep.

ROWING (single sculls) Women

YEAR	PLACE	NAME	COUNTRY
1976	1	**Christine Scheiblich**	**German Dem. Rep.**
	2	Joan Lind	U.S.A.
	3	Elena Antonova	U.S.S.R.
1980	1	**Sanda Toma**	**Rumania**
	2	Antonina Makhina	U.S.S.R.
	3	Martina Schroter	German Dem. Rep.

ROWING (double sculls) Men

YEAR	PLACE	NAME	COUNTRY
1904	1	**J. Mulcahy/W. Varley**	**U.S.A.**
	2	J. McLoughlin/J. Hoben	U.S.A.
	3	J. Ravanack/J. Wells	U.S.A.
1920	1	**J. Kelly/P. Costello**	**U.S.A.**
	2	E. Dones/P Annoni	Italy
	3	A. Plé/G. Giran	France
1924	1	**J. Kelly/P. Costello**	**U.S.A.**
	2	J. Stock/M. Detton	France
	3*	R. Bosshard/H. Thoma	Switzerland
1928	1	**C. McIlvaine/ P. Costello**	**U.S.A.**
	2	J. Guest/J. Wright	Canada
	3	V. Flessl/L. Losert	Austria
1932	1	**W. Garret-Gilmore/ K. Myers**	**U.S.A.**
	2	G. Boetzelen/H. Buhtz	Germany
	3	N. de Mille/C. Pratt	Canada
1936	1	**L. Southwood/ J. Beresford**	**Great Britain**
	2	J. Pirsch/W. Kaidel	Germany
	3	J. Ustupski/R. Verey	Poland
1948	1	**B.H. Bushnell/ R. Burnell**	**Great Britain**
	2	A. Larsen/E. Parsner	Denmark
	3	J. Rodriguez/W. Jones	Uruguay
1952	1	**T. Cappozzo/ E. Guerrero**	**Argentina**
	2	G. Schilin/I. Yerntschuk	U.S.S.R.
	3	M. Seijas/J. Rodriguez	Uruguay
1956	1	**A. Berkutov/ Y. Tyukalov**	**U.S.S.R.**
	2	B. Costello/J. Gardiner	U.S.A.
	3	M. Riley/M. Wood	Australia
1960	1	**V. Kozak/P. Schmidt**	**Czechoslovakia**
	2	A. Berkutov/Y. Tyukalov	U.S.S.R.
	3	H. Hürlimann/R. Larcher	Switzerland
1964	1	**C. Tyurin/ B. Dubrovsky**	**U.S.S.R.**
	2	S. Cromwell/J. Storm	U.S.A.
	3	V. Andrs/P. Hofman	Czechoslovakia
1968	1	**A. Sass/A. Timoschinin**	**U.S.S.R.**
	2	L.F. van Dis/H. Droog	Netherlands
	3	W. Maher/J. Nunn	U.S.A.
1972	1	**A. Timoschinin/ G. Korschikov**	**U.S.S.R.**
	2	F. Hansen/S. Thogersen	Norway
	3	J. Boehmer/H. Schmied	East Germany
1976	1	**Frank Hansen/ Alf Hansen**	**Norway**
	2	Chris Baillieu/ Michael Hart	Great Britain
	3	Hans-Ulrich Schmied/ Jurgen Berton	East Germany
1980	1	**Joach Dreifke/ Klaus Kroppelien**	**East Germany**
	2	Zoran Pancic/ Milorad Stanulov	Yugoslavia
	3	Zdenek Pecka/ Vaclav Vochoska	Czechoslovakia

* Fouled—time not recorded

ROWING (double sculls) Women

YEAR	PLACE	COUNTRY
1976	1	**Bulgaria**
	2	East Germany
	3	U.S.S.R.
1980	1	**U.S.S.R.**
	2	East Germany
	3	Rumania

ROWING (coxed pairs) Men

YEAR	PLACE	COUNTRY
1900	1	**Netherlands**
	2	France
	3	France
1920	1	**Italy**
	2	France
	3	Switzerland
1924	1	**Switzerland**
	2	Italy
	3*	U.S.A.
1928	1	**Switzerland**
	2	France
	3	Belgium
1932	1	**U.S.A.**
	2	Poland
	3	France
1936	1	**Germany**
	2	Italy
	3	France
1948	1	**Denmark**
	2	Italy
	3	Hungary
1952	1	**France**
	2	Germany
	3	Denmark
1956	1	**U.S.A.**
	2	Germany
	3	U.S.S.R.
1960	1	**Germany**
	2	U.S.S.R.
	3	U.S.A.
1964	1	**U.S.A.**
	2	France
	3	Netherlands
1968	1	**Italy**
	2	Netherlands
	3	Denmark
1972	1	**East Germany**
	2	Czechoslovakia
	3	Rumania
1976	1	**East Germany**
	2	U.S.S.R.
	3	Czechoslovakia
1980	1	**East Germany**
	2	U.S.S.R.
	3	Yugoslavia

* Fouled—time not recorded

ROWING (coxed fours) Women
New Olympic Event—1976

YEAR	PLACE	COUNTRY
1976	1	**East Germany**
	2	Bulgaria
	3	U.S.S.R.
1980	1	**East Germany**
	2	Bulgaria
	3	U.S.S.R.

ROWING (coxswainless pairs)—Men

YEAR	PLACE	NAME	COUNTRY
1908	1	**J. Fenning/ G. Thomson**	**Great Britain**
	2	G. Fairbairn/P Verdon	Great Britain
	3	Toms/Jacks	Canada
1924	1	**W. Rösingh/A. Beijnen**	**Netherlands**
	2	M. Bouton/G. Piot	France
	3*		
1928	1	**B. Müller/ K. Möschter**	**Germany**
	2	R.A. Nisbet/T. O'Brien	Great Britain
	3	J. Schmitt/P. McDowell	U.S.A.
1932	1	**H. Edwards/L. Clive**	**Great Britain**
	2	F. Thompson/C. Stiles	New Zealand
	3	J. Mikolajczyk/ H. Budzynski	Poland
1936	1	**H. Strauss/W. Eichhorn**	**Germany**
	2	H. Larsen/R. Olsen	Denmark
	3	J. Curatella/H. Podesta	Argentina
1948	1	**J. Wilson/W.S. Laurie**	**Great Britain**
	2	J. Kalt/H. Kalt	Switzerland
	3	B. Boni/F. Fanetti	Italy
1952	1	**C. Logg/T. Price**	**U.S.A.**
	2	M. Knuysen/R. Baetens	Belgium
	3	K. Schmid/H. Kalt	Switzerland
1956	1	**J. Fifer/D. Hecht**	**U.S.A.**
	2	I. Buldakov/V. Ivanov	U.S.S.R.
	3	J. Kloimstein/A. Sageder	Austria
1960	1	**V. Boreyko/ O. Golovanov**	**U.S.S.R.**
	2	J. Kloimstein/A. Sageder	Austria
	3	V. Lehtela/T. Pitkänen	Finland
1964	1	**G. Hungerford/ R. Jackson**	**Canada**
	2	S. Blaisse/Veenemans	Netherlands
	3	M. Schwan/ W. Hottenrott	Germany
1968	1	**J. Lucke/H-J. Bothe**	**East Germany**
	2	L. Hough/P. Johnson	U.S.A.
	3	P. Christiansen/I. Larsen	Denmark
1972	1	**S. Brietzke/W. Mager**	**East Germany**
	2	H. Fischer/A. Bachmann	Switzerland
	3	R. Luynenburg/ R. Stokvis	Netherlands

YEAR	PLACE		COUNTRY
1976	1	**Jorg Landvoigt/ Benard Landvoigt**	**East Germany**
	2	Calvin Coffey/ Michael Staines	U.S.A.
	3	Peter Vanroye/ Thomas Strauss	Germany
1980	1	**Jorg Landvoigt/ Bernd Landvoigt**	**East Germany**
	2	Yuriy Pimenov/ Nikolai Pimenov	U.S.S.R.
	3	Charles Wiggin/ Malcolm Carmichael	Great Britain

* 1924 — The team that was eligible for this final (Great Britain) did not take part.

ROWING (coxswainless pairs) Women

YEAR	PLACE	COUNTRY
1976	1	**Bulgaria**
	2	East Germany
	3	West Germany
1980	1	**East Germany**
	2	Poland
	3	Bulgaria

ROWING (coxswainless fours) Men

YEAR	PLACE	COUNTRY
1904	1	**U.S.A.**
	2	U.S.A.
	dna	
1908	1	**Great Britain**
	2	Great Britain
	dna	
1924	1	**Great Britain**
	2*	Canada
	3*	Switzerland
1928	1	**Great Britain**
	2	U.S.A.
	3	Italy
1932	1	**Great Britain**
	2	Germany
	3	Italy
1936	1	**Germany**
	2	Great Britain
	3	Switzerland
1948	1	**Italy**
	2	Denmark
	3	U.S.A.
1952	1	**Yugoslavia**
	2	France
	3	Finland
1956	1	**Canada**
	2	U.S.A.
	3	France
1960	1	**U.S.A.**
	2	Italy
	3	U.S.S.R.
1964	1	**Denmark**
	2	Great Britain
	3	U.S.A.
1968	1	**East Germany**
	2	Hungary
	3	Italy
1972	1	**East Germany**
	2	New Zealand
	3	West Germany

* Fouled — time not recorded

ROWING (coxswainless quadruple sculls) New Olympic Event — 1976

YEAR	PLACE	COUNTRY
1976	1	**East Germany**
	2	Norway
	3	U.S.S.R.
1980	1	**East Germany**
	2	U.S.S.R.
	3	Great Britain

ROWING (coxed fours) Men

YEAR	PLACE	COUNTRY
1900*	1	**Germany**
	2	Netherlands
	3	Germany
1912	1	**Germany**
	2	Great Britain
	3	Norway/Denmark
1920	1	**Switzerland**
	2	U.S.A.
	3	Norway
1924	1	**Switzerland**
	2	France
	3**	U.S.A.
1928	1	**Italy**
	2	Switzerland
	3	Poland
1932	1	**Germany**
	2	Italy
	3	Poland
1936	1	**Germany**
	2	Switzerland
	3	France
1948	1	**U.S.A.**
	2	Switzerland
	3	Denmark
1952	1	**Czechoslovakia**
	2	Switzerland
	3	U.S.A.
1956	1	**Italy**
	2	Sweden
	3	Finland
1960	1	**Germany**
	2	France
	3	Italy
1964	1	**Germany**
	2	Italy
	3	Netherlands
1968	1	**New Zealand**
	2	East Germany
	3	Switzerland
1972	1	**Germany**
	2	East Germany
	3	Czechoslovakia
1976	1	**U.S.S.R.**
	2	E. Germany
	3	W. Germany
1980	1	**E. Germany**
	2	U.S.S.R.
	3	Poland

* Rowing was not declared an official Olympic Sport until 1908 when four events were held. Coxed fours were added in 1912.
** Fouled — time not recorded.

ROWING (coxed eights) Men

YEAR	PLACE	COUNTRY
1900	1	**U.S.A.**
	2	Belgium
	3	Netherlands
1904	1	**U.S.A.**
	2	Canada
	dna	
1908	1	**Great Britain**
	2	Belgium
	3	Great Britain/Canada
1912	1	**Great Britain**
	2	Great Britain
	3	Germany
1920	1	**U.S.A.**
	2	Great Britain
	3	Norway
1924	1	**U.S.A.**
	2	Canada
	3	Italy
1928	1	**U.S.A.**
	2	Great Britain
	3	Canada
1932	1	**U.S.A.**
	2	Italy
	3	Canada
1936	1	**U.S.A.**
	2	Italy
	3	Germany
1948	1	**U.S.A.**
	2	Great Britain
	3	Norway
1952	1	**U.S.A.**
	2	U.S.S.R.
	3	Australia
1956	1	**U.S.A.**
	2	Canada
	3	Australia
1960	1	**Germany**
	2	Canada
	3	Czechoslovakia
1964	1	**U.S.A.**
	2	Germany
	3	Czechoslovakia
1968	1	**Germany**
	2	Australia
	3	U.S.S.R.
1972	1	**New Zealand**
	2	U.S.A.
	3	East Germany
1976	1	**E. Germany**
	2	Great Britain
	3	New Zealand
1980	1	**East Germany**
	2	Great Britain
	3	U.S.S.R.

ROWING (coxed eights) Women

YEAR	PLACE	COUNTRY
1976	1	**East Germany**
	2	U.S.S.R.
	3	U.S.A.
1980	1	**East Germany**
	2	U.S.S.R.
	3	Rumania

ROWING (coxed quadruple sculls) Women

YEAR	PLACE	COUNTRY
1976	1	**East Germany**
	2	U.S.S.R.
	3	Rumania
1980	1	**East Germany**
	2	U.S.S.R.
	3	Bulgaria

SHOOTING

EVENT	DATE		SITE TO BE DETERMINED	

JULY	**29**	Free pistol/Sport pistol/Clay target-trap	**AUGUST**	**2**	Small-bore rifle 3 positions/Rapid-fire pistol Clay target-skeet
	30	Small-bore rifle English match Clay target-trap/Running game target		**3**	Air rifle/Clay target-skeet
	31	Clay target-trap/ Running game target/Air rifle		**4**	Clay target-skeet
AUGUST	**1**	Small-bore rifle 3 positions Rapid-fire pistol			

HISTORY

Marksmanship began with the invention of the gun. Hitting a target gave the gun purpose and meaning. Unfortunately, the target was usually an enemy in war or argument. The establishment of shooting clubs turned the gun from primarily a weapon of destruction to an enjoyable sport.

Along with the variety of guns, came a variety of shooting events which have been shuffled, sifted and sorted out for present day competition. When target shooting was included in the 1896 Olympic Games, there were eight medals awarded in four events.

Six events, including trap shooting, were added to the 1900 Games and a team competition was included in 1904. There were 15 shooting events in the 1912 Games, and the total climbed to 17 for the 1920 Games. By this time a debate began to rage over the vast number of Olympic shooting events. When the 1924 Games were held in Paris, the shooting events were pared back to six, all featuring military-type weapons.

Shooting was omitted from the 1928 Games. When it was included in the 1932 Los Angeles Games programme, military guns had dropped out of fashion and competition was restricted to the target-shooting smallbore rifle and pistol. Throughout the years events were constantly added and subtracted. By 1956, the programme was back to the 1924 total of six events. Skeet shooting was added in 1968 and the Running Game event was included in 1972. For the 1984 Games in Los Angeles, the air rifle events for men and women have been added. There will also be smallbore rifle events and a pistol match for women.

GENERAL DESCRIPTION

The greatest technical skill in Olympic sports is found in shooting. Few can visualize the finesse, steady nerves and muscle control required to hold a pistol at arm's length while attempting to score a bull's-eye 50 metres away from a target that is only about the size of a half-dollar.

Shooting is demanding. It requires top-notch physical form, a keen eye and a steady hand.

The constant improvement in results over the years can be attributed to the meticulous search for the best physiological conditions. The slightest mental error or problems from fatigue or balance can be costly to the shooter. An even greater amount of research has gone into the development of firearms. There is no room for the slightest mechanical failure in the Olympics.

PROCEDURE

Each country is allowed two competitors in each event. A variety of methods are used to select competitors. Canada, for instance, will hold Olympic trials in several events and will name competitors in other events from results in international competition.

Rapid-fire pistol – men — This .22-calibre match is fired from 25 metres at a bank of five silhouette-targets. Each target has 10 scoring zones. Firing is divided into two courses of 30 shots each, with a maximum score of 600 points.

The shooter, presented with five silhouettes appearing for eight seconds, must fire one shot at each. The series is repeated. The shooter fires two more five-shot series, but is permitted to see the five silhouettes for only six seconds. Finally, the course is completed by firing two five-shot series in four seconds each. After all competitors have completed the first 30-shot course, the entire process is repeated.

Competitors must begin each series with pistols pointed downward at an angle not less than 45 degrees from the horizontal. Only as the targets begin to turn toward the shooter may pistols be raised.

Free Pistol – Men — As the name implies, there are few restrictions placed on the firearm used in the match. Regulations specify that it be a .22-calibre pistol with metallic (open) sights. This is the only International Shooting Union calibre pistol event fired at 50 metres. The bull's-eye target has a 5.08-centimetre centre, 10-point ring and shooters fire 60 single shots in 2 hours 30 minutes to attempt a perfect score of 600.

Sport Pistol – Women — This is the International Shooting Union "Standard Pistol." It is .22-calibre, has a maximum allowable weight of 1,400 grams, barrel length of 153 millimetres and a trigger-pull weight of at least 1,000 grams. Special accessories or grips that enclose the hand are not allowed.

The match consists of 60 shots at 25 metres. Thirty shots are fired on the Precision (Free Pistol) target, and 30 shots on a single Rapid Fire target (Duel). In the Duel course, one shot is fired when the target is exposed for 3 seconds. There is an interval of 7 seconds between 3 second exposures.

Smallbore Free Rifle – three positions — this match consists of 120 shots, 40 in each position: prone, standing and kneeling. It is fired with a .22-calibre free rifle from 50 metres on the same target used in the English Match. The free rifle has a weight limit of eight kilograms. Only metallic sights are allowed, however, special accessories are permitted. The maximum score is 1,200 and the shooter is given the following time allowance: prone, 1 hour 30 minutes; standing, 2 hours; kneeling, 1 hour 45 minutes.

Smallbore English Match — This event consists of 60 shots fired from the prone position within two hours. Shooters aim for a maximum score of 600, firing from 50 metres at a target with a 10-ring of 12.4 millimetres in diameter. All .22-calibre long rifles are permitted provided they do not exceed eight kilograms including accessories. Metallic sights are used. A sling is used to help support the rifle.

Air Rifle — rules permit the use of any air-or-gas-powered rifles having a bore of 4.5 millimetres weighing not more than five kilograms. Matches consist of 40 shots for women and 60 shots for men fired at a distance of 10 metres on a bull's-eye target having a centre one millimetre in diameter. All firing is done from the standing position. Time limits are 1 hour 30 minutes for 40 shots and 2 hours 15 minutes for 60 shots. A perfect score is 400 or 600 points.

Smallbore Rifle Three Positions (Standard Rifle) — open to women. It is similar to the Free Rifle Match for men, except that competitors must use a Standard Rifle with a 5-kilogram weight limit and meet dimensional limits. Twenty shots are fired from each position. The total time limit for all shots is 2 hours and 30 minutes.

Running Game — also known as Running Boar. First fired in the world championships in 1966, it became part of the Olympic programme in 1972. It is fired with a .22-calibre rifle which almost invariably is equipped with telescopic sights.

The target is a lithograph of a wild boar in full charge running at right angles to the shooter, over which is superimposed a 60 millimetre 10-ring target. The target is on a track and travels alternately left and right across a 10-metre wide opening for five seconds for slow runs and 2.5 seconds for fast runs. A match consists of 30 slow-run shots and 30 fast-run shots for a possible score of 600.

Shotgun or Clay Target shooting — is divided into two forms, *skeet* and *trap*. Easily broken saucer-shaped targets 110 millimetres in diameter and 25 millimetres thick are used in both forms. A "round" consists of 25 targets with competitions usually comprising eight rounds of 200 targets.

In *skeet*, the targets are thrown on a fixed flight path from two traphouses facing each other 36.8 metres apart. There are seven stations arranged in a semicircle between the two houses with an eighth station in the centre. One target at a time is thrown from each house.

The target flight distance is a minimum of 65 metres and there is a delay of between zero to three seconds between the call and the appearance of each target. The gun butt must be held at the waistline until the target appears.

In *trap* events, competitors use the Olympic Trench installations. These are five stations arranged three metres apart in a straight line, 15 metres behind a long, ground-level trench in which the traps are located. There are three traps one metre apart in front of each shooting station. Each time a shooter calls for a target, one of the three traps throws the target at an unknown angle and height. The target flight distance is 70 metres. Two shots may be fired at each target. The shooters fire at only one target from each of the five stations.

EQUIPMENT

Free pistol — a .22-calibre firearm without restrictions on weight, barrel length or trigger. The grip may be adjusted to the users' hand, but it may not support the wrist. Optical sights are not permitted.

Smallbore rifle — a .22-calibre firearm classified as "free". There are no restrictions on the type of trigger, a sling

is used for support, a hook butt-plate, which is placed against the shoulder and in the armpit for more stability, may also be used. Optical sights are not permitted and the weight of the rifle may not exceed eight kilograms.

Shotgun — 12 gauge guns are used for both the skeet and clay events. Shells use 32 grams of shot.

Running Game rifle — must be of .22-calibre with at least 500 grams pressure required to release the trigger. It may not weigh more than five kilograms. Any type of sight, including telescopic, is permitted.

Rapid-fire pistol — only .22-calibre pistols are permitted, normally of the semiautomatic type. They use special low-velocity .22-calibre short-range ammunition to minimize recoil, thus permitting rapid recovery of aim after each shot and accurate movement from one target to the next.

Target — it is divided into concentric bands marked from 10 to 1, starting at the bull's-eye (centre). The target is of heavy paper or tagboard. In the case of the Smallbore, Prone, and Three Positions events, competitors will be aiming at a roundmark which is 112.4 millimetres wide, with a 12.4-millimetre diameter bull's-eye.

Clay targets — a breakable disc, usually made of pitch, 110 millimetres in diameter; 25 – 26 millimetres thick and weighing 105 grams. Used in skeet and trap events.

Running Game target — shaped like a boar with a round bull's-eye and scoring rings counting from 1 to 10 points. The ring is 60 millimetres in diameter.

TECHNICAL TERMS

Air rifle/pistol — a compressed air, spring or CO_2 rifle or pistol using an hourglass-shaped ("waisted") lead pellet of 4.5-millimetre calibre.

Any sights — any sights without restriction as to material or construction, including telescopes.

Bull's-eye — an aiming point printed on a target card. The aiming point for shooting is usually circular and contains concentric numbered rings for scoring. Also can refer to the 10-ring.

Clay target — a breakable disc, usually made of pitch, 110 millimetres in diameter, 25 – 28 millimetres in height and weighing 105 grams.

Facing targets — in international pistol competition, the turning of the targets at a 90-degree angle to the firing line before shooting begins.

Firing line — the line immediately in front of the several firing points from which distance to the targets is measured. Also used to indicate the line of shooters at their respective firing points.

Firing point — that part of the range provided for each competitor immediately in the rear of the firing line.

Free rifle — rifles for international competition under U.I.T. rules at 50 metres or 300 metres, virtually free from restrictions, except that it may not weigh more than 8 kilograms and its calibre must be either .22 Long Rifle or not exceed 8 millimetres respectively.

Match — a complete event as described in the program for the award of certain specific prizes. A match may consist of one or several stages.

Metallic sights — any sighting system, constructed of metal or equivalent, which provides a method of aiming or aligning two separate but visible sights or reference points mounted on the rifle. Magnifying optics are not allowed.

Rapid fire — generally, a series of shots fired without reloading. In international competitions, a particular pistol match (see above).

Sighting (sighter) shots — practice shots fired at a target provided for that purpose and used to obtain desired information relative to adjustment of sights for the match which immediately follows.

Smallbore free rifle — a 5.56 millimetre (.22 calibre long rifle) subject to the regulations for free rifles (see above).

Stage — in a match fired at more than one range or in more than one position, each range or position is referred to as a "stage" of the match.

Standard rifle — a rifle conforming to strict U.I.T. rules which proscribe palm rests, hook buttplates and other accoutrements of free rifles. Weight must not exceed 5 kilograms with the rifle not exceeding detailed dimensional limits.

String or series — a series of shots (usually 5 or 10 shots) forming a part of a stage.

Target — a surface, usually paper or tagboard, containing one or more aiming marks.

U.I.T. — International Shooting Union (Union international de tir), the worldwide governing body of target shooting.

TOP COMPETITORS

Competitors from the United States and the Soviet Union are expected to be top contenders but no country has been able to call shooting its private domain. Past winners in events have come from Switzerland, Sweden, Finland, East Germany, Norway, Canada, Czechoslovakia, France, Brazil, the United States and, the Soviet Union, and a host of other countries.

TOP CANADIANS

Susan Nattrass of Edmonton is a six-time women's world champion in trap shooting. She was the first female competitor in that event in the Olympics when she placed 25th in 1976. She was third in the 1983 world championship women's event.

John Primrose of Edmonton has won the men's trap world championships twice; in 1975 and 1983. He also won the Commonwealth Games twice in 1974 and 1978, and is a 10-time Canadian champion.

Linda Thom of Ottawa placed second in the Match Pistol at the 1983 Pan-American Games while Jean-François Senecal of Montreal finished 15th in the men's Air Rifle event at the 1983 World Championships.

MEDAL WINNERS

SHOOTING (free pistol)

YEAR	PLACE	NAME	COUNTRY
1896	1	S. Paine	U.S.A.
	2	V. Jensen	Denmark
	3	H. Nielsen	Denmark
1900	1	K. Röderer	Switzerland
	2	A. Paroche	France
	3	K. Stäheli	Switzerland
1912	1	A. Lane	U.S.A.
	2	P. Dolfen	U.S.A.
	3	C.E. Stewart	Great Britain
1920	1	C. Frederick	U.S.A.
	2	A. da Costa	Brazil
	3	A. Lane	U.S.A.
1936	1	T. Ullman	Sweden
	2	E. Krempel	Germany
	3	C. des Jammonières	France
1948	1	C. Vasquez	Peru
	2	R. Schnyder	Switzerland
	3	T. Ullman	Sweden
1952	1	H. Benner	U.S.A.
	2	A. de Gozalo	Spain
	3	A. Balogh	Hungary
1956	1	P. Linnosvuo	Finland
	2	M. Umarov	U.S.S.R.
	3	O. Pinion	U.S.A.
1960	1	A. Guschtschin	U.S.S.R.
	2	M. Umarov	U.S.S.R.
	3	Y. Yoshikawa	Japan
1964	1	V. Markkanen	Finland
	2	F. Green	U.S.A.
	3	Y. Yoshikawa	Japan
1968	1	G. Kossykh	U.S.S.R.
	2	M. Mertel	Germany
	3	H. Vollmar	East Germany
1972	1	R. Skanaker	Sweden
	2	D. Iuga	Rumania
	3	R. Dollinger	Austria
1976	1	Uwe Potteck	German Dem. Rep.
	2	Harald Vollmar	German Dem. Rep.
	3	Rudolf Dollinger	Austria
1980	1	Aleksandr Melentev	U.S.S.R.
	2	Harald Vollmar	German Dem. Rep.
	3	Lubtcho Diakov	Bulgaria

SHOOTING (small-bore rifle — prone)

YEAR	PLACE	NAME	COUNTRY
1908	1	A. Carnell	Great Britain
	2	H.R. Humby	Great Britain
	3	G. Barnes	Great Britain
1912	1	F. Hird	U.S.A.
	2	W. Milne	Great Britain
	3	H. Burt	Great Britain
1920	1	L. Nuesslein	U.S.A.
	2	A. Rothrock	U.S.A.
	3	D. Fenton	U.S.A.
1924	1	P. Coquelin de Lisle	France
	2	M. Dinwiddie	U.S.A.
	3	J. Hartmann	Switzerland
1932	1	B. Rönnmark	Sweden
	2	G. Huet	Mexico
	3	Z. Hradetsky-Soós	Hungary
1936	1	W. Rögeberg	Norway
	2	R. Berzsenyi	Hungary
	3	W. Karas	Poland
1948	1	A. Cook	U.S.A.
	2	W. Tomsen	U.S.A.
	3	J. Jonsson	Sweden
1952	1	I. Sirbu	Rumania
	2	B. Andreyev	U.S.S.R.
	3	A. Jackson	U.S.A.
1956	1	G. Ouellette	Canada
	2	V. Borisov	U.S.S.R.
	3	G. Boa	Canada
1960	1	P. Kohnke	Germany
	2	J. Hill	U.S.A.
	3	E. Pelliccioni	Venezuela

YEAR	PLACE	NAME	COUNTRY
1964	1	L. Hammerl	Hungary
	2	L. Wigger	U.S.A.
	3	T. Pool	U.S.A.
1968	1	J. Kurka	Czechoslovakia
	2	L. Hammerl	Hungary
	3	I. Ballinger	New Zealand
1972	1	H. Jun Li	North Korea
	2	V. Auer	U.S.A.
	3	N. Rotaru	Rumania
1976	1	Karlheinz Smieszek	Germany
	2	Ulrich Lind	Germany
	3	Gennadi Lushchikov	U.S.S.R.
1980	1	Karoly Varga	Hungary
	2	Hellfried Heilfort	German Dem. Rep.
	3	Petar Zaprianov	Bulgaria

SHOOTING (smal-bore rifle — three positions)

YEAR	PLACE	NAME	COUNTRY
1952	1	E. Kongshaug	Norway
	2	V. Ylönen	Finland
	3	B. Andreyev	U.S.S.R.
1956	1	A. Bogdanov	U.S.S.R.
	2	O. Hofinek	Czechoslovakia
	3	N. Sundberg	Sweden
1960	1	V. Schamburkin	U.S.S.R.
	2	M. Niyason	U.S.S.R.
	3	K. Zähringer	Germany
1964	1	L. Wigger	U.S.A.
	2	V. Khristov	Bulgaria
	3	L. Hammerl	Hungary
1968	1	B. Klingner	Germany
	2	J. Writer	U.S.A.
	3	V. Parkhimovitsch	U.S.S.R.
1972	1	J. Writer	U.S.A.
	2	L. Bassham	U.S.A.
	3	W. Lippoldt	East Germany
1976	1	Lanny Bassham	U.S.A.
	2	Margaret Murdock	U.S.A.
	3	Werner Seibold	Germany
1980	1	Viktor Vlasov	U.S.S.R.
	2	Bernd Hartstein	German Dem. Rep.
	3	Sven Johansson	Sweden

SHOOTING (rapid-fire pistol)

YEAR	PLACE	NAME	COUNTRY
1896	1	J. Phrangoudis	Greece
	2	G. Orphanidis	Greece
	3	H. Nielsen	Denmark
1900	1	M. Larrouy	France
	2	L. Moreaux	France
	3	E. Balme	France
1908	1	P. van Asbroeck	Belgium
	2	R. Storms	Belgium
	3	J. Gorman	U.S.A.
1912	1	A.P. Lane	U.S.A.
	2	P. Palèn	Sweden
	3	H. von Holst	Sweden
1920	1	G. Paraense	Brazil
	2	R. Bracken	U.S.A.
	3	F. Zulauf	Switzerland
1924	1	H. Bailey	U.S.A.
	2	V. Carlberg	Sweden
	3	L. Hannelius	Finland
1932	1	R. Morigi	Italy
	2	H. Hax	Germany
	3	D. Matteucci	Italy
1936	1	C. van Oyen	Germany
	2	H. Hax	Germany
	3	T. Ullman	Sweden
1948	1	K. Takács	Hungary
	2	C. Valiente	Argentina
	3	S. Lundqvist	Sweden
1952	1	K. Takács	Hungary
	2	S. Kun	Hungary
	3	G. Lichiardopol	Rumania
1956	1	S. Petrescu	Rumania
	2	Y. Tscherkassov	U.S.S.R.
	3	G. Lichiardopol	Rumania
1960	1	W. McMillan	U.S.A.
	2	P. Linnosvuo	Finland
	3	A. Zabelin	U.S.S.R.

1964	1	**P. Linnosvuo**	**Finland**
	2	I. Tripsa	Rumania
	3	L. Nacovsky	Czechoslovakia
1968	1	**J. Zapedski**	**Poland**
	2	M. Rosca	Rumania
	3	R. Suleimanov	U.S.S.R.
1972	1	**J. Zapedski**	**Poland**
	2	L. Faita	Czechoslovakia
	3	V. Torschin	U.S.S.R.
1976	1	**Norbert Klaar**	**German Dem. Rep.**
	2	Jurgen Wiefel	German Dem. Rep.
	3	Roberto Ferraris	Italy
1980	1	**Corneliu Ion**	**Rumania**
	2	Jurgen Wiefel	German Dem. Rep.
	3	Gerhard Petritsch	Austria

SHOOTING (trap)

YEAR	PLACE	NAME	COUNTRY
1900	1	**R. Barbarin**	**France**
	2	R. Guyot	France
	3	J. de Clary	France
1908	1	**W. Ewing**	**Canada**
	2	G. Beattie	Canada
	3	A. Maunder/	Great Britain/
		A. Metaxes	Greece
1912	1	**J. Graham**	**U.S.A.**
	2	A. Goldel	Germany
	3	H. Blau	Russia
1920	1	**M. Arie**	**U.S.A.**
	2	F. Troeh	U.S.A.
	3	F. Wright	U.S.A.
1924	1	**G. Halasy**	**Hungary**
	2	K. Huber	Finland
	3	F. Hughes	U.S.A.
1952	1	**G. Genereux**	**Canada**
	2	K. Holmqvist	Sweden
	3	H. Liljedahl	Sweden
1956	1	**G. Rossini**	**Italy**
	2	A. Smelczynski	Poland
	3	A. Ciceri	Italy
1960	1	**I. Dumitrescu**	**Rumania**
	2	G. Rossini	Italy
	3	S. Kalinin	U.S.S.R.
1964	1	**E. Mattarelli**	**Italy**
	2	P. Senitschev	U.S.S.R.
	3	W. Morris	U.S.A.
1968	1	**R. Braithwaite**	**Great Britain**
	2	T. Garrigus	U.S.A.
	3	K. Czekalla	East Germany
1972	1	**A. Scalzone**	**Italy**
	2	M. Carrega	France
	3	S. Basagni	Italy
1976	1	**Donald Haldeman**	**U.S.A.**
	2	Armando Silva Marques	Portugal
	3	Ubaldesc Baldi	Italy
1980	1	**Luciano Giovannetti**	**Italy**
	2	Rustan Yambulatov	U.S.S.R.
	3	Jorg Damme	German Dem. Rep.

SHOOTING (skeet)

YEAR	PLACE	NAME	COUNTRY
1968	1	**E. Petrov**	**U.S.S.R.**
	2	R. Garagnani	Italy
	3	K. Wirnhier	Germany
1972	1	**K. Wirnhier**	**Germany**
	2	E. Petrov	U.S.S.R.
	3	M. Bucheim	East Germany
1976	1	**Josef Panacek**	**Czechoslovakia**
	2	Eric Swinkels	Netherland
	3	Wieslaw Gawlikowski	Poland
1980	1	**Hans Kjeld Rasmussen**	**Denmark**
	2	Lars-Goran Carlsson	Sweden
	3	Roberto Castrillo	Cuba

SHOOTING (moving target)

YEAR	PLACE	NAME	COUNTRY
1972	1	**L. Zhelezniak**	**U.S.S.R.**
	2	H. Bellingrodt	Colombia
	3	J. Kynoch	Great Britain
1976	1	**Alexander Gazov**	**U.S.S.R.**
	2	Alexander Kedyardv	U.S.S.R.
	3	Jerzy Greszkiewicz	Poland
1980	1	**Igor Sokolov**	**U.S.S.R.**
	2	Thomas Pfeffer	German Dem. Rep.
	3	Alexandr Gazov	U.S.S.R.

SWIMMING

The butterfly stroke

HISTORY

The history of Olympic swimming has been spotted with controversy both in the pool and out. Yet, outstanding performances have been the norm despite the trials and tribulations cast upon the individuals.

The greatest individual performance in Olympic swimming history took place in Munich in 1972. Tall and slender Mark Spitz of the United States astounded the swimming world by winning seven gold medals. In a remarkable performance, he swam 13 races over 18 days.

Only a few hours after Spitz earned his seventh gold medal, the Olympic scene was in an uproar. A terrorist group from the Palestinian Liberation Organization killed 11 members of the Israeli Olympic team. Spitz, a Jew, was stunned and outraged and American officials feared for his life. He was placed under heavy guard and a few hours after the massacre, he was on a plane home.

The heroics of Spitz in the water enabled the Olympic committee to downplay an incident involving Rick Demont of the United States. Demont, 16, was the apparent winner of the men's 400-metre freestyle but he was stripped of the medal on drug charges. An asthmatic since childhood, Demond had taken an ephedrine medication, which is banned by the Olympic medical commission.

A glass of champagne got lovely Eleanor Holm of the United States into hot water. A gold medal winner at the 1932 Olympics, Holm was on her way to the 1936 Games in Berlin by boat when she was photographed with a glass of champagne in her hand. The U.S. Olympic committee ordered her home for "immoral" behaviour.

Holm went home a hero, the American public loved her free spirit, and she became a *cause célèbre*. She accepted a movie offer and later gained more notoriety by marrying and then divorcing famed U.S. showbusiness personality Billy Rose.

All Olympic competitors swim to the best of their ability, but America's Lance Larson discovered that doing your best and being the best sometimes is not good enough. In the 100-metre freestyle final in the 1960 Rome Games, Larson had the best electronic time but the "visual"

McDonald's USC Swim Stadium is the site for the swimming and diving events.

EVENT DATE		UNIVERSITY OF SOUTHERN CALIFORNIA
JULY	29	Heats—100m freestyle, women/Heats—100m breaststroke, men/Heats—400m l. medley, men/Heats—200m freestyle, men/Finals—100m freestyle, women/Finals—100m breaststroke, men/Finals—400m l. medley, women/Finals—200m freestyle, men
	30	Heats—100m butterfly, men/Heats—200m freestyle, women/Heats—400m l. medley, men/Heats—200m breaststroke, women/Heats—4 x 200m freestyle relay, men/Finals—100m butterfly, men/Finals—200m freestyle, women/Finals—400m l. medley, men/Finals—200m breaststroke, women/Finals—4 x 200m freestyle relay, men
	31	Heats—400m freestyle, women/Heats—100m freestyle, men/Heats—100m backstroke, women/Heats—200m backstroke, men/Heats—4 x 100m freestyle relay, women/Finals—400m freestyle, women/Finals—100m freestyle, men/Finals—100m backstroke, women/Finals—200m backstroke, men/Finals—4 x 100m freestyle relay, women
AUGUST	2	Heats—400m freestyle, men/Heats—100m butterfly, women/Heats—200m breaststroke, men/Heats—100m breaststroke, women/Heats—4 x 100m freestyle relay, men/Heats—800m freestyle, women/Finals—400m freestyle, men/Finals—100m butterfly, women/Finals—200m breaststroke, men/Finals—100m breaststroke, women/Finals—4 x 100m freestyle relay, men
	3	Heats—200m l. medley, women/Heats—200m butterfly, men/Heats—100m backstroke, men/Heats—4 x 100 medley relay, women/Heats—1500m freestyle, men/Finals—200m l. medley, women/Finals—200m butterfly, men/Finals—800m freestyle, women/Finals—100m backstroke, men/Finals—4 x 100m medley relay, women
	4	Heats—200m l. medley, men/Heats—200m butterfly, women/Heats—200m backstroke, women/Heats—4 x 100m medley relay, men/Finals—200m l. medley, men/Finals—200m butterfly, women/Finals—1500m freestyle, men/Finals—200m backstroke, women/Finals—4 x 100 medley relay, men

Synchronized Swimming

AUGUST	6	Duet routines preliminary
	8	Duet routines figures
	9	Duet routines final

judges were not sure if Larson had made the finishing touch before Australian John Devitt. The chief judge cast the deciding vote for Devitt, touching off an uproar by both the American swimmers and public. The decision stayed. Larson remarked later, ''not winning is what I'm remembered for.''

The Americans also unleashed some anger in a controversy at the 1912 Games in Stockholm. Three racers were eliminated when they missed the semifinals of the men's 100-metre freestyle. The racers argued that they had been told there would be no semifinal race, and upon investigation, officials accepted their story. As a concession to the Americans, the officials decided to hold a special qualifying race for the three racers. Those that bettered the slowest time posted in the semifinal would be eligible for the final. Duke Kahanamoka of Hawaii set a world record in the qualifying race and went on to win the final.

Kahanamoka was involved in another controversy when he won the final of the 100-metre event in the 1920 Antwerp Games. William Herald from Australia protested that he had been impeded by American Norman Ross. There were no lane markers to restrict the swimmers in those days. The officials upheld Herald's protest and ordered a new final. Kahanomoka won that race too.

Perhaps the most embarrassing incident in Olympic aquatic history took place in the platform diving event at the 1928 Games in Amsterdam. Having been told that he was the winner, the Egyptian Earid Simaika quite properly took the winner's spot on the podium for the formalities of the medal presentations.

In the meantime, diving officials discovered they had made an error in calculation. Simaika was not the winner, in fact he was second to American Peter Desjardins. The officials had only one move and they took it. They interrupted the presentation ceremony and asked Simaika to switch places with Desjardins. It was the second gold medal for the Canadian-born Desjardins who had won the springboard event earlier.

Despite its problems, Olympic swimming has had its share of great athletes. There were Americans Johnny Weissmuller, Buster Crabbe, Kahanamoka, John Nabor, and Shirley Babashoff;

Dawn Fraser and Murray Rose from Australia; and Roland Mathes and Kornelia Ender, from East Germany. Some of the names may be familiar to the reader. Weissmuller became famous as the movies ''Tarzan,'' while Crabbe had featured roles in both movies and television. He is best known for his Buck Rogers TV role.

It is believed that man took to the water as soon as he saw animals splashing about in it, but it took a long time before swimming reached the sophisticated stage it enjoys today. The performances of modern-day swimmers overshadow the successful efforts of past Olympians. There has been tremendous advancement through better health care and new training methods and techiques.

Swimming was an outdoor sport until the British discovered it could be enjoyed indoors. By the mid-nineteenth century, there were thousands of Englishmen swimming in large ''tanks.'' The English were content to

move idly in the water. The swimming style of the day was the breaststroke. Speed did not creep into swimming until the ''crawl'' was introduced by Arthur Trudgen, who had returned to England in 1860 after a visit to South America. Trudgen noticed that the natives rapidly moved through the water, the speed generated by an over-the-head stroke while alternating the arm movement. It was this action that Trudgen introduced as a ''crawl.''

Another observant Englishman, Frederick Cavill, was to make an important ''discovery'' a decade later. Cavill had gone to Australia to manage some swim tanks and noticed that the natives were not only using the overhead motion but were also generating added speed through the use of flutter kicks with the feet. He quickly set about to refine this ''Australian crawl.'' His sons Richard and Sydney left for England and the United States to promote the technique.

The technique became popular. No longer did swimmers have to dawdle

Diving off the starting platforms

along in the water by using the breast-stroke and tiring frog-kick. Speed swimming was here to stay and records became even faster when the tumble-turn was invented. By doing a tumble at the end of the pool, a swimmer could use his feet to "push off" from the wall.

Since entering the Olympic swim competitions in the 1904 St. Louis Games, the United States has earned a remarkable 296 medals, 125 of them gold. Australia has picked up 89 medals. And East Germany has emerged as a new power with 64 medals. The East Germans won 11 of 13 events at the 1980 Moscow Olympics. The United States did not participate in the Moscow Games.

Canadian swimmers have also earned considerable respect in Olympic competition. Canada's only gold medal winner is George Hodgson who won the 400- and 1,500-metre freestyle events at the 1912 Games in Stockholm. However, they have won numerous silvers: George Venot in the 1,500-metre freestyle at the 1920 Antwerp Games; famed "Mighty Mouse" Elaine Tanner in the 100- and 200-metre backstroke in the 1968 Games in Mexico City; Ralph Hutton in the 400-metre freestyle, also in 1968; Bruce Robertson in the 100-metre butterfly and Leslie Cliff in the 400-metre individual medley at the 1972 Munich Games; Cheryl Gibson in the 400-metre individual medley at Montreal in 1976 where the men's team of Stephen Pickell, Graham Smith, Clay Evans and Gary MacDonald earned a silver in the 400-metre medley relay. Add to that an impressive 11 bronzes for a grand Olympic total of 21 medals.

GENERAL DESCRIPTION

Swimming is both an individual and team sport. All Olympic races, regardless of distance, are held in a pool that must be 50-metres long and 21-metres wide. This sized pool is known as an "Olympic-size" pool and is used in the Olympic Games. All races are electronically timed.

The swimmers use four strokes. They are: the butterfly, the breaststroke, the backstroke, and the freestyle. There are individual and team events in the Olympics for all four strokes. Some "medley" events require the use of all four strokes by the individual or team.

Here is a list of the various events for all strokes for both men and women scheduled for the Los Angeles Games:

Men

Freestyle (individual) — 100 metres, 200 metres, 400 metres and 1,500 metres.

Freestyle (team) — 4 x 100-metres and 4 x 200-metre relays.

Breaststroke (individual) — 100 metres and 200 metres

Backstroke (individual) — 100 metres and 200 metres

Butterfly (individual) — 100 metres and 200 metres.

Medley (individual) — 200 metres (50-metre legs in each of the butterfly, backstroke, breaststroke and freestyle) and 400 metres (100-metre legs in each of the four strokes).

Medley (team) — 4 x 100 metres (one swimmer for each of the four strokes). The sequence is backstroke, breaststroke, butterfly and freestyle.

Women

Freestyle (individual) — 100 metres,

200 metres, 400 metres, and 800 metres.

Freestyle (team) — 100 metres relay for each of the four team competitors.

Backstroke (individual) — 100 metres and 200 metres.

Breaststroke (individual) — 100 metres and 200 metres

Butterfly (individual) — 100 metres and 200 metres.

Medley (individual) — 200 metres (50-metre legs of the butterfly, backstroke, breaststroke and freestyle in sequence and 400 metres (100-metre legs for the four strokes).

Medley (team) — 4 x 100 metres (one swimmer for each of the four strokes). The medley sequence is backstroke, breaststroke, butterfly and freestyle.

To appreciate the physical demands on the swimmer, let us look at each of the four strokes:

Backstroke — requires the competitor to swim on his or her back throughout the whole race. A somersault may be used to facilitate turns but the swimmer must be on the back before the feet leave the wall. Swimmers use a flutter kick synchronized with the arm strokes.

Breaststroke — the swimmer must keep both shoulders parallel to the water surface while the hands are pushed forward together from the breast and then brought back on or under the surface of the water. All arm movements must be simultaneous. In addition, the legs must do the frog kick and action must be simultaneous. The dolphin kick (a thrashing of both legs) is forbidden.

The head of the racer must not break the surface of the water except at the start or at the turn when the swimmer may take one leg kick and one arm stroke while submerged. The touch at the turns, however, must be made with both hands simultaneously, above or below the water.

Butterfly — requires that the swimmer bring the arms forward to enter the water at some point in front of the shoulders with the arms then being pulled backward simultaneously under the water. From the beginning of the first stroke at the start and on the turns, both shoulders must be parallel to the surface of the water and the swimmer must keep his or her body forward on the breast.

The use of the feet must be simultaneous and any up and down motions in the vertical plane are permitted. Alternating kicks are not permitted. One or more leg kicks, however, is permitted at the start and the turns to bring the swimmer to the surface. In the turn and at the finish, the hands must touch at the same time and at the same level.

Freestyle — the term is used to describe any stroke other than the butterfly, breaststroke or backstroke. The most popular of the freestyle strokes (because it is fastest) is the crawl. In the crawl, the swimmer alternates the arm action, bringing the arm out of the water, over the head, into the water and pulling back. At the same time, the swimmer alternates the kicking action thus giving him or her a steady pull-push motion from arms and legs. The swimmer keeps his or her head in the water, turning the head to one side as desired to gain air.

EQUIPMENT

Pool — for Olympic events, the pool must be 50-metres long and at least 21-metres wide. The pool must have an overall depth of 1.8 metres. For racing, the pool is divided into eight lanes that are 2.5-metres wide and separated by floating markers. The lane markers are usually coloured floats and they must have a distinctive colour change within five metres of each end of the pool.

Starting platforms — are used for races other than backstroke where racers start in the pool. The platforms show the lane number. The nonskid surface should be at least 50-centimetres square.

Timer — electric timers that relate in 100ths of a second.

Dress — men must wear swim trunks and women must wear one-piece suits with no front opening.

TOP COMPETITORS
Women

The competition in the Los Angeles Games is shaping up as a strong battle between the United States and East Germany for the team title. Both countries have outstanding talent.

Ute Geweniger of East Germany is the world-record holder for the 200-metre individual medley and the world-record holder in the 100-metre breaststroke. Teammate Petra Schneider is the world-record holder in the 400-metre individual medley and won that event in the 1980 Games. Cornelia Sirch, the world-

record holder in the 200-metre backstroke, is another member of the East German squad.

American Mary Meagher holds world records for the 100-metre and 200-metre butterfly, while Cynthia Woodhead is the world-record holder in the 200-metre freestyle.

Men

There could be a three-way battle for the team title among the United States, West Germany and the Soviet Union. All of these teams have great talent.

The pride of the Soviet squad is freestyle specialist Vladimir Salnikov who holds world records in the 400 and 1,500 metres and is particularly dominant in the longer distance. He is the first man to swim 1,500 metres in under 15 minutes.

American Rick Carey holds the world records for 100- and 200-metre backstroke while Michael Gross of West Germany is the world-record holder in the 200-metre freestyle and 200-metre butterfly.

TOP CANADIANS
Women

Anne Ottenbrite had the third fastest time in the world for the 100-metre and 200-metre breaststroke in 1983, while Julie Daigneault has been improving in the 400-metre freestyle and was sixth fastest in the world in 1983.

Men

Victor Davis, who recovered from mononucleosis is the world-record holder in the 200-metre breaststroke. Alex Baumann is the world record holder in the 200-metre individual medley event and posted the fastest time for the 400-metre individual medley in 1983.

DIVING

EVENT DATE   **UNIVERSITY OF SOUTHERN CALIFORNIA**

AUGUST	5	Springboard preliminaries, women
	6	Springboard finals, women
	7	Springboard preliminaries, men
	8	Springboard finals, men
	9	Platform preliminaries, women

AUGUST	10	Platform finals, women
	11	Platform preliminaries, men
	12	Platform finals, men

Debbie Fuller, Canada's national tower champion

GENERAL DESCRIPTION

Olympic diving events are restricted to the three-metre springboard and the 10-metre platform (or tower) for both men and women. There are different requirements for each sex.

In platform competition, the men must make four voluntary dives (selected by the diver), each with a limited degree of difficulty as set out in a table issued by the Federation Internationale de Nation Amateur (FINA), the sport's international ruling body, and six voluntary dives without a difficulty limit in the 10-metre event. The women make four voluntary dives with a limited degree of difficulty and four voluntary dives without limit.

In the springboard competition, the men must make five voluntary dives with a limited degree of difficulty and six voluntary dives without limit. The women must make five voluntary dives with a limited degree of difficulty and five voluntary dives without limit.

Prior to the competition, the competitors select their dives from the FINA handbook, which outlines the degree of difficulty for each of the dives. The competitors must write down their choice of dives and how they will execute them — straight, piked, with tuck or free. The written submissions, which also must contain choice of board, must be made at least 24 hours before competition begins.

By selecting the dives in advance, the judges know what to expect when the diver comes to the board. The judges consider each dive for its run, takeoff, flight and entry and must consider the technique and execution of the dive. To find the score for the dive, the high and low marks are discarded and the other scores are multiplied by the official degree of difficulty. Three fifths of this total is the diver's score.

Preliminary or qualifying rounds have become common in recent years with the growth of the sport. The top 12 divers in each of the preliminary events advance to the final round. Competitors must perform all their selected dives in each round.

The dives fall into two groups, those with a maximum degree of difficulty and those without limit. Divers, however, cannot use the same dive in each group. The dives are as follows: a forward dive with the body facing the water; a backward dive with the body facing the board; a reverse dive with the body facing the water; an inward dive with the body facing the board; a twist dive with the body changing direction in the air; and armstand dives, only allowed off the platform.

TECHNICAL TERMS

Start — must be free and unaffected. Can be taken by standing or running forward, backward standing or by handstand (platform only).

Flight — the body may be straight, piked, in a tuck or deemed free.

Straight — the body must be straight at the knees and hips with the feet together and the toes pointed.

Pike — requires the body to be bent at the hips with the legs straight at the knees and with the feet together and toes pointed.

Tuck — requires the body to be bent at the knees and at the hips. The knees and feet should be together with the hands on the lower legs and toes pointed.

Free — requires only that the legs be together and the toes pointed.

Flying somersault — requires that a straight position should be held for half the somersault. The straight position usually comes at the takeoff.

Twist — the diver rotates on a head-through-toes axis and must be within 90 degrees of the dive specified. In straight dives with one half or full twist, the twisting should be done from the board. In the pike, the twist should not be made until the pike position has been reached. The twist can be performed anytime during a somersault dive.

Entry — divers try to enter the water in a vertical position, the body straight, the feet together and the toes pointed. In head-first entries, the arms should stretch beyond the head in line with the body. In feet-first entries, the arms should be held close to the body in a straight line.

EQUIPMENT

Pool — must be a minimum of 1.8-metres deep with a deeper area immediately below the diving boards. There must be a depth of five metres beneath the 10-metre board and at least four metres for the three-metre springboard divers.

Boards — the three-metre springboard and the 10-metre platform are used in the Olympics. Both should be covered with nonskid material. Platforms are surrounded by handrails and reached by steps. Springboards can be adjusted for divers.

Dress — men must wear swim trunks while women must wear one-piece suits.

TOP PERFORMERS

They should come from the United States, Soviet Union and East Germany which have dominated the events in recent Olympics. Falk Hoffman of East Germany won the men's platform title in 1980 in Moscow succeeding Klaus Dibiasi of Italy who had won the title in the three previous Olympics.

Alexsandr Portnov of the Soviet Union won the men's springboard championship at the 1980 Games with Martina Jaschke of East Germany taking the women's platform honours and Irina Kalinina of the Soviet Union taking the women's springboard title.

The Chinese have made remarkable advances in diving and are expected to send some high quality competitors to the Games in Los Angeles.

TOP CANADIANS

Sylvie Bernier of Montreal is the Canadian champion in the springboard event. She won bronze medals at the World University Games and at the 1983 Pan American Games in Venezuela.

Debbie Fuller of Calgary won the platform event at the Canadian championships and earned a silver medal at the Swedish Cup.

Kathy Kelemen of Calgary won the gold medal in the platform event at an international meet in Innsbruck, Austria last summer, with Debbie Fuller taking the silver medal.

*Canadian Robin Wittmeier
in the pike position*

*Wendy Fuller of the
Canadian team in the tuck position*

Canada's David Snively in the flight position

MEDAL WINNERS

SWIMMING (100 metres freestyle) Women

YEAR	PLACE	NAME	COUNTRY
1912	1	**F. Durack**	**Australia**
	2	W. Wylie	Australia
	3	J. Fletcher	Great Britain
1920	1	**E. Bleibtrey**	**U.S.A.**
	2	I. Guest	U.S.A.
	3	F. Schroth	U.S.A.
1924	1	**E. Lackie**	**U.S.A.**
	2	M. Wehselau	U.S.A.
	3	G. Ederle	U.S.A.
1928	1	**A. Osipowich**	**U.S.A.**
	2	E. Garatti	U.S.A.
	3	M. Cooper	Great Britain
1932	1	**H. Madison**	**U.S.A.**
	2	W. den Ouden	Netherlands
	3	E. Saville-Garatti	Netherlands
1936	1	**H. Mastenbroek**	**Netherlands**
	2	J. Campbell	Argentina
	3	G. Arendt	Germany
1948	1	**G. Andersen**	**Denmark**
	2	A. Curtis	U.S.A.
	3	M. Vaessen	Netherlands
1952	1	**K. Szöke**	**Hungary**
	2	J. Termeulen	Netherlands
	3	J. Temes	Hungary
1956	1	**D. Fraser**	**Australia**
	2	L. Crapp	Australia
	3	F. Leech	Australia
1960	1	**D. Fraser**	**Australia**
	2	C. von Saltza	U.S.A.
	3	N. Steward	Great Britain
1964	1	**D. Fraser**	**Australia**
	2	S. Stouder	U.S.A.
	3	K. Ellis	U.S.A.
1968	1	**J. Henne**	**U.S.A.**
	2	S. Pedersen	U.S.A.
	3	L. Gustavson	U.S.A.
1972	1	**S. Neilson**	**U.S.A.**
	2	S. Babashoff	U.S.A.
	3	S. Gould	Australia
1976	1	**K. Enders**	**German Dem. Rep.**
	2	P. Priemer	German Dem. Rep.
	3	E. Brigitha	Holland
1980	1	**B. Krause**	**German Dem. Rep.**
	2	C. Metschuk	German Dem. Rep.
	3	I. Diers	German Dem. Rep.

SWIMMING (200 metres freestyle) Women

YEAR	PLACE	NAME	COUNTRY
1968	1	**D. Meyer**	**U.S.A.**
	2	J. Henne	U.S.A.
	3	J. Barkman	U.S.A.
1972	1	**S. Gould**	**Australia**
	2	S. Babashoff	U.S.A.
	3	K. Rothhammer	U.S.A.
1976	1	**K. Enders**	**German Dem. Rep.**
	2	S. Babashoff	U.S.A.
	3	E. Brigitha	Netherlands
1980	1	**A. Krause**	**German Dem. Rep.**
	2	I. Diers	German Dem. Rep.
	3	C. Schmidt	German Dem. Rep.

SWIMMING (400 metres freestyle) Women

YEAR	PLACE	NAME	COUNTRY
1920	1	**E. Bleibtrey (300m)**	**U.S.A.**
	2	M. Woodbridge	U.S.A.
	3	F. Schroth	U.S.A.
1924	1	**M. Norelius**	**U.S.A.**
	2	H. Wainwright	U.S.A.
	3	G. Ederle	U.S.A.
1928	1	**M. Norelius**	**U.S.A.**
	2	M. Braun	Netherlands
	3	J. McKim	U.S.A.
1932	1	**H. Madison**	**U.S.A.**
	2	L. Kight	U.S.A.
	3	J. Makaal	South Africa

YEAR	PLACE	NAME	COUNTRY
1936	1	H. Mastenbroek	Netherlands
	2	R. Hveger	Denmark
	3	L. Wingard-Kight	U.S.A.
1948	1	A. Curtis	U.S.A.
	2	K. Harup	Denmark
	3	C. Gibson	Great Britain
1952	1	V. Gyenge	Hungary
	2	E. Novák	Hungary
	3	E. Kawamoto	U.S.A.
1956	1	L. Crapp	Australia
	2	D. Fraser	Australia
	3	S. Ruuska	U.S.A.
1960	1	C. Von Saltza	U.S.A.
	2	J. Cederqvist	Sweden
	3	C. Lagerberg	Netherlands
1964	1	V. Duenkel	U.S.A.
	2	M. Ramenofsky	U.S.A.
	3	T. Stickles	U.S.A.
1968	1	D. Meyer	U.S.A.
	2	L. Gustavson	U.S.A.
	3	K. Moras	Australia
1972	1	S. Gould	Australia
	2	N. Calligaris	Italy
	3	G. Wegner	East Germany
1976	1	P. Thuemer	German Dem. Rep.
	2	S. Babashoff	U.S.A.
	3	S. Smith	Canada
1980	1	I. Diers	German Dem. Rep.
	2	P. Schneider	German Dem. Rep.
	3	C. Schmidt	German Dem. Rep.

SWIMMING (800 metres freestyle) Women

YEAR	PLACE	NAME	COUNTRY
1968	1	D. Meyer	U.S.A.
	2	P. Kruse	U.S.A.
	3	M. Ramirez	Mexico
1972	1	K. Rothhammer	U.S.A.
	2	S. Gould	Australia
	3	N. Calligaris	Italy
1976	1	P. Thuemer	German Dem. Rep.
	2	S. Babashoff	U.S.A.
	3	W. Weinberg	U.S.A.
1980	1	M. Ford	Australia
	2	I. Diers	German Dem. Rep.
	3	H. Dahne	German Dem. Rep.

SWIMMING (100 metres backstroke) Women

YEAR	PLACE	NAME	COUNTRY
1924	1	S. Bauer	U.S.A.
	2	P. Harding	Great Britain
	3	A. Riggin	U.S.A.
1928	1	M. Braun	Netherlands
	2	E. King	Great Britain
	3	M. Cooper	Great Britain
1932	1	E. Holm	U.S.A.
	2	P. Mealing	Australia
	3	E. Davies	Great Britain
1936	1	D. Senff	Netherlands
	2	H. Mastenbroek	Netherlands
	3	A. Bridges	U.S.A.
1948	1	K. Harup	Denmark
	2	S. Zimmerman	U.S.A.
	3	J.J. Davies	Australia
1952	1	J. Harrison	South Africa
	2	G. Wielema	Netherlands
	3	J. Stewart	New Zealand
1956	1	J. Grinham	Great Britain
	2	C. Cone	U.S.A.
	3	M. Edwards	Great Britain
1960	1	L. Burke	U.S.A.
	2	N. Steward	Great Britain
	3	S. Tanaka	Japan
1964	1	C. Ferguson	U.S.A.
	2	C. Caron	France
	3	V. Duenkel	U.S.A.
1968	1	K. Hall	U.S.A.
	2	E. Tanner	Canada
	3	J. Swaggerty	U.S.A.
1972	1	M. Belote	U.S.A.
	2	A. Gyarmati	Hungary
	3	S. Atwood	U.S.A.

YEAR	PLACE	NAME	COUNTRY
1976	1	U. Richter	German Dem. Rep.
	2	B. Treiber	German Dem. Rep.
	3	N. Garapick	Canada
1980	1	R. Reinisch	German Dem. Rep.
	2	I. Kleber	German Dem. Rep.
	3	P. Reidel	German Dem. Rep.

SWIMMING (200 metres backstroke) Women

YEAR	PLACE	NAME	COUNTRY
1968	1	P. Watson	U.S.A.
	2	E. Tanner	Canada
	3	K. Hall	U.S.A.
1972	1	M. Belote	U.S.A.
	2	S. Atwood	U.S.A.
	3	D. Gurr	Canada
1976	1	U. Richter	German Dem. Rep.
	2	B. Treiber	German Dem. Rep.
	3	N. Garapick	Canada
1980	1	R. Reinisch	German Dem. Rep.
	2	C. Polit	German Dem. Rep.
	3	B. Treiber	German Dem. Rep.

SWIMMING (100 metres breaststroke) Women

YEAR	PLACE	NAME	COUNTRY
1968	1	D. Bjedov	Yugoslavia
	2	G. Prozumen-schtschikova	U.S.S.R.
	3	S. Wichman	U.S.A.
1972	1	C. Carr	U.S.A.
	2	G. Stepanova	U.S.S.R.
	3	B. Whitfield	Australia
1976	1	H. Anke	German Dem. Rep.
	2	L. Rusanova	U.S.S.R.
	3	M. Koshevaia	U.S.S.R.
1980	1	U. Geweniger	German Dem. Rep.
	2	E. Vasilkova	U.S.S.R.
	3	S. Neilsson	Denmark

SWIMMING (200 metres breaststroke) Women

YEAR	PLACE	NAME	COUNTRY
1924	1	L. Morton	Great Britain
	2	A. Geraghty	U.S.A.
	3	G. Carson	Great Britain
1928	1	H. Schrader	Germany
	2	M. Baron	Netherlands
	3	L. Mühe-Hildensheim	Germany
1932	1	C. Dennis	Australia
	2	H. Maehata	Japan
	3	E. Jacobsen	Denmark
1936	1	H. Maehata	Japan
	2	M. Genenger	Germany
	3	I. Sörensen	Denmark
1948	1	P. van Vliet	Netherlands
	2	B. Lyons	Australia
	3	E. Novák	Hungary
1952	1	E. Székely	Hungary
	2	E. Novak	Hungary
	3	H. Gordon	Great Britain
1956	1	U. Happe	Germany
	2	E. Székely	Hungary
	3	E. Ten Elsen	Germany
1960	1	A. Lonsbrough	Great Britain
	2	W. Urselmann	Germany
	3	B. Göbel	Germany
1964	1	G. Prozumen-schtschikova	U.S.S.R.
	2	C. Kolb	U.S.A.
	3	S. Babanina	U.S.S.R.
1968	1	S. Wichman	U.S.A.
	2	D. Bjedov	Yugoslavia
	3	G. Prozumen-schtschikova	U.S.S.R.
1972	1	B. Whitfield	Australia
	2	D. Schoenfield	U.S.A.
	3	G. Stepanova	U.S.S.R.
1976	1	M. Koshevaia	U.S.S.R.
	2	M. Iurchenia	U.S.S.R.
	3	L. Rusanova	U.S.S.R.
1980	1	L. Kachushite	U.S.S.R.
	2	S. Varganova	U.S.S.R.
	3	Y. Bogdanova	U.S.S.R.

SWIMMING (100 metres butterfly) Women

YEAR	PLACE	NAME	COUNTRY
1956	1	S. Mann	U.S.A.
	2	N.J. Ramey	U.S.A.
	3	M.J. Sears	U.S.A.
1960	1	C. Schuler	U.S.A.
	2	M. Heemskerk	Netherlands
	3	J. Andrew	Australia
1964	1	S. Stouder	U.S.A.
	2	A. Kok	Netherlands
	3	K. Ellis	U.S.A.
1968	1	L. McClements	Australia
	2	E. Daniel	U.S.A.
	3	S. Shields	U.S.A.
1972	1	M. Aoki	Japan
	2	R. Beier	Germany
	3	A. Gyarmati	Hungary
1976	1	K. Ender	German Dem. Rep.
	2	A. Pollack	German Dem. Rep.
	3	W. Boglioli	U.S.A.
1980	1	C. Metschuck	German Dem. Rep.
	2	A. Pollack	German Dem. Rep.
	3	C. Knacke	German Dem. Rep.

SWIMMING (200 metres butterfly) Women

YEAR	PLACE	NAME	COUNTRY
1968	1	A. Kok	Netherlands
	2	H. Lindner	East Germany
	3	E. Daniel	U.S.A.
1972	1	K. Moe	U.S.A.
	2	L. Colella	U.S.A.
	3	E. Daniel	U.S.A.
1976	1	A. Pollack	German Dem. Rep.
	2	U. Tauber	German Dem. Rep.
	3	R. Gabriel	German Dem. Rep.
1980	1	I. Geissler	German Dem. Rep.
	2	S. Schonrock	German Dem. Rep.
	3	M. Ford	Australia

SWIMMING (400 metres individual medley) Women

YEAR	PLACE	NAME	COUNTRY
1964	1	D. de Varona	U.S.A.
	2	S. Finneran	U.S.A.
	3	M. Randall	U.S.A.
1968	1	C. Kolb	U.S.A.
	2	L. Vidali	U.S.A.
	3	S. Steinbach	East Germany
1972	1	G. Neall	Australia
	2	L. Cliff	Canada
	3	N. Calligaris	Italy
1976	1	U. Tauber	German Dem. Rep.
	2	C. Gibson	Canada
	3	B. Smith	Canada
1980	1	P. Schneider	German Dem. Rep.
	2	S. Davies	United Kingdom
	3	A. Czopek	Poland

SWIMMING (400 metres freestyle relay) Women

YEAR	PLACE	NAME	COUNTRY
1912	1		Great Britain
	2		Germany
	3		Austria
1920	1		U.S.A.
	2		Great Britain
	3		Sweden
1924	1		U.S.A.
	2		Great Britain
	3		Sweden
1928	1		U.S.A.
	2		Great Britain
	3		South Africa
1932	1		U.S.A.
	2		Netherlands
	3		Great Britain
1936	1		Netherlands
	2		Germany
	3		U.S.A.
1948	1		U.S.A.
	2		Denmark
	3		Netherlands

YEAR	PLACE	NAME	COUNTRY
1952	1		**Hungary**
	2		Netherlands
	3		U.S.A.
1956	1		**Australia**
	2		U.S.A.
	3		South Africa
1960	1		**U.S.A.**
	2		Australia
	3		Germany
1964	1		**U.S.A.**
	2		Australia
	3		Netherlands
1968	1		**U.S.A.**
	2		East Germany
	3		Canada
1972	1		**U.S.A.**
	2		East Germany
	3		Germany
1976	1		**U.S.A.**
	2		East Germany
	3		Canada
1980	1		**East Germany**
	2		Sweden
	3		Netherlands

SWIMMING (400 metres medley relay) Women

YEAR	PLACE	NAME	COUNTRY
1960	1		**U.S.A.**
	2		Australia
	3		Germany
1964	1		**U.S.A.**
	2		Netherlands
	3		U.S.S.R.
1968	1		**U.S.A.**
	2		Australia
	3		Germany
1972	1		**U.S.A.**
	2		East Germany
	3		Germany
1976	1		**East Germany**
	2		U.S.A.
	3		Canada
1980	1		**East Germany**
	2		Great Britain
	3		U.S.S.R.

SWIMMING (100 metres freestyle) Men

YEAR	PLACE	NAME	COUNTRY
1896	1	**A. Hajos**	**Hungary**
	2	E. Choraphas	Greece
	3	O. Herschmann	Austria
1904	1	**Z. Halmay (100 yds)**	**Hungary**
	2	C. Daniels	U.S.A.
	3	S. Leary	U.S.A.
1908	1	**C. Daniels**	**U.S.A.**
	2	Z. Halmay	Hungary
	3	H. Julin	Sweden
1912	1	**D. Kahanamoku**	**U.S.A.**
	2	C. Healy	Australia
	3	K. Huszagh	U.S.A.
1920	1	**D. Kahanamoku**	**U.S.A.**
	2	P. Kealoha	U.S.A.
	3	W. Harris	U.S.A.
1924	1	**J. Weissmuller**	**U.S.A.**
	2	D. Kahanamoku	U.S.A.
	3	S. Kahanamoku	U.S.A.
1928	1	**J. Weissmuller**	**U.S.A.**
	2	I. Bárány	Hungary
	3	K. Takaishi	Japan
1932	1	**Y. Miyazaki**	**Japan**
	2	T. Kawaishi	Japan
	3	S. Schwartz	U.S.A.
1936	1	**F. Csik**	**Hungary**
	2	M. Yusa	Japan
	3	S. Arai	Japan
1948	1	**W. Ris**	**U.S.A.**
	2	A. Ford	U.S.A.
	3	G. Kádas	Hungary
1952	1	**C.C. Scholes**	**U.S.A.**
	2	H. Suzuki	Japan
	3	G. Larsson	Sweden
1956	1	**J. Henricks**	**Australia**
	2	J. Devitt	Australia
	3	G. Chapman	Australia
1960	1	**J. Devitt**	**Australia**
	2	L. Larson	U.S.A.
	3	M. dos Santos	Brazil
1964	1	**D. Schollander**	**U.S.A.**
	2	R. McGregor	Great Britain
	3	H-J. Klein	Germany
1968	1	**M. Wenden**	**Australia**
	2	K. Walsh	U.S.A.
	3	M. Spitz	U.S.A.
1972	1	**M. Spitz**	**U.S.A.**
	2	J. Heidenreich	U.S.A.
	3	V. Bure	U.S.S.R.
1976	1	**J. Montgomery**	**U.S.A.**
	2	J. Babashoff	U.S.A.
	3	P. Nocke	W. Germany
1980	1	**J. Woithe**	**German Dem. Rep.**
	2	P. Holmertz	Sweden
	3	P. Johansson	Sweden

SWIMMING (200 metres freestyle) Men

YEAR	PLACE	NAME	COUNTRY
1900	1	**F. Lane**	**Australia**
	2	Z. Halmay	Hungary
	3	K. Ruberl	Austria
1904	1	**C. Daniels**	**U.S.A.**
	2	F. Gailey	U.S.A.
	3	E. Rausch	Germany
1968	1	**M. Wendon**	**Australia**
	2	D. Schollander	U.S.A.
	3	J. Nelson	U.S.A.
1972	1	**M. Spitz**	**U.S.A.**
	2	S. Genter	U.S.A.
	3	W. Lampe	Germany
1976	1	**B. Furniss**	**U.S.A.**
	2	J. Naber	U.S.A.
	3	J. Montgomery	U.S.A.
1980	1	**S. Kopliakov**	**U.S.S.R.**
	2	A. Krylov	U.S.S.R.
	3	G. Brewer	Australia

SWIMMING (400 metres freestyle) Men

YEAR	PLACE	NAME	COUNTRY
1896	1	**P. Neumann (500m)**	**Austria**
	2	A. Pepanos	Greece
	3	E. Choraphas	Greece
1904	1	**C. Daniels (440 yds)**	**U.S.A.**
	2	F. Gailey	U.S.A.
	3	O. Wahle	Austria
1908	1	**H. Taylor**	**Great Britain**
	2	F. Beaurepaire	Australia
	3	O. Scheff	Austria
1912	1	**G. Hodgson**	**Canada**
	2	J. Hatfield	Great Britain
	3	H. Hardwick	Australia
1920	1	**N. Ross**	**U.S.A.**
	2	L. Langer	U.S.A.
	3	G. Vernot	Canada
1924	1	**J. Weissmuller**	**U.S.A.**
	2	A. Borg	Sweden
	3	A. Charlton	Australia
1928	1	**A. Zorilla**	**Argentina**
	2	A. Charlton	Australia
	3	A. Borg	Sweden
1932	1	**C. Crabbe**	**U.S.A.**
	2	J. Taris	France
	3	T. Oyokota	Japan
1936	1	**J. Medica**	**U.S.A.**
	2	S. Uto	Japan
	3	S. Makino	Japan
1948	1	**W. Smith**	**U.S.A.**
	2	J. McLane	U.S.A.
	3	J. Marshall	Australia
1952	1	**J. Boiteux**	**France**
	2	F. Konno	U.S.A.
	3	P. Östrand	Sweden
1956	1	**M. Rose**	**Australia**
	2	T. Yamanaka	Japan
	3	G. Breen	U.S.A.
1960	1	**M. Rose**	**Australia**
	2	T. Yamanaka	Japan
	3	J. Konrads	Australia
1964	1	**D. Schollander**	**U.S.A.**
	2	F. Wiegand	Germany
	3	A. Wood	Australia
1968	1	**M. Burton**	**U.S.A.**
	2	R. Hutton	Canada
	3	A. Mosconi	France
1972	1*	**R. Demont**	**U.S.A.**
	2	B. Cooper	Australia
	3	S. Genter	U.S.A.
1976	1	**B. Goodell**	**U.S.A.**
	2	T. Shaw	U.S.A.
	3	Y. Raskatov	U.S.S.R.
1980	1	**V. Salnikov**	**U.S.S.R.**
	2	A. Krylov	U.S.S.R.
	3	I. Stukolkin	U.S.S.R.

* Disqualified by positive dope test from receiving medal — record still stands.

SWIMMING (1,500 metres freestyle) Men

YEAR	PLACE	NAME	COUNTRY
1896	1	**A. Hajós (1200m)**	**Hungary**
	2	J. Andreou	Greece
	3	E. Choraphas	Greece
1900	1	**J. Jarvis (1000m)**	**Great Britain**
	2	O. Wahle	Austria
	3	Z. Halmay	Hungary
1904	1	**E. Rausch (1 mile)**	**Germany**
	2	G. Kiss	Hungary
	3	F. Gailey	U.S.A.
1908	1	**H. Taylor**	**Great Britain**
	2	T. Battersby	Great Britain
	3	F. Beaurepaire	Australia
1912	1	**G. Hodgson**	**Canada**
	2	J. Hatfield	Great Britain
	3	H. Hardwick	Australia
1920	1	**N. Ross**	**U.S.A.**
	2	G. Vernot	Canada
	3	F. Beaurepaire	Australia
1924	1	**A. Charlton**	**Australia**
	2	A. Borg	Sweden
	3	F. Beaurepaire	Australia
1928	1	**A. Borg**	**Sweden**
	2	A. Charlton	Australia
	3	C. Crabbe	U.S.A.
1932	1	**K. Kitamura**	**Japan**
	2	S. Makino	Japan
	3	J. Christy	U.S.A.
1936	1	**N. Terada**	**Japan**
	2	J. Medica	U.S.A.
	3	S. Uto	Japan
1948	1	**J. McLane**	**U.S.A.**
	2	J. Marshall	Australia
	3	G. Mitró	Hungary
1952	1	**F. Konno**	**U.S.A.**
	2	S. Hashizume	Japan
	3	T. Okamoto	Brazil
1956	1	**M. Rose**	**Australia**
	2	T. Yamanaka	Japan
	3	G. Breen	U.S.A.
1960	1	**J. Konrads**	**Australia**
	2	M. Rose	Australia
	3	G. Breen	U.S.A.
1964	1	**R. Windle**	**Australia**
	2	J. Nelson	U.S.A.
	3	A. Wood	Australia
1968	1	**M. Burton**	**U.S.A.**
	2	J. Kinsella	U.S.A.
	3	G. Brough	Australia
1972	1	**M. Burton**	**U.S.A.**
	2	G. Windeatt	Australia
	3	D. Northway	U.S.A.
1976	1	**B. Goodell**	**U.S.A.**
	2	B. Hackett	U.S.A.
	3	S. Holland	Australia
1980	1	**V. Salnikov**	**U.S.S.R.**
	2	A. Chaev	U.S.S.R.
	3	M. Metzker	Australia

SWIMMING (100 metres backstroke) Men

YEAR	PLACE	NAME	COUNTRY
1904	1	**W. Brack (100 yds)**	**Germany**
	2	G. Hoffmann	Germany
	3	G. Zacharias	Germany
1908	1	**A. Bieberstein**	**Germany**
	2	L. Dam	Denmark
	3	H.N. Haresnape	Great Britain
1912	1	**H. Hebner**	**U.S.A.**
	2	O. Fahr	Germany
	3	P. Kellner	Germany
1920	1	**W. Kealoha**	**U.S.A.**
	2	R.K. Kegeris	U.S.A.
	3	G. Blitz	Belgium
1924	1	**W. Kealoha**	**U.S.A.**
	2	P. Wyatt	U.S.A.
	3	K. Bartha	Hungary
1928	1	**G. Kojac**	**U.S.A.**
	2	W. Laufer	U.S.A.
	3	P. Wyatt	U.S.A.
1932	1	**M. Kiyokawa**	**Japan**
	2	T. Irie	Japan
	3	K. Kawatsu	Japan
1936	1	**A. Kiefer**	**U.S.A.**
	2	A. Van de Weghe	U.S.A.
	3	M. Kiyokawa	Japan
1948	1	**A. Stack**	**U.S.A.**
	2	R. Cowell	U.S.A.
	3	G. Vallerey	France
1952	1	**Y. Oyakawa**	**Japan**
	2	G. Bozon	France
	3	J. Taylor	U.S.A.
1956	1	**D. Theile**	**Australia**
	2	J. Monckton	Australia
	3	F. McKinney	U.S.A.
1960	1	**D. Theile**	**Australia**
	2	F. McKinney	U.S.A.
	3	R. Bennett	U.S.A.
1968	1	**R. Matthes**	**East Germany**
	2	C. Hickcox	U.S.A.
	3	R. Mills	U.S.A.
1972	1	**R. Matthes**	**East Germany**
	2	M. Stamm	U.S.A.
	3	J. Murphy	U.S.A.
1976	1	**J. Naber**	**U.S.A.**
	2	P. Rocca	U.S.A.
	3	R. Mathes	German Dem. Rep.
1980	1	**B. Baron**	**Sweden**
	2	V. Kuznetsov	U.S.S.R.
	3	V. Dolgov	U.S.S.R.

SWIMMING (200 metres backstroke) Men

YEAR	PLACE	NAME	COUNTRY
1900	1	**E. Hoppenburg**	**Germany**
	2	K. Ruberl	Austria
	3	J. Drost	Netherlands
1964	1	**J. Graef**	**U.S.A.**
	2	G. Dilley	U.S.A.
	3	R. Bennett	U.S.A.
1968	1	**R. Matthes**	**East Germany**
	2	M. Ivey	U.S.A.
	3	J. Horsley	U.S.A.
1972	1	**R. Matthes**	**East Germany**
	2	M. Stamm	U.S.A.
	3	M. Ivey	U.S.A.
1976	1	**J. Naber**	**U.S.A.**
	2	P. Rocca	U.S.A.
	3	D. Harrigan	U.S.A.
1980	1	**S. Wladar**	**Hungary**
	2	Z. Verraszto	Hungary
	3	M. Kerry	Australia

SWIMMING (100 metres breaststroke) Men

YEAR	PLACE	NAME	COUNTRY
1968	1	**D. McKenzie**	**U.S.A.**
	2	V. Kossinsky	U.S.S.R.
	3	N. Pankin	U.S.S.R.
1972	1	**N. Taguchi**	**Japan**
	2	T. Bruce	U.S.A.
	3	J. Hencken	U.S.A.
1976	1	**J. Hencken**	**U.S.A.**
	2	D. Wilkie	United Kingdom
	3	A. Ivozaytis	U.S.S.R.
1980	1	**D. Goodhew**	**United Kingdom**
	2	A. Miskarov	U.S.S.R.
	3	P. Evans	Australia

SWIMMING (200 metres breaststroke) Men

YEAR	PLACE	NAME	COUNTRY
1908	1	**F. Holman**	**Great Britain**
	2	W. Robinson	Great Britain
	3	P. Hansson	Sweden
1912	1	**W. Bathe**	**Germany**
	2	W. Lützow	Germany
	3	K. Malisch	Germany
1920	1	**H. Malmroth**	**Sweden**
	2	T. Henning	Sweden
	3	A. Aaltonen	Finland
1924	1	**R. Skelton**	**U.S.A.**
	2	J. de Combe	Belgium
	3	W. Kirschbaum	U.S.A.
1928	1	**Y. Tsuruta**	**Japan**
	2	E. Rademacher	Germany
	3	T. Yldefonzo	Philippines
1932	1	**Y. Tsuruta**	**Japan**
	2	R. Koike	Japan
	3	T. Yldefonzo	Philippines
1936	1	**T. Hamuro**	**Japan**
	2	E. Sietas	Germany
	3	R. Koike	Japan
1948	1	**J. Verdeur**	**U.S.A.**
	2	K. Carter	U.S.A.
	3	R. Sohl	U.S.A.
1952	1	**J. Davies**	**Australia**
	2	B. Stassforth	U.S.A.
	3	H. Klein	Germany
1956	1	**M. Furukawa**	**Japan**
	2	M. Yoshimura	Japan
	3	C. Yunitschev	U.S.S.R.
1960	1	**W. Mulliken**	**U.S.A.**
	2	Y. Osaki	Japan
	3	W. Mensonides	Netherlands
1964	1	**I. O'Brien**	**Australia**
	2	G. Prokopenko	U.S.S.R.
	3	C. Jastremski	U.S.A.
1968	1	**F. Muñoz**	**Mexico**
	2	V. Kossinsky	U.S.S.R.
	3	B. Job	U.S.A.
1972	1	**J. Hencken**	**U.S.A.**
	2	D. Wilkie	Great Britain
	3	N. Taguchi	Japan
1976	1	**D. Wilkie**	**United Kingdom**
	2	J. Hencken	U.S.A.
	3	R. Colella	U.S.A.
1980	1	**R. Zulpa**	**U.S.S.R.**
	2	A. Vermes	Hungary
	3	A. Miskarov	U.S.S.R.

SWIMMING (100 metres butterfly) Men

YEAR	PLACE	NAME	COUNTRY
1968	1	**D. Russell**	**U.S.A.**
	2	M. Spitz	U.S.A.
	3	R. Wales	U.S.A.
1972	1	**M. Spitz**	**U.S.A.**
	2	B. Robertson	Canada
	3	J. Heidenreich	U.S.A.
1976	1	**M. Vogel**	**U.S.A.**
	2	J. Bottom	U.S.A.
	3	G. Hall	U.S.A.
1980	1	**P. Arvidsson**	**Sweden**
	2	R. Pyttel	United Kingdom
	3	D. Lopaz	Spain

SWIMMING (200 metres butterfly) Men

YEAR	PLACE	NAME	COUNTRY
1956	1	**W. Yorzyk**	**U.S.A.**
	2	T. Ishimoto	Japan
	3	G. Tumpek	Hungary
1960	1	**M. Troy**	**U.S.A.**
	2	N. Hayes	Australia
	3	J.D. Gillanders	U.S.A.

YEAR	PLACE	NAME	COUNTRY
1964	1	**K. Berry**	**Australia**
	2	C. Robie	U.S.A.
	3	F. Schmidt	U.S.A.
1968	1	**C. Robie**	**U.S.A.**
	2	M. Woodroffe	Great Britain
	3	J. Ferris	U.S.A.
1972	1	**M. Spitz**	**U.S.A.**
	2	G. Hall	U.S.A.
	3	R. Backhaus	U.S.A.
1976	1	**M. Bruner**	**U.S.A.**
	2	S. Gregg	U.S.A.
	3	W. Forrester	U.S.A.
1980	1	**S. Fesenko**	**U.S.S.R.**
	2	P. Hubble	United Kingdom
	3	R. Pyttel	German Dem. Rep.

SWIMMING (400 metres individual medley) Men

YEAR	PLACE	NAME	COUNTRY
1964	1	**R. Roth**	**U.S.A.**
	2	R. Saari	U.S.A.
	3	G. Hetz	Germany
1968	1	**C. Hickcox**	**U.S.A.**
	2	G. Hall	U.S.A.
	3	M. Holthaus	Germany
1972	1	**G. Larsson**	**Sweden**
	2	T. McKee	U.S.A.
	3	A. Hargitay	Hungary
1976	1	**R. Strachan**	**U.S.A.**
	2	T. McGee	U.S.A.
	3	A. Smirnov	U.S.S.R.
1980	1	**A. Sidorenko**	**U.S.S.R.**
	2	S. Fesenko	U.S.S.R.
	3	Z. Verraszto	Hungary

SWIMMING (400 metres medley relay) Men

YEAR	PLACE	COUNTRY
1960	1	**U.S.A.**
	2	Australia
	3	Japan
1964	1	**U.S.A.**
	2	Germany
	3	Australia
1968	1	**U.S.A.**
	2	East Germany
	3	U.S.S.R.
1972	1	**U.S.A.**
	2	East Germany
	3	Canada
1976	1	**U.S.A.**
	2	Canada
	3	W. Germany
1980	1	**Australia**
	2	U.S.S.R.
	3	United Kingdom

SWIMMING (800 metres freestyle relay) Men

YEAR	PLACE	COUNTRY
1908	1	**Great Britain**
	2	Hungary
	3	U.S.A.
1912	1	**Australia**
	2	U.S.A.
	3	Great Britain
1920	1	**U.S.A.**
	2	Australia
	3	Great Britain
1924	1	**U.S.A.**
	2	Australia
	3	Sweden
1928	1	**U.S.A.**
	2	Japan
	3	Canada
1932	1	**Japan**
	2	U.S.A.
	3	Hungary
1936	1	**Japan**
	2	U.S.A.
	3	Hungary
1948	1	**U.S.A.**
	2	Hungary
	3	France

YEAR	PLACE	NAME	COUNTRY
1952	1		U.S.A.
	2		Japan
	3		France
1956	1		Australia
	2		U.S.A.
	3		U.S.S.R.
1960	1		U.S.A.
	2		Japan
	3		Australia
1964	1		U.S.A.
	2		Germany
	3		Japan
1968	1		U.S.A.
	2		Australia
	3		U.S.S.R.
1972	1		U.S.A.
	2		Germany
	3		U.S.S.R.
1976	1		U.S.A.
	2		U.S.S.R.
	3		United Kingdom
1980	1		U.S.S.R.
	2		E. Germany
	3		Brazil

DIVING (springboard) Men

YEAR	PLACE	NAME	COUNTRY
1908	1	A. Zürner	Germany
	2	R. Behrens	Germany
	3	G.W. Gaidzik	U.S.A.
1912	1	P. Günther	Germany
	2	H. Luber	Germany
	3	K. Behrens	Germany
1920	1	L. Kuehn	U.S.A.
	2	C. Pinkston	U.S.A.
	3	L. Balbach	U.S.A.
1924	1	A. White	U.S.A.
	2	P. Desjardins	U.S.A.
	3	C. Pinkston	U.S.A.
1928	1	P. Desjardins	U.S.A.
	2	M. Galitzen	U.S.A.
	3	F. Simaika	Egypt
1932	1	M. Galitzen	U.S.A.
	2	H. Smith	U.S.A.
	3	R. Degener	U.S.A.
1936	1	R. Degener	U.S.A.
	2	M. Wayne	U.S.A.
	3	A. Greene	U.S.A.
1948	1	B. Harlan	U.S.A.
	2	M. Anderson	U.S.A.
	3	S. Lee	U.S.A.
1952	1	D. Browning	U.S.A.
	2	M. Anderson	U.S.A.
	3	R. Clotworthy	U.S.A.
1956	1	R. Clotworthy	U.S.A.
	2	D. Harper	U.S.A.
	3	J.C. Pérez	Mexico
1960	1	G. Tobian	U.S.A.
	2	S. Hall	U.S.A.
	3	J. Botella	Mexico
1964	1	K. Sitzberger	U.S.A.
	2	F. Gorman	U.S.A.
	3	L. Andreasen	U.S.A.
1968	1	B. Wrightson	U.S.A.
	2	K. Dibiasi	Italy
	3	J. Henry	U.S.A.
1972	1	V. Vasin	U.S.S.R.
	2	F. Cagnotto	Italy
	3	C. Lincoln	U.S.A.
1976	1	P. Boggs	U.S.A.
	2	F. Cagnotto	Italy
	3	A. Kosenkov	U.S.S.R.
1980	1	A. Portnov	U.S.S.R.
	2	C. Giron	Mexico
	3	F. Cagnotto	Italy

DIVING (platform) Men

YEAR	PLACE	NAME	COUNTRY
1904	1	G. Sheldon	U.S.A.
	2	G. Hoffmann	Germany
	3	A. Braunschweiger/ F.H. Kehoe	Germany/ U.S.A.
1908	1	H. Johansson	Sweden
	2	K. Malström	Sweden
	3	A. Spangberg	Sweden
1912	1	E. Adlerz	Sweden
	2	A. Zürner	Germany
	3	G. Blomgren	Sweden
1920	1	C. Pinkston	U.S.A.
	2	E. Adlerz	Sweden
	3	H. Prieste	U.S.A.
1924	1	A. White	U.S.A.
	2	D. Fall	U.S.A.
	3	C. Pinkston	U.S.A.
1928	1	P. Desjardins	U.S.A.
	2	F. Simaika	Egypt
	3	M. Galitzen	U.S.A.
1932	1	H. Smith	U.S.A.
	2	M. Galitzen	U.S.A.
	3	F. Kurtz	U.S.A.
1936	1	M. Wayne	U.S.A.
	2	E. Root	U.S.A.
	3	H. Stork	Germany
1948	1	S. Lee	U.S.A.
	2	B. Harlan	U.S.A.
	3	J.C. Pérez	Mexico
1952	1	S. Lee	U.S.A.
	2	J.C. Pérez	Mexico
	3	G. Haase	Germany
1956	1	J.C. Pérez	Mexico
	2	G. Tobian	U.S.A.
	3	R. Connor	U.S.A.
1960	1	R. Webster	U.S.A.
	2	G. Tobian	U.S.A.
	3	B. Phelps	Great Britain
1964	1	R. Webster	U.S.A.
	2	K. Dibiasi	Italy
	3	T. Gompf	U.S.A.
1968	1	K. Dibiasi	Italy
	2	A. Gaxiola	Mexico
	3	E. Young	U.S.A.
1972	1	K. Dibiasi	Italy
	2	R. Rydze	U.S.A.
	3	F. Cagnotto	Italy
1976	1	K. Dibiasi	Italy
	2	G. Louganis	U.S.A.
	3	V. Aleynik	U.S.S.R.
1980	1	F. Hoffmann	German Dem. Rep.
	2	V. Aleinik	U.S.S.R.
	3	D. Ambartsumyan	U.S.S.R.

DIVING (springboard) Women

YEAR	PLACE	NAME	COUNTRY
1920	1	A. Riggin	U.S.A.
	2	H. Wainwright	U.S.A.
	3	T. Payne	U.S.A.
1924	1	E. Becker	U.S.A.
	2	A. Riggin	U.S.A.
	3	C. Fletcher	U.S.A.
1928	1	H. Meany	U.S.A.
	2	D. Poynton	U.S.A.
	3	G. Coleman	U.S.A.
1932	1	G. Coleman	U.S.A.
	2	K. Rawls	U.S.A.
	3	J. Fauntz	U.S.A.
1936	1	M. Gestring	U.S.A.
	2	K. Rawls	U.S.A.
	3	D. Hill-Poynton	U.S.A.
1948	1	V. Draves	U.S.A.
	2	Z.A. Olsen	U.S.A.
	3	P. Elsener	U.S.A.
1952	1	P. McCormick	U.S.A.
	2	M. Moreau	France
	3	Z.A. Jensen-Olsen	U.S.A.
1956	1	P. McCormick	U.S.A.
	2	J. Stunyo	U.S.A.
	3	I. MacDonald	Canada
1960	1	I. Engel-Krämer	Germany
	2	P.J. Pope-Myers	U.S.A.
	3	E. Ferris	Great Britain
1964	1	I. Engel-Krämer	Germany
	2	J. Collier	U.S.A.
	3	M. Willard	U.S.A.
1968	1	S. Gossick	U.S.A.
	2	T. Pogoscheva	U.S.S.R.
	3	K. O'Sullivan	U.S.A.
1972	1	M. King	U.S.A.
	2	U. Knape	Sweden
	3	M. Janicke	East Germany
1976	1	J. Chandler	U.S.A.
	2	C. Kohler	German Dem. Rep.
	3	C. McIngvale	U.S.A.
1980	1	I. Kalinina	U.S.S.R.
	2	M. Proeber	German Dem. Rep.
	3	K. Guthke	German Dem. Rep.

DIVING (platform) Women

YEAR	PLACE	NAME	COUNTRY
1912	1	G. Johansson	Sweden
	2	L. Regnell	Sweden
	3	I. White	Great Britain
1920	1	S. Fryland-Clausen	Denmark
	2	E. Armstrong	Great Britain
	3	E. Ollivier	Sweden
1924	1	C. Smith	U.S.A.
	2	E. Becker	U.S.A.
	3	H. Töpel	Sweden
1928	1	E. Pinkston-Becker	U.S.A.
	2	G. Coleman	U.S.A.
	3	L. Sjöqvist	Sweden
1932	1	D. Poynton	U.S.A.
	2	G. Coleman	U.S.A.
	3	M. Roper	U.S.A.
1936	1	D. Hill-Poynton	U.S.A.
	2	V. Dunn	U.S.A.
	3	K. Köhler	Germany
1948	1	V. Draves	U.S.A.
	2	P. Elsener	U.S.A.
	3	B. Christoffersen	Denmark
1952	1	P. McCormick	U.S.A.
	2	P.J. Myers	U.S.A.
	3	J. Irwin-Stover	U.S.A.
1956	1	P. McCormick	U.S.A.
	2	J. Irwin	U.S.A.
	3	P.J. Myers	U.S.A.
1960	1	I. Engel-Krämer	Germany
	2	P.J. Pope-Myers	U.S.A.
	3	N. Krutova	U.S.S.R.
1964	1	L. Bush	U.S.A.
	2	I. Engel-Krämer	Germany
	3	G. Alekseyeva	U.S.S.R.
1968	1	M. Duchková	Czechoslovakia
	2	N. Lobanova	U.S.S.R.
	3	A. Peterson	U.S.A.
1972	1	U. Knape	Sweden
	2	M. Duchková	Czechoslovakia
	3	M. Janicke	East Germany
1976	1	E. Vaytsekhovskaya	U.S.S.R.
	2	U. Knape	Sweden
	3	D. Wilson	U.S.A.
1980	1	M. Jaschke	German Dem. Rep.
	2	S. Emirzyan	U.S.S.R.
	3	L. Tsotadze	U.S.S.R.

SYNCHRONIZED

Synchronized swimming was first demonstrated at the 1952 Summer Olympics in Helsinki, Finland.

HISTORY

Synchronized swimming originated in Montreal where women swimming enthusiasts in the 1920s developed a series of routines that were both demanding and entertaining. In 1924, the first championship was held using rules based upon the techniques required by the Royal Lifesaving Society for its highest awards. The following year, regulations were finalized for the Canadian championships and in 1926 the Frances C. Gale trophy, named after a patron of the sport, was presented for "graceful and ornamental swimming."

In North America, the sport spread slowly, perhaps because of the rarity of practice pools or because synchronized swimming demands so much from a competitor. As one of the best conditioned athletes in the world, the synchronized swimmer must have superb breath control while performing a multitude of movements.

Yet, it was this tremendous demand on a person's physical capabilities and creativity that helped the sport grow in the past decades. It was "demonstrated" by swimmers from the United States and Canada at the 1952 Olympic Games in Helsinki, Finland. They were captivating, and impressed representatives from Holland, Germany and France who went home determined to start synchronized swimming programmes. By the time world championships took place in Copenhagen in 1970, there were teams from 11 countries with Canada winning gold medals in duet and team, and silver and bronze in solo.

Canada, the main booster of the sport, has taken an active part in its growth. In 1977, Canada held "Synchro Camp '77," the first international training camp for synchronized swimming. Sixteen enthusiastic countries attended the camp.

A major breakthrough for the sport came with the inclusion of a duet competition in the 1984 Olympics. And synchronized swimmers have reached another milestone. The event will be included in the 1986 Commonwealth Games scheduled for Edinburgh, Scotland.

Participants in the duet competition

A beautiful yet physically demanding sport where creative routines are synchronized to music.

GENERAL DESCRIPTION

Limited to women, synchronized swimming is a beautiful yet physically demanding sport of creative routines synchronized to music. The competitors are given a free rein for self-expression. Athletes must possess superb aquatic skills and have highly developed strength, endurance, breath control, flexibility and balance.

The figures are divided into four categories:

1. Ballet leg figures — synonymous with synchronized swimming. One leg is lifted vertically into the air while the athlete floats on her back. This category has many variations, some of which require the athlete to either vertically lift both legs or rotate them into an inverted position (head in the water and feet above water line).

2. Dolphin figures — to perform the dolphin and its family of variations, the athlete traces a complete circle forward (feet first) or backward (head first) underwater while floating on her back.

3. Somersault figures — these forward or backward tumbling moves are similar to gymnastics, though performed in water. These rolls are performed in a pike or tuck position (see Technical Terms), and may also include lifts, splits and/or other variations.

4. Other figures — figures that do not fit into any of the above named categories; an example is the swordfish, where the athlete arches her body and flips over, all the while remaining as close to the surface as possible; or a walkover.

PROCEDURE

Synchronized swimming is a new event for the Olympics and is limited to duet competition. Swim officials are hopeful that there will be competition in solos and teams in future Olympics.

Countries choose their own entries in whichever manner they desire. Canada, for instance, has decided to hold trials from January through May of 1984.

At the Olympics, the entries will face a two-part competition — the figures and the routine. The time limit for the duet is four minutes, including twenty seconds of deck movements.

The athletes must perform six figures, chosen 30 hours before the competition, from a possible 36 figures. The athletes must perform the figures and their routines twice. The preliminary competition, which is the first time the figures and routines are performed, helps to determine starting order for the second and final round.

One alternate is permitted, which means that a coach will have three competitors with her. The alternate will compete only if one of the other athletes cannot compete.

SCORING

There is quite a crowd involved in scoring: a referee, scorers, timers, clerks, runners and a music man, in addition to five or seven judges.

Considered in the judgment of figures are qualities of slowness, height and control, clearly defined figure sections and uniform motion. Routines are judged for flowing rhythm, choice of music and movement, choreography, perfection of strokes, figures and variations, variety, degree of difficulty, pool pattern, interpretation of music, manner of presentation, and synchronization.

The judges use half-points in scoring figures on a table ranging from 0 to 10. They use 1/10 points for scoring routines also on a table of 0 to 10. As in figure skating, the high and low marks are cancelled.

	Figures	Routines
Completely failed	0	0
Unsatisfactory	½-2½	0.1-2.9
Deficient	3-4½	3.0-4.9
Satisfactory	5-6½	5.0-6.9
Good	7-8½	7.0-8.9
Very Good	9-10	9.0-10

The Olympic winner with the highest score is proclaimed when the figure results and final routine results are tabulated.

EQUIPMENT

Pool — must have a water depth of three metres over a maximum area of 12 metres by 12 metres. This area may be extended for routines but a minimum depth of 1.7 metres must be maintained for at least eight metres.

Apparel — athletes must wear a black bathing suit and white cap for figures. Apparel for routines must conform to international rules and currently tends to complement and dramatize the choice of music and choreography. Noseclips are worn for both events.

VIEWING TIPS

Just sit back and enjoy. The abundance of grace and beauty in this event should not overshadow your appreciation of the physical demands on the competitors.

TOP COMPETITORS

Tracie Ruiz of the United States won the 1983 Pan-American Games solo and teamed with Candy Costie to take the gold medal in the duet event.

TOP CANADIANS

Identical twins Penny and Vicky Vilagos of Dollard des Ormeaux, Quebec, won the silver medal in duet at the 1983 Pan-American Games. Sharon Hambrook and Kelly Kryczka, the world champion duet from Calgary, won the 1983 Pan-Pacific championship and they were runners-up to Ruiz and Costie in the 1983 American Cup.

TECHNICAL TERMS

Transition — a change, bridge, link, between positions, movements, locations, directions.

Hybrids — variations and/or combinations or strokes and/or figures.

Pattern — harder than formation with two or more swimmers stationary or moving but linked in some manner.

Formation — simple pattern involving two or more swimmers, no links.

Sequence — combination or series of Synchro Swim skills.

Routine Composition — the technique of combining a series of Synchro Swim skills—strokes, sculls, figures, hybrids, transitions, patterns, formations—for one or more people with accompaniment.

Music Analysis — the breaking down of a piece of music into its components.

Accent — emphasis or stress on one tone or chord.

Beat — regular pulse of equal units of time, synchronization.

Metre — basic grouping of beats into 2's or 3's, indicated by time signature.

Rhythm — the innumerable patterns formed within the basic metric framework by the various arrangements of smaller or larger note values.

Tempo — rate of speed, indicated by tempo or metronome marks.

Volume — degree of intensity of music, e.g. adagio.

Synchronization — performing movements identically, at precisely the same time.

Eggbeater — vertical from head to hips, with arms extended along the surface; perform an alternating rotating kick-forward, backward, sideways left, sideways right, keeping water level constant with shoulders at or above the surface.

Sculling — movement of the hands designed to apply continuous pressure against the water to support, balance and propel the body.

Support Scull — a type of stationary scull, used when the body is inverted; enables the legs to be lifted and held high out of the water.

Crane Position — body extended vertically, head downward; head, hips and ankle in line with the body and the other leg at a right angle to the trunk and parallel to the surface of the water.

Inverted Vertical Position — body extended, head downward; head, hips and ankles in line and perpendicular to the surface of the water; water level at any point between the ankles and hips.

Split Position — trunk in arched position; head downward; legs evenly split forward and backward with feet and hips as near the surface as possible.

Ballet Leg — body extended in back layout, one leg extended perpendicular to the surface of the water.

Dolphin — started and finished in a back layout position. With the head leading, the body follows the circumference of a circle which has the diameter of approximately 2½ metres. Movement continues until the body surfaces in back layout position.

Front Walkover — front layout position; trunk moves downward toward a front pike position and buttock, legs and feet travel along the surface of the water; one leg is lifted in an arc to the surface of the water; the opposite leg describes a similar arc to meet the first leg; continue until in a back layout position.

Kip — in back layout position; the knees are drawn toward the chest, with the knees and toes at the surface of the water until a tuck position is assumed. A partial tuck somersault is executed until the legs, from knees to toes, are perpendicular to the surface of the water. The body assumes a vertical position on a line through the hips and the vertical line through head and legs.

Porpoise — in a front layout position; as the trunk moves downward to assume a front pike position, the legs are raised and the body assumes a vertical position.

Somersub — front layout position; perform a partial front pike somersault until the legs are vertical with the water level no lower than the ankles; one leg is lowered parallel to the surface of the water; body rises holding the ballet leg position until the face is out of water; finish as a single ballet leg.

Swordfish — front layout position; bent knee; body arches and the foot of the extended leg describes an arc to the surface of the water; bent knee straightens and the body arches up to a back layout position.

Pike Position — the body is bent at the hips, the legs straight at the knees, feet are together and toes pointed.

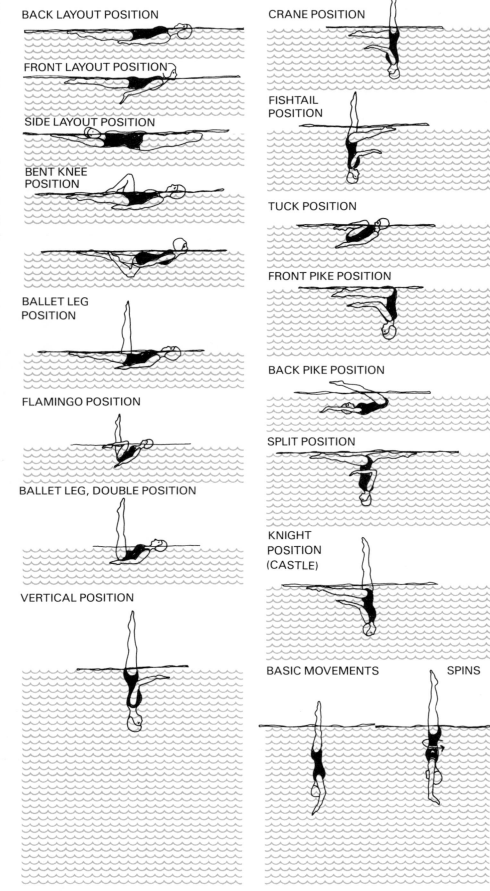

BACK LAYOUT POSITION

FRONT LAYOUT POSITION

SIDE LAYOUT POSITION

BENT KNEE POSITION

BALLET LEG POSITION

FLAMINGO POSITION

BALLET LEG, DOUBLE POSITION

VERTICAL POSITION

CRANE POSITION

FISHTAIL POSITION

TUCK POSITION

FRONT PIKE POSITION

BACK PIKE POSITION

SPLIT POSITION

KNIGHT POSITION (CASTLE)

BASIC MOVEMENTS   SPINS

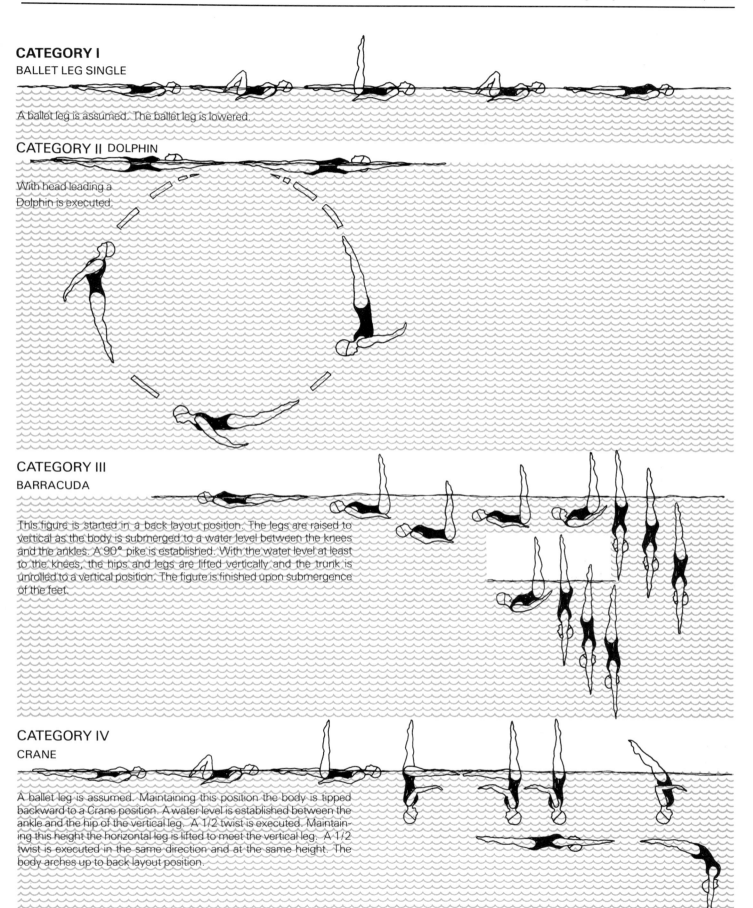

CATEGORY I
BALLET LEG SINGLE

A ballet leg is assumed. The ballet leg is lowered.

CATEGORY II DOLPHIN

With head leading a Dolphin is executed.

CATEGORY III
BARRACUDA

This figure is started in a back layout position. The legs are raised to vertical as the body is submerged to a water level between the knees and the ankles. A 90° pike is established. With the water level at least to the knees, the hips and legs are lifted vertically and the trunk is unrolled to a vertical position. The figure is finished upon submergence of the feet.

CATEGORY IV
CRANE

A ballet leg is assumed. Maintaining this position the body is tipped backward to a Crane position. A water level is established between the ankle and the hip of the vertical leg. A 1/2 twist is executed. Maintaining this height the horizontal leg is lifted to meet the vertical leg. A 1/2 twist is executed in the same direction and at the same height. The body arches up to back layout position.

WATER POLO

EVENT DATE			PEPPERDINE UNIVERSITY, MALIBU		
AUGUST	1	6 games—preliminaries	AUGUST	7	6 games—final round
	2	6 games—preliminaries		9	6 games—final round
	3	6 games—preliminaries		10	6 games—final round
	6	6 games—final round			

Setting up to make the save

The action rarely stops

Receiving a pass

Surrounding the opposition

HISTORY

Since its inception, water polo has been a fantastically demanding sport. Its players must either tread water or swim during the 28-minute contest, for there are no shallow ends where a player can touch bottom to gain relief. To appreciate water polo is to play it.

The game is believed to have originated in 1870 in England. Played with a soft ball, it was commonly called water soccer.

Water polo in its infancy was a tough, rugged game, often marked by fighting. The very nature of the sport led to violence. It was a common tactic to hold an opponent beneath the surface to get the ball away from him. When he came up for air, he usually came up swinging. With all the splashing around, the turbulent waters also presented opportunities for the sneak player to kick an opponent or to simply grab his trunks to hold him back.

Refinements came gradually. A fully inflated ball and several rule changes made over the past 20 years, helped to eliminate stalling and made water polo a much faster game than the rugged one played in the sport's early years. The quick, one-handed passes mixed with carefully plotted offensive strategies have shaped the game into the swift-paced action expected by modern sports fans.

The game's physical, technical and psychological demands have made it unique among team sports. Yet, water polo players often toil in obscurity. Though exacting and fast, characteristics treasured by the North American sport psyche, the game has a low profile here.

Despite its relative obscurity, water polo is one of the oldest team sports in the Olympics. Formally introduced in 1900 at the Paris Games, its medal was won by Great Britain, which went on to capture four of the first five gold medals awarded in the sport. But rugged individualists around the world were taking to the pool and water polo, and Great Britain was soon to learn that the game wasn't its private domain. In 1928, Hungary won a silver medal and experts recognized a new power was stepping forward.

Hungary went on to become the most dominant country in water polo. Since the 1928 Games in Amsterdam, it has captured a dozen Olympic medals, six of them gold. The country won its last gold in 1976. In the 1980 Games, the Soviet Union emerged as champion, with Yugoslavia taking the silver medal and Hungary the bronze.

GENERAL DESCRIPTION

Take the elements of basketball and soccer, blend them with a team of six players and a goalie and stir in a pool that is 30-metres long and 20-metres wide. The result is water polo, one of the most fascinating team sports in the Olympics.

A distinguishing characteristic of the game is that all the players, except the goalie, may handle the ball with only one hand at a time. In addition, they must constantly swim or tread water.

Penalties can be confusing but they are simply broken down into major and minor. Major penalties call for players to be excluded from the action for 45 seconds or until a goal is scored. The exclusion sets up a power-play situation similar to that found in hockey. Common major fouls are for holding and for sinking or pulling an opponent who is not touching the ball.

The game consists of four, seven-minute quarters. The goalie guards a net that is 3-metres wide and .90-metres high. Goals may be scored by using any part of the body except the closed fist. One point is awarded for each goal.

VIEWING TIPS

The key to water polo is that all players (except the goalie) may only handle the ball with one hand at a time, so be prepared for some snappy passing with players trying to ''outmuscle'' defenders.

Do not be alarmed by the frequency of whistles from the referee. Unlike most sports, the action rarely stops when the whistle sounds. It merely indicates a player has been awarded a free throw because of a minor foul, such as splashing or pushing. On the free throw, players will seek out key offensive positions while the player with the ball either swims with it or passes it off. He cannot shoot directly at the net and defenders cannot interfere with the player taking the free throw.

The two referees most common duty is to signal where and by whom a free throw is to be taken. To signal infractions, the referees have flags with blue and white markings to correspond with the caps worn by opposing teams.

PROCEDURE

There are a total of 12 teams. The host country gets a bye and is joined by the top six teams from the preceding world championships — U.S.S.R., Hungary, West Germany, Cuba, Yugoslavia, the Netherlands — and the top five teams from the Olympic qualification tournament.

TECHNICAL TERMS

Free throw — means a victim of a minor penalty such as splashing may play the ball without interference.

Holeman — the player who sets up in front of the opponent's net.

Power Play — when one team has a manpower advantage because a player has been removed for 45 seconds due to a major penalty such as holding or sinking.

SOME TOP PLAYERS

Goal — Eugeniy Sharonov, USSR, in the 1980 Olympic and 1982 world championship teams.

Field — Gyorgy Gerendas of Hungary and Manuel Estiarte of Spain; the leading scorers in the 1980 Olympics and 1982 world championships. Another outstanding player is Gianni De Magistris of Italy.

TOP CANADIANS

Paul Pottier and George Gross have played in more than 100 international matches. René Bol was a top scorer in the 1983 World Student Games.

MEDAL WINNERS

SWIMMING (water polo) Men

YEAR	PLACE	COUNTRY
1900	1	**Great Britain**
	2	Belgium
	3	France
1904	1	**U.S.A.** *
	2	U.S.A. **
	3	U.S.A. ***
1908	1	**Great Britain**
	2	Belgium
	3	Sweden
1912	1	**Great Britain**
	2	Sweden
	3	Belgium
1920	1	**Great Britain**
	2	Belgium
	3	Sweden
1924	1	**France**
	2	Belgium
	3	U.S.A.
1928	1	**Germany**
	2	Hungary
	3	France
1932	1	**Hungary**
	2	Germany
	3	U.S.A.
1936	1	**Hungary**
	2	Germany
	3	Belgium
1948	1	**Italy**
	2	Hungary
	3	Netherlands
1952	1	**Hungary**
	2	Yugoslavia
	3	Italy
1956	1	**Hungary**
	2	Yugoslavia
	3	U.S.S.R.
1960	1	**Italy**
	2	U.S.S.R.
	3	Hungary
1964	1	**Hungary**
	2	Yugoslavia
	3	U.S.S.R.
1968	1	**Yugoslavia**
	2	U.S.S.R.
	3	Hungary
1972	1	**U.S.S.R.**
	2	Hungary
	3	U.S.A.
1976	1	**Hungary**
	2	Italy
	3	Netherlands
1980	1	**U.S.S.R.**
	2	Yugoslavia
	3	Hungary

* New York A.C.
** Chicago A.C.
*** Missouri A.C.

TRACK AND FIELD

Concentration at the start

EVENT	DATE	LOS ANGELES MEMORIAL COLISEUM
AUGUST	3	Heptathlon 100m hurdles, high jump/Triple jump qualifying/400m hurdles 1st round, men/400m 1st round, women/Shot put qualifying, women/100m 1st & 2nd rounds, men/70m women, 90m men/800m 1st round, women/Heptathlon shot put, 200m/800m 1st round, men/20 km walk final (start & finish)/Shot put final, women/10,000m 1st round
	4	Heptathlon long jump/400m 1st round, men/400m 2nd round, women/Javelin throw qualifying, men/100m 1st round, women/100m 2nd round, women/Heptathlon javelin throw, 800m (final event)/100m semifinal, men/800m semifinal, women/800m 2nd round, men/Triple jump final/400m hurdles semifinal, men/100m final. men
	5	Marathon, women (finish)/Javelin throw qualifying, women/400m hurdles 1st round, women/110m hurdles 1st round/Hammer throw qualifying/100m semifinal & final, women/Long jump qualifying, men/110m hurdles 2nd round/400m 2nd round, men/400m semifinal, women/Javelin throw final, men/800m semifinal, men/400m hurdles final, men
	6	Pole vault qualifying/200m 1st & 2nd rounds, men/3000m 1st round/110m hurdles semifinal & final/Hammer throw final/400m hurdles semifinal, women/400m semifinal, men/400m final, women/800m final, women/Long jump final, men/800m final, men/Javelin throw final, women/3,000m steeplechase 1st round/10,000m final
AUGUST	8	Decathlon 100m, long jump, shot put/Discus throw qualifying, men/200m 1st & 2nd rounds, women/1,500m 1st round, women/200m semifinal & final, men/Decathlon high jump, 400m/Pole vault final/400m hurdles final, women/400m final, men/5,000m 1st round/Long jump qualifying, women/3,000m semifinal/3,000m steeplechase semifinal
	9	Decathlon discus throw, 110m, hurdles, pole vault/100m hurdles 1st round/High jump qualifying, women/200m semifinal & final, women/Decathlon javelin throw, 1,500m (final event)/1,500m 1st round, men/1,500m semifinal, women/Long jump final, women/5,000m semifinal
	10	High jump qualifying, men/4 x 400m relay 1st round, women/4 x 400m relay 1st round, men/Discus throw qualifying, women/4 x 100m relay 1st round, women/4 x 100m relay 1st round, men/High jump final, women/100m hurdles semifinal/4 x 400m relay semifinal, men/4 x 400m relay semifinal, women/Discus throw final, men/1,500m semifinal, men/100m hurdles final/3,000m final/3,000m steeplechase final
	11	50km walk final (start & finish)/Shot put qualifying, men/4 x 100m relay semifinal, women/4 x 100m relay semifinal, men/Discus throw final, women/4 x 100m relay final, women/High jump final, men/4 x 100m relay final, men/4 x 400m relay final, women/4 x 400m relay final, men/Shot put final, men/1,500m final, men/1,500m final, women/men/5,000m final
	12	Marathon, men (finish)

The Los Angeles Memorial Coliseum is the site of the track and field competition.

HISTORY

Cirtius, Altius, Fortius. The Olympic motto means faster, higher, stronger. It is also a fitting description of the track and field performances at the Olympic Games (see General Description for events involved in track and field). Historians one day may want to add drama to the list when they talk of track and field history. The events have been full of it since 1896.

One of the more memorable dramatic moments revolved around the finish of the marathon race in the 1908 Games in London. The day was hot and humid and the 58 runners were perspiring heavily when they went to the starting line. The runners knew their reserves would be taxed heavily in the run of 26 miles, 385 yards.

The 385 yards had been added to the original course of 26 miles so that the runners would finish opposite the Queen's royal box in the stadium. Included in the starting field was the Canadian Indian, Tom Longboat, from a reserve near Hamilton, Ontario. Longboat was the prerace favourite and he was permitted to start only after the officials were satisfied that he had not run as a professional in North America.

This day, Longboat was not at his best. At 17 miles, with his strength and energy sapped by the heat, he was forced into a walk before dropping out of the race. Spectators at the finish area in the stadium looked anxiously at the downhill ramp the runners would take into the stadium for the final lap to the finish line.

The first runner was the Italian Dorando Pietri, who came down the ramp stumbling like a drunk. His arms flopped around, and his legs were wobbly. Sheer determination drove him on. When he reached the track, Pietri turned the wrong way for the final lap. He stopped when shouting fans and officials attracted his attention. He seemed in a daze but was able to comprehend that the officials were pointing for him to go in the other direction. Pietri turned and staggered on. It was a remarkable display of courage and it proved too much for some officials. They grabbed him by the arms, helped him across the line and declared him the winner.

But while Pietri was going through

those last agonizing steps, the American Johnny Hayes had entered the stadium and was circling the track. When he hit the finish line another chapter in the drama unfolded. The Americans claimed Hayes should be the winner and Pietri should be disqualified for having received assistance from the officials. After hours of soul-searching, the committee named Hayes the winner, although there was some argument as to whether officials had actually touched Pietri in the race.

Pietri's courage was not forgotten. The next day he was back in the stadium and accepted a gold cup, a replica of Hayes' award, from Queen Alexandra. To Pietri, it mattered not that the inscription on the cup referred to him as Pietri Dorando.

After the American Indian Jim Thorpe won the pentathlon and decathlon (track and field events) in the 1912 Games in Stockholm, the Swedish king, Gustav V, proclaimed him the world's most wonderful athlete. There was little argument. Thorpe performed in 15 events, five in the pentathlon and 10 in the decathlon, and won seven of them.

A few months after returning home, Thorpe found himself the centre of a drama built around a story that he was a professional when competing in Stockholm. A newspaper claimed that Thorpe had received $60 a month for playing professional baseball under an alias. Officials from the U.S. Amateur Athletic Union (USAAU) investigated and ruled Thorpe was a professional. Thorpe was forced to return his medals.

For many years, Thorpe and his family fought to have the medals restored and his performances put back into the record books. Thorpe died an unhappy man in 1953. Twenty years after his death, the U.S. Olympic Committee restored Thorpe to its honour roll and in late 1982, the International Olympic Committee ordered the medals returned to Thorpe's family.

A new type of drama occurred in the 1936 Games in Berlin. It focused on racism. Hitler and the Nazi government were in power in Germany preaching the supremacy of the Aryan race. There was no question that Germany wanted to use the Olympic Games as a propaganda vehicle for Hitler. Some countries, in-

cluding the United States, talked of staying out of the Games, but they decided to participate.

When the Americans marched into the stadium, there were 10 blacks on the track team. Among them was the quiet Jesse Owens who was to put on one of the greatest track shows in Olympic history. Owens won the 100 and 200 metres and the long jump, and ran on the 4 x 100-metre team that sped to a world record of 39.8 seconds.

Much has been written about the fact that Hitler did not offer any personal congratulations to Owens as he did to German winners on the opening day of track events. In fact, Hitler was asked by the Olympic committee to refrain from offering congratulations, which was a duty reserved for Olympic officials. That didn't stop Hitler from meeting German champions in private.

Thirty-two years later, another drama unfolded, this time in Mexico City in 1968. The International Olympic Committee had reinstated South Africa as a member in good standing, much to the chagrin of black nations who were against South Africa's apartheid policy of racial segregation. Some 40 black nations threatened to pull out and stayed only when the IOC once again barred South Africa.

The racial situation was soon all but forgotten and harmony between black and white existed in the Olympic village. When winner Tommie Smith and third-place finisher John Carlos of the United States joined second-place finisher Peter Norman of Australia for the medal presentations after the men's 200-metre final, Olympic officials had no idea a new drama would unfold. As the American flag was being raised on the pole and the strains of the American national anthem floated across the stadium, Carlos and Smith turned their backs to the flag, bowed their heads and held gloved, clenched right fists high in the air. It was the Black Power salute and its impact was staggering.

The U.S. Olympic committee gave Carlos and Smith 48 hours to get out of Mexico. The IOC censured the pair; Carlos in particular for being the instigator. Last fall Carlos, who currently works for the 1984 Los Angeles Committee, said he has no regrets. "People see it

clearly now. What we did was hardly what you would call violent and that blew everyone's mind — the calmness of it, very soft, very powerful."

The track and field competitions are dramatic in themselves. Athletes of the world are performing faster, higher and are stronger than ever before. Just how far the athletes have come can be found by comparing recent Olympic performances to those in the early modern Games. The differences are staggering. For instance, the United States' Lee Evans won the 400 metres in 43.8 seconds at Mexico in 1968. Tom Burke of the United States won the event in 54.2 back in 1896. When American Frank Foss set a world record of 4.09 metres to win the pole vault at the 1920 Games, spectators were very impressed. In 1980, Poland's Wladislaw Kozakiewicz cleared 5.78 metres, setting a new world record and winning the event in Moscow. Also in Moscow, East Germany's Ilona Slupianek won the women's shot put with a mighty heave of 22.41 metres. It took a throw of only 13.75 metres for Micheline Ostermeyer of France to win the gold medal in 1948.

There are many such one-sided comparisons and just how much faster, higher and stronger the athletes will get remains to be seen. People ran and jumped as a natural course of events until their energies were directed into competition, and competition is the heartbeat of Olympic track and field.

GENERAL DESCRIPTION

Aside from the marathon races for both men and women and the 20- and 50-kilometre walks for men, all track and field events are held in the main stadium, which will be the Coliseum in Los Angeles for the 1984 Games.

The track is a distance of 400 metres with eight lanes around for the 100-metre sprints, the 100-metre hurdles for women and the 110-metre hurdles for men on an eight-lane straightaway. In the 200-metre sprint competitors are faced with running at high speeds around one half of the track, while 400-metre runners and 400-metre hurdlers must run around one lap of the track.

For the 800-metre run, competitors must stay in their lanes until the first turn has been completed. Then they can jockey and break for the inside position

Closing in on the finish line

Running in their lanes for the short sprint

and set their tactics into motion.

For the sprints, the athletes settle themselves into starting blocks, which enable the runners to get a solid push with their feet. For races up to 400 metres, the starter will call out "on your marks" then "set." When all runners are steady the starter will signal a "go" by firing a pistol which also activates an electronic photo-finish clock. Racers are allowed one warning for a false start. A second false start by the individual calls for disqualification. In events up to and including the 400-metre sprints, the runners must stay in their respective lanes.

The photo-finish camera is used to help determine time and placings in close finishes. It takes a sequence of pictures at the finish line and times the athlete to 1/100th of a second in the sprints.

It should be noted that for races of 200 metres or less, records will not be ratified unless the wind speed is under two metres per second or 7.19 kilometres an hour.

Race officials watch the action closely. If there is any jostling or obstruction of a runner, the offending runner may be disqualified.

For the hurdles and steeplechase events, competitors are not penalized for knocking down the metal-wood hurdles. It just slows them down. In the steeplechase, the competitors must make seven water jumps and be concerned with clearing 28 hurdles.

For relay events sheer speed is not enough. There must be excellent timing in the exchange of the baton. Runners preparing to accept the baton in the 4 x 100-metre event may start drifting toward the oncoming runner up to 10 metres outside the 20-metre exchange zone, but must effect the takeover before the end of the zone is reached. In the 4 x 400-metre relay, the exchange must be made in the zone. In case of a dropped baton, the only runner allowed to retrieve it is the one who dropped it.

Competitors for the marathon are permitted to have something to eat and drink after the first 11 kilometres, and may have further refreshment every five kilometres. Water and sponging is available between feeding stations and all food and drink is provided by the athletes or by the Olympic committee.

Working to a full stride

A speed walker

The relay race

In the starting blocks

In walking events, the competitors must maintain unbroken contact with the ground with their toe-heel steps. The leg must be straightened at the knee for at least one moment. A competitor is cautioned once if he stops walking within the definition, and judges mark the caution with a white flag where the infraction occurred. If the competitor is given the red flag, he is disqualified and must leave the course.

Olympic officials try to have a dozen finalists for each of the field events. The finalists in the long and triple jumps and the four throws (javelin, discus, shot and hammer) have three trials each. The eight leading performers then earn three more trials to determine final placings and medals.

In the high jump, the competitors must take off from one foot and the bar must be cleared. Three consecutive failures at any height disqualifies a competitor from further jumping.

A tie is broken by declaring the competitor with the fewest jumps at the tieing height, the winner. If there is still a tie, then the winner will be the competitor with the fewest failures at any height. If a tie is still in effect, the winner shall be the competitor with the fewest jumps. If a tie for first place still remains, more jumps will be taken with the bar lowered and raised until a winner is declared.

The pole vault allows a competitor three trials at each height and he or she must clear the bar. If the pole knocks down the bar, the jump is voided. Ties are broken with the same procedure used in the high jump.

In the long jump, a competitor makes the takeoff from a board that is 20-centimetres wide. If a competitor touches the ground beyond the board, it is called a foul jump and does not count. Good jumps are measured from the nearest break in the sand made by any part of the body or limbs, back to the takeoff board.

For the triple jump, the same rules used for the long jump apply. In the "hop" the triple jumper must land on the same foot used at takeoff and in the "step" the competitor must land on the other foot.

Shot-putters must cradle the shot on the shoulder. They use one hand only, are forbidden to throw from behind the shoulder and they must remain in the designated throwing circle. There is also a circle for the discus and hammer throwers while javelin throwers must stay on the runway, which is 4-metres wide and up to 36.5-metres long.

Placings for running events are determined by times while placings in other events are determined by the height achieved or the throwing distances made.

VIEWING TIPS

There is no set physical requirement for success in track and field. Men and women come in all sizes and shapes; lean and lithe in the sprints, muscular and big in the field events.

Today's athletes are generally bigger, stronger and faster than those from the past. If past performances hold true, we should see several records established.

It is especially important to watch the sprint starts. An "explosive" or extremely fast start can be the key to success just as a poor or late start can mean disaster. The sprinters starts are assisted by start blocks. In the 100-metre dash, there is virtually no room for error and no time for a viewer's attention to wander.

For the races of 800 metres and longer, the viewers should watch for the competitor's strategy. How a competitor runs the race is as important as sheer physical ability. Watch how the race favourites jockey for position or force the pace to suit their abilities.

In the relays, keep an eye on the exchange of batons for this is a crucial area. Faulty exchanges can result in dropped batons or runners crashing into each other. Spills are also common in hurdle events when competitors fail to cleanly clear the hurdle.

When the television camera focuses on the faces of competitors it captures the tension as the drama builds for such field events as the high jump, pole vault and power events — the discus, shot put and javelin. Competition is intense so watch for the reaction of performers after they successfully meet or fail to meet their objectives.

The best viewing tip is to try to learn a bit about what the track and field athletes are attempting to do (see General Description). To appreciate their efforts is to increase your personal viewing enjoyment.

EQUIPMENT

Hurdles — made of metal with a wood topping. For the women's 100-metre event, they are set at a height of .84 metres and for the 400-metre event are set at .762 metres. For the men, the hurdles are set at .914 metres for the 400-metre test and 1.067 metres for the 110-metre event.

Javelin — of uniform thickness, the wood-metal javelin for men is about 2.7-metres long and weighs just over 800 grams. The head of the javelin is sharply pointed and there is a cord grip for the thrower. The women's javelin weighs just over 600 grams and is about 2.3-metres long. Competitors must use javelins provided by the Olympic committee.

Discus — made of wood with a metal rim. Both sides must be uniform. The men's discus weighs just over two kilograms, is about 45-centimetres thick and has a circumference of about 220 millimetres. The women's discus must weigh at least one kilogram and is about 181 millimetres in diameter. Competitors must use the discus provided by the Olympic committee.

Discus Circle — athletes toss the discus from a circle that is about 2.5 metres in diameter. The circle is surrounded on three sides by a wire cage to catch any errant throws.

Shot — made of metal, smooth and spherical. For men the shot weighs just over 7.26 kilograms and is about 120 millimetres in diameter. The women's shot weighs just over four kilograms and its diameter ranges from 95 to 110 millimetres. Competitors must use the shot provided by the Olympic committee.

Shot area — with an inside diameter of around 2.13 metres, the circle is covered with a nonskid material and is slightly below the metal band that fronts the circle and contains the feet of the thrower.

Hammer — a spherical, metal ball that is joined by a wire attached to a grip. The ball must be between 110 and 130 millimetres in diameter. The complete hammer must weigh at least 7.26 kilograms and measure no longer than 1.175 metres from the inside of the grip. Competitors must use the hammers provided by the Olympic committee.

Hammer circle — is about 2.13 metres in diameter and is covered with a nonskid material and is only slightly below the iron band that covers the circumference of the circle. The circle is surrounded on three sides by a wire cage.

Long Jump — a runway of at least 45 metres is needed. There is a takeoff board about 20-centimetres wide that the competitor hits on his last step before landing in a sandpit. The pit is raked for each competitor.

Triple Jump — a runway of at least 45 metres is needed. There is a 20-centimetre wide takeoff board, 13 metres from the pit in order to accommodate the hop, step and jump.

High Jump — the crossbar is made of wood or metal and is almost 4-metres long and weighs just .under two kilograms. The crossbar must be able to fall freely when hit by a competitor. The crossbar sits on the supports of the uprights. The landing area must be deeply padded. The run-up area must be at least 25 metres from the bar.

Pole vault — the crossbar is made of wood or metal and is almost 4.52-metres long. The crossbar sits on supports on the uprights and it must fall freely when hit by the competitor.

Track — must handle a straightaway 100-metre race. Staggered starts are used on the curves for races of 200 metres to 800 metres. There is no staggered start for races of 1,500 metres or more. The track is made of a synthetic material to offer conformity for the runners who race in lanes that are 1.22-metres wide for the sprints.

Steeplechase — competitors are required to make seven water jumps over the one water obstacle constructed just on the inside of the infield. The competitor runs off the main track and its obstacle hurdles to make the water jump.

Footwear — a competitor's choice. He or she can race with one shoe, two shoes or barefoot. Track shoes are allowed only six spikes in the sole and two in the heel. Competitors in the high jump and javelin may have four spikes in their heels.

Dress — Competitors must wear shorts and shirts.

TOP CONTENDERS

Women

The East Germans gave strong performances at the 1983 world championships in Helsinki. Marlies Goehr (100 metres), Marita Koch (200 metres), Bettine Jahn (100-metre hurdles), Heike Daute (long jump), Martina Opitz (discus) and Ramona Neubert (heptathlon) were winners in Helsinki.

The most dominating runner at the world championships was Jarmila Kratochvilova of Czechoslovakia who set a world record of 47.99 seconds in the 400 metres and also won the 800 metres.

Mary Decker of the United States won the 1,500-and 3,000-metre test while the Soviet Union saw Tamara Bykova win the high jump and Ekaterina Fessenko win the 400-metre hurdles.

Men

The United States once again has a powerful sprint team. Carl Lewis is being hailed as the new "Jesse Owens." He won the 100 metres and long jump at Helsinki. Carl Smith won the 200 metres, also for the United States.

Defending Olympic champion Daley Thompson of Great Britain won the decathlon at Helsinki ahead of two West Germans. Gennady Avdeenko of the Soviet Union took the high jump honours with a leap of 2.32 metres and Jianhua Zhu of China finished third. Later in 1983, Zhu set the world record of 2.38 metres in a high jump event in China. Soviets Sergy Bubka and Konstantin Volkov were first and second in the pole vault in the world championships.

TOP CANADIANS

The Canadians failed to win any medals at the world championships last summer in Helsinki, Finland, but they earned a lot of respect. They had 13 athletes among the top eight performers in each event. Overall, the Canadians were seventh in team standings and Canadian experts hailed that as a major achievement. They are optimistic about Canadian performances at the Los Angeles Olympic Games.

Women

Angela Bailey of Toronto was a finalist in the 100 metres (finishing fifth), the 200 metres (finishing seventh) and the 4 x 100 metres relay (finishing fifth).

Marita Payne of Toronto is steadily improving her times in the 400 metres. She set a Commonwealth record of 50.06 seconds, the 10th fastest time ever, although she failed to win a medal at the world championships, finishing fifth.

Brit McRoberts of Vancouver was eighth in the women's 1,500 metres at the world championships but she too is steadily improving her times. Her time of 4:05.73 at Helsinki was a Canadian record.

Men

Dave Steen of Toronto missed the world championship decathlon event because of an ankle injury. Previously, he had won the gold at the World University Games in Edmonton and the gold medal at the Pan-American Games in Venezuela last summer.

High jumper Milt Ottey of Toronto was one of the best in the world before a leg injury sidelined him for most of 1983. He was back jumping late in the year. How much he can work his way back to his previous form is the big question mark for this outstanding athlete.

Hurdler Mark McKoy of Toronto grabbed a fourth-place finish in the world championships at Helsinki and is rated as one of the world's best at the 110-metre event.

François Lapointe and Guillaume Leblanc, both of Montreal, are among Canada's top walkers. Lapointe was sixth at Helsinki in the 50-kilometre event. Leblanc was eighth in the 20-kilometre test at Helsinki.

Laslo Babits of Penticton, B.C., won the javelin at the Pan-American Games while the Toronto quartet of Ben Johnson, Tony Sharpe, Desai Williams and Sterling Hinds teamed to win a gold medal in the 4 x 100 metres relay in the international summer Games meet last summer in Los Angeles.

Running the hurdles

The hammer throw

The high jump athlete

A javelin competitor

Sheer strength is the key to success for a discus thrower.   *Up and over*

MEDAL WINNERS

ATHLETICS (100 metres) Men

YEAR	PLACE	NAME	COUNTRY
1896	1	T. Burke	U.S.A.
	2	F. Hofmann	Germany
	3	A. Szokolyi	Hungary
1900	1	F. Jarvis	U.S.A.
	2	W. Tewksbury	U.S.A.
	3	S. Rowley	Australia
1904	1	A. Hahn	U.S.A.
	2	N. Cartmell	U.S.A.
	3	W. Hogenson	U.S.A.
1908	1	R. Walker	South Africa
	2	J. Rector	U.S.A.
	3	R. Kerr	Canada
1912	1	R. Craig	U.S.A.
	2	A. Meyer	U.S.A.
	3	D. Lippincott	U.S.A.
1920	1	C. Paddock	U.S.A.
	2	M. Kirksey	U.S.A.
	3	H. Edward	Great Britain
1924	1	H. Abrahams	Great Britain
	2	J. Scholz	U.S.A.
	3	A. Porritt	New Zealand
1928	1	P. Williams	Canada
	2	J. London	Great Britain
	3	G. Lammers	Germany
1932	1	E. Tolan	U.S.A.
	2	R. Metcalfe	U.S.A.
	3	A. Jonath	Germany
1936	1	J. Owens	U.S.A.
	2	R. Metcalfe	U.S.A.
	3	M. Osendarp	Netherlands
1948	1	W.H. Dillard	U.S.A.
	2	H.N. Ewell	U.S.A.
	3	L. LaBeach	Panama
1952	1	L. Remigino	U.S.A.
	2	H. McKenley	Jamaica
	3	E. Bailey	Great Britain
1956	1	R. Morrow	U.S.A.
	2	W.T. Baker	U.S.A.
	3	H. Hogan	Australia
1960	1	A. Hary	Germany
	2	D. Sime	U.S.A.
	3	P. Radford	Great Britain
1964	1	R. Hayes	U.S.A.
	2	E. Figuerola	Cuba
	3	H. Jerome	Canada
1968	1	J. Hines	U.S.A.
	2	L. Miller	Jamaica
	3	C. Greene	U.S.A.
1972	1	V. Borzov	U.S.S.R.
	2	R. Taylor	U.S.A.
	3	L. Miller	Jamaica
1976	1	Hasely Crawford	Trinidad and Tobago
	2	Donald Quarrie	Jamaica
	3	Valeriy Borzov	U.S.S.R.
1980	1	Allan Wells	United Kingdom
	2	Silvio Leonard	Cuba
	3	Petar Petrov	Bulgaria

ATHLETICS (200 metres) Men

YEAR	PLACE	NAME	COUNTRY
1900	1	J.W. Tewksbury	U.S.A.
	2	N. Pritchard	India
	3	S. Rowley	Australia
1904	1	A. Hahn	U.S.A.
	2	N. Cartmell	U.S.A.
	3	W. Hogenson	U.S.A.
1908	1	R. Kerr	Canada
	2	R. Cloughen	U.S.A.
	3	N. Cartmell	U.S.A.
1912	1	R. Craig	U.S.A.
	2	D. Lippincott	U.S.A.
	3	W. Applegarth	Great Britain
1920	1	A. Woodring	U.S.A.
	2	C. Paddock	U.S.A.
	3	H. Edward	Great Britain

YEAR	PLACE	NAME	COUNTRY
1924	1	J. Scholz	U.S.A.
	2	C. Paddock	U.S.A.
	3	E. Liddell	Great Britain
1928	1	P. Williams	Canada
	2	W. Rangeley	Great Britain
	3	H. Körnig	Germany
1932	1	E. Tolan	U.S.A.
	2	G. Simpson	U.S.A.
	3	R. Metcalfe	U.S.A.
1936	1	J. Owens	U.S.A.
	2	M. Robinson	U.S.A.
	3	M. Osendarp	Netherlands
1948	1	M. Patton	U.S.A.
	2	H.N. Ewell	U.S.A.
	3	L. LaBeach	Panama
1952	1	A. Stanfield	U.S.A.
	2	W.T. Baker	U.S.A.
	3	J. Gathers	U.S.A.
1956	1	R. Morrow	U.S.A.
	2	A. Stanfield	U.S.A.
	3	W.T. Baker	U.S.A.
1960	1	L. Berruti	Italy
	2	L. Carney	U.S.A.
	3	A. Seye	France
1964	1	H. Carr	U.S.A.
	2	P. Drayton	U.S.A.
	3	E. Roberts	Trinidad
1968	1	T. Smith	U.S.A.
	2	P. Norman	Australia
	3	J. Carlos	U.S.A.
1972	1	V. Borzov	U.S.S.R.
	2	L. Black	U.S.A.
	3	P. Mennea	Italy
1976	1	Donald Quarrie	Jamaica
	2	Millard Hampton	U.S.A.
	3	Dwayne Evans	U.S.A.
1980	1	Pietro Mennea	Italy
	2	Allan Wells	United Kingdom
	3	Donald Quarrie	Jamaica

ATHLETICS (400 metres) Men

YEAR	PLACE	NAME	COUNTRY
1896	1	T. Burke	U.S.A.
	2	H. Jamison	U.S.A.
	3	E. Hofmann	Germany
1900	1	M. Long	U.S.A.
	2	W. Holland	U.S.A.
	3	E. Schultz	Denmark
1904	1	H. Hillman	U.S.A.
	2	F. Waller	U.S.A.
	3	H.C. Groman	U.S.A.
1908	1	W. Halswell	Great Britain
		Race ordered rerun due to disqualification. Others refused and Halswell ran alone.	
1912	1	C. Reidpath	U.S.A.
	2	H. Braun	Germany
	3	E. Lindberg	U.S.A.
1920	1	B. Rudd	South Africa
	2	G. Butler	Great Britain
	3	N. Engdahl	Sweden
1924	1	E. Liddell	Great Britain
	2	H. Fitch	U.S.A.
	3	G. Butler	Great Britain
1928	1	R. Barbuti	U.S.A.
	2	J. Ball	Canada
	3	J. Buchner	Germany
1932	1	W. Carr	U.S.A.
	2	B. Eastman	U.S.A.
	3	A. Wilson	Canada
1936	1	A. Williams	U.S.A.
	2	A.G. Brown	Great Britain
	3	J. LuValle	U.S.A.
1948	1	A. Wint	Jamaica
	2	H. McKenley	Jamaica
	3	M. Whitfield	U.S.A.
1952	1	G. Rhoden	Jamaica
	2	H. McKenley	Jamaica
	3	O. Matson	U.S.A.
1956	1	C. Jenkins	U.S.A.
	2	K. Haas	Germany
	3	V. Hellsten/ A. Ignatyev	Finland/ U.S.S.R.

ATHLETICS (800 metres) Men

YEAR	PLACE	NAME	COUNTRY
1960	1	O. Davis	U.S.A.
	2	C. Kaufmann	Germany
	3	M. Spence	South Africa
1964	1	M. Larrabee	U.S.A.
	2	W. Mottley	Trinidad
	3	A. Badenski	Poland
1968	1	L. Evans	U.S.A.
	2	L. James	U.S.A.
	3	R. Freeman	U.S.A.
1972	1	V. Matthews	U.S.A.
	2	W. Collett	U.S.A.
	3	J. Sang	Kenya
1976	1	Alberto Juantorena	Cuba
	2	Fred Newhouse	U.S.A.
	3	Herman Frazier	U.S.A.
1980	1	Viktor Markin	U.S.S.R.
	2	Richard Mitchell	Australia
	3	Frank Schaffer	German Dem. Rep.

YEAR	PLACE	NAME	COUNTRY
1896	1	E. Flack	Australia
	2	N. Dani	Hungary
	3	D. Golemis	Greece
1900	1	A. Tysoe	Great Britain
	2	J. Cregan	U.S.A.
	3	D. Hall	U.S.A.
1904	1	J. Lightbody	U.S.A.
	2	H. Valentine	U.S.A.
	3	E. Breitkreutz	U.S.A.
1908	1	M. Sheppard	U.S.A.
	2	E. Lunghi	Italy
	3	H. Braun	Germany
1912	1	J. Meredith	U.S.A.
	2	M. Sheppard	U.S.A.
	3	I. Davenport	U.S.A.
1920	1	A. Hill	Great Britain
	2	E. Eby	U.S.A.
	3	B. Rudd	South Africa
1924	1	D. Lowe	Great Britain
	2	P. Martin	Switzerland
	3	S. Enck	U.S.A.
1928	1	D. Lowe	Great Britain
	2	E. Bylehn	Sweden
	3	H. Engelhard	Germany
1932	1	T. Hampson	Great Britain
	2	A. Wilson	Canada
	3	P. Edwards	Canada
1936	1	J. Woodruff	U.S.A.
	2	M. Lanzi	Italy
	3	P. Edwards	Canada
1948	1	M. Whitfield	U.S.A.
	2	A. Wint	Jamaica
	3	M. Hansenne	France
1952	1	M. Whitfield	U.S.A.
	2	A. Wint	Jamaica
	3	H. Ulzheimer	Germany
1956	1	T. Courtney	U.S.A.
	2	D. Johnson	Great Britain
	3	A. Boysen	Norway
1960	1	P. Snell	New Zealand
	2	R. Moens	Belgium
	3	G. Kerr	West Indies
1964	1	P. Snell	New Zealand
	2	W. Crothers	Canada
	3	W. Kiprugut	Kenya
1968	1	R. Doubell	Australia
	2	W. Kiprugut	Kenya
	3	T. Farrell	U.S.A.
1972	1	D. Wottle	U.S.A.
	2	E. Arzhanov	U.S.S.R.
	3	M. Boit	Kenya
1976	1	Alberto Juantorena	Cuba
	2	Ivo Van Damme	Belgium
	3	Richard Wohlhuter	U.S.A.
1980	1	Steven Ovett	United Kingdom
	2	Sebastian Coe	United Kingdom
	3	Nikolai Kirov	U.S.S.R.

ATHLETICS (1,500 metres) Men

YEAR	PLACE	NAME	COUNTRY
1896	1	**E. Flack**	**Australia**
	2	A. Blake	U.S.A.
	3	A. Lermusiaux	France
1900	1	**C. Bennett**	**Great Britain**
	2	H. Deloge	France
	3	J. Bray	U.S.A.
1904	1	**J. Lightbody**	**U.S.A.**
	2	F. Verner	U.S.A.
	3	L. Hearn	U.S.A.
1908	1	**M. Sheppard**	**U.S.A.**
	2	H. Wilson	Great Britain
	3	N. Hallows	Great Britain
1912	1	**A. Jackson**	**Great Britain**
	2	A. Kiviat	U.S.A.
	3	N. Taber	U.S.A.
1920	1	**A. Hill**	**Great Britain**
	2	P. Baker	Great Britain
	3	L. Shields	U.S.A.
1924	1	**P. Nurmi**	**Finland**
	2	W. Scharer	Switzerland
	3	H. Stallard	Great Britain
1924	1	**H. Larva**	**Finland**
	2	J. Ladoumègue	France
	3	E. Purje	Finland
1932	1	**L. Beccali**	**Italy**
	2	J. Cornes	Great Britain
	3	P. Edwards	Canada
1936	1	**J. Lovelock**	**New Zealand**
	2	G. Cunningham	U.S.A.
	3	L. Beccali	Italy
1948	1	**H. Eriksson**	**Sweden**
	2	L. Strand	Sweden
	3	W. Slijkhuis	Netherlands
1952	1	**J. Barthel**	**Luxembourg**
	2	R. McMillen	U.S.A.
	3	W. Lueg	Germany
1956	1	**R. Delany**	**Eire**
	2	K. Richtzenhain	Germany
	3	J. Landy	Australia
1960	1	**H. Elliott**	**Australia**
	2	M. Jazy	France
	3	I. Rozsavolgyi	Hungary
1964	1	**P. Snell**	**New Zealand**
	2	J. Odlozil	Czechoslovakia
	3	J. Davies	New Zealand
1968	1	**K. Keino**	**Kenya**
	2	J. Ryun	U.S.A.
	3	B. Tummler	Germany
1972	1	**P. Vasala**	**Finland**
	2	K. Keino	Kenya
	3	R. Dixon	New Zealand
1976	1	**John Walker**	**New Zealand**
	2	Ivo Van Damme	Belgium
	3	Paul Heinz Wellmann	West Germany
1980	1	**Sebastian Coe**	**United Kingdom**
	2	Jurgen Straub	German Dem. Rep.
	3	Steven Ovett	United Kingdom

ATHLETICS (5,000 metres) Men

YEAR	PLACE	NAME	COUNTRY
1912	1	**H. Kolehmainen**	**Finland**
	2	J. Bouin	France
	3	G. Hutson	Great Britain
1920	1	**J. Guillemot**	**France**
	2	P. Nurmi	Finland
	3	E. Backman	Sweden
1924	1	**P. Nurmi**	**Finland**
	2	V. Ritola	Finland
	3	E. Wide	Sweden
1928	1	**V. Ritola**	**Finland**
	2	P. Nurmi	Finland
	3	E. Wide	Sweden
1932	1	**L. Lehtinen**	**Finland**
	2	R. Hill	U.S.A.
	3	L. Virtanen	Finland
1936	1	**G. Höckert**	**Finland**
	2	L. Lehtinen	Finland
	3	H. Jonsson	Sweden

1948	1	**G. Reiff**	**Belgium**
	2	E. Zatopek	Czechoslovakia
	3	W. Slijkhuis	Netherlands
1952	1	**E. Zatopek**	**Czechoslovakia**
	2	A. Mimoun	France
	3	H. Schade	Germany
1956	1	**V. Kuts**	**U.S.S.R.**
	2	G. Pirie	Great Britain
	3	D. Ibbotson	Great Britain
1960	1	**M. Halberg**	**New Zealand**
	2	H. Grodotzki	Germany
	3	K. Zimny	Poland
1964	1	**R. Schul**	**U.S.A.**
	2	H. Norpoth	Germany
	3	W. Dellinger	U.S.A.
1968	1	**M. Gammoudi**	**Tunisia**
	2	K. Keino	Kenya
	3	N. Temu	Kenya
1972	1	**L. Viren**	**Finland**
	2	M. Gammoudi	Tunisia
	3	I. Stewart	Great Britain
1976	1	**L. Viren**	**Finland**
	2	D. Quax	New Zealand
	3	K-P Hildenbrand	West Germany
1980	1	**M. Yifter**	**Ethiopia**
	2	S. Nyambui	Tanzania
	3	K. Maaninka	Finland

ATHLETICS (10,000 metres) Men

YEAR	PLACE	NAME	COUNTRY
1912	1	**H. Kolemainen**	**Finland**
	2	L. Tewanima	U.S.A.
	3	A. Stenroos	Finland
1920	1	**P. Nurmi**	**Finland**
	2	J. Guillemot	France
	3	J. Wilson	Great Britain
1924	1	**V. Ritola**	**Finland**
	2	E. Wide	Sweden
	3	E. Berg	Finland
1928	1	**P. Nurmi**	**Finland**
	2	V. Ritola	Finland
	3	E. Wide	Sweden
1932	1	**J. Kusocinski**	**Poland**
	2	V. Iso-Hollo	Finland
	3	L. Virtanen	Finland
1936	1	**I. Salminen**	**Finland**
	2	A. Askola	Finland
	3	V. Iso-Hollo	Finland
1948	1	**E. Zatopek**	**Czechoslovakia**
	2	A. Mimoun	France
	3	B. Albertsson	Sweden
1952	1	**E. Zatopek**	**Czechoslovakia**
	2	A. Mimoun	France
	3	A. Anufriyev	U.S.S.R.
1956	1	**V. Kuts**	**U.S.S.R.**
	2	J. Kovacs	Hungary
	3	A. Lawrence	Australia
1960	1	**P. Bolotnikov**	**U.S.S.R.**
	2	H. Grodotzki	Germany
	3	D. Power	Australia
1964	1	**W. Mills**	**U.S.A.**
	2	M. Gammoudi	Tunisia
	3	R. Clarke	Australia
1968	1	**N. Temu**	**Kenya**
	2	M. Wolde	Ethiopia
	3	M. Gammoudi	Tunisia
1972	1	**I. Viren**	**Finland**
	2	E. Puttemans	Belgium
	3	M. Yifter	Ethiopia
1976	1	**Lasse Viren**	**Finland**
	2	Carlos Lopes	Portugal
	3	Brendan Foster	United Kingdom
1980	1	**Miruts Yifter**	**Ethiopia**
	2	Kaarlo Maaninka	Finland
	3	Mohammed Kedir	Ethiopia

ATHLETICS (marathon) Men

YEAR	PLACE	NAME	COUNTRY
1896	1	**S. Louis**	**Greece**
	2	C. Vasilakos	Greece.
	3	G. Kellner	Hungary
1900	1	**M. Théato**	**France**
	2	E. Champion	France
	3	E. Fast	Sweden
1904	1	**T. Hicks**	**U.S.A.**
	2	A. Corey	U.S.A.
	3	A. Newton	U.S.A.
1908	1	**J. Hayes**	**U.S.A.**
	2	C. Hefferon	South Africa
	3	J. Forshaw	U.S.A.
1912	1	**K. McArthur**	**South Africa**
	2	C. Gitsham	South Africa
	3	G. Strobino	U.S.A.
1920	1	**H. Kolehmainen**	**Finland**
	2	J. Lossman	Estonia
	3	V. Arri	Italy
1924	1	**A. Stenroos**	**Finland**
	2	R. Bertini	Italy
	3	C. DeMar	U.S.A.
1928	1	**M. Ouafi**	**France**
	2	M. Plaza	Chile
	3	M. Marttelin	Finland
1932	1	**J.C. Zabala**	**Argentina**
	2	S. Ferris	Great Britain
	3	A. Toivonen	Finland
1936	1	**K. Son**	**Japan**
	2	E. Harper	Great Britain
	3	S. Nan	Japan
1948	1	**D. Cabrera**	**Argentina**
	2	T. Richards	Great Britain
	3	E. Gailly	Belgium
1952	1	**E. Zatopek**	**Czechoslovakia**
	2	R. Gorno	Argentina
	3	G. Jansson	Sweden
1956	1	**A. Mimoun**	**France**
	2	F. Mihalic	Yugoslavia
	3	V. Karvonen	Finland
1960	1	**A. Bikila**	**Ethiopia**
	2	R.B. Abdesselem	Morocco
	3	B. Magee	New Zealand
1964	1	**A. Bikila**	**Ethiopia**
	2	B. Heatley	Great Britain
	3	K. Tsuburaya	Japan
1968	1	**M. Wolde**	**Ethiopia**
	2	K. Kimihara	Japan
	3	M. Ryan	New Zealand
1972	1	**F. Shorter**	**U.S.A.**
	2	K. Lismont	Belgium
	3	M. Wolde	Ethiopia
1976	1	**Waldemar Cierpinski**	**German Dem. Rep.**
	2	Frank Shorter	U.S.A.
	3	Karel Lismont	Belgium
1980	1	**Waldemar Cierpinski**	**German Dem. Rep.**
	2	Gerard Nijboer	Netherlands
	3	Setymkul Bzhumanazarov	U.S.S.R.

ATHLETICS (400 metres relay) Men

YEAR	PLACE	COUNTRY
1912	1	**Great Britain**
	2	Sweden
		Germany placed second but was disqualified.
1920	1	**U.S.A.**
	2	France
	3	Sweden
1924	1	**U.S.A.**
	2	Great Britain
	3	Netherlands
1928	1	**U.S.A.**
	2	Germany
	3	Great Britain
1932	1	**U.S.A.**
	2	Germany
	3	Italy
1936	1	**U.S.A.**
	2	Italy
	3	Germany

YEAR	PLACE	COUNTRY
1948	1	U.S.A.
	2	Great Britain
	3	Italy
1952	1	U.S.A.
	2	U.S.S.R.
	3	Hungary
1956	1	U.S.A.
	2	U.S.S.R.
	3	Germany
1960	1	Germany
	2	U.S.S.R.
	3	Great Britain
1964	1	U.S.A.
	2	Poland
	3	France
1968	1	U.S.A.
	2	Cuba
	3	France
1972	1	U.S.A.
	2	U.S.S.R.
	3	Germany
1976	1	U.S.A.
	2	East Germany
	3	U.S.S.R.
1980	1	U.S.S.R.
	2	Poland
	3	France

ATHLETICS (1,600 metres relay) Men

YEAR	PLACE	COUNTRY
1908	1	U.S.A.
	2	Germany
	3	Hungary
1912	1	U.S.A.
	2	France
	3	Great Britain
1920	1	Great Britain
	2	South Africa
	3	France
1924	1	U.S.A.
	2	Sweden
	3	Great Britain
1928	1	U.S.A.
	2	Germany
	3	Canada
1932	1	U.S.A.
	2	Great Britain
	3	Canada
1936	1	Great Britain
	2	U.S.A.
	3	Germany
1948	1	U.S.A.
	2	France
	3	Sweden
1952	1	Jamaica
	2	U.S.A.
	3	Germany
1956	1	U.S.A.
	2	Australia
	3	Great Britain
1960	1	U.S.A.
	2	Germany
	3	British W.I.
1964	1	U.S.A.
	2	Great Britain
	3	Trinidad
1968	1	U.S.A.
	2	Kenya
	3	Germany
1972	1	Kenya
	2	Great Britain
	3	France
1976	1	U.S.A.
	2	Poland
	3	West Germany
1980	1	U.S.S.R.
	2	East Germany
	3	Italy

ATHLETICS (110 metres hurdle) Men

YEAR	PLACE	NAME	COUNTRY
1896	1	T. Curtis	U.S.A.
	2	G. Goulding	Great Britain
		Only two competitors took part in the final.	
1900	1	A. Kraenzlein	U.S.A.
	2	J. McLean	U.S.A.
	3	F. Moloney	U.S.A.
1904	1	F. Schule	U.S.A.
	2	T. Shideler	U.S.A.
	3	L. Ashburner	U.S.A.
1908	1	F. Smithson	U.S.A.
	2	J. Garrets	U.S.A.
	3	A. Shaw	U.S.A.
1912	1	F. Kelly	U.S.A.
	2	J. Wendell	U.S.A.
	3	M. Hawkins	U.S.A.
1920	1	E. Thomson	Canada
	2	H. Barron	U.S.A.
	3	F. Murray	U.S.A.
1924	1	D. Kinsey	U.S.A.
	2	S. Atkinson	South Africa
	3	S. Pettersson	Sweden
1928	1	S. Atkinson	South Africa
	2	S. Anderson	U.S.A.
	3	J. Collier	U.S.A.
1932	1	G. Saling	U.S.A.
	2	P. Beard	U.S.A.
	3	D. Finlay	Great Britain
1936	1	F. Towns	U.S.A.
	2	D. Finlay	Great Britain
	3	F. Pollard	U.S.A.
1948	1	W. Porter	U.S.A.
	2	C. Scott	U.S.A.
	3	C. Dixon	U.S.A.
1952	1	W.H. Dillard	U.S.A.
	2	J. Davis	U.S.A.
	3	A. Barnard	U.S.A.
1956	1	L. Calhoun	U.S.A.
	2	J. Davis	U.S.A.
	3	J. Shankle	U.S.A.
1960	1	L. Calhoun	U.S.A.
	2	W. May	U.S.A.
	3	H. Jones	U.S.A.
1964	1	H. Jones	U.S.A.
	2	B. Lindgren	U.S.A.
	3	A. Mikhailov	U.S.S.R.
1968	1	W. Davenport	U.S.A.
	2	E. Hall	U.S.A.
	3	E. Ottoz	Italy
1972	1	R. Milburn	U.S.A.
	2	G. Drut	France
	3	T. Hill	U.S.A.
1976	1	Guy Drut	France
	2	Alejandro Casanas	Cuba
	3	Willie Davenport	U.S.A.
1980	1	Thomas Munkelt	German Dem. Rep.
	2	Alejandro Casanas	Cuba
	3	Aleksandr Punchkov	U.S.S.R.

ATHLETICS (400 metres hurdle) Men

YEAR	PLACE	NAME	COUNTRY
1900	1	J.W. Tewksbury	U.S.A.
	2	H. Tauzin	France
	3	G. Orton	Canada
1904	1	H. Hillman	U.S.A.
	2	F. Waller	U.S.A.
	3	G. Poage	U.S.A.
1908	1	C. Bacon	U.S.A.
	2	H. Hillman	U.S.A.
	3	L. Tremeer	Great Britain
1920	1	F. Loomis	U.S.A.
	2	J. Norton	U.S.A.
	3	A. Desch	U.S.A.
1924	1	F.M. Taylor	U.S.A.
	2	E. Vilen	Finland
	3	I. Riley	U.S.A.
1928	1	D. Burghley	Great Britain
	2	F. Cuhel	U.S.A.
	3	F.M. Taylor	U.S.A.

YEAR	PLACE	NAME	COUNTRY
1932	1	R. Tisdall	Eire
	2	G. Hardin	U.S.A.
	3	F.M. Taylor	U.S.A.
1936	1	G. Hardin	U.S.A.
	2	J. Loaring	Canada
	3	M. White	Philippines
1948	1	R. Cochran	U.S.A.
	2	D. White	Ceylon
	3	R. Larsson	Sweden
1952	1	C. Moore	U.S.A.
	2	Y. Lituyev	U.S.S.R.
	3	J. Holland	New Zealand
1956	1	G. Davis	U.S.A.
	2	S.E. Southern	U.S.A.
	3	J. Culbreath	U.S.A.
1960	1	G. Davis	U.S.A.
	2	C. Cushman	U.S.A.
	3	R. Howard	U.S.A.
1964	1	W. Cawley	U.S.A.
	2	J. Cooper	Great Britain
	3	S. Morale	Italy
1968	1	D. Hemery	Great Britain
	2	G. Hennige	Germany
	3	J. Sherwood	Great Britain
1972	1	J. Akii Bua	Uganda
	2	R. Mann	U.S.A.
	3	D. Hemery	Great Britain
1976	1	Edwin Moses	U.S.A.
	2	Michael Shine	U.S.A.
	3	Evgenity Gavrilenko	U.S.S.R.
1980	1	Volker Beck	German Dem. Rep.
	2	Vasily Arkhipenko	U.S.S.R.
	3	Gary Oakes	United Kingdom

ATHLETICS (3,000 metres steeplechase) Men

YEAR	PLACE	NAME	COUNTRY
1900	1	G. Orton	Canada
	2	S. Robinson	Great Britain
	3	J. Chastanié	France
1904	1	J. Lightbody	U.S.A.
	2	J. Daly	Great Britain
	3	A. Newton	U.S.A.
1908	1	A. Russell	Great Britain
	2	A.J. Robertson	Great Britain
	3	J.L. Eisele	U.S.A.
1920	1	P. Hodge	Great Britain
	2	P. Flynn	U.S.A.
	3	E. Ambrosini	Italy
1924	1	V. Ritola	Finland
	2	E. Katz	Finland
	3	P. Bontemps	France
1928	1	T. Loukola	Finland
	2	P. Nurmi	Finland
	3	O. Andersen	Finland
1932	1	V. Iso-Hollo	Finland
	2	T. Evenson	Great Britain
	3	J. McCluskey	U.S.A.
1936	1	V. Iso-Hollo	Finland
	2	K. Tuominen	Finland
	3	A. Dompert	Germany
1948	1	T. Sjöstrand	Sweden
	2	E. Elmsäter	Sweden
	3	G. Hagström	Sweden
1952	1	H. Ashenfelter	U.S.A.
	2	V. Kazantzev	U.S.S.R.
	3	J. Disley	Great Britain
1956	1	C. Brasher	Great Britain
	2	S. Rozsnyoi	Hungary
	3	E. Larsen	Norway
1960	1	Z. Krzyszkowiak	Poland
	2	N. Sokolov	U.S.S.R.
	3	S. Rshischtschin	U.S.S.R.
1964	1	G. Roelants	Belgium
	2	M. Herriott	Great Britain
	3	I. Belyayev	U.S.S.R.
1968	1	A. Biwott	Kenya
	2	B. Kogo	Kenya
	3	G. Young	U.S.A.
1972	1	K. Keino	Kenya
	2	B. Jipcho	Kenya
	3	T. Kantanen	Finland

1976	1	Anders Garderud	Sweden
	2	Bronislaw Malinowski	Poland
	3	Frank Baumgartl	German Dem. Rep.
1980	1	Bronislaw Malinowski	Poland
	2	Filbert Bayi	Tanzania
	3	Eshetu Tura	Ethiopia

ATHLETICS (20 km walk) Men

YEAR	PLACE	NAME	COUNTRY
1908	1	G.E. Larner (3.5km)	Great Britain
	2	E.J. Webb	Great Britain
	3	H.E. Kerr	Australia
1912	1	G.H. Goulding (10km)	Canada
	2	E.J. Webb	Great Britain
	3	F. Altimani	Italy
1920	1	U. Frigerio (10km)	Italy
	2	J.B. Pearman	U.S.A.
	3	C.E.J. Gunn	Great Britain
1924	1	U. Frigerio (10km)	Italy
	2	G. Goodwin	Great Britain
	3	C. MacMaster	South Africa
1948	1	J.F. Mikaelsson (10km)	Sweden
	2	I. Johansson	Sweden
	3	F. Schwab	Switzerland
1956	1	L. Spirin	U.S.S.R.
	2	A. Mikenas	U.S.S.R.
	3	B. Yunk	U.S.S.R.
1960	1	V. Golubnitschy	U.S.S.R.
	2	N. Freeman	Australia
	3	S. Vickers	Great Britain
1964	1	K. Matthews	Great Britain
	2	D. Lindner	Germany
	3	V. Golubnitschy	U.S.S.R.
1968	1	V. Golubnitschy	U.S.S.R.
	2	J. Pedraza	Mexico
	3	N. Smaga	U.S.S.R.
1972	1	P. Frenkel	East Germany
	2	V. Golubnitschy	U.S.S.R.
	3	H. Reimann	East Germany
1976	1	Daniel Bautista	Mexico
	2	Hans Reimann	German Dem. Rep.
	3	Peter Frenkel	German Dem. Rep.
1980	1	Maurizio Damilano	Italy
	2	Pyotr Pochinchuk	U.S.S.R.
	3	Roland Wieser	German Dem. Rep.

ATHLETICS (running high jump) Men

YEAR	PLACE	NAME	COUNTRY
1896	1	E. Clark	U.S.A.
	2	J. Connolly	U.S.A.
	3	R. Garrett	U.S.A.
1900	1	I. Baxter	U.S.A.
	2	P. Leahy	Great Britain
	3	L. Gönczy	Hungary
1904	1	S. Jones	U.S.A.
	2	G.P. Serviss	U.S.A.
	3	P. Weinstein	Germany
1908	1	H. Porter	U.S.A.
	2	C. Leahy/ I. Somodi G. Andre	Great Britain/ Hungary France
1912	1	A. Richards	U.S.A.
	2	H. Liesche	Germany
	3	G. Horine	U.S.A.
1920	1	R. Landon	U.S.A.
	2	H. Muller	U.S.A.
	3	B. Ekelund	Sweden
1924	1	H. Osborn	U.S.A.
	2	L. Brown	U.S.A.
	3	P. Lewden	France
1928	1	R. King	U.S.A.
	2	B. Hedges	U.S.A.
	3	C. Menard	France
1932*	1	D. McNaughton	Canada
	2	R. Van Osdel	U.S.A.
	3	S. Toribio	Philippines
1936	1	C. Johnson	U.S.A.
	2	D. Albritton	U.S.A.
	3	D. Thurber	U.S.A.
1948	1	J. Winter	Australia
	2	B. Paulsen	Norway
	3	G. Stanich	U.S.A.

1952	1	W. Davis	U.S.A.
	2	K. Wiesner	U.S.A.
	3	J.T. Conceicao	Brazil
1956	1	C. Dumas	U.S.A.
	2	C. Porter	Australia
	3	I. Kachkarov	U.S.S.R.
1960	1	R. Schavlakadze	U.S.S.R.
	2	V. Brumel	U.S.S.R.
	3	J. Thomas	U.S.A.
1964	1	V. Brumel	U.S.S.R.
	2	J. Thomas	U.S.A.
	3	J. Rambo	U.S.A.
1968	1	R. Fosbury	U.S.A.
	2	E. Caruthers	U.S.A.
	3	V. Gavrilov	U.S.S.R.
1972	1	Y. Tarmak	U.S.S.R.
	2	S. Junge	East Germany
	3	D. Stones	U.S.A.
1976	1	Jacek Wszola	Poland
	2	Greg Joy	Canada
	3	Dwight E. Stones	U.S.A.
1980	1	Gerd Wessig	German Dem. Rep.
	2	Jacek Wszola	Poland
	3	Jorg Freimuth	German Dem. Rep.

* The first four places were decided in a jump-off.

ATHLETICS (pole vault) Men

YEAR	PLACE	NAME	COUNTRY
1896	1	W. Hoyt	U.S.A.
	2	A. Tyler	U.S.A.
	3	E. Damaskos	Greece
1900	1	I. Baxter	U.S.A.
	2	M.B. Colkett	U.S.A.
	3	C.A. Andersen	Norway
1904	1	C. Dvorak	U.S.A.
	2	L. Samse	U.S.A.
	3	L. Wilkins	U.S.A.
1908	1	A. Gilbert/E. Cook	U.S.A.
	3	E. Archibald/C.S. Jacobs B. Söderström	Canada/U.S.A. Sweden
1912	1	H. Babcock	U.S.A.
	2	F. Nelson/M. Wright	U.S.A.
	3	B. Uggla/W. Happenny F. Murphy	Sweden/Canada
1920	1	F. Foss	U.S.A.
	2	H. Petersen	Denmark
	3	E. Myers	U.S.A.
1924	1	L. Barnes	U.S.A.
	2	G. Graham	U.S.A.
	3	J. Brooker	U.S.A.
1928	1	S. Carr	U.S.A.
	2	W. Droegemuller	U.S.A.
	3	C. McGinnis	U.S.A.
1932	1	W. Miller	U.S.A.
	2	S. Nishida	Japan
	3	G. Jefferson	U.S.A.
1936	1	E. Meadows	U.S.A.
	2	S. Nishida	Japan
	3	S. Oe	Japan
1948	1	O.G. Smith	U.S.A.
	2	E. Kataja	Finland
	3	R. Richards	U.S.A.
1952	1	R. Richards	U.S.A.
	2	D. Laz	U.S.A.
	3	R. Lundberg	Sweden
1956	1	R. Richards	U.S.A.
	2	R. Gutowski	U.S.A.
	3	G. Roubanis	Greece
1960	1	D. Bragg	U.S.A.
	2	R. Morris	U.S.A.
	3	E. Landström	Finland
1964	1	F. Hansen	U.S.A.
	2	W. Reinhardt	Germany
	3	K. Lehnertz	Germany
1968	1	R. Seagren	U.S.A.
	2	C. Schiprowski	Germany
	3	W. Nordwig	East Germany
1972	1	W. Nordwig	East Germany
	2	R. Seagren	U.S.A.
	3	J. Johnson	U.S.A.

1976	1	Tadeusz Slusarski	Poland
	2	Antti Kalliomaki	Finland
	3	David Roberts	U.S.A.
1980	1	Wladyslaw Kozakiewicz	Poland
	2	Konstantin Volkov	U.S.S.R.
	3	Tadeusz Slusarski	Poland

ATHLETICS (long jump) Men

YEAR	PLACE	NAME	COUNTRY
1896	1	E. Clark	U.S.A.
	2	R. Garrett	U.S.A.
	3	J. Connolly	U.S.A.
1900	1	A. Kraenzlein	U.S.A.
	2	M. Prinstein	U.S.A.
	3	P. Leahy	Great Britain
1904	1	M. Prinstein	U.S.A.
	2	D. Frank	U.S.A.
	3	R. Stangland	U.S.A.
1908	1	F. Irons	U.S.A.
	2	D. Kelly	U.S.A.
	3	C. Bricker	Canada
1912	1	A. Gutterson	U.S.A.
	2	C. Bricker	Canada
	3	G. Aberg	Sweden
1920	1	W. Pettersson	Sweden
	2	C. Johnson	U.S.A.
	3	E. Abrahamsson	Sweden
1924	1	W. De Hart Hubbard	U.S.A.
	2	E. Gourdin	U.S.A.
	3	S. Hansen	Norway
1928	1	E. Hamm	U.S.A.
	2	S. Cator	Haiti
	3	A. Bates	U.S.A.
1932	1	E. Gordon	U.S.A.
	2	C.L. Redd	U.S.A.
	3	C. Nambu	Japan
1936	1	J. Owens	U.S.A.
	2	L. Long	Germany
	3	N. Tajima	Japan
1948	1	W. Steele	U.S.A.
	2	T. Bruce	Australia
	3	H. Douglas	U.S.A.
1952	1	J. Biffle	U.S.A.
	2	M. Gourdine	U.S.A.
	3	O. Foldessy	Hungary
1956	1	G. Bell	U.S.A.
	2	J. Bennett	U.S.A.
	3	J. Valkama	Finland
1960	1	R. Boston	U.S.A.
	2	I. Roberson	U.S.A.
	3	I. Ter-Ovanesyan	U.S.S.R.
1964	1	L. Davies	Great Britain
	2	R. Boston	U.S.A.
	3	I. Ter-Ovanesyan	U.S.S.R.
1968	1	R. Beamon	U.S.A.
	2	K. Beer	East Germany
	3	R. Boston	U.S.A.
1972	1	R. Williams	U.S.A.
	2	H. Baumgartner	Germany
	3	A. Robinson	U.S.A.
1976	1	Arnie Robinson	U.S.A.
	2	Randy L. Williams	U.S.A.
	3	Frank Wartenberg	German Dem. Rep.
1980	1	Lutz Dombrowski	German Dem. Rep.
	2	Frank Paschek	German Dem. Rep.
	3	Valery Podluzhnyi	U.S.S.R.

ATHLETICS (triple jump) Men

YEAR	PLACE	NAME	COUNTRY
1896	1	J. Connelly	U.S.A.
	2	A. Tuffere	France
	3	I. Persakis	Greece
1900	1	M. Prinstein	U.S.A.
	2	J. Connolly	U.S.A.
	3	L. Sheldon	U.S.A.
1904	1	M. Prinstein	U.S.A.
	2	E. Englehardt	U.S.A.
	3	R. Stangland	U.S.A.
1908	1	T. Ahearne	Great Britain
	2	G. MacDonald	Canada
	3	E. Larsen	Norway

1912	1	**G. Lindblom**	**Sweden**
	2	G. Aberg	Sweden
	3	E. Almlöf	Sweden
1920	1	**V. Tuulos**	**Finland**
	2	F. Jansson	Sweden
	3	E. Almlöf	Sweden
1924	1	**A. Winter**	**Australia**
	2	L. Bruneto	Argentina
	3	V. Tuulos	Finland
1928	1	**M. Oda**	**Japan**
	2	L. Casey	U.S.A.
	3	V. Tuulos	Finland
1932	1	**C. Nambu**	**Japan**
	2	E. Svensson	Sweden
	3	K. Oshima	Japan
1936	1	**N. Tajima**	**Japan**
	2	M. Harada	Japan
	3	J. Metcalfe	Australia
1948	1	**A. Ahman**	**Sweden**
	2	G. Avery	Australia
	3	R. Sarialp	Turkey
1952	1	**A.F. da Silva**	**Brazil**
	2	L. Schtscherbakov	U.S.S.R.
	3	A. Devonish	Venezuela
1956	1	**A.F. da Silva**	**Brazil**
	2	V. Einarsson	Iceland
	3	V. Kreyer	U.S.S.R.
1960	1	**J. Schmidt**	**Poland**
	2	V. Goryayev	U.S.S.R.
	3	V. Kreyer	U.S.S.R.
1964	1	**J. Schmidt**	**Poland**
	2	O. Fedoseyev	U.S.S.R.
	3	V. Kravtschenko	U.S.S.R.
1968	1	**V. Saneyev**	**U.S.S.R.**
	2	N. Prudencio	Brazil
	3	G. Gentile	Italy
1972	1	**V. Saneyev**	**U.S.S.R.**
	2	J. Drehmel	East Germany
	3	N. Prudencio	Brazil
1976	1	**Viktor Saneyev**	**U.S.S.R.**
	2	James Butts	U.S.A.
	3	Joao de Oliveira	Brazil
1980	1	**Jaak Uudmae**	**U.S.S.R.**
	2	Viktor Saneyev	U.S.S.R.
	3	Joao de Oliveira	Brazil

ATHLETICS (shot put) Men

YEAR	PLACE	NAME	COUNTRY
1896	1	**R. Garrett**	**U.S.A.**
	2	M. Gouskos	Greece
	3	G. Papasideris	Greece
1900	1	**R. Sheldon**	**U.S.A.**
	2	J. McCracken	U.S.A.
	3	R. Garrett	U.S.A.
1904	1	**R. Rose**	**U.S.A.**
	2	W. Coe	U.S.A.
	3	L.B. Feuerbach	U.S.A.
1908	1	**R. Rose**	**U.S.A.**
	2	D. Horgan	Great Britain
	3	J. Garrels	U.S.A.
1912	1	**P. McDonald**	**U.S.A.**
	2	R. Rose	U.S.A.
	3	L. Whitney	U.S.A.
1920	1	**V. Pörhölä**	**Finland**
	2	E. Niklander	Finland
	3	H. Liversedge	U.S.A.
1924	1	**C. Houser**	**U.S.A.**
	2	G. Hartranft	U.S.A.
	3	R. Hills	U.S.A.
1928	1	**J. Kuck**	**U.S.A.**
	2	H. Brix	U.S.A.
	3	E. Hirschfield	Germany
1932	1	**L. Sexton**	**U.S.A.**
	2	H. Rothert	U.S.A.
	3	F. Douda	Czechoslovakia
1936	1	**H. Woellke**	**Germany**
	2	S. Bärlund	Finland
	3	G. Stöck	Germany
1948	1	**W. Thompson**	**U.S.A.**
	2	J. Delaney	U.S.A.
	3	J. Fuchs	U.S.A.
1952	1	**W.P. O'Brien**	**U.S.A.**
	2	D. Hooper	U.S.A.
	3	J. Fuchs	U.S.A.
1956	1	**W.P. O'Brien**	**U.S.A.**
	2	W. Nieder	U.S.A.
	3	J. Skobla	Czechoslovakia
1960	1	**W. Nieder**	**U.S.A.**
	2	W.P. O'Brien	U.S.A.
	3	D. Long	U.S.A.
1964	1	**D. Long**	**U.S.A.**
	2	R. Matson	U.S.A.
	3	V. Varju	Hungary
1968	1	**R. Matson**	**U.S.A.**
	2	G. Woods	U.S.A.
	3	E. Guschtschin	U.S.S.R.
1972	1	**W. Komar**	**Poland**
	2	G. Woods	U.S.A.
	3	H. Briesenick	East Germany
1976	1	**Udo Beyer**	**German Dem. Rep.**
	2	Evgenity Mironov	U.S.S.R.
	3	Alexandr Baryshnikov	U.S.S.R.
1980	1	**Vladimir Kiselyov**	**U.S.S.R.**
	2	Alexandr Baryshnikov	U.S.S.R.
	3	Udo Beyer	German Dem. Rep.

ATHLETICS (hammer throw) Men

YEAR	PLACE	NAME	COUNTRY
1900	1	**J. Flanagan**	**U.S.A.**
	2	T. Hare	U.S.A.
	3	J. McCracken	U.S.A.
1904	1	**J. Flanagan**	**U.S.A.**
	2	J. DeWitt	U.S.A.
	3	R. Rose	U.S.A.
1908	1	**J. Flanagan**	**U.S.A.**
	2	M. McGrath	U.S.A.
	3	C. Walsh	U.S.A.
1912	1	**M. McGrath**	**U.S.A.**
	2	D. Gillis	Canada
	3	C. Childs	U.S.A.
1920	1	**P. Ryan**	**U.S.A.**
	2	C.J. Lind	Sweden
	3	B. Bennet	U.S.A.
1924	1	**F. Tootell**	**U.S.A.**
	2	M. McGrath	U.S.A.
	3	M. Nokes	Great Britain
1928	1	**P. O'Callaghan**	**Eire**
	2	O. Skiöld	Sweden
	3	E. Black	U.S.A.
1932	1	**P. O'Callaghan**	**Eire**
	2	V. Pörhölä	Finland
	3	P. Zaremba	U.S.A.
1936	1	**K. Hein**	**Germany**
	2	E. Blask	Germany
	3	F. Warngard	Sweden
1948	1	**I. Nemeth**	**Hungary**
	2	I. Gubijan	Yugoslavia
	3	R. Bennett	U.S.A.
1952	1	**J. Csermak**	**Hungary**
	2	K. Storch	Germany
	3	I. Nemeth	Hungary
1956	1	**H. Connolly**	**U.S.A.**
	2	M. Krivonosov	U.S.S.R.
	3	A. Samotsvyetov	U.S.S.R.
1960	1	**V. Rudenkov**	**U.S.S.R.**
	2	G. Zsivotzky	Hungary
	3	T. Rut	Poland
1964	1	**R. Klim**	**U.S.S.R.**
	2	G. Zsivotzky	Hungary
	3	U. Beyer	Germany
1968	1	**G. Zsivotzky**	**Hungary**
	2	R. Klim	U.S.S.R.
	3	L. Lovasz	Hungary
1972	1	**A. Bondarchuk**	**U.S.S.R.**
	2	J. Sachse	East Germany
	3	V. Khmelevski	U.S.S.R.
1976	1	**Y. Sedykh**	**U.S.S.R.**
	2	A. Spiridonov	U.S.S.R.
	3	A. Bondarchuk	U.S.S.R.
1980	1	**Y. Sedykh**	**U.S.S.R.**
	2	S. Litvinov	U.S.S.R.
	3	Y. Tamm	---

ATHLETICS (discus throw) Men

YEAR	PLACE	NAME	COUNTRY
1896	1	**R. Garrett**	**U.S.A.**
	2	P. Parasakevopoulos	Greece
	3	S. Versis	Greece
1900	1	**R. Bauer**	**Hungary**
	2	F. Janda-Suk	Bohemia
	3	R. Sheldon	U.S.A.
1904	1	**M. Sheridan**	**U.S.A.**
	2	R. Rose	U.S.A.
	3	N. Georgantos	Greece
1908	1	**M. Sheridan**	**U.S.A.**
	2	M.H. Griffin	U.S.A.
	3	M. Horr	U.S.A.
1912	1	**A. Taipale**	**Finland**
	2	R. Byrd	U.S.A.
	3	J. Duncan	U.S.A.
1920	1	**E. Niklander**	**Finland**
	2	A. Taipale	Finland
	3	A. Pope	U.S.A.
1924	1	**C. Houser**	**U.S.A.**
	2	V. Niittymaa	Finland
	3	T. Lieb	U.S.A.
1928	1	**C. Houser**	**U.S.A.**
	2	A. Kivi	Finland
	3	J. Corson	U.S.A.
1932	1	**J. Anderson**	**U.S.A.**
	2	H. Laborde	U.S.A.
	3	P. Winter	France
1936	1	**K. Carpenter**	**U.S.A.**
	2	G. Dunn	U.S.A.
	3	G. Oberweger	Italy
1948	1	**A. Consolini**	**Italy**
	2	G. Tosi	Italy
	3	F. Gordien	U.S.A.
1952	1	**S. Iness**	**U.S.A.**
	2	A. Consolini	Italy
	3	J. Dillion	U.S.A.
1956	1	**A. Oerter**	**U.S.A.**
	2	F. Gordien	U.S.A.
	3	D. Koch	U.S.A.
1960	1	**A. Oerter**	**U.S.A.**
	2	R. Babka	U.S.A.
	3	R. Cochran	U.S.A.
1964	1	**A. Oerter**	**U.S.A.**
	2	L. Danek	Czechoslovakia
	3	D. Weill	U.S.A.
1968	1	**A. Oerter**	**U.S.A.**
	2	L. Milde	East Germany
	3	L. Danek	Czechoslovakia
1972	1	**L. Danek**	**Czechoslovakia**
	2	J. Silvester	U.S.A.
	3	R. Bruch	Sweden
1976	1	**M. MacWilkins**	**U.S.A.**
	2	W. Schmidt	German Dem. Rep.
	3	J. Powell	U.S.A.
1980	1	**V. Rasschupkin**	**U.S.S.R.**
	2	I. Bugav	Czechoslovakia
	3	L. Delis	Cuba

ATHLETICS (javelin throw — free style) Men

YEAR	PLACE	NAME	COUNTRY
1908	1	**E. Lemming**	**Sweden**
	2	A. Halse	Norway
	3	O. Nilsson	Sweden
1912	1	**E. Lemming**	**Sweden**
	2	J. Saaristo	Finland
	3	M. Koczan	Hungary
1920	1	**J. Myyrä**	**Finland**
	2	U. Peltonen	Finland
	3	P.J. Johansson	Finland
1924	1	**J. Myyrä**	**Finland**
	2	G. Lindstrom	Sweden
	3	E. Oberst	U.S.A.
1928	1	**E. Lundkvist**	**Sweden**
	2	B. Szepes	Hungary
	3	O. Sunde	Norway
1932	1	**M. Järvinen**	**Finland**
	2	M. Sippala	Finland
	3	E. Penttilä	Finland

1936	1	G. Stöck	Germany
	2	Y. Nikkanen	Finland
	3	K. Toivonen	Finland
1948	1	T. Rautavaara	Finland
	2	S. Seymour	U.S.A.
	3	J. Varszegi	Hungary
1952	1	C. Young	U.S.A.
	2	W. Miller	U.S.A.
	3	T. Hyytiäinen	Finland
1956	1	E. Danielsen	Norway
	2	J. Sidlo	Poland
	3	V. Tsybulenko	U.S.S.R.
1960	1	V. Tsybulenko	U.S.S.R.
	2	W. Krüger	Germany
	3	G. Kulcsar	Hungary
1964	1	P. Nevala	Finland
	2	G. Kulscar	Hungary
	3	J. Lusis	U.S.S.R.
1968	1	J. Lusis	U.S.S.R.
	2	J. Kinnunen	Finland
	3	G. Kulcsar	Hungary
1972	1	K. Wolfermann	Germany
	2	J. Lusis	U.S.S.R.
	3	W. Schmidt	U.S.A.
1976	1	M. Nemeth	Hungary
	2	H. Siitonen	Finland
	3	G. Megelea	Rumania
1980	1	D. Kula	U.S.S.R.
	2	A. Makarov	U.S.S.R.
	3	W. Hanisch	German Dem. Rep.

ATHLETICS (decathlon) Men

YEAR	PLACE	NAME	COUNTRY
1912*	1	H. Wieslander	Sweden
	2	C. Lomberg	Sweden
	3	G. Holmer	Sweden
1920	1	H. Lovland	Norway
	2	B. Hamilton	U.S.A.
	3	B. Ohlson	Sweden
1924	1	H. Osborn	U.S.A.
	2	E. Norton	U.S.A.
	3	A. Klumberg	Estonia
1928	1	P. Yrjölä	Finland
	2	A. Järvinen	Finland
	3	K. Doherty	U.S.A.
1932	1	J. Bausch	U.S.A.
	2	A. Järvinen	Finland
	3	W. Eberle	Germany
1936	1	G. Morris	U.S.A.
	2	R. Clark	U.S.A.
	3	J. Parker	U.S.A.
1948	1	R. Mathias	U.S.A.
	2	I. Heinrich	France
	3	F. Simmons	U.S.A.
1952	1	R. Mathias	U.S.A.
	2	M. Campbell	U.S.A.
	3	F. Simmons	U.S.A.
1956	1	M. Campbell	U.S.A.
	2	R. Johnson	U.S.A.
	3	V. Kuznyetsov	U.S.S.R.
1960	1	R. Johnson	U.S.A.
	2	C.K. Yang	Taiwan
	3	V. Kuznyetsov	U.S.S.R.
1964	1	W. Holdorf	Germany
	2	R. Aun	U.S.S.R.
	3	H. Walde	Germany
1968	1	W. Toomey	U.S.A.
	2	H. Walde	Germany
	3	K. Bendlin	Germany
1972	1	N. Avilov	U.S.S.R.
	2	L. Litvenenko	U.S.S.R.
	3	R. Katus	Poland
1976	1	Bruce Jenner	U.S.A.
	2	Guido Kratschmer	West Germany
	3	Nikolai Avilov	U.S.S.R.
1980	1	Daley Thompson	United Kingdom
	2	Yuri Kutsenko	U.S.S.R.
	3	Sergei Zhelanov	U.S.S.R.

*The decathlon was introduced in 1904 but was considerably different to that which followed when re-introduced in 1912.

ATHLETICS (100 metres) Women

YEAR	PLACE	NAME	COUNTRY
1928	1	E. Robinson	U.S.A.
	2	E. Rosenfeld	Canada
	3	E. Smith	Canada
1932	1	S. Walasiewicz	Poland
	2	H. Strike	Canada
	3	W. von Bremen	U.S.A.
1936	1	H. Stephens	U.S.A.
	2	H. Walasiewicz	Poland
	3	K. Krauss	Germany
1948	1	F. Blankers-Koen	Netherlands
	2	D. Manley	Great Britain
	3	S. Strickland	Australia
1952	1	M. Jackson	Australia
	2	D. Hasenjager-Robb	South Africa
	3	S. de la Hunty-Strickland	Australia
1956	1	B. Cuthbert	Australia
	2	C. Stubnick	Germany
	3	M. Matthews	Australia
1960	1	W. Rudolph	U.S.A.
	2	D. Hyman	Great Britain
	3	G. Leone	Italy
1964	1	W. Tyus	U.S.A.
	2	E. McGuire	U.S.A.
	3	E. Klobukowska	Poland
1968	1	W. Tyus	U.S.A.
	2	B. Ferrell	U.S.A.
	3	I. Szewinska-Kirszenstein	Poland
1972	1	R. Stecher	East Germany
	2	R. Boyle	Australia
	3	S. Chivas	Cuba
1976	1	A. Richter	West Germany
	2	R. Stecher	German Dem. Rep.
	3	J. Helten	West Germany
1980	1	L. Kondrateva	U.S.S.R.
	2	M. Gohr	German Dem. Rep.
	3	J. Auerswald	German Dem. Rep.

ATHLETICS (200 metres) Women

YEAR	PLACE	NAME	COUNTRY
1948	1	F. Blankers-Koen	Netherlands
	2	A. Williamson	Great Britain
	3	A. Patterson	U.S.A.
1952	1	M. Jackson	Australia
	2	B. Brouwer	Netherlands
	3	N. Khnykina	U.S.S.R.
1956	1	B. Cuthbert	Australia
	2	C. Stubnick	Germany
	3	M. Matthews	Australia
1960	1	W. Rudolph	U.S.A.
	2	J. Heine	Germany
	3	D. Hyman	Great Britain
1964	1	E. McGuire	U.S.A.
	2	I. Kirszenstein	Poland
	3	M. Black	Australia
	3	I. Szewinska-Kirszenstein	Poland
	2	R. Boyle	Australia
	3	J. Lamy	Australia
1972	1	R. Stecher	East Germany
	2	R. Boyle	Australia
	3	I. Szewinska-Kirszenstein	Poland
1976	1	B. Eckert	German Dem. Rep.
	2	A. Richter	West Germany
	3	R. Stecher	German Dem. Rep.
1980	1	B. Wockel	German Dem. Rep.
	2	N. Bochina	U.S.S.R.
	3	M. Ottey	Jamaica

ATHLETICS (400 metres) Women

YEAR	PLACE	NAME	COUNTRY
1964	1	B. Cuthbert	Australia
	2	A. Packer	Great Britain
	3	J. Amoore	Australia
1968	1	C. Besson	France
	2	L. Board	Great Britain
	3	N. Petschenkina	U.S.S.R.

1972	1	M. Zehrt	East Germany
	2	R. Wilden	Germany
	3	K. Hammond	U.S.A.
1976	1	I. Szewinska	Poland
	2	C. Brehmer	German Dem. Rep.
	3	E. Streidt	German Dem. Rep.
1980	1	M. Kuch	German Dem. Rep.
	2	J. Kratochvilova	Czechoslovakia
	3	C. Lathan	German Dem. Rep.

ATHLETICS (800 metres) Women

YEAR	PLACE	NAME	COUNTRY
1928	1	L. Radke-Batschauer	Germany
	2	K. Hitomi	Japan
	3	I. Gentzel	Sweden
1960	1	L. Schevtsova	U.S.S.R.
	2	B. Jones	Australia
	3	U. Donath	Germany
1964	1	A. Packer	Great Britain
	2	M. Dupureur	France
	3	A. Chamberlain	New Zealand
1968	1	M. Manning	U.S.A.
	2	I. Silai	Rumania
	3	M. Gommers	Netherlands
1972	1	H. Falck	Germany
	2	N. Sabaite	U.S.S.R.
	3	G. Hoffmeister	East Germany
1976	1	T. Kazankina	U.S.S.R.
	2	N. Chtereva	Bulgaria
	3	E. Zinn	German Dem. Rep.
1980	1	N. Olizarenko	U.S.S.R.
	2	O. Mineyeva	U.S.S.R.
	3	T. Providokhina	U.S.S.R.

ATHLETICS (1,500 metres) Women

YEAR	PLACE	NAME	COUNTRY
1972	1	L. Bragina	U.S.S.R.
	2	G. Hoffmeister	East Germany
	3	P. Cacchi	Italy
1976	1	T. Kazankina	U.S.S.R.
	2	G. Hoffmeister	German Dem. Rep.
	3	V. Klapezgnski	German Dem. Rep.
1980	1	T. Kazankina	U.S.S.R.
	2	C. Wartenberg	German Dem. Rep.
	3	N. Olizarenko	U.S.S.R.

ATHLETICS (400 metres relay) Women

YEAR	PLACE	COUNTRY
1928	1	Canada
	2	U.S.A.
	3	Germany
1932	1	U.S.A.
	2	Canada
	3	Great Britain
1936	1	U.S.A.
	2	Great Britain
	3	Canada
1948	1	Netherlands
	2	Australia
	3	Canada
1952	1	U.S.A.
	2	Germany
	3	Great Britain
1956	1	Australia
	2	Great Britain
	3	U.S.A.
1960	1	U.S.A.
	2	Germany
	3	Poland
1964	1	Poland
	2	U.S.A.
	3	Great Britain
1968	1	U.S.A.
	2	Cuba
	3	U.S.S.R.
1972	1	Germany
	2	East Germany
	3	Cuba

YEAR	PLACE	COUNTRY
1976	1	East Germany
	2	West Germany
	3	U.S.S.R.
1980	1	East Germany
	2	U.S.S.R.
	3	United Kingdom

ATHLETICS (1,600 metres relay) Women

YEAR	PLACE	COUNTRY
1972	1	East Germany
	2	U.S.A.
	3	Germany
1976	1	East Germany
	2	U.S.A.
	3	U.S.S.R.
1980	1	U.S.S.R.
	2	East Germany
	3	United Kingdom

ATHLETICS (80 metres hurdle*) Women

YEAR	PLACE	NAME	COUNTRY
1932	1	M. Didrikson	U.S.A.
	2	E. Hall	U.S.A.
	3	M. Clark	South Africa
1936	1	T. Valla	Italy
	2	A. Steuer	Germany
	3	E. Taylor	Canada
1948	1	F. Blankers-Koen	Netherlands
	2	M. Gardner	Great Britain
	3	S. Strickland	Australia
1952	1	S. de la Hunty-Strickland	Australia
	2	M. Golubnitschaya	U.S.S.R.
	3	M. Sander	Germany
1956	1	S. de la Hunty-Strickland	Australia
	2	G. Kohler	Germany
	3	N. Thrower	Australia
1960	1	I. Press	U.S.S.R.
	2	C. Quinton	Great Britain
	3	G. Birkemeyer-Kohler	Germany
1964	1	K. Balzer	Germany
	2	T. Ciepla	Poland
	3	P. Kilborn	Australia
1968	1	M. Caird	Australia
	2	P. Kilborn	Australia
	3	C. Cheng	Taiwan
1972	1	A. Ehrhardt (100m)	East Germany
	2	V. Bufanu	Rumania
	3	K. Balzer	East Germany
1976	1	J. Schaller(100m)	German Dem. Rep.
	2	T. Anisimova	U.S.S.R.
	3	N. Lebedeva	U.S.S.R.
1980	1	V. Komisova	U.S.S.R.
	2	J. Klier	German Dem. Rep.
	3	L. Langer	Poland

*In 1972 this event was changed to 100 meters, and will be run as such in 1976.

ATHLETICS (highjump) Women

YEAR	PLACE	NAME	COUNTRY
1928	1	E. Catherwood	Canada
	2	C. Gisolf	Netherlands
	3	M. Wiley	U.S.A.
1932	1	J. Shiley	U.S.A.
	2	M. Didrikson	U.S.A.
	3	E. Dawes	Canada
1936	1	I. Csak	Hungary
	2	D. Odam	Great Britain
	3	E. Kaun	Germany
1948	1	A. Coachman	U.S.A.
	2	D. Tyler-Odam	Great Britain
	3	M. Ostermeyer	France
1952	1	E. Brand	South Africa
	2	S. Lerwill	Great Britain
	3	A. Tschudina	U.S.S.R.
1956	1	M. McDaniel	U.S.A.
	2	T. Hopkins/	Great Britain/
	3	M. Pissaryeva	U.S.S.R.
1960	1	I. Balas	Rumania
	2	J. Jozwiakowska/	Poland/
	3	D. Shirley	Great Britain
1964	1	I. Balas	Rumania
	2	M. Brown-Mason	Australia
	3	T. Tschentschik	U.S.S.R.
1968	1	M. Rezkova	Czechoslovakia
	2	A. Okorokova	U.S.S.R.
	3	V. Kozyr	U.S.S.R.
1972	1	U. Mayfarth	Germany
	2	Y. Blagoeva	Bulgaria
	3	I. Gusenbauer	Austria
1976	1	R. Ackermann	East Germany
	2	S. Simeoni	Italy
	3	Y. Blagoyeva	Bulgaria
1980	1	S. Simeoni	Italy
	2	V. Kielan	Poland
	3	J. Kirst	East Germany

ATHLETICS (shotput) Women

YEAR	PLACE	NAME	COUNTRY
1948	1	M. Ostermeyer	France
	2	A. Piccinini	Italy
	3	I. Schäffer	Austria
1952	1	G. Zybina	U.S.S.R.
	2	M. Werner	Germany
	3	K. Totschenova	U.S.S.R.
1956	1	T. Tyschkevitsch	U.S.S.R.
	2	G. Zybina	U.S.S.R.
	3	M. Werner	Germany
1960	1	T. Press	U.S.S.R.
	2	J. Lüttge	Germany
	3	E. Brown	U.S.A.
1964	1	T. Press	U.S.S.R.
	2	R. Garisch	Germany
	3	G. Zybina	U.S.S.R.
1968	1	M. Gummel-Heimboldt	East Germany
	2	M. Lange	East Germany
	3	N. Tschischova	U.S.S.R.
1972	1	N. Tschischova	U.S.S.R.
	2	M. Gummel	East Germany
	3	I. Christova	Bulgaria
1976	1	I. Khristova	Bulgaria
	2	N. Chizhova	U.S.S.R.
	3	H. Fibinerova	Czechoslovakia
1980	1	I. Slupianek	East Germany
	2	S. Krachevskaya	U.S.S.R.
	3	M. Pufe	East Germany

ATHLETICS (discus) Women

YEAR	PLACE	NAME	COUNTRY
1928	1	H. Konopacka	Poland
	2	L. Copeland	U.S.A.
	3	R. Svedberg	Sweden
1932	1	L. Copeland	U.S.A.
	2	R. Osburn	U.S.A.
	3	J. Wajsowna	Poland
1936	1	G. Mauermayer	Germany
	2	J. Wajsowna	Poland
	3	P. Mollenhauer	Germany
1948	1	M. Ostermeyer	France
	2	V.E. Gentile-Cordiale	Italy
	3	J. Mazeas	France
1952	1	N. Romaschkova	U.S.S.R.
	2	Y. Bagryantseva	U.S.S.R.
	3	N. Dumbadze	U.S.S.R.
1956	1	O. Fikotova	Czechoslovakia
	2	I. Beglyakova	U.S.S.R.
	3	N. Ponomaryeva-Romanschkova	U.S.S.R.
1960	2	T. Press	U.S.S.R.
	3	L. Manoliu	Rumania
1964	1	T. Press	U.S.S.R.
	2	I. Lotz	Germany
	3	L. Manoliu	Rumania
1968	1	L. Manoliu	Rumania
	2	L. Westermann	Germany
	3	J. Kleiber	Hungary
1972	1	F. Melnik	U.S.S.R.
	2	A. Menis	Rumania
	3	V. Stoyeva	Bulgaria
1976	1	E. Schlaak	East Germany
	2	M. Vergova	Bulgaria
	3	G. Hinzmann	East Germany
1980	1	E. Jahl	East Germany
	2	M. Petkova	Bulgaria
	3	T. Lesovaya	U.S.S.R.

ATHLETICS (javelin) Women

YEAR	PLACE	NAME	COUNTRY
1932	1	M. Didrikson	U.S.A.
	2	E. Braumüller	Germany
	3	T. Fleischer	Germany
1936	1	T. Fleischer	Germany
	2	L. Krüger	Germany
	3	M. Kwasniewska	Poland
1948	1	H. Bauma	Austria
	2	K. Parviäinen	Finland
	3	L. Carlstedt	Denmark
1952	1	D. Zatopkova	Czechoslovakia
	2	A. Tschudina	U.S.S.R.
	3	Y. Gortschakova	U.S.S.R.
1956	1	I. Yaunzeme	U.S.S.R.
	2	M. Ahrens	Chili
	3	N. Konyayeva	U.S.S.R.
1960	1	E. Ozolina	U.S.S.R.
	2	D. Zatopkova	Czechoslovakia
	3	B. Kalediene	U.S.S.R.
1964	1	M. Penes	Rumania
	2	M. Rudas	Hungary
	3	Y. Gortschakova	U.S.S.R.
1968	1	A. Nemeth	Hungary
	2	M. Penes	Rumania
	3	E. Janko	Austria
1972	1	R. Fuchs	East Germany
	2	I. Todten	East Germany
	3	K. Schmidt	U.S.A.
1976	1	R. Fuchs	East Germany
	2	M. Becker	East Germany
	3	K. Schmidt	U.S.A.
1980	1	M. Colon	Cuba
	2	S. Gunba	U.S.S.R.
	3	U. Hommola	East Germany

ATHLETICS (pentathlon) Women

YEAR	PLACE	NAME	COUNTRY
1964	1	I. Press	U.S.S.R.
	2	M. Rand	Great Britain
	3	G. Bystrova	U.S.S.R.
1968	1	I. Becker	Germany
	2	L. Prokop	Austria
	3	A. Toth-Kovacs	Hungary
1972	1	M. Peters	Great Britain
	2	H. Rosendahl	Germany
	3	B. Pollak	East Germany
1976	1	S. Siegl	East Germany
	2	C. Laser	East Germany
	3	B. Pollack	East Germany
1980	1	N. Tkachenko	U.S.S.R.
	2	D. Rukavishnikova	U.S.S.R.
	3	O. Kuragina	U.S.S.R.

ATHLETICS (longjump) Women

YEAR	PLACE	NAME	COUNTRY
1948	1	O. Gyarmati	Hungary
	2	S. de Portela	Argentina
	3	A. Leyman	Sweden
1952	1	Y. Williams	New Zealand
	2	A. Tschudina	U.S.S.R.
	3	S. Cawley	Great Britain
1956	1	E. Krzesinska	Poland
	2	W. White	U.S.A.
	3	N. Dvalischvili	U.S.S.R.
1960	1	V. Krepkina	U.S.S.R.
	2	E. Krzesinska	Poland
	3	H. Claus	Germany
1964	1	M. Rand	Great Britain
	2	I. Kirszenstein	Poland
	3	T. Schtschelkanova	U.S.S.R.
1968	1	V. Viscopoleanu	Rumania
	2	S. Sherwood	Great Britain
	3	T. Talysheva	U.S.S.R.
1972	1	H. Rosendahl	Germany
	2	D. Yorgova	Bulgaria
	3	E. Suranova	Czechoslovakia
1976	1	A. Voigt	East Germany
	2	K. McMillan	U.S.A.
	3	L. Alfeyeva	U.S.S.R.
1980	1	T. Kolpakova	U.S.S.R.
	2	B. Wujak	East Germany
	3	T. Skachko	U.S.S.R.

VOLLEYBALL

EVENT DATE   **LONG BEACH SPORTS ARENA**

JULY	**29**	4 matches—preliminaries, men	**AUGUST**	**5**	2 matches—semifinals (5-8 places), women 2 matches—semifinals (1-4 places), women
	30	4 matches—preliminaries, women		**6**	4 matches—preliminaries, men
	31	4 matches—preliminaries, men		**7**	2 matches—finals (5-8 places), women/1 match—final (3-4 places), women/1 match—final (1-2 places), women
AUGUST	**1**	4 matches—preliminaries, women		**8**	4 matches—semifinals, men 1 match—final (9-10 places), men
	2	4 matches—preliminaries, men		**10**	2 matches—finals (5-8 places), men
	3	4 matches—preliminaries, women		**11**	1 match—final (3-4 places), men 1 match—final (1-2 places), men
	4	4 matches—preliminaries, men			

A fast and exciting game where defence is as important as offence

HISTORY

William G. Morgan is credited with inventing this team game back in 1895 in Holyoke, Massachusetts. At that time, Morgan was an athletic director at a Young Men's Christian Association (YMCA) club which was the centre of local, indoor sports activity.

The "new" game, basketball, which had been invented four years earlier, had a strong foothold in the YMCA gymnasium and was bringing many a youngster indoors. But while there was this new stream of youngsters, there was still a group of older people coming into the gym. Morgan thought about creating a game that old and young could play together.

One day, he strung a tennis net across the gymnasium and split a group of gym visitors into teams. Morgan tossed a ball to them and told them to hit it over the net with their hands. Volleyball was born. Aside from refinements in skill and equipment, the basic concept of the game has remained very much the same. Though several versions have sprung up it has only been in the past 40 years that the world has recognized volleyball as a fine game.

The game had been confined to the United States and Canada through YMCA programmes until it was picked up on a very minor basis by a few other countries. Then came the Second World War. Whenever U.S. soldiers had a break, they would string up a net, get a ball and play a version of volleyball. As well as having fun, they were introducing the sport to their European allies.

The sport's popularity spread quickly and it is currently played in 145 countries. Reasons for its growth stem from its minimal initial training requirements and low equipment cost factor to its inclusion in the school curriculum of many countries. Another reason for its popularity is that volleyball can be a co-ed game. Sitting on a beach you will inevitably see men and women playing impromptu volleyball.

The impact of volleyball on the sports world led to its inclusion in the Olympic Games in 1964. The Soviet Union has won three of the first five men's titles while its women have won three golds. There has been considerable competitive development in both the United States and Canada in recent years, and they are being considered serious rivals for medals.

GENERAL DESCRIPTION

Volleyball is a fast and exciting game, demanding a high level of skill and tactical awareness when played internationally.

As the sport grew, countries started to develop varied and interesting styles. There is the power of the Soviet Union, the technical skill of Czechoslovakia, the emotion of Rumania, the speed of Korea, the jumping of Cuba, the teamwork of Japan and the strength of Bulgaria.

only score a point when it has the serve. Each team is allowed three contacts before having to return the ball over the net to the opponent's court.

PROCEDURE

There are two pools in the men's division and 10 teams fill the five spots in each pool for the 1984 Olympic Games.

In the A pool, the United States, as the host country, automatically is given a berth. Another automatic choice is Brazil, the country that won the 1982 world championship.

Argentina rates a berth in the A pool because it is the South American champion and Poland rates a spot because it is

Long Beach Sports Arena is the site of the Olympic volleyball competition.

The game is played on a court that is 18-metres long and 9-metres wide. The net for men is 2.43-metres high and 2.24-metres high for women.

Each team consists of six players, three located in the front row and three in the back. The front row players may "attack" the ball (hit it above the height of the net) within the attack zone, while the back row players may attack only if their last floor contact was within the court, behind the attack line. All six players may play the ball below the height of the net. The game starts by one player serving the ball over the net from behind the right-end zone. A team can

the European champion. The final berth is filled by Bulgaria, the Olympic qualifying tournament winner.

In the B pool, the Soviet Union is an automatic choice, being the defending Olympic champion. Cuba also has a spot from its 1981 World Cup victory and Canada has a berth as the champion for the NORCECA area (North and Central America and the Caribbean islands). The other two berths in pool B will be filled by Japan, the Asian champion, and Egypt, the African champion.

The top two teams from each pool advance to the medal round. Team 1 crosses over to meet Team 2 from the other pool, and vice-versa. These two matches then constitute the semifinals, with winners of both contests meeting in the gold medal match.

There are also two pools (A and B) for the women but each pool will only have four teams.

The United States qualifies for Pool A because it is the host country. China is in as the 1982 world champion while East Germany as European champion and Peru as the 1982 world silver medallist are also in the group.

The Soviet Union tops Pool B as defending champion in the Olympics. Cuba is the NORCECA representative while Japan represents Asia and Brazil represents South America.

The top two teams advance from the pool round-robin competition into the medal round.

SCORING

A team can only score a point when it has the serve. A point is scored each time the nonserving team cannot return the ball over the net using a maximum three contacts, or when the ball is returned but lands outside the court.

The first team to reach 15 points by a margin of at least two points wins the set. For example, 15-13, 16-14 or 17-15. A team wins the match when it has won a majority of sets. International matches require three sets won (best of five).

VIEWING TIPS

There is a lot of strategy in this swift game, despite the fact that a team is allowed to hit the ball only three times before sending it over the net (not including the block). When a team has the ball, it is common for the first tap of the ball to go to the setter in the attack zone, who in turn sets up a teammate for a spike. At the same time, the opposing team's defence tries to anticipate the offensive movements by moving into position to block the spike.

The court is divided into two zones (attack and back) with three players in each zone. When a team earns a serve, the players rotate clockwise so that each player ends up playing all six positions. This eliminates a specialist in one fixed position, such as in blocking or defence.

After a coin toss to determine sides and first serve, the ball is put in play from the service area behind the end line. The serve must clear the net cleanly and land in the opposing team's territory. Once a team has won the serve, the same server continues to put the ball into play until his team loses possession. Remember, only the team with a serve can score a point. There is no point awarded when the serving team loses possession.

The referee is positioned above one end of the net and is responsible for the conduct of the game. There is also an umpire positioned on the floor and facing the referee. He is known as the second referee. The linesmen, located at two diagonally opposite corners of the court, are responsible for declaring if a ball is ''in'' or ''out'' of the playing area.

TECHNICAL TERMS

Ace — a point scored as the direct result of the serve.

Block — a defensive play by one or more players who attempt to intercept a ball at the point where it crosses the net, by either returning it immediately to the offensive team's court or deflecting it so that it can be played by a teammate.

Stuff — a blocked ball that is returned directly to the opposing floor for a point or side-out.

Save — a contact with the ball below waist level with a solid surface formed by the forearms or the heel of the hand. Primarily, the dig (a scooping motion) is used to recover a spike.

Dink or Tip — a faked spike in which the attacking player merely taps the ball down on the opposite side of the net or over the outstretched hands of the waiting blockers.

Double Hit — when a player hits the ball twice in succession (an illegal move).

Held ball — a ball that comes to rest momentarily in the hands, arms or any other part of the body. The ball must be cleanly hit.

Kill — a spike that is put away for a point or to recover the serve for the team.

Rotation — the movement of the players during the game. Each player moves one position clockwise when his team receives the ball for service.

Service — the act of putting the ball into play.

Float Serve — a ball hit in such a manner that the ball has no spin and has an unpredictable flight such as shifting from side to side. Like a screwball in baseball.

Set — usually the second contact of the ball by a team. The objective of the set is to direct the ball to the spiker, using the overhead pass skill.

Spiking — the act of hitting the ball downward with great force, usually from the top of a jump, into the opponent's court. The objective of the spike is to direct the ball with such power or placement that it cannot be returned by the opponents.

Switch — the movement of players into their proper rotational positions after the ball has been served.

Throw — to catch the ball and throw it. An illegal move.

Tip — a hit made to an area not covered by players, usually just over the hands of the blockers.

Volley — the basic skill of the game in which the ball is contacted by the hands and propelled forward and upward. The continuous action until the ball becomes dead.

Attack area — the zone between the attack line and centre line. A back row player may only attack above the height of the net if the last floor contact by that player was within the court, behind the attack line.

Foot fault — stepping on or over the end line while serving or completely over the centre line during play, or touching the floor outside the playing area when play is started by a nonserver.

TOP TEAMS

Men — the Soviet Union rates the nod here and not just because it is the defending champion in the Olympic Games. The Soviets seem to be in a class by themselves.

The United States has depth and home court advantage. If you think that is not much of an edge, just recall the United States triumph over the Soviets in the 1980 Olympic hockey series.

Brazil is the only team to beat the Soviets in the past couple of years, while Japan is a perennial contender and Poland traditionally has strong teams.

Canada, for the first time, has qualified for an Olympic berth. Canada appeared in the 1976 Olympics because it was the host nation and has a legitimate chance at a medal for 1984. Given that first place will likely go to the U.S.S.R. and last to Egypt, Canada's main com-

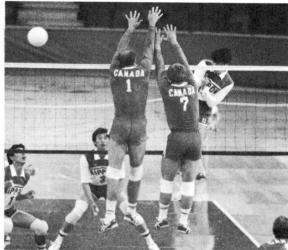

The block is an effective defensive play

Passing off the ball

Setting up to spike the ball

The ready defensive position

petition will be from Cuba and Japan, two teams we have consistently defeated in the past two years.

Women — The United States has height (eight players over six-foot) and home court advantage. China also has a tall team while the Cubans have some of the best jumpers. Japan is always strong and the Soviet Union, the defending champion, has had a history of a strong competitor feeder system.

INDIVIDUALS

Men — Alexander Savin of the Soviet Union is considered the world's best player as middle blocker. Poland's Tomasz Vojtowicz and Raul Vilches of Cuba are highly rated as are Dusty Dvorak and Karch Kilraly of the United States.

Women — at 6 feet, 5 inches, Flo Hyman has been a standout player for the United States for years. Rita Crockett of the United States is a big leaper and rated one of the world's top spikers.

Kermi Nakada and Yumi Egami give Japan some strength while Mercedes Perez and Nancy Gonzales head up the Cuban Team. Lang Ping will give China some punch.

CANADA'S BEST

Paul Gratton of Ottawa, is the captain of the team and is rated one of the best power hitters in the world. He is also an outstanding leaper.

Tom Jones of New Westminster, B.C., is a super setter and is acknowledged as one of the game's finest players. Other veteran players include Dan Saxton, a middle-blocker from Saskatchewan, Al Coulter, an offside player from London, Ontario, John Barrett, a power hitter from Toronto and Glenn Hoag, a middle-blocker from Gatineau, Quebec.

MEDAL WINNERS

VOLLEYBALL—Women

YEAR	PLACE	COUNTRY
1964	1	**Japan**
	2	U.S.S.R.
	3	Poland
1968	1	**U.S.S.R.**
	2	Japan
	3	Poland
1972	1	**U.S.S.R.**
	2	Japan
	3	North Korea
1976	1	**Japan**
	2	U.S.S.R.
	3	Korea
1980	1	**U.S.S.R.**
	2	East Germany
	3	Bulgaria

VOLLEYBALL—Men

YEAR	PLACE	COUNTRY
1964	1	**U.S.S.R.**
	2	Czechoslovakia
	3	Japan
1968	1	**U.S.S.R.**
	2	Japan
	3	Czechoslovakia
1972	1	**Japan**
	2	East Germany
	3	U.S.S.R.
1976	1	**Poland**
	2	U.S.S.R.
	3	Cuba
1980	1	**U.S.S.R.**
	2	Bulgaria
	3	Rumania

WEIGHTLIFTING

EVENT DATE					LOYOLA MARYMOUNT UNIVERSITY, WESTCHESTER		
JULY	29	Up to 52 kg, groups A and B		AUGUST	5	Up to 90 kg, groups A, B and C
	30	Up to 56 kg, groups A and B			6	Up to 100 kg, groups A and B
	31	Up to 60 kg, groups A and B			7	Up to 110 kg, groups A and B
AUGUST	1	Up to 67.5 kg, groups A, B and C			8	Over 110 kg, groups A and B
	2	Up to 75 kg, groups A, B and C				
	4	Up to 82.5 kg, groups A, B and C				

A weightlifter in the "clean" position

HISTORY

Feats of strength entrance everyone. The little boy sits in wide-eyed amazement as the circus strongman performs his incredible routines, and the dignified world leader sits stoically and politely applauds the spectacular achievements of today's weightlifters.

From the superbly muscled mighty mites who weigh up to 52-kilograms, to the mammoth hulks in the super heavyweight class of more than 110 kilograms, weightlifters have a unique charisma. It's one that tends to captivate and hold a viewer to his or her seat.

As outstanding as the mighty mites may be, much of the sport's spotlight falls on the big boys — the super heavyweights. They are imposing figures, huge hunks of men whose manner ex-

target for international acclaim for the Soviet Union and it has enjoyed considerable success in recent years.

Much of the growth of the sport must be credited to the 151.5-kilogram Vassili Alexeev who, with a full schedule of competitions, continued to add to his world records. With each lift, he gave the sport another boost. In the 1972 Games, the Russian lifted a remarkable total of 640 kilograms in the press, the snatch and the clean and jerk. He was again Games champion in 1976, the same year the press was dropped from competition. He had a combined total of 440 kilograms; a total matched by his compatriot Sultan Rakhmanov, who took the title in the 1980 Games.

Today's modern strongmen are a product of intense research and develop-

gland. When the Olympic Games were revived in 1896, weightlifting was included with the one and two-handed lifting of dumbbells. Launceston Elliott of Great Britain won the one-handed event with 71 kilograms, and Denmark's Viggo Jensen took the two-handed competition with a 111-kilogram total.

These events were held again in 1904 and 1920, but then gave way to a set of uniform rules that were standardized in 1928. With standardization came a worldwide federation, the International Weightlifting Organization, with 14-member countries. Membership hit 103 by the mid-1970s and continues to grow. Weightlifting will be a Games fixture as long as tests of strength are viewed with a sense of wonder.

GENERAL DESCRIPTION

Competitors fit into various weight classes and in the Olympics they will compete in the snatch and clean and jerk events to determine their final total.

Each country is allowed two competitors and a couple of spares for each event. They qualify for the Games by meeting minimum standards established either by their own country or by using the Olympic formula.

Before the competition, lifters weigh in two hours before the event. The overweight competitors can return within an hour for another weigh-in. During that hour a number of weight-reducing methods may be attempted — from taking a steam bath to taking a diuretic. If on the second weigh-in the competitor fails to meet the weight limit for his class, he can choose to enter the higher weight division, unless of course, his country already has two representatives in that group.

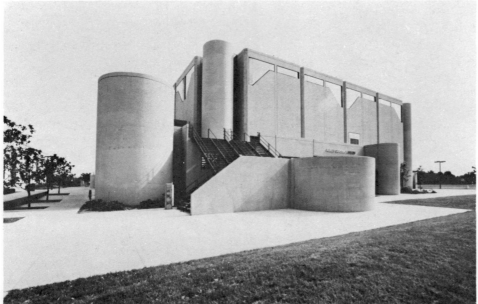

The Albert Gersten Pavilion is the site of the weightlifting competition.

udes power, for that's what weightlifting is all about.

And powerful these men are. When the Soviet Union team marched around Olympic Stadium for the opening of the 1976 Olympic Games in Montreal, it was a weightlifter who carried the flag in an unforgettable manner. He held the pole in one hand at full arm's length, seemingly as though the powerful arm had been frozen stiff. Less brawny Olympic flag carriers have held the pole with two hands and a leather support.

In a way, it was fitting for a weightlifter to be the Soviet Union standard bearer. Weightlifting has been a prime

ment. Competitors with proper builds are sought out and developed by national organizations who institute rigid training programmes and strength-building diets. Because the sport requires well-timed movements to hoist great amounts of weights, it calls for a special physique to provide the natural leverage. If the super heavyweights appear ponderous about the waist, there's a reason for it. Super heavyweights have been known to put away enough food at one sitting to feed a family of four for several days.

The first weightlifting world championship was held in 1891 in London, En-

SCORING

The winner is the lifter who attains the highest total in the two lifts, that is the total weight boosted in the snatch and the clean and jerk. In the case of a tie, the lifter with the lowest body weight is declared the winner and receives the appropriate Olympic medal.

Should two lifters have identical weights and identical lift totals, they are called co-champions and receive the same medals. Should such a situation arise for first place, both lifters would receive gold medals with the next-placed finisher being awarded the bronze medal.

Each competitor is allowed three attempts in the snatch and the clean and jerk. The lifter with the lightest weights starts first and the weights are increased as requested. Before the event, each lifter must declare at which weight he plans to start.

VIEWING TIPS

To appreciate weightlifting is to know the sport, and so the best tips for viewing we can offer are descriptions of what the lifters are doing.

Snatch — The bar is placed horizontally in front of the lifter's legs. It is gripped, palms downward, and pulled in a single movement from the ground to the full extent of both arms above the head while either splitting (moving one leg forward to maintain balance) or bending the legs. The bar shall pass with a continuous movement along the body. No part of the body other than the feet may touch the ground during the execution of the lift.

The weight that has been lifted must be maintained in the final motionless position, the arms and legs extended, the feet on the same line, until the referee signals to replace the bar on the platform.

The turning over of the wrists must not take place until the bar has passed the top of the lifter's head. The lifter may recover from a split or squat in his own time, and his feet must be on the same line, parallel to the plane of the trunk and barbell.

The referee's signal is given as soon as the lifter becomes absolutely motionless.

CLEAN AND JERK

Clean — The bar is placed horizontally in front of the lifter's legs. It is gripped, palms downward, and brought in a single movement from the ground to the shoulders, while either splitting or bending the legs.

During this movement, the bar may slide along the thighs and the lap (the upper thigh). The bar must *not* touch the chest before the final position. It then rests on the clavicles or on the chest above the nipples or on the fully bent arms. The feet return to the same line,

legs straight, before performing the jerk. The lifter may make this recovery in his own time and his feet must be on the same line, parallel to the plane of his trunk and barbell.

Jerk — The lifter bends his legs and extends them and his arms to bring the bar to the full vertical stretch of the arms. He then returns his feet to the same line, arms and legs extended and awaits the referee's signal to replace the bar on the platform.

WEIGHT LIMITS

1. Up to 52 kilograms (114.4 pounds)
2. Up to 56 kilograms (123.3 pounds)
3. Up to 60 kilograms (132.3 pounds)
4. Up to 67.5 kilograms (148.8 pounds)
5. Up to 75 kilograms (165.4 pounds)
6. Up to 82.5 kilograms (181.9 pounds)
7. Up to 90 kilograms (198.4 pounds)
8. Up to 100 kilograms (220.5 pounds)
9. Up to 110 kilograms (242.5 pounds)
10. More than 110 kilograms

EQUIPMENT

The weight used is a barbell, a steel bar, or rod, to which metal (cast iron) or rubber disc weights are fastened on a revolving sleeve at each end. The range of weights is 25 kilograms, 20 kilograms, 15 kilograms, 10 kilograms, 5 kilograms, 2½ kilograms, 1¼ kilograms.

The lifts are performed on a 4-metre square wooden platform. If a lifter steps off this platform during the course of the lift, the lift will not be recognized.

Weightlifter's shoe

TOP CONTENDERS

Anatoli Pisarenko and Alexander Kurlovich of the Soviet Union are standouts in the plus 110-kilogram category, while Hungary's Jacso Jozsef is prominent in the 110-kilogram category.

TOP CANADIANS

Jacques Demers of St. Hubert, Quebec, won the gold medal in the clean and jerk event in the 75-kilogram category at the Pan-American Games last summer in Venezuela. He was a silver medal winner in the overall total placings.

Mario Parente of Montreal picked up a couple of silver medals at the Pan-American Games; one in the clean and jerk for the 90-kilogram category and the other in the overall total placings.

MEDAL WINNERS

WEIGHTLIFTING* (up to 52 kg)

YEAR	PLACE	NAME	COUNTRY
1972	1	**Z. Smalcerz**	**Poland**
	2	L. Szücs	Hungary
	3	S. Holczreiter	Hungary
1976	1	**A. Voronin**	**U.S.S.R.**
	2	G. Koszegi	Hungary
	3	M. Nassiri	Iran
1980	1	**K. Osmanoliev**	**U.S.S.R.**
	2	Bong Chol Ho	Dem. People's Rep. of Korea
	3	Gyong Si Han	Dem. People's Rep. of Korea

WEIGHTLIFTING* (up to 56 kg)

YEAR	PLACE	NAME	COUNTRY
1948	1	**J. de Pietro**	**U.S.A.**
	2	J. Creus	Great Britain
	3	R. Tom	U.S.A.
1952	1	**I. Udodov**	**U.S.S.R.**
	2	M. Namdjou	Iran
	3	A. Mirzai	Iran
1956	1	**C. Vinci**	**U.S.A.**
	2	V. Stogov	U.S.S.R.
	3	M. Namdjou	Iran
1960	1	**C. Vinci**	**U.S.A.**
	2	Y. Miyake	Japan
	3	E. Khan	Iran
1964	1	**A. Vakhonin**	**U.S.S.R.**
	2	I. Földi	Hungary
	3	S. Ichinoseki	Japan
1968	1	**M. Nassiri**	**Iran**
	2	I. Földi	Hungary
	3	H. Trebicki	Poland
1972	1	**I. Földi**	**Hungary**
	2	M. Nassiri	Iran
	3	G. Chetin	U.S.S.R.
1976	1	**Norair Nurikyan**	**Bulgaria**
	2	Grzegorz Cziura	Poland
	3	Kenkichi Ando	Japan
1980	1	**Daniel Nunez**	**Cuba**
	2	Yurik Sarkisian	U.S.S.R.
	3	Tadeusz Demboncsyk	Poland

* The weights used as records, from 1928–1972, have been a cumulative total of the press, the snatch and the clean and jerk. The press has been dropped for the 1976 Games.

WEIGHTLIFTING* (up to 60 kg)

YEAR	PLACE	NAME	COUNTRY
1920**	1	**F. de Haes**	**Belgium**
	2	A. Schmidt	Estonia
	3	E. Ryther	Switzerland
1924***	1	**P. Gabetti**	**Italy**
	2	A. Stadler	Austria
	3	A. Reinmann	Switzerland

1928	1	**F. Andrysek**	**Austria**
	2	P. Gabetti	Italy
	3	H. Wölpert	Germany
1932	1	**R. Suvigny**	**France**
	2	H. Wölpert	Germany
	3	A. Terlazzo	U.S.A.
1936	1	**A. Terlazzo**	**U.S.A.**
	2	S.M. Soliman	Egypt
	3	I. Shams	Egypt
1948	1	**M. Fayad**	**Egypt**
	2	R. Wilkes	Trinidad
	3	J. Salmassi	Iran
1952	1	**R. Tschimischkyan**	**U.S.S.R.**
	2	N. Saksonov	U.S.S.R.
	3	R. Wilkes	Trinidad
1956	1	**I. Berger**	**U.S.A.**
	2	Y. Minayev	U.S.S.R.
	3	M. Zielinski	Poland
1960	1	**Y. Minayev**	**U.S.S.R.**
	2	I. Berger	U.S.A.
	3	S. Mannironi	Italy
1964	1	**Y. Miyake**	**Japan**
	2	I. Berger	U.S.A.
	3	M. Nowak	Poland
1968	1	**Y. Miyake**	**Japan**
	2	D. Schanidze	U.S.S.R.
	3	Yoshiyuki Miyake	Japan
1972	1	**N. Nourikian**	**Bulgaria**
	2	D. Schanidze	U.S.S.R.
	3	J. Benedek	Hungary
1976	1	**Nikolai Kolesnikov**	**U.S.S.R.**
	2	Georgi Todorov	Bulgaria
	3	Kuzumasa Hirai	Japan
1980	1	**Viktor Mazin**	**U.S.S.R.**
	2	Stefan Dimitrov	Bulgaria
	3	Marek Seweryn	Poland

* The weights used as records, from 1928-1972, have been a cumulative total of the press, the snatch and the clean and jerk. The press has been dropped for the 1976 Games.
** The lifts used in 1920 were the one hand snatch, one hand jerk and two hands jerk.
*** The lifts used in 1924 were one hand snatch, one hand jerk, two hands press, two hands snatch and two hands jerk.

WEIGHTLIFTING* (up to 67.5 kg)

YEAR	PLACE	NAME	COUNTRY
1920**	1	**A. Neuland**	**Estonia**
	2	R. Williquet	Belgium
	3	F. Rooms	Belgium
1924***	1	**E. Decottignies**	**France**
	2	A. Zwerina	Austria
	3	B. Durdis	Czechoslovakia
1928	1	**K. Helbig/**	**Germany/**
		H. Haas	**Austria**
	3	F. Arnout	France
1932	1	**R. Duverger**	**France**
	2	H. Haas	Austria
	3	G. Pierini	Italy
1936	1	**M. Mesbah/**	**Egypt/**
		R. Fein	**Austria**
	3	K. Jansen	Germany
1948	1	**I. Shams**	**Egypt**
	2	A. Hamouda	Egypt
	3	J. Halliday	Great Britain
1952	1	**T. Kono**	**U.S.A.**
	2	Y. Lopatin	U.S.S.R.
	3	V. Barberis	Australia
1956	1	**I. Rybak**	**U.S.S.R.**
	2	R. Khabutdinov	U.S.S.R.
	3	C.H. Kim	Korea
1960	1	**V. Buschuyev**	**U.S.S.R.**
	2	H.L. Tan	Singapore
	3	A.W. Aziz	Iraq
1964	1	**W. Baszanowski**	**Poland**
	2	V. Kaplunov	U.S.S.R.
	3	M. Zielinski	Poland
1968	1	**W. Baszanowski**	**Poland**
	2	P. Jalayer	Iran
	3	M. Zielinski	Poland
1972	1	**M. Kirzhinov**	**U.S.S.R.**
	2	M. Koutchev	Bulgaria
	3	Z. Kaczmarek	Poland
1976	1	**Piotr Korol**	**U.S.S.R.**
	2	Daniel Senet	France
	3	Kazimierz Czarnecki	Poland
1980	1	**Yanko Rousseu**	**U.S.S.R.**
	2	Joachim Kunz	German Dem. Rep.
	3	Mincho Pachou	Bulgaria

* The weights used as records, from 1928-1972, have been a cumulative total of the press, the snatch and the clean and jerk. The press has been dropped for the 1976 Games.
** The lifts used in 1920 were the one hand snatch, one hand jerk and two hands jerk.
*** The lifts used in 1924 were one hand snatch, one hand jerk, two hands press, two hands snatch and two hands jerk.

WEIGHTLIFTING* (up to 75 kg)

YEAR	PLACE	NAME	COUNTRY
1920**	1	**H. Gance**	**France**
	2	P. Bianchi	Italy
	3	A. Pettersson	Sweden
1924***	1	**C. Galimberti**	**Italy**
	2	A. Neuland	Estonia
	3	J. Kikas	Estonia
1928	1	**R. Francois**	**France**
	2	C. Galimberti	Italy
	3	A. Scheffer	Netherlands
1932	1	**R. Ismayr**	**Germany**
	2	C. Galimberti	Italy
	3	K. Hipfinger	Austria
1936	1	**K. el Touni**	**Egypt**
	2	R. Ismayr	Germany
	3	A. Wagner	Germany
1948	1	**F. Spellman**	**U.S.A.**
	2	P. George	U.S.A.
	3	S. Kim	Korea
1952	1	**P. George**	**U.S.A.**
	2	G. Gratton	Canada
	3	S. Kim	Korea
1956	1	**F. Bogdanovsky**	**U.S.S.R.**
	2	P. George	U.S.A.
	3	E. Pignatti	Italy
1960	1	**A. Kurynov**	**U.S.S.R.**
	2	T. Kono	U.S.A.
	3	G. Veres	Hungary
1964	1	**H. Zdrazila**	**Czechoslovakia**
	2	V. Kurentsov	U.S.S.R.
	3	M. Ouchi	Japan
1968	1	**V. Kurentsov**	**U.S.S.R.**
	2	M. Ouchi	Japan
	3	K. Bakos	Hungary
1972	1	**Y. Bikov**	**Bulgaria**
	2	M. Trabulsi	Lebanon
	3	A. Silvino	Italy
1976	1	**Yordan Mitkov**	**Bulgaria**
	2	Vartan Militosyan	U.S.S.R.
	3	Peter Wenzel	German Dem. Rep.
1980	1	**Assen Zlatev**	**Bulgaria**
	2	Alexander Pervy	U.S.S.R.
	3	Nedeltcho Kolev	Bulgaria

* The weights used as records, from 1928-1972, have been a cumulative total of the press, the snatch and the clean and jerk. The press has been dropped for the 1976 Games.
** The lifts used in 1920 were the one hand snatch, one hand jerk and two hands jerk.
*** The lifts used in 1924 were one hand snatch, one hand jerk, two hands press, two hands snatch and two hands jerk.

WEIGHTLIFTING* (up to 82.5 kg)

YEAR	PLACE	NAME	COUNTRY
1920**	1	**E. Cadine**	**France**
	2	F. Hünenberger	Switzerland
	3	E. Pettersson	Sweden
1924***	1	**C. Rigoulot**	**France**
	2	F. Hünenberger	Switzerland
	3	L. Friedrich	Austria
1928	1	**S. Nosseir**	**Egypt**
	2	L. Hostin	France
	3	J. Verheijen	Netherlands
1932	1	**L. Hostin**	**France**
	2	S. Olsen	Denmark
	3	H. Duey	U.S.A.
1936	1	**L. Hostin**	**France**
	2	E. Deutsch	Germany
	3	I. Wasif	Egypt
1948	1	**S. Stanczyk**	**U.S.A.**
	2	H. Sakata	U.S.A.
	3	G. Magnusson	Sweden
1952	1	**T. Lomakin**	**U.S.S.R.**
	2	S. Stanczyk	U.S.A.
	3	**A. Vorobyov**	**U.S.S.R.**
1956	1	**T. Kono**	**U.S.A.**
	2	V. Stepanov	U.S.S.R.
	3	J. George	U.S.A.
1960	1	**I. Palinski**	**Poland**
	2	J. George	U.S.A.
	3	J. Bochenek	Poland
1964	1	**R. Plukfelder**	**U.S.S.R.**
	2	G. Tóth	Hungary
	3	G. Veres	Hungary
1968	1	**B. Selitsky**	**U.S.S.R.**
	2	V. Belyayev	U.S.S.R.
	3	N. Ozimek	Poland
1972	1	**L. Jenssen**	**Norway**
	2	N. Ozimek	Poland
	2	G. Horvath	Hungary
1976	1	**Valeri Schary**	**U.S.S.R.**
	2	Trendachil Stoichev	Bulgaria
	3	Peter Baczako	Hungary
1980	1	**Yurik Vardanyan**	**U.S.S.R.**
	2	Blagoi Blagoev	Bulgaria
	3	Dusan Poliacik	Czechoslovakia

* The weights used as records, from 1928-1972, have been a cumulative total of the press, the snatch and the clean and jerk. The press has been dropped for the 1976 Games.
** The lifts used in 1920 were the one hand snatch, one hand jerk and two hands jerk.
*** The lifts used in 1924 were one hand snatch, one hand jerk, two hands press, two hands snatch and two hands jerk.

WEIGHTLIFTING* (up to 90 kg)

YEAR	PLACE	NAME	COUNTRY
1952	1	**N. Schemansky**	**U.S.A.**
	2	G. Novak	U.S.S.R.
	3	L. Kilgour	Trinidad
1956	1	**A. Vorobyov**	**U.S.S.R.**
	2	D. Sheppard	U.S.A.
	3	J. Debuf	France
1960	1	**A. Vorobyov**	**U.S.S.R.**
	2	T. Lomakin	U.S.S.R.
	3	L. Martin	Great Britain
1964	1	**V. Golovanov**	**U.S.S.R.**
	2	L. Martin	Great Britain
	3	I. Palinski	Poland
1968	1	**K. Kangasniemi**	**Finland**
	2	Y. Talts	U.S.S.R.
	3	M. Golab	Poland
1972	1	**A. Nikolov**	**Bulgaria**
	2	A. Chopov	Bulgaria
	3	H. Bettembourg	Sweden
1976	1	**David Rigert**	**U.S.S.R.**
	2	Lee James	U.S.A.
	3	Atanas Shopov	Bulgaria
1980	1	**Peter Baczako**	**U.S.S.R.**
	2	Roumen Alexandrov	Bulgaria
	3	Frank Mantek	German Dem. Rep.

* The weights used as records, from 1928-1972, have been a cumulative total of the press, the snatch and the clean and jerk. The press has been dropped for the 1976 Games.

WEIGHTLIFTING (up to 100 kg)

YEAR	PLACE	NAME	COUNTRY
1980	1	**Ota Zaremba**	**Czechoslovakia**
	2	Igor Nikitin	U.S.S.R.
	3	Alberto Blanco Fernandez	Cuba

WEIGHTLIFTING* (up to 110 kg)

YEAR	PLACE	NAME	COUNTRY
1920**	1	**F. Bottino**	**Italy**
	2	J. Alzin	Luxembourg
	3	L. Bernot	France
1924***	1	**G. Tonani**	**Italy**
	2	F. Aigner	Austria
	3	H. Tammer	Estonia
1928	1	**J. Strassberger**	**Germany**
	2	A. Luhaar	Estonia
	3	J. Skobla	Czechoslovakia
1932	1	**J. Skobla**	**Czechoslovakia**
	2	V. Psenicka	Czechoslovakia
	3	J. Strassberger	Germany
1936	1	**J. Manger**	**Germany**
	2	V. Psenicka	Czechoslovakia
	3	A. Luhaar	Estonia
1948	1	**J. Davis**	**U.S.A.**
	2	N. Schemansky	U.S.A.
	3	A. Charité	Netherlands
1952	1	**J. Davis**	**U.S.A.**
	2	J. Bradford	U.S.A.
	3	H. Selvetti	Argentina
1956	1	**P. Anderson**	**U.S.A.**
	2	H. Selvetti	Argentina
	3	A. Pigaiani	Italy
1960	1	**Y. Vlassov**	**U.S.S.R.**
	2	J. Bradford	U.S.A.
	3	N. Schemansky	U.S.A.
1964	1	**L. Schabotinsky**	**U.S.S.R.**
	2	Y. Vlassov	U.S.S.R.
	3	N. Schemansky	U.S.A.
1968	1	**L. Schabotinsky**	**U.S.S.R.**
	2	S. Reding	Belgium
	3	J. Dube	U.S.A.
1972	1	**Y. Talts**	**U.S.S.R.**
	2	A. Kraitchev	Bulgaria
	3	S. Grützner	East Germany
1976	1	**Yuri Zaitsev**	**U.S.S.R.**
	2	Krastio Semerdjiev	Bulgaria
	3	Tadeusz Rutkowski	Poland
1980	1	**Leonid Taranenko**	**U.S.S.R.**
	2	Valentin Khristov	Bulgaria
	3	Gyorgy Szlai	Hungary

WEIGHTLIFTING* (over 110 kg)

YEAR	PLACE	NAME	COUNTRY
1972	1	**V. Alexeev**	**U.S.S.R.**
	2	R. Mang	West Germany
	3	G. Bonk	East Germany
1976	1	**Vassili Alexeev**	**U.S.S.R.**
	2	Gerd Bonk	German Dem. Rep.
	3	Helmut Losch	German Dem. Rep.
1980	1	**Sultan Rakhmanov**	**U.S.S.R.**
	2	Jurgen Heuser	German Dem. Rep.
	3	Tadeusz Rutkowski	Poland

** The lifts used in 1920 were the one hand snatch, one hand jerk and two hands jerk.
*** The lifts used in 1924 were one hand snatch, one hand jerk, two hands press, two hands snatch and two hands jerk.

WRESTLING

EVENT DATE   **ANAHEIM CONVENTION CENTER**

JULY	30	Greco-Roman Style Preliminaries—48, 62, 90 kg
	31	Preliminaries—48, 52, 62, 74, 90, over 100 kg
AUGUST	1	Preliminaries—52, 57, 68, 74, 82, 100, over 100 kg Semifinals—48, 62, 90 kg/over 100 kg/Finals—48, 62, 90 kg
	2	Preliminaries—57, 68, 82, 100 kg/Semifinals—52, 74, over 100 kg/Finals—52, 74, over 100 kg
	3	Preliminaries—57, 68, 82, 100 kg Semifinals/finals—57, 68, 82, 100 kg
	7	Freestyle Preliminaries—48, 62, 90 kg Preliminaries—48, 62, 90 kg

AUGUST	8	Preliminaries—48, 52, 62, 74, 90, over 100 kg
	9	Preliminaries—52, 57, 68, 74, 82, 100, over 100 kg Semifinals—48, 62, 90 kg/Finals—48, 62, 90 kg
	10	Preliminaries—57, 68, 82, 100 kg Semifinals—52, 74, over 100 kg/Finals—52, 74, over 100 kg
	11	Preliminaries/Semifinals/finals—57, 68, 82, 100 kg

HISTORY

The sport of wrestling is as old as mankind. Though its precise origin cannot be traced, the sport is linked to prehistoric man through drawings discovered on cave walls throughout the world.

Wrestling stirs the combative spirit and probably started when one person reached out to touch another. It is common to see youngsters wrestling playfully in parks, on the streets and yes, even on the couch in the living room; not unlike our prehistoric ancestors depicted in the cave drawings.

Aside from high school and college exposure in the classic, competitive events of true wrestling, most of us have been exposed to the wacky, albeit wonderful world of professional wrestling. The professional matches, with their dazzling array of characters and occasional bursts of brutality to stir up the fans, are little more than plain, old-fashioned showbusiness.

The Olympic programme has no room for the professional package and all its flamboyancy. The Olympics feature two demanding and competitive types of wrestling — the freestyle and Greco-Roman.

As its name suggests, Greco-Roman is a combination of rules used by the Greeks and Romans. Unlike freestyle, the Greco-Roman competition forbids any holds below the hips. Its rules force the competitors to rely on skillful holds, agility, quickness and strength. There is no room for the dirty tactics so common in professional wrestling.

When wrestling was introduced to the ancient Olympic Games, there were no weight categories. A competitor often found himself facing a bigger, more powerful opponent and mismatches were common.

Such was the case when the modern-day Olympics were revived in 1896 in Athens. Wrestling was omitted from the 1900 Games but came back in 1904 when freestyle events in seven weight groups were introduced. In 1908, the Greco-Roman purists decided they too would have weight categories.

The time limit has also been a blessing for wrestlers. They no longer have to face long, drawn out bouts that had become so prevalent in Greco-Roman wrestling. The historic battle between middle-

The Anaheim Convention Center, site of the 1984 Olympic wrestling competition.

weights Martin Klein of the Soviet Union and Finland's Alfred Asikainen in the 1912 Stockholm Games was the longest Olympic Greco-Roman event. They wrestled almost 12 hours, doing little more than pushing and shoving in the late stages. When it was over, Klein, who was actually from Estonia, was declared the winner. However, he was too tired to go into the final the next day and Claes Johansson of Sweden won the gold medal by default. Klein settled for the silver and Asikainen got the bronze.

The same year, Anders Ahlgren of Sweden and Ivar Bohling of Finland wrestled for nine hours in the light-heavyweight final. The bout was called a draw and officials gave both of them silver medals. The decision to award no gold medal is still being debated today.

More than 100 countries recognized by the sport's international ruling body, the Federation Internationale de Lutte Amateur, ensure a steady stream of talent for future Olympic Games.

GENERAL DESCRIPTION

The object of the competition is for one athlete to hold his opponent's shoulder blades flat on the mat for one full second. This pin or fall ends the match.

The competitors will compete in two classes, either the freestyle or the Greco-Roman. In the latter, wrestlers are barred from applying any holds below the hips.

There are 10 different weight catego-ries for each type of wrestler and under Olympic rules a country may only enter one athlete in each weight class in a discipline. Olympic fields usually consist of 20 to 30 competitors in each weight class.

The bouts consist of two, three-minute rounds. This time limit leads to intense competition and a need for speed and strength.

If there is no fall or pin, the match is decided on a point-scoring basis. Points are awarded by the referee, three mat judges and the mat chairman. A wrestler can earn either one, two, three or four points for a variety of moves which are covered in the Scoring Section.

The various weight classes are: up to 48 kilograms (105.8 pounds); up to 52 kilograms (114.6 pounds); up to 57 kilograms (125.7 pounds); up to 62 kilograms (136.7 pounds); up to 68 kilograms (149.9 pounds); up to 74 kilograms (163.1 pounds); up to 82 kilograms (180.8 pounds); up to 90 kilograms (198.4 pounds); up to 100 kilograms (220.5 pounds); and 100-plus kilograms.

PROCEDURE

Each of the 10 weight classes in freestyle and Greco-Roman events are divided into two pools (A and B) by random draw.

The athletes in each pool compete in a round-robin session. Two losses are the criteria for elimination.

The round robin establishes the top three wrestlers in each pool. Then the finals are held. The top wrestler in pool A wrestles the first-place wrestler in pool B to determine the gold and silver medal winners. The two second-place finishers in the pools meet for the bronze medal and fourth place while the third-place finishers in the pools wrestle to determine the fifth and sixth-place standings.

Each match consists of two, three-minute rounds with a minute break. If there is no pin or fall, the outcome of the bout will be determined by points (see Scoring).

VIEWING TIPS

Watching a wrestling match can be like watching a mongoose battle a snake. The action is quick and furious. Turn your head and you might miss a pin or a fall.

Keep an eye on the tactics used by the wrestlers as they take advantage of passivity rules or move out of bounds to plot their next move.

Freestyle allows all the legal holds but in Greco-Roman events, wrestlers are forbidden to take hold below the waist or to grab the head with more than one arm.

Since the object of wrestling is to pin an opponent's shoulders flat on the mat for a full second, keep an eye on the wrestler in control. Watch him use his expertise and experience when the man underneath gives him an opening to apply the pin hold. At the same time, the wrestler in control makes it difficult for the man underneath to escape.

SCORING

Points are awarded by the officiating team made up of the referee, one mat judge and the mat chairman.

In each bout, one wrestler wears a blue singlet (uniform), and the other wears a red singlet. The referee on the mat wears a shirt with a right blue sleeve and left red sleeve. The referee indicates points scored by raising the appropriate number of fingers on the appropriate arm. So, as well as keeping your eyes on the wrestlers, keep an eye on the referee and how he is scoring the bout.

One point is scored for the following actions:

Takedown — one wrestler takes his opponent to the mat and controls him momentarily with three points of contact, one of which must be a knee.

Reversal — a wrestler in the defensive position (down) executes a hold which now puts him in control of his opponent and usually behind him.

Exposure — in the sitting position, a man may be faced toward the mat even though he does not touch the mat with his elbow, shoulder or head.

Illegal hold — a completion of a hold is prevented due to an illegal hold such as a choke hold. In addition, a caution is also awarded against the offender.

Fleeing the mat — a wrestler purposely steps off the mat to avoid a possible takedown by his opponent.

Two points are awarded for the following actions:

Exposure plus mat contact — when a wrestler forces his opponent toward the mat so that an elbow, shoulder or back of head touch the mat. This is called a danger position.

Three points are awarded for the following:

Low amplitude — one wrestler throws his opponent into a danger position.

Four points are awarded for the following:

Grande amplitude — a wrestler throws his opponent in a spectacular high arc. He maintains dominant control throughout the throw so that the opponent lands on his back and remains in a danger position.

TECHNICAL TERMS

Most of the technical terms are included in the Scoring section, but here are a few other important terms.

Great technical superiority — when one wrestler is winning a match by a point differential of 12 or more, the match is automatically stopped and the bout awarded to the leading wrestler.

Passivity — the action of a wrestler, who, contrary to the spirit of continuous wrestling, avoids or obstructs the progress of the match.

Gut Wrench — a hold where a wrestler, by virtue of a tight waist lock hold, brings his opponent into the danger position. This move can be executed a maximum of two consecutive times.

Danger position — is signalled when a wrestler holds an opponent's shoulders to the mat at a 90-degree angle for five seconds.

Caution — awarded against a wrestler who commits an act that is against the rules, such as an illegal hold or passivity. Three cautions mean automatic disqualification.

Supplé — a back-bending throw usually executed with grande amplitude.

Singlet — the red or blue uniform worn by wrestlers.

F.I.L.A. — the sport's international governing body, the Federation Internationale de Lutte Amateur.

SPECIAL EQUIPMENT

The only special equipment needed for wrestling is a mat, usually made of high density, shock-absorbing polyfoam from one- to two-inches thick.

The mat has a starting point, a competitive area, a passivity zone and a protection zone .

TOP COMPETITORS

The 1983 European championships were dominated by Bulgaria, winning 10 of the 20 gold medals available in both freestyle and Greco-Roman events. The usually strong Soviet Union team was made up of mostly young, inexperienced competitors. The Soviets won only two golds. It was the first time a Soviet team had done so poorly in the European championships. Yet, in the 1983 world championships, the Soviets won seven out of 10 gold medals in freestyle and five out of 10 golds in Greco-Roman.

Hungary's Ferenc Kocsis won his fourth European championship at 74 kilograms in the Greco-Roman division. He is the defending Olympic champion in this event.

The wrestling action in Los Angeles figures to be a three-nation struggle between Bulgaria, the Soviet Union and the United States, with a few outsiders grabbing the occasional medal.

CANADA'S BEST

Richard Deschatelets of Sturgeon Falls, Ontario was ninth in the 1983 world championships in the 100-kilogram class. He was a silver medalist in the 1983 Pan-American Games and was fourth in the 1979 world championships.

Clark Davis of Clemersport, N.S., has been the Canadian champion in the 90-kilogram class for the past five years, and was sixth in the 1983 world championships.

Super heavyweight (over 100 kilograms) Bob Molle of Vancouver was fifth in the 1983 freestyle event at the world championships in Kiev and is rated among the up and coming talent.

Doug Yeats and Louis Santerre of Montreal have been showing steady improvement in the 62- and 82-kilogram divisions of Greco-Roman. Ray Takahashi of Ottawa won the gold medal in the 52-kilogram freestyle event at the Pan-American Games and is an Olympic prospect for Los Angeles.

MEDAL WINNERS

WRESTLING FREESTYLE (paperweight)

YEAR	PLACE	NAME	COUNTRY
1904*	1	**R. Curry**	**U.S.A.**
	2	J. Heim	U.S.A.
	3	G. Thiefenthaler	U.S.A.
1972	1	**R. Dmitriev**	**U.S.S.R.**
	2	O. Nikolov	Bulgaria
	3	E. Javadpour	Iran
1976	1	**K. Issaev**	**Bulgaria**
	2	R. Dmitriev	U.S.S.R.
	3	A. Kudo	Japan
1980	1	**C. Pollio**	**Italy**
	2	S. Hong Jang	Dem. People's Rep. of Korea
	3	S. Kornilaev	U.S.S.R.

* Event not held 1908–1968

WRESTLING FREESTYLE (Flyweight)

YEAR	PLACE	NAME	COUNTRY
1904*	1	**I.G. Mehnert**	**U.S.A.**
	2	G. Bauers	U.S.A.
	3	W. Nelson	U.S.A.
1948	1	**L. Viitala**	**Finland**
	2	H. Balamir	Turkey
	3	T. Johansson	Sweden
1952	1	**H. Gemici**	**Turkey**
	2	Y. Kitano	Japan
	3	H. Mollaghassemi	Iran
1956	1	**M. Tsalkalamanidze**	**U.S.S.R.**
	2	M. Khojastehpour	Iran
	3	H. Akbas	Turkey
1960	1	**A. Bilek**	**Turkey**
	2	M. Matsubara	Japan
	3	M.S. Saidababi	Iran
1964	1	**Y. Yoshida**	**Japan**
	2	C. Chang	Korea
	3	S.A. Haydari	Iran
1968	1	**S. Nakata**	**Japan**
	2	R. Sanders	U.S.A.
	3	S. Sukhbaatar	Mongolia
1972	1	**K. Kato**	**Japan**
	2	A. Alakhverdiev	U.S.S.R.
	3	H. Kim Gwong	North Korea
1976	1	**Y. Takada**	**Japan**
	2	A. Ivanov	U.S.S.R.
	3	H. Jeon	Korea
1980	1	**A. Beloglazov**	**U.S.S.R.**
	2	W. Stecyk	Poland
	3	N. Selimov	Bulgaria

* Event not held 1908–1936

WRESTLING FREESTYLE (bantamweight)

YEAR	PLACE	NAME	COUNTRY
1904	1	**I. Niflot**	**U.S.A.**
	2	A. Wester	U.S.A.
	3	Z. Strebler	U.S.A.
1908*	1	**G. Mehnert**	**U.S.A.**
	2	W.J. Press	Great Britain
	3	A. Côté	Canada
1924	1	**K. Pihlajamäki**	**Finland**
	2	K. Mäkinen	Finland
	3	B. Hines	U.S.A.
1928	1	**K. Mäkinen**	**Finland**
	2	E. Spapen	Belgium
	3	J. Trifunov	Canada
1932	1	**R. Pearce**	**U.S.A.**
	2	O. Zombori	Hungary
	3	A. Jaskari	Finland
1936	1	**O. Zombori**	**Hungary**
	2	R. Flood	U.S.A.
	3	J. Herbert	Germany
1948	1	**N. Akar**	**Turkey**
	2	G. Leeman	U.S.A.
	3	C. Kouyos	France
1952	1	**S. Ishli**	**Japan**
	2	R. Mamedbekov	U.S.S.R.
	3	K. Jadav	India

1956	1	**M. Dagistanli**	**Turkey**
	2	M. Yaghoubi	Iran
	3	M. Schakhov	U.S.S.R.
1960	1	**T. McCann**	**U.S.A.**
	2	M. Zalev	Bulgaria
	3	T. Trojanowski	Poland
1964	1	**Y. Uetake**	**Japan**
	2	H. Akbas	Turkey
	3	A. Ibragimov	U.S.S.R.
1968	1	**Y. Uetake**	**Japan**
	2	D. Behm	U.S.A.
	3	A. Gorgori	Iran
1972	1	**H. Yanagida**	**Japan**
	2	R. Sanders	U.S.A.
	3	L. Klinga	Hungary
1976	1	**V. Umin**	**U.S.S.R.**
	2	H. Bruchert	German Dem. Rep.
	3	M. Arai	Japan
1980	1	**S. Beloglazov**	**U.S.S.R.**
	2	H. Li	Dem. People's Rep. of Korea
	3	D. Quinbold	Mongolia

WRESTLING FREESTYLE (featherweight)

YEAR	PLACE	NAME	COUNTRY
1904	1	**B. Bradshaw**	**U.S.A.**
	2	T. McLear	U.S.A.
	3	C. Clapper	U.S.A.
1908*	1	**G. Dole**	**U.S.A.**
	2	J. Slim	Great Britain
	3	W. McKie	Great Britain
1920	1	**C. Ackerly**	**U.S.A.**
	2	S. Gerson	U.S.A.
	3	P. Bernard	Great Britain
1924	1	**R. Reed**	**U.S.A.**
	2	C. Newton	U.S.A.
	3	K. Naito	Japan
1928	1	**A. Morrison**	**U.S.A.**
	2	K. Pihlajmäki	Finland
	3	H. Minder	Switzerland
1932	1	**H. Pihlajamäki**	**Finland**
	2	E. Nemir	U.S.A.
	3	E. Karlsson	Sweden
1936	1	**K. Pihlajamäki**	**Finland**
	2	F. Millard	U.S.A.
	3	G. Jönsson	Sweden
1948	1	**G. Bilge**	**Turkey**
	2	I. Sjölin	Sweden
	3	A. Müller	Switzerland
1952	1	**B. Sit**	**Turkey**
	2	N. Guivehtchi	Iran
	3	J. Henson	U.S.A.
1956	1	**S. Sasahara**	**Japan**
	2	J. Mewis	Belgium
	3	E. Penttilä	Finland
1960	1	**M. Dagistanli**	**Turkey**
	2	S. Ivanov	Bulgaria
	3	V. Rubaschvili	U.S.S.R.
1964	1	**O. Watanabe**	**Japan**
	2	S. Ivanov	Bulgaria
	3	N. Khokhaschvili	U.S.S.R.
1968	1	**M. Kaneko**	**Japan**
	2	E. Todorov	Bulgaria
	3	S. Seyed-Abassy	Iran
1972	1	**Z. Abdulbekov**	**U.S.S.R.**
	2	V. Akdag	Turkey
	3	I. Krastev	Bulgaria
1976	1	**J. Yang**	**Korea**
	2	Z. Oidov	Mongolia
	3	G. Davis	U.S.A.
1980	1	**M. Abushev**	**U.S.S.R.**
	2	M. Doukov	Bulgaria
	3	G. Hadjioannidis	Greece

* Event not held 1912

WRESTLING FREESTYLE (lightweight)

YEAR	PLACE	NAME	COUNTRY
1904	1	**O. Roehm**	**U.S.A.**
	2	R. Tesing	U.S.A.
	3	A. Zirkel	U.S.A.
1908*	1	**G. de Relwyskow**	**Great Britain**
	2	W. Wood	Grat Britain
	3	A. Gingell	Great Britain
1920	1	**K. Anttila**	**Finland**
	2	G. Svensson	Sweden
	3	P. Wright	Great Britain
1924	1	**R. Vis**	**U.S.A.**
	2	V. Vikström	Finland
	3	A. Haavisto	Finland
1928	1	**O. Käpp**	**Estonia**
	2	C. Pacôme	France
	3	E. Leino	Finland
1932	1	**C. Pacôme**	**France**
	2	K. Kárpáti	Hungary
	3	G. Klarén	Sweden
1936	1	**K. Kárpáti**	**Hungary**
	2	W. Ehrl	Germany
	3	H. Pihlajamäki	Finland
1948	1	**C. Atik**	**Turkey**
	2	G. Frändfors	Sweden
	3	H. Baumann	Switzerland
1952	1	**O. Anderberg**	**Sweden**
	2	T. Evans	U.S.A.
	3	D. Tovfighe	Iran
1956	1	**E. Habibi**	**Iran**
	2	S. Kasahara	Japan
	3	A. Bestayev	U.S.S.R.
1960	1	**S. Wilson**	**U.S.A.**
	2	V. Sinyavsky	U.S.S.R.
	3	E. Dimov	Bulgaria
1964	1	**E. Valtschev**	**Bulgaria**
	2	K. Rost	Germany
	3	I. Horiuchi	Japan
1968	1	**A.M. Ardabili**	**Iran**
	2	E. Valtschev	Bulgaria
	3	S. Danzandarjaa	Mongolia
1972	1	**D. Gable**	**U.S.A.**
	2	K. Wada	Japan
	3	R. Ashuraliev	U.S.S.R
1976	1	**P. Pinigin**	**U.S.S.R.**
	2	L. Keaser	U.S.A.
	3	Y. Saga wara	Japan
1980	1	**S. Absaidov**	**U.S.S.R.**
	2	I. Yankov	Bulgaria
	3	S. Sejdi	Yugoslavia

* Event not held 1912

WRESTLING FREESTYLE (welterweight)

YEAR	PLACE	NAME	COUNTRY
1904	1	**C. Erickson**	**U.S.A.**
	2	W. Beckmann	U.S.A.
	3	J. Winholtz	U.S.A.
1928*	1	**A. Haavisto**	**Finland**
	2	L. Appleton	U.S.A.
	3	M. Letchford	Canada
1932	1	**J. van Bebber**	**U.S.A.**
	2	D. MacDonald	Canada
	3	E. Leino	Finland
1936	1	**F. Lewis**	**U.S.A.**
	2	T. Andersson	Sweden
	3	J. Schleimer	Canada
1948	1	**Y. Dogu**	**Turkey**
	2	R. Garrard	Australia
	3	L. Merrill	U.S.A.
1952	1	**W. Smith**	**U.S.A.**
	2	P. Berlin	Sweden
	3	A. Modjtabavi	Iran
1956	1	**M. Ikeda**	**Japan**
	2	I. Zengin	Turkey
	3	V. Balavadze	U.S.S.R.
1960	1	**D. Blubaugh**	**U.S.A.**
	2	I. Ogan	Turkey
	3	M. Bashir	Pakistan

1964	1	**I. Ogan**	**Turkey**
	2	G. Sagaradze	U.S.S.R.
	3	M. Sanatkaran	Iran
1968	1	**M. Atalay**	**Turkey**
	2	D. Robin	France
	3	D. Purev	Mongolia
1972	1	**W. Wells**	**U.S.A.**
	2	J. Karlsson	Sweden
	3	A. Seger	Germany
1976	1	**J. Date**	**Japan**
	2	M. Barzegar	Iran
	3	S. Dziedzic	U.S.A.
1980	1	**V. Raitchev**	**Bulgaria**
	2	J. Davaajav	Mongolia
	3	D. Karabin	Czechoslovakia

WRESTLING FREESTYLE (middleweight)

YEAR	PLACE	NAME	COUNTRY
1908*	1	**S. Bacon**	**Great Britain**
	2	G. de Relwyskow	Great Britain
	3	F. Beck	Great Britain
1920	1	**E. Leino**	**Finland**
	2	V. Penttala	Finland
	3	C. Johnson	U.S.A.
1924	1	**F. Haggmann**	**Switzerland**
	2	P. Ollivier	Belgium
	3	V. Pekkala	Finland
1928	1	**E. Kyburz**	**Switzerland**
	2	D. Stockton	Canada
	3	S. Rabin	Great Britain
1932	1	**I. Johansson**	**Sweden**
	2	K. Luukko	Finland
	3	T. Tunyogi	Hungary
1936	1	**E. Poilvé**	**France**
	2	R. Voliva	U.S.A.
	3	A. Kirecci	Turkey
1948	1	**G. Brand**	**U.S.A.**
	2	A. Candemir	Turkey
	3	E. Lindén	Sweden
1952	1	**D. Tsimakuridze**	**U.S.S.R.**
	2	G. Takhti	Iran
	3	G. Gurics	Hungary
1956	1	**N. Stantschev**	**Bulgaria**
	2	D. Hodge	U.S.A.
	3	G. Skhirtladze	U.S.S.R.
1960	1	**H. Güngör**	**Turkey**
	2	G. Skhirtladze	U.S.S.R.
	3	H. Antonsson	Sweden
1964	1	**P. Gardschev**	**Bulgaria**
	2	H. Güngör	Turkey
	3	D. Brand	U.S.A.
1968	1	**B. Gurevitsch**	**U.S.S.R.**
	2	M. Jigjid	Mongolia
	3	P. Gardschev	Bulgaria
1972	1	**L. Tediashvili**	**U.S.S.R.**
	2	J. Peterson	U.S.A.
	3	V. Jorga	Rumania
1976	1	**J. Peterson**	**U.S.A.**
	2	V. Novojilov	U.S.S.R.
	3	A. Seger	W. Germany
1980	1	**I. Abilov**	**Bulgaria**
	2	M. Aratsilov	U.S.S.R.
	3	I. Kovacs	Hungary

* Event not held 1912

WRESTLING FREESTYLE (light heavyweight)

YEAR	PLACE	NAME	COUNTRY
1920	1	**A. Larsson**	**Sweden**
	2	C. Courant	Switzerland
	3	W. Maurer	U.S.A.
1924	1	**J. Spellman**	**U.S.A.**
	2	R. Svensson	Sweden
	3	C. Courant	Switzerland
1928	1	**T. Sjöstedt**	**Sweden**
	2	A. Bögli	Switzerland
	3	H. Lefèbre	France
1932	1	**P. Mehringer**	**U.S.A.**
	2	T. Sjöstedt	Sweden
	3	E. Scarf	Australia

YEAR	PLACE	NAME	COUNTRY
1936	1	K. Fridell	Sweden
	2	A. Neo	Estonia
	3	F. Siebert	Germany
1948	1	H. Wittenberg	U.S.A.
	2	F. Stöckli	Switzerland
	3	B. Fahlkvist	Sweden
1952	1	W. Palm	Sweden
	2	H. Wittenberg	U.S.A.
	3	A. Atan	Turkey
1956	1	G. Takhti	Iran
	2	B. Kulayev	U.S.S.R.
	3	P. Blair	U.S.A.
1960	1	I. Atli	Turkey
	2	G. Takhti	Iran
	3	A. Albul	U.S.S.R.
1964	1	A. Medved	U.S.S.R.
	2	A. Ayik	Turkey
	3	S. Mustafov	Bulgaria
1968	1	A. Ayik	Turkey
	2	S. Lomidze	U.S.S.R.
	3	J. Csátari	Hungary
1972	1	B. Peterson	U.S.A.
	2	G. Strakhov	U.S.S.R.
	3	K. Bajko	Hungary
1976	1	L. Tediashivili	U.S.S.R.
	2	B. Peterson	U.S.A.
	3	S. Morcov	Rumania
1980	1	S. Oganesyan	U.S.S.R.
	2	U. Neupert	German Dem. Rep.
	3	A. Cichon	Poland

WRESTLING FREESTYLE (heavyweight)

YEAR	PLACE	NAME	COUNTRY
1904	1	B. Hansen	U.S.A.
	2	F. Kungler	U.S.A.
	3	F. Warmbold	U.S.A.
1908*	1	G.C. O'Kelly	Great Britain
	2	J. Gundersen	Norway
	3	E. Barrett	Great Britain
1920	1	R. Roth	Switzerland
	2	N. Pendleton	U.S.A.
	3	E. Nilsson/	Sweden/
		F. Meyer	U.S.A.
1924	1	H. Steele	U.S.A.
	2	H. Wernli	Switzerland
	3	A. McDonald	Great Britain
1928	1	J. Richthoff	Sweden
	2	A. Sihvola	Finland
	3	E. Dame	France
1932	1	J. Richthoff	Sweden
	2	J. Riley	U.S.A.
	3	N. Hirschl	Austria
1936	1	K. Palusalu	Estonia
	2	J. Klapuch	Czechoslovakia
	3	H. Nyström	Finland
1948	1	G. Bóbis	Hungary
	2	B. Antonsson	Sweden
	3	J. Armstrong	Australia
1952	1	A. Mekokischvili	U.S.S.R.
	2	B. Antonsson	Sweden
	3	K. Richmond	Great Britain
1956	1	H. Kaplan	Turkey
	2	H. Mekhmedov	Bulgaria
	3	T. Kangasniemi	Finland
1960	1	W. Dietrich	Germany
	2	H. Kaplan	Turkey
	3	S. Dzarassov	U.S.S.R.
1964	1	A. Ivanitsky	U.S.S.R.
	2	L. Dschiber	Bulgaria
	3	H. Kaplan	Turkey
1968	1	A. Medved	U.S.S.R.
	2	O. Duralyev	Bulgaria
	3	W. Dietrich	Germany
1972	1	I. Yarygin	U.S.S.R.
	2	K. Baianmunkh	Mongolia
	3	J. Csatari	Hungary
1976	1	I. Yarygin	U.S.S.R.
	2	R. Hellickson	U.S.A.
	3	D. Kostov	Bulgaria
1980	1	I. Mate	U.S.S.R.
	2	S. Tchervenkov	Bulgaria
	3	J. Strnisko	Czechoslovakia

* Event not held 1912

WRESTLING FREESTYLE (super heavyweight)

YEAR	PLACE	NAME	COUNTRY
1972	1	A. Medved	U.S.S.R.
	2	O. Duralyev	Bulgaria
	3	C. Taylor	U.S.A.
1976	1	S. Andiev	U.S.S.R.
	2	J. Balla	Hungary
	3	L. Simon	Rumania
1980	1	S. Andiev	U.S.S.R.
	2	J. Balla	Hungary
	3	A. Sandruski	Poland

WRESTLING GRECO-ROMAN STYLE (paperweight)

YEAR	PLACE	NAME	COUNTRY
1972	1	G. Berceanu	Rumania
	2	R. Aliabadi	Iran
	3	S. Anghelov	Bulgaria
1976	1	A. Shumakov	U.S.S.R.
	2	G. Berceanu	Rumania
	3	S. Anghelov	Bulgaria
1980	1	Z. Ushkempirov	U.S.S.R.
	2	G. Alexandru	Rumania
	3	F. Seres	Hungary

WRESTLING GRECO-ROMAN STYLE (flyweight)

YEAR	PLACE	NAME	COUNTRY
1948	1	P. Lombardi	Italy
	2	K. Olcay	Turkey
	3	R. Kangasmäki	Finland
1952	1	B. Gurevitsch	U.S.S.R.
	2	I. Fabra	Italy
	3	L. Honkala	Finland
1956	1	N. Solovyov	U.S.S.R.
	2	I. Fabra	Italy
	3	D. Egribas	Turkey
1960	1	D. Pirvulescu	Rumania
	2	O. Sayed	United Arab Republic
	3	M. Paziraye	Iran
1964	1	T. Hanahara	Japan
	2	A. Kerezov	Bulgaria
	3	D. Pirvulescu	Rumania
1968	1	P. Kirov	Bulgaria
	2	U. Bakulin	U.S.S.R.
	3	M. Zeman	Czechoslovakia
1972	1	P. Kirov	Bulgaria
	2	K. Hirayama	Japan
	3	G. Bognanni	Italy
1976	1	V. Konstantinov	U.S.S.R.
	2	N. Ginga	Rumania
	3	K. Hirayama	Japan
1980	1	V. Blagidze	U.S.S.R.
	2	L. Racz	Hungary
	3	M. Mladenov	Bulgaria

WRESTLING GRECO-ROMAN STYLE (bantamweight)

YEAR	PLACE	NAME	COUNTRY
1924	1	E. Pütsep	Estonia
	2	A. Ahlfors	Finland
	3	V. Ikonen	Finland
1928	1	K. Leucht	Germany
	2	J. Maudr	Czechoslovakia
	3	G. Gozzi	Italy
1932	1	J. Brendel	Germany
	2	H. Nizzola	Italy
	3	L. Francois	France
1936	1	M. Lörincz	Hungary
	2	E. Svensson	Sweden
	3	J. Brendel	Germany
1948	1	K. Pettersén	Sweden
	2	A.M. Hassan	Egypt
	3	H. Kaya	Turkey
1952	1	I. Hódos	Hungary
	2	Z. Chihab	Lebanon
	3	A. Teryan	U.S.S.R.
1956	1	K. Vyrupayev	U.S.S.R.
	2	E. Vesterby	Sweden
	3	F. Horvat	Rumania

YEAR	PLACE	NAME	COUNTRY
1960	1	O. Karavayev	U.S.S.R.
	2	I. Cernea	Rumania
	3	P. Dinko	Bulgaria
1964	1	M. Ichiguchi	Japan
	2	V. Trostyansky	U.S.S.R.
	3	I. Cernea	Rumania
1968	1	J. Varga	Hungary
	2	I. Baciu	Rumania
	3	I. Kotschergin	U.S.S.R.
1972	1	R. Kazakov	U.S.S.R.
	2	H. Veil	Germany
	3	B. Björlin	Finland
1976	1	P. Ukkola	Finland
	2	I. Frgic	Yugoslavia
	3	F. Mustafin	U.S.S.R.
1980	1	S. Serikov	U.S.S.R.
	2	J. Lipien	Poland
	3	B. Ljungbeck	Sweden

WRESTLING GRECO-ROMAN STYLE (featherweight)

YEAR	PLACE	NAME	COUNTRY
1912	1	K. Koskelo	Finland
	2	G. Gerstacker	Germany
	3	O. Lasanen	Finland
1920	1	O. Friman	Finland
	2	K. Käkhönen	Finland
	3	F. Svensson	Sweden
1924	1	K. Anttila	Finland
	2	A. Toivola	Finland
	3	E. Malmberg	Sweden
1928	1	V. Väli	Estonia
	2	E. Malmberg	Sweden
	3	G. Quaglia	Italy
1932	1	G. Gozzi	Italy
	2	W. Ehrl	Germany
	3	L. Koskela	Finland
1936	1	Y. Erkan	Turkey
	2	A. Reini	Finland
	3	E. Karlsson	Sweden
1948	1	M. Oktav	Turkey
	2	O. Anderberg	Sweden
	3	F. Tóth	Hungary
1952	1	Y. Punkin	U.S.S.R.
	2	I. Polyák	Hungary
	3	A. Rashed	Egypt
1956	1	R. Mäkinen	Finland
	2	I. Polyák	Hungary
	3	R. Dzneladze	U.S.S.R.
1960	1	M. Sille	Turkey
	2	I. Polyak	Hungary
	3	K. Vyrupayev	U.S.S.R.
1964	1	I. Polyák	Hungary
	2	R. Rurua	U.S.S.R.
	3	B. Martinovic	Yugoslavia
1968	1	R. Rurua	U.S.S.R.
	2	H. Fujimoto	Japan
	3	S. Popescu	Rumania
1972	1	G. Markov	Bulgaria
	2	H. Wehling	East Germany
	3	K. Lipien	Poland
1976	1	K. Lipien	Poland
	2	N. Davidian	U.S.S.R.
	3	L. Reczi	Hungary
1980	1	S. Migiakis	Greece
	2	I. Toth	Hungary
	3	B. Kramorenko	U.S.S.R.

WRESTLING GRECO-ROMAN STYLE (lightweight)

YEAR	PLACE	NAME	COUNTRY
1908	1	E. Porro	Italy
	2	N. Orlov	Russia
	3	A. (Lindén) Linko	Finland
1912	1	E. Väre	Finland
	2	G. Malmström	Sweden
	3	E. Matiasson	Sweden
1920	1	E. Väre	Finland
	2	T. Tamminen	Finland
	3	F. Andersen	Norway
1924	1	O. Friman	Finland
	2	L. Keresztes	Hungary
	3	K. Vesterlund	Finland

YEAR	PLACE	NAME	COUNTRY
1928	1	**L. Keresztes**	**Hungary**
	2	E. Sperling	Germany
	3	E. Vesterlund	Finland
1932	1	**E. Malmberg**	**Sweden**
	2	A. Kurland	Denmark
	3	E. Sperling	Germany
1936	1	**L. Koskela**	**Finland**
	2	J. Herda	Czechoslovakia
	3	V. Vali	Estonia
1948	1	**G. Freij**	**Sweden**
	2	A. Eriksen	Norway
	3	K. Ferencz	Hungary
1952	1	**S. Safin**	**U.S.S.R.**
	2	G. Freij	Sweden
	3	M. Athanasov	Czechoslovakia
1956	1	**K. Lehtonen**	**Finland**
	2	R. Dogan	Turkey
	3	C. Tóth	Hungary
1960	1	**A. Koridze**	**U.S.S.R.**
	2	B. Martinovic	Yugoslavia
	3	G. Freij	Sweden
1964	1	**K. Ayvaz**	**Turkey**
	2	V. Bularca	Rumania
	3	D. Gvantseladze	U.S.S.R.
1968	1	**M. Munemura**	**Japan**
	2	S. Horvat	Yugoslavia
	3	P. Galaktopoulos	Greece
1972	1	**S. Khisamutdinov**	**U.S.S.R.**
	2	S. Apostolov	Bulgaria
	3	G. Ranzi	Italy
1976	1	**S. Nalbandyan**	**U.S.S.R.**
	2	S. Rusu	Rumania
	3	H. Wehling	German Dem. Rep.
1980	1	**S. Rusu**	**Rumania**
	2	A. Supron	Poland
	3	L. Skiold	Sweden

WRESTLING GRECO-ROMAN STYLE (welterweight)

YEAR	PLACE	NAME	COUNTRY
1932	1	**I. Johansson**	**Sweden**
	2	V. Kajander-Kajukorpi	Finland
	3	E. Gallegatti	Italy
1936	1	**R. Svedberg**	**Sweden**
	2	F. Schäfer	Germany
	3	E. Virtanen	Finland
1948	1	**G. Andersson**	**Sweden**
	2	M. Szilvási	Hungary
	3	H. Hansen	Denmark
1952	1	**M. Szilvási**	**Hungary**
	2	G. Andersson	Sweden
	3	K. Taha	Lebanon
1956	1	**M. Bayrak**	**Turkey**
	2	M. Maneyev	U.S.S.R.
	3	P. Berlin	Sweden
1960	1	**M. Bayrak**	**Turkey**
	2	G. Maritschnigg	Germany
	3	R. Schiermeyer	France
1964	1	**A. Kolesov**	**U.S.S.R.**
	2	C. Todorov	Bulgaria
	3	B. Nyström	Sweden
1968	1	**R. Vesper**	**East Germany**
	2	D. Robin	France
	3	K. Bajkó	Hungary
1972	1	**V. Macha**	**Czechoslovakia**
	2	P. Galaktopoulos	Greece
	3	J. Karlsson	Sweden
1976	1	**A. Bykov**	**U.S.S.R.**
	2	V. Macha	Czechoslovakia
	3	K. Helbing	W. Germany
1980	1	**F. Kocsis**	**Hungary**
	2	A. Bykov	U.S.S.R.
	3	M. Huntala	Finland

WRESTLING GRECO-ROMAN STYLE (middleweight)

YEAR	PLACE	NAME	COUNTRY
1908	1	**F. Martensson**	**Sweden**
	2	M. Andersson	Sweden
	3	A. Andersen	Denmark
1912	1	**C. Johansson**	**Sweden**
	2	M. Klein	Russia
	3	A. Asikainen	Finland
1920	1	**C. Westergren**	**Sweden**
	2	A. Lindfors	Finland
	3	M. Perttilä	Finland
1924	1	**E. Vesterlund**	**Finland**
	2	A. Lindfors	Finland
	3	R. Steinberg	Estonia
1928	1	**V. Kokkinen**	**Finland**
	2	L. Papp	Hungary
	3	A. Kusnets	Estonia
1932	1	**V. Kokkinen**	**Finland**
	2	J. Földeák	Germany
	3	A. Cadier	Sweden
1936	1	**I. Johansson**	**Sweden**
	2	L. Schweickert	Germany
	3	J. Palotás	Hungary
1948	1	**A. Grönberg**	**Sweden**
	2	M. Tayfur	Turkey
	3	E. Gallegati	Italy
1952	1	**A. Grönberg**	**Sweden**
	2	R. Rauhala	Finland
	3	N. Byelov	U.S.S.R.
1956	1	**G. Kartoziya**	**U.S.S.R.**
	2	D. Dobrev	Bulgaria
	3	K. Jansson	Sweden
1960	1	**D. Dobrev**	**Bulgaria**
	2	L. Metz	Germany
	3	I. Taranu	Rumania
1964	1	**B. Simic**	**Yugoslavia**
	2	J. Kormanik	Czechoslovakia
	3	L. Metz	East Germany
1968	1	**L. Metz**	**East Germany**
	2	V. Olenik	U.S.S.R.
	3	B. Simic	Yugoslavia
1972	1	**C. Hegedus**	**Hungary**
	2	A. Nazarenko	U.S.S.R.
	3	M. Nenadic	Yugoslavia
1976	1	**M. Petkovic**	**Yugoslavia**
	2	V. Cheboksarov	U.S.S.R.
	3	I. Kolev	Bulgaria
1980	1	**G. Korban**	**U.S.S.R.**
	2	J. Dolgowicz	Poland
	3	Pavlov	Bulgaria

WRESTLING GRECO-ROMAN STYLE (light heavyweight)

YEAR	PLACE	NAME	COUNTRY
1908	1	**V. Weckman**	**Finland**
	2	Y. Saarela	Finland
	3	C. Jensen	Denmark
1912	2*	**A. Ahlgren/**	**Sweden/**
	2*	**I. Bohling**	**Finland**
	3	B. Varga	Hungary
1920	1	**C. Johansson**	**Sweden**
	2	E. Rosenqvist	Finland
	3	J. Eriksen	Denmark
1924	1	**C. Westergren**	**Sweden**
	2	R. Svensson	Sweden
	3	O. Pellinen	Finland
1928	1	**I. Moustafa**	**Egypt**
	2	A. Rieger	Germany
	3	O. Pellinen	Finland
1932	1	**R. Svensson**	**Sweden**
	2	O. Pellinen	Finland
	3	M. Gruppioni	Italy
1936	1	**A. Cadier**	**Sweden**
	2	E. Bietags	Lithuania
	3	A. Neo	Estonia
1948	1	**K. Nilsson**	**Sweden**
	2	K. Gröndahl	Finland
	3	I. Orabi	Egypt
1952	1	**K. Gröndahl**	**Finland**
	2	S. Tschikhladze	U.S.S.R.
	3	K. Nilsson	Sweden
1956	1	**V. Nikolayev**	**U.S.S.R.**
	2	S. Sirakov	Bulgaria
	3	K. Nilsson	Sweden
1960	1	**T. Kis**	**Turkey**
	2	K. Bimbalov	Bulgaria
	3	G. Kartoziya	U.S.S.R.
1964	1	**B. Radev**	**Bulgaria**
	2	P. Svensson	Sweden
	3	H. Kiehl	Germany
1968	1	**B. Radev**	**Bulgaria**
	2	N. Yakovenko	U.S.S.R.
	3	N. Martinescu	Rumania
1972	1	**V. Rezantsev**	**U.S.S.R.**
	2	J. Corak	Yugoslavia
	3	C. Kwiecinski	Poland
1976	1	**V. Rezantsev**	**U.S.S.R.**
	2	S. Ivanov	Bulgaria
	3	C. Kwiecinski	Poland
1980	1	**N. Nottny**	**Hungary**
	2	I. Kanygin	U.S.S.R.
	3	P. Dicu	Rumania

WRESTLING GRECO-ROMAN STYLE (heavyweight)

YEAR	PLACE	NAME	COUNTRY
1896	1	**K. Schuhmann**	**Germany**
	2	G. Tsitos	Greece
	3	S. Christopoulos	Greece
1908	1	**R. Weisz**	**Hungary**
	2	A. Petrov	Russia
	3	S. Jensen	Denmark
1912	1	**Y. Saarela**	**Finland**
	2	J. Olin	Finland
	3	S. Jensen	Denmark
1920	1	**A. Lindfors**	**Finland**
	2	P. Hansen	Denmark
	3	M. Nieminen	Finland
1924	1	**H. Deglane**	**France**
	2	E. Rosenqvist	Finland
	3	R. Badó	Hungary
1928	1	**R. Svensson**	**Sweden**
	2	H. Nyström	Finland
	3	G. Gehring	Germany
1932	1	**C. Westergren**	**Sweden**
	2	J. Urban	Czechoslovakia
	3	N. Hirschl	Austria
1936	1	**K. Palusalu**	**Estonia**
	2	J. Nyman	Sweden
	3	K. Hornfischer	Germany
1948	1	**A. Kirecci**	**Turkey**
	2	T. Nilsson	Sweden
	3	G. Fantoni	Italy
1952	1	**J. Kotkas**	**U.S.S.R.**
	2	J. Ruzicka	Czechoslovakia
	3	T. Kovanen	Finland
1956	1	**A. Parfenov**	**U.S.S.R.**
	2	W. Dietrich	Germany
	3	A. Bulgarelli	Italy
1960	1	**I. Bogdan**	**U.S.S.R.**
	2	W. Dietrich	Germany
	3	B. Kubat	Czechoslovakia
1964	1	**I. Kozma**	**Hungary**
	2	A. Roschtschin	U.S.S.R.
	3	W. Dietrich	Germany
1968	1	**I. Kozma**	**Hungary**
	2	A. Roschtschin	U.S.S.R.
	3	P. Kment	Czechoslovakia
1972	1	**N. Martinescu**	**Rumania**
	2	N. Yakovenko	U.S.S.R.
	3	F. Kiss	Hungary
1976	1	**N. Bolboshin**	**U.S.S.R.**
	2	K. Goranov	Bulgaria
	3	A. Skrzylewski	Poland
1980	1	**G. Raikov**	**Bulgaria**
	2	R. Bierla	Poland
	3	V. Andrei	Rumania

WRESTLING GRECO-ROMAN STYLE (super heavyweight)

YEAR	PLACE	NAME	COUNTRY
1972	1	**A. Roschtschin**	**U.S.S.R.**
	2	A. Tomov	Bulgaria
	3	V. Dolipschi	Rumania
1976	1	**A. Kolchinski**	**U.S.S.R.**
	2	A. Tomov	Bulgaria
	3	R. Codreanu	Rumania
1980	1	**A. Kolchinski**	**U.S.S.R.**
	2	A. Tomov	Bulgaria
	3	H. Bchara	Lebanon

YACHTING

EVENT DATE			OLYMPIC YACHTING CENTER, LONG BEACH		
JULY	31	First race	AUGUST	6	Fifth race
AUGUST	1	Second race		7	Sixth race
	2	Third race		8	Seventh race
	3	Fourth race			

Trying to counter the strong winds

HISTORY

When man mastered the use of sails, he opened up world exploration and created a whole new style of competition. The most famous yacht competition, the America's Cup, started in 1851 and captured the imagination of the world. The prized trophy resided in the United States until last fall, when Australia won it after a series of suspenseful events.

The glamorous 12-metre yachts in the America's Cup are a far cry from the first "yachts" of the fifteenth century: sleek, swift boats designed to fight pirates. From these hit-and-run vessels evolved small boats used for pleasure and then racing.

While the sport of yachting is said to have originated in the Netherlands, historians tend to credit Great Britain with the sport's development. As sailing knowledge grew, so did the sport. Sailors were determined to display their seamanship and skill wherever there was water and wind. The sailor would hit the water with little more than a board and sail. The one-man boat race quickly caught on as a test of toughness; an individual's ability against the elements. Multiple-man yachts, where teamwork was needed as well as ability, were also catching on.

Since the sport of yachting had gripped most of the world by the time the Olympic Games were revived in 1896, it was readily included in the programme. But this auspicious introduction to the Games was less than historic. Inclement weather forced cancellation of the events, and sailors could only sit around and talk about what might have been.

From that somewhat dubious start, yachting has become firmly entrenched in the Games, and like most sports has undergone considerable change. From the 15 classes that competed in the 1920 Games at Antwerp, Belgium, there are now a tidy seven classes. The classes, all illustrated in this book, are the Finn, Star, Tornado, Flying Dutchman, 470, Soling and Windglider. The Soling, with a crew of three, is the largest class.

The flags of many nations have been flown in yachting competitions over the years, but in the Finn class events of 1952, 1956 and 1960, most observers trained binoculars on the Danish flag. Denmark's Paul Elvstrom captured Olympic golds in each of those games. He also won the Firefly class in 1948. Like the 25.5-kilogram shotput, the Firefly class is Olympics history.

When the 1984 Olympic entrants take their boats into the Pacific Ocean off Long Beach, California, they will be competing in seven classes, including a new boardsailing class, Windglider. Introduced to the Games this year, boardsailing was born in the surf and sunshine of California. With an estimated 20,000 new enthusiasts each year, it is a natural to include in the Los Angeles Games.

The Olympic Yachting Center hosts the yachting competition.

GENERAL DESCRIPTION

The races are sailed on the Olympic course with each race expected to take about three hours. They are started by an anchored committee boat firing a warning gun and hoisting a white flag ten minutes before the start. Five minutes later, another shot is fired and a blue flag is hoisted. Officially, the race is on when the last shot is fired and a red flag is hoisted.

The start is crucial. It is important to hit the starting line at full speed, so there is much jockeying around by the sailors. They want to catch full wind to avoid being trapped by "dead air" and left bobbing like a motorboat with a dead engine.

Each competitor must sail the entire Olympic course, rounding each buoy in the proper sequence. All boats must finish between the finish boat and the finishing marker.

Rules are enforced by a jury that floats on the water in a powerboat and carefully observes the racing boats. If the jury feels an infraction has been made, it can conduct a hearing with the competitor after the race. A competitor may protest another competitor by hoisting a red flag in his rigging. After the race, a written complaint is made to the jury, which investigates the charge.

As in highway traffic acts, there are rules to prevent collisions while racing. These must be obeyed by all competitors. In yachting, an infringement of the rules results in disqualification from the race. Obviously, such infractions can be very expensive to a competitor. Knowing the rules and applying them in a traffic jam is an important ingredient for the successful sailor.

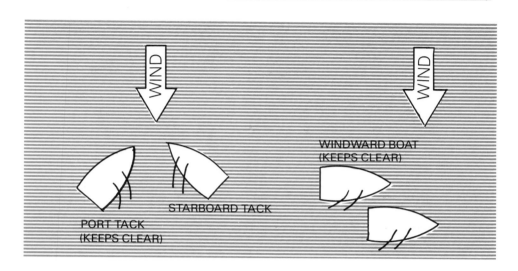

THE TWO BASIC RULES ARE:

1. Starboard tack boat (wind blows across the sailboat from right to left) has the right-of-way over port tack boat (wind blows from across sailboat from left to right).

2. Leeward boat has the right-of-way over windward boat (boat closest to wind).

SCORING

The winner of each race receives 0 points with competitors receiving a higher number of points based on their finishes. Remember that this is a sport in which the competitor with the least penalty points wins.

The Canadian Yachting Association, in 1972, produced a chart that outlines the scoring system designed to reward top performance. Briefly, the system stresses that it is tougher to move from second place to first than it is to move from 50th to 49th.

Under the system, second place is worth 3 points; third is worth 5.7 points; fourth is worth 8 points; fifth is worth 10 points; sixth is worth 11.7 points; and seventh is worth 13 points. Beyond seventh, the points awarded are placing plus six: if a boat finishes 20th that boat would have 26 points.

To better understand the scoring, imagine a line that curves up at the end. The degree of difficulty moves up with positions.

Each competitor can discard his worst race of the seven sailed. The gold medalist is the sailor with the least number of penalty points.

VIEWING TIPS

Aside from television, the best seat for watching a yachting race is aboard another boat near the buoys where the competitors make their turns.

The flatter the sailors keep their boats (the nearer the masts are to vertical), the faster they will travel.

When the yachts are racing downwind (the wind at their backs), the spinnakers, those multicoloured front sails that bellow out when catching wind, should be full and not flapping.

There is considerable excitement at the start. The strategic movements and near collisions add to the thrill as the boats jockey for positions while trying to hit the starting line at full speed the instant the start flag is hoisted.

All in all, yachting is a spectacle that grabs anyone who has experienced the pleasure of a sleek boat slicing through the water with the help of a brisk wind.

TECHNICAL TERMS

Sailors have a jargon all of their own. Unless one has spent a lot of time in boats, the jargon is hard to grasp for a first-time viewer. Television commentators try to avoid technical terms because the wind, and sensing its direction, is very difficult for the listener to comprehend.

PROCEDURE

Each country can enter one yacht (plus reserves) and must supply their own yacht with the exception of the Finn and Windglider classes where competitors draw for boats provided by the host country.

Because all boats must be measured to ensure they meet the rules of their International Associations, activity at the Olympic Harbour usually starts two weeks before the Games open.

The first race begins July 31, and one race per day in each event is held for four days. Spare days are then scheduled to allow the organizers the opportunity to catch up on any races postponed or

Multi-coloured sails catch the strong winds

Strategy is the key to winning

The race to the finish

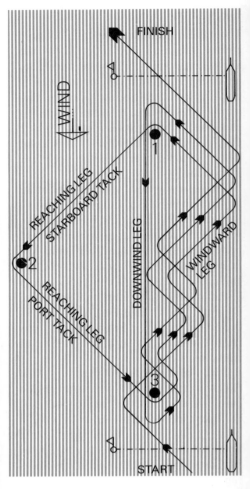

abandoned because of poor weather. The final three races are held one per day after the scheduled spare days.

The events are: Finn class, 470 class, Flying Dutchman class, Star class, Soling class, Tornado class and Windglider class.

TOP CANADIANS

Terry McLaughlin and Evert Bastet—Flying Dutchman. McLaughlin was the skipper of Canada 1 in the America's Cup trials. He won the 1980 world championship in the Flying Dutchman class and in early 1983, he and Bastet placed third in the world championships.

Terry Neilson—Finn. Neilson has been racing in the Finn class for three years. He is a world Laser champion and was fifth and sixth in the world Finn championships in 1982 and 1983.

Hans Fogh, John Kerr and Steve Calder—Soling. Fogh won an Olympic silver medal in the Flying Dutchman class in 1960 when competing for Denmark. He won the European Soling championship in 1982 and 1983.

FINN CLASS

Specifications
Length   4m50 14'9"
Beam   1m46 4'10"
Draft
Weight   145 Kg 319 lbs
Typical Use
Racer
Crew
One

470 CLASS

Specifications
Length   4m7 15.39'
Beam   1m7 5.56'
Draft   1m2 3.93'
Weight   120 Kg 264 lbs
Typical Use
Racer
Crew
Two

FLYING DUTCHMAN CLASS

Specifications
Length   6m05 19'10"
Beam   1m70 5'7"
Draft
Weight   165.5 Kg 364 lbs
Typical Use
Racer
Crew
Two

SOLING CLASS

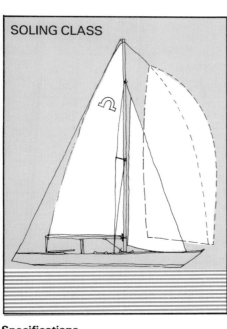

Specifications
Length   8m2 26'9"
Beam   1m9 6'3"
Draft   1m3 4'3"
Weight   1000 Kg 2200 lbs
Typical Use
Racer
Crew
Three

STAR CLASS

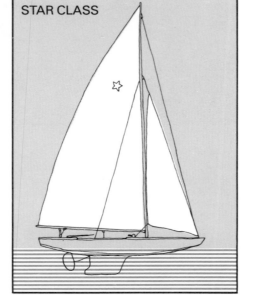

Specifications
Length   6m92 22'8"
Beam   1m73 5'8"
Draft   1m02 3'4"
Weight   677.3 Kg 1490 lbs
Typical Use
Racer
Crew
Two

TORNADO CLASS

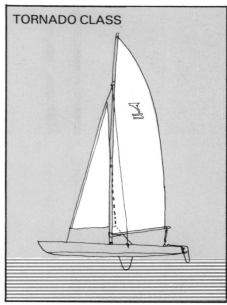

Specifications
Length   6m10 20'
Beam   3m05 10'
Draft   15cm-43cm 6"-2'6"
Weight   153.7 Kg 340 lbs
Typical Use
Racer
Crew
Two

BOARDSAILING CLASS

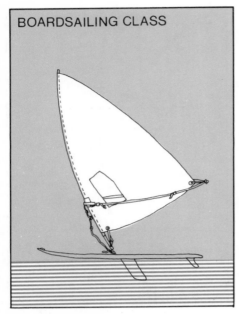

Specifications

Length	ca 12 ft
Beam	ca 2 ft 2 in.
Draft, daggerboard down	ca 2 ft
Hull weight	ca 53 lbs
Total weight	ca 66 lbs
Sail area	59 sq. ft

MEDAL WINNERS

SOLING CLASS

YEAR	PLACE	NAME	COUNTRY
1972	1	**H. Melges/ W. Bentsen/ W. Allen**	**U.S.A.**
	2	S. Wennerström/ L. Poslund/B. Knape/ S. Krook	Sweden
	3	D. Miller/J. Ekels/ P. Cote	Canada
1976	1	**P. Jensen/ V. Bandolowski/ E. Hansen**	**Denmark**
	2	J. Kolius/W. Glasgow/ R. Hoepfner	U.S.A.
	3	D. Below/M. Zachries/ O. Engelhardt	East Germany
1980	1	**P. Jensen/ V. Bandolowski/ E. Hansen**	**Denmark**
	2	B. Budnikov/ A. Budnikov/ N. Polyakov	U.S.S.R.
	3	A. Boudouris/ A. Gavrilis/ A. Rapanakis	Greece

YACHTING (international star class)

YEAR	PLACE	NAME	COUNTRY
1896- 1928		**Event not held**	
1932	1	**Gilbert Gray/ Andrew Libano, Jr.**	**U.S.A.**
	2	Colin Ratsey/ Peter Jaffe	Great Britain
	3	Gunnar Asther/ Daniel Sunden-Cullberg	Sweden
1936	1	**Peter Bischoff/ Hans-Joachim Weise**	**Germany**
	2	Arved Laurin/ Uno Wallentin	Sweden
	3	Adriaan Maas/ Willem de Vries Lentsch	Netherlands
1948	1	**Hilary Smart/ Paul Smart**	**U.S.A.**
	2	Carlos de Cardenas/ Carlos de Cardenas Jr.	Cuba
	3	Adriaan Maas/ Edward Stutterheim	Netherlands
1952	1	**Agostino Straulino/ Nicolo Rode**	**Italy**
	2	John Reid/ John Price	U.S.A.
	3	Francisco de Andrade/ Joaquim Fiuza	Portugal
1956	1	**Herbert Williams/ Lawrence Low**	**U.S.A.**
	2	Agostino Straulino/ Nicolo Rode	Italy
	3	Durward Knowles/ Sloan Farrington	Bahamas
1960	1	**Timir Pinegin/ Fyedor Shutkov**	**U.S.S.R.**
	2	Mario Quina/ José Quina	Portugal
	3	William Parks/ Robert Halperin	U.S.A.
1964	1	**Durward Knowles/ Cecil Cooke**	**Bahamas**
	2	Richard Stearns/ Lynn Williams	U.S.A.
	3	Pelle Pettersson/ Holger Sundstrom	Sweden
1968	1	**Lowell North/ Peter Barrett**	**U.S.A.**
	2	Peder Lunde/ Per Olav Wiken	Norway
	3	Franco Cavallo/ Camillo Gargano	Italy
1972	1	**David Forbes/ John Anderson**	**Australia**
	2	Pelle Pettersson/ Stellan Westerdahl	Sweden
	3	Willi Kuhweide/ Karsten Meyer	West Germany

YEAR	PLACE	NAME	COUNTRY
1976		**Event not held**	
1980	1	**Valentin Mankin/ Aleksandr Muzychenko**	**U.S.S.R.**
	2	Hubert Raudaschl/ Karl Ferstl	Austria
	3	Giorgio Gorla/ Alfio Peraboni	Italy

FLYING DUTCHMAN CLASS

YEAR	PLACE	NAME	COUNTRY
1960	1	**P. Lundejun/ B. Bervall**	**Norway**
	2	H. Fogh/O. Petersen	Denmark
	3	R. Mulka/ I. Von Bredow/ A. Kadelback	Germany
1964	1	**H. Pedersen/E. Wells**	**New Zealand**
	2	F. Musto/A. Morgan	Great Britain
	3	H. Melges/W. Bentsen	U.S.A.
1968	1	**R. Pattisson/ I. MacDonald-Smith**	**Great Britain**
	2	U. Libor/P. Naumann	Germany
	3	R. Conrad/B. Cordes	Brazil
1972	1	**R. Pattisson/ C. Davies**	**Great Britain**
	2	V. Pajot/M. Pajot	France
	3	U. Libor/P. Naumann	Germany
1976	1	**J. Diesch/E. Diesch**	**West Germany**
	2	R. Pattisson/ J. Brooke Houghton	Great Britain
	3	R. Conrad/P. Ficker	Brazil
1980	1	**A. Abascal/ M. Noguer**	**Spain**
	2	D. Wilkins/J. Wilkinson	Ireland
	3	S. Detre/Z. Detre	Hungary

INTERNATIONAL 470 CLASS

YEAR	PLACE	NAME	COUNTRY
1976	1	**F. Huebner/H. Bode**	**West Germany**
	2	A. Gorostegui/P. Millet	Spain
	3	I. Brown/I. Ruff	Australia
1980	1	**M. Soares/E. Penido**	**Brazil**
	2	J. Borowski/ E. Swensson	East Germany
	3	J. Lindgren/G. Tallberg	Finland

FINN CLASS

YEAR	PLACE	NAME	COUNTRY
1956	1	**P. Elvström**	**Denmark**
	2	A. Nelis	Belgium
	3	J. Marvin	U.S.A.
1960	1	**P. Elvström**	**Denmark**
	2	A. Tschutschelov	U.S.S.R.
	3	A. Nelis	Belgium
1964	1	**K. Kuhwelde**	**Germany**
	2	P. Barrett	U.S.A.
	3	H. Wind	Denmark
1968	1	**V. Mankin**	**U.S.S.R.**
	2	H. Raudaschl	Austria
	3	F. Albarelli	Italy
1972	1	**S. Maury**	**France**
	2	I. Hatzipavlis	Greece
	3	V. Potapov	U.S.S.R.
1976	1	**J. Schumann**	**East Germany**
	2	A. Balashov	U.S.S.R.
	3	J. Bertrand	Australia
1980	1	**E. Rechardt**	**Finland**
	2	W. Mayrhofer	Austria
	3	A. Balashov	U.S.S.R.

TORNADO CLASS

YEAR	PLACE	NAME	COUNTRY
1976	1	**R. White/J. Osborn**	**Great Britain**
	2	D. McFaull/ M. Rothwell	U.S.A.
	3	J. Spengler/ J. Schmall	West Germany
1980	1	**A. Welter/ L. Bjorkstrom**	**Brazil**
	2	P. Due/P. Kjergard	Denmark
	3	G. Marstrom/ J. Ragnarsson	Sweden

BASEBALL

EVENT DATE					DODGER STADIUM
JULY	31	2 games—preliminaries	AUGUST	4	2 games—preliminaries
AUGUST	1	2 games—preliminaries		5	2 games—preliminaries
	2	2 games—preliminaries		6	2 games—semifinals
	3	2 games—preliminaries		7	2 games—finals

Baseball is a demonstration sport at this year's Olympic Games.

Dodger Stadium, the site of the 1984 Olympic baseball competition

HISTORY

Americans refer to baseball as their national pastime. True, the game is deeply embedded in that country's history. But there is nothing parochial about the game, which is now being played in many corners of the world. Amateur baseball can be found in Italy, North and South Korea, Colombia, Venezuela, Cuba, Mexico, the Dominican Republic, Taiwan, Brazil, Canada, and a dozen other countries.

The heart of baseball, though, is the professional game in North America with 26 teams in the American and National Leagues. The American League has a team in Toronto, the Blue Jays, while the Montreal Expos are in the National League.

Professional baseball also is flourishing in Japan, which has two major leagues. Although rated below the American and National Leagues in player ability, the Japanese game is adding to its reputation each year. Some players are imported from North America (each team is limited to two imported players). The North Americans have aided the sport in Japan but Japan's real strength comes from the patience to wait as its own talent develops.

Talent may be found anywhere a boy plays with a bat and a ball. It could be in the well manicured infields of Little Leagues in the United States or the rough, pebbled sandlots of Latin America.

Although baseball was played in Latin America for many years, the players did not see much hope for major league careers. That changed when Jackie Robinson broke the colour barrier with the Montreal Royals in 1946 and joined the major-league Brooklyn Dodgers in 1947. Until then, major-league baseball was limited to whites. American blacks and Latin American Hispanics could only look forward to playing as professionals in the Negro leagues.

The influx of blacks and Latin-American players has steadily grown, and now most major league teams have many such players either on their 25-man roster or in their minor league systems. The achievements of the Latin Americans has helped promote the game in their countries.

Cuba, in particular, was a good source for major-league talent in the 1950s. That flow dried up, however, when Fidel Castro took over the island in 1958. Although he stopped the movement of Cubans to the majors, Castro, a former pitcher, has supported the game in his country. Today, Cuba is the dominant country in world amateur championship play.

Today, much of the success of professional baseball must be attributed to television. The major leagues have lined up long-term, lucrative packages from the television networks. Some clubs are also enriching themselves with private pay-TV deals. Television money makes it possible for the Expos to pay catcher Gary Carter $2 million a year. The Expos have an annual TV revenue of $12 million.

Money, and the invention of jet aircraft it seems, have steered much of baseball's recent history. The prospect of greater profits has led to the shifting of team franchises, the most notable being the move to Los Angeles by the Brooklyn Dodgers and the move to San Francisco by the New York Giants in 1958. The Dodgers have become one of the wealthiest clubs in baseball and last year averaged about 45,000 fans for each of its 81 home games.

The Olympic demonstration baseball events will be held at Dodger Stadium in the Chavez Ravine area of Los Angeles. Major league scouts will be in the stands rating the talent for possible signings.

By nature, baseball is a low-key sport and generally free of the violence that seems to permeate other sports. There have been brawls, usually precipitated when a pitcher hits a batter with a ball or when a sliding base runner slides hard into a player covering the base.

One of the beautiful things about baseball is that it has been able to retain much of its implemented character. Aside from the "designated hitter" rule, implemented by the American League in 1973, the game has stayed relatively the same for more than 100 years. The "designated hitter" rule allows the team manager to use a player to bat for the pitcher. The National League still requires the pitcher to bat.

The origins of baseball are debatable. Some historians say the game was the brainchild of Abner Doubleday in 1839 in Cooperstown, N.Y. The city is now the home of the Baseball Hall of Fame. Other historians claim baseball owes its origins to the English game of rounders, which has been played in several parts of the United States prior to 1839.

The establishment of the Knickerbocker Club in New York in 1845 was a boost for baseball. The club promoted the game's development, and in 1846, it played another New York City team under what is believed to be the first set of rules written for the sport.

Amateur baseball was jolted in 1869 when the Red Stockings team in Cincinnati declared it was going professional and would pay its players through increased ticket prices. The "Reds" then took their team on tour. It was such a great success, concerned amateur officials felt professionalism would destroy amateur baseball.

Far-sighted promoters felt the future of the game was in professional players. In 1876, the National League came into being and was followed by the American League in 1900. Three years later, the two leagues had their champions meet in the first World Series. Boston, of the AL, defeated Pittsburgh of the NL, five games to three.

The 1919 World Series was to give baseball its darkest hour. After the Cincinnati Reds of the NL defeated the AL's Chicago White Sox, five games to three, charges were levelled that eight of the White Sox players had conspired to throw the game. A year after the charges were first mentioned, American League President Ban Johnson suspended White Soxers Joe Jackson, Oscar Felsch, Arnold Gandil, George Weaver, Charles Risberg, Fred McMullin, Eddie Cicotte and Claude Williams from organized baseball.

Such isolated cases as the "Black Sox" scandal have failed to hurt the overall integrity and popularity of the game.

The home-run hitting heroics of Babe Ruth and many subsequent stars eradicated memory of the White Sox scandal and the game has flourished. Baseball has had many outstanding players since Ruth such as Joe DiMaggio, Henry Aaron, and in recent years, Reggie Jackson.

GENERAL DESCRIPTION

Baseball is a skilful game played on a field with nine players on each team. A bat and a ball are the key components.

The field is made up of two parts, the "infield" and the "outfield." The infield is where home plate and three bases are located and is often called a diamond. It is 90 feet from home plate to first base and the same distance between the other bases.

Home plate has outlined batter boxes on either side where the batter stands as he faces the pitch thrown by the pitcher, who is on a slightly elevated mound (up to 18 inches), 60 feet 6 inches away in the centre of the infield.

The catcher stands behind the batter. His job is to catch the balls that are not hit by the batter. The other players on the field are the first baseman, second baseman, third baseman, shortstop, left fielder, centre fielder and right fielder.

The outfielders, of course, play in the "outfield" which varies in size, although most modern baseball stadiums are being standardized for professional and amateur play. Most "outfields" are restricted by fences or stands.

Once the defensive players take the field, the umpires signal the start of the game by yelling, "play ball." Usually there are four umpires, but in classics such as the professional World Series there are six. The home plate umpire is the umpire chief and his duty is to call the balls and strikes along with the plays in his vicinity.

The other umpires are usually stationed at the foul lines near first and third base and near second base. The line umpires signal if a batted ball stayed in the field of play or was "foul," and the first base umpire signals "safe" or "out" when a batted ground ball is picked up by an infielder and thrown to first base. A batter is "out" if the ball reaches first base before he does on a ground ball.

Each team is allowed three "outs" in its half of the inning. Each team bats in an inning and games are scheduled for nine innings. Extra innings, however, can be used to end tie games.

For the team at bat, the object is to score as many runs as possible until the three "outs" are registered. A "run" is scored when the batter safely works his way from home plate, around the bases and back to home plate. This is not easy. The batter may face 100-mile-an-hour pitches. In addition, he may face pitches that suddenly curve or drop unexpectedly. The batter has only about four-fifths of a second to make up his mind to swing at the pitch.

If the batter does hit the ball, the defence comes into play. Skilled infielders and fleet outfielders grab many of the batted balls and turn them into "outs." Outs are made by throwing the batted ground ball to first base before the batter reaches the base, or by catching the ball on the fly.

If the batter cleanly hits the pitch and reaches first base safely, he is credited with a "single." If he reaches second base off the hit, he has a "double" and if he makes it to third base he is credited with a "triple." If the batter is able to circle the bases, he has a "home run" which generally comes by hitting the ball over the outfield fence although "inside-the-park" homers do occur at times.

The batter can also reach base on an "error" by a defensive player. An "error" occurs when a player does not make a play or an "out" on a batted ball that in the opinion of the scorer should have been handled cleanly.

The batter can also reach base on a "walk," which happens when the batter has watched four balls being thrown outside the "strike zone." The "strike zone" is an area the width of the home plate which is 17-inches wide and between imaginary horizontal lines from the batter's knees to his armpits. The ruling on the pitches comes from the home plate umpire.

The pitcher, however, can make an "out" by throwing three pitches into the "strike zone." Should a batter foul tip or swing and miss a pitched ball, the call by the umpire is a strike. A third strike, however, cannot be called on foul-tipped pitches.

If in the case of an errant pitch the batter is struck by the ball, he is automatically awarded first base. The batter is declared a "hit batsman" and is not credited with an official time at bat.

The official times at bat are used to calculate the player's "batting average," which is the number of times he has hit safely in relation to the number of times he has batted. For the pitcher, the earned run average (ERA) is important. The ERA is the ratio of earned runs charged to the pitcher and the number of innings he pitched.

PROCEDURE

The United States and five other countries will participate in the demonstration of baseball at the 1984 Olympic Games in Los Angeles. The games will be played at Dodger Stadium, home of the Los Angeles Dodgers.

Joining the United States in the round-robin tournament will be South Korea, which gets in for winning the last world amateur championship; Taiwan, the winner of an Asian playoff; Italy, winner of the European Championship in 1983; Cuba which won the 1983 Pan-American Games title; and Nicaragua, the runnerup in the Pan-American Games.

Canada missed an opportunity to participate in the baseball demonstration because it did not win a medal at the Pan-American Games.

TECHNICAL TERMS

Base hit — when a batter reaches first base or any succeeding base on a ball hit into fair territory (field of play).

An Error — a miscue that permits a batter to reach or advance a base.

Strikeout — credited to the pitcher after a batter takes three strikes. Strikes are called by the umpire when the pitch crosses the plate in the strike zone (an area designated by an imaginary line at the knees to an imaginary line at the armpits).

Base of balls — a batter is awarded first base when the pitcher throws four balls outside the strike zone.

Putout — is credited to a fielder who makes an out on the batter, either by catching a fly ball, fielding a ball hit on the ground and throwing to a base before the runner arrives, or by tagging the runner off the base with the ball.

Run batted in — is credited to a batter when the ball he hits scores a runner from one of the other bases.

Stolen base — is credited to a base runner when he advances unaided by other action such as a ground ball or base hit.

Double play — happens when two base runners are put out in a single play after the ball is put into play with a base hit or ground ball.

Umpire — official in charge of the game. The home plate umpire calls the balls and strikes. There may be as many as six umpires in a game to rule on plays in the infield and outfield as well as at the plate.

EQUIPMENT

Bat — is made of one piece of solid wood or from a block of wood consisting of two or more pieces bonded together in such a way that the grain direction is parallel to the length of the bat. It can be as long as 42 inches and must not exceed a diameter of 2-3/4 inches at its thickest part. Tape or another sticky substance may be applied to the handle to permit a better grip, but should not be higher than 18 inches up the handle.

Ball — a cork centre wrapped with yarn and then covered with cowhide or horsehide and stitched tightly. White in colour, the ball weighs about five ounces and has a circumference of about nine inches.

Field — can be of various dimensions, usually enclosed. The bases must be 90 feet apart with the pitcher's mound 60 feet 6 inches away from home plate.

Dress — players wear uniforms and shoes with cleats for traction when playing on a grass field. Rubberized footware is used for play on artificial turf.

Gloves — vary according to position and personal taste. The catcher, for instance, uses a thickly-padded "mitt" to handle the speedy pitches thrown by the pitcher. Infielders prefer wide, lightweight gloves while the first baseman uses a thicker, fingerless glove to snare the throws from the infielders.

Shin guards — plastic guards wrapped around a catcher's shins for protection against foul-tipped balls.

Chest protector — worn around the chest by the catcher as protection against foul-tipped balls.

Mask — worn to protect the head from foul-tipped balls, often made of three metal strands attached to a frame.

Bases — 15-inch squares of padded material that runners must touch when scoring a run.

Sliding safely into second base

Delivering a blistering fast ball

TENNIS

HISTORY

Tennis, one of the most popular games of this generation, has had an in-and-out history with the International Olympic Committee. It was included in the Olympic Games programme from 1896 through 1924, and then was dropped. Perhaps, the IOC felt the amateur competitions were too prominent or the game was the private preserve of the wealthy.

In the boom that followed the Second World War, tennis grew as swiftly as inflation. It no longer remained a game for the monied people. Tennis courts sprang up in thousands of public parks around the world.

As interest increased, tennis administrators once again sought to have the sport included in the Olympic programme. The IOC allowed it to be demonstrated in the 1968 Games in Mexico City, possibly believing its growth was just a fad. But the growth continued, and after tennis is demonstrated at the 1984 Olympic Games in Los Angeles, it will be fully restored to the programme during the 1988 Games in Seoul, South Korea.

The origins of the name and game are debatable. There have been strong claims from both England and France, where early versions of tennis as we know it were played seven hundred years ago.

The Canadian Lawn Tennis Association was founded in 1890. One year later, the U.S. Lawn Tennis Association was formed and a standard set of rules was written.

The sport was given an international boost when it was added to the programme for the modern Olympic Games in Athens in 1896. By this time, the tennis rivalry between England and the United States was starting to build. It increased in 1900 when the American Dwight Davis, a civic leader and tennis patron, offered a challenge cup to represent tennis supremacy between the two countries. A few years later, other nations were allowed to compete for the cup.

The Davis Cup became a prestigious amateur event and the foremost team competition. Yet, it was a relative newcomer when compared to the Wimbledon tournament which started with a men's singles event in 1877. Women's play at Wimbledon started in 1884.

Both Wimbledon and the Davis Cup competitions had stringent rules concerning amateur play. But professional tennis was catching on and it soon became apparent amateur play would not last, especially after the Second World War.

The professional ranks started innocently enough in 1927 when the U.S. Professional Lawn Tennis Association was formed. The purists at first, didn't consider the pro game a threat to the amateur one but they were slowly forced to change their minds. It soon became clear that amateur tournaments were mere training grounds for players bent on professional careers.

Wimbledon and Davis Cup officials, who tried desperately to keep their events free from the play-for-pay players, soon knew it was a losing battle. In 1968, Wimbledon opened its door to professionals. The Davis Cup soon followed Wimbledon's lead, for most of the top players were pros. With peace restored between the professional promoters and the amateur ones by declaring the "open" tournaments, tennis officials settled back and watched the sport grow. Increasingly, tennis made its niche in the world of athletics.

As the numbers of players soared, there were those ready to take advantage of the game. With the help of some Texas oil money anted by Lamar Hunt, World Championship Tennis (WCT) was formed for men and a series of international pro events were started in 1971. Shortly after, the women's pro league started to flourish.

These events drew the best from every country. Playing for a king-sized purse were such talents as Australian John Newcombe, Ilie Nastase of Rumania and Billie Jean King of the United States, to be followed later, by Bjorn Borg of Sweden, Martina Navratilova and Ivan Lendl of Czechoslovakia, Yannick Noah of France, and Tracy Austin, Jimmy Connors and John McEnroe of the United States.

The health of tennis has never been better.

GENERAL DESCRIPTION

Tennis is a game of both power and finesse. One may overcome the other at times, but the best players are solid in both aspects of the game.

Tennis is played with a racquet and a ball on a court divided by a net which is 3-feet high in the middle and 3 feet 6 inches at the sides. The game may be played in either the singles, doubles or mixed doubles format.

The object is to hit the ball over the net, landing on the court surface. A point is scored when the opponent is unable to "return" the shot and keep the ball in play.

Scoring in tennis is unique. Each player starts out at "love" or no score. The first point scored is posted as "15" and a second point ups the total to "30." A third point takes the total to "40" and a fourth point wins the game. Should the score be tied at 15-15 or 30-30, the announcer will often refer to the score as being 15-all or 30-all. When the score is tied at 40-40 it is referred to as a "deuce." "Deuce" means that a player must have a margin of two points to win the game. The first point scored after a "deuce" is called an "advantage" and if the score again is tied, the situation reverts back to "deuce."

Six games make up a "set" and a match is made up of a player winning three sets in a best-of-five series or two sets in a best-of-three series. Sets must be won by a margin of two games.

To avoid extremely long sets, the "tiebreaker" comes into play when the players find themselves tied at six games apiece. The winner of each rally earns one point, and the first player (or pairs) to reach seven points with at least a two-point edge wins the tiebreaker. Play must continue until the two-point margin is established.

The court may be either grass or of synthetic material. It is 78-feet long and 36-feet wide and has markings for single (78 by 27 feet) and doubles play.

In both singles and doubles play, the right to serve is retained for a whole game by the individual or pairs. In singles, the player starts serving from behind his or her right-hand court diagonally across the court. For subsequent points the serve is alternated from the right to the left side of the court.

In doubles, the serves must also be diagonal ones. The server must alternate from the right and left court areas so that he or she serves to each of the opposing players.

So that no player or pairs of players have court advantage, there is a shifting of ends. The players change ends at the conclusion of all odd-numbered games (one, three, five, etc.).

PROCEDURE

The format for the demonstration of tennis at the Olympic Games in Los Angeles was established by the International Tennis Federation (ITF) and will consist solely of singles events for men and women.

Professional players are eligible even though there is no prize money or medals. The players must be in the 20-and-under age group (born in 1964 or later).

The ITF format calls for 32 players in each of the men's and women's divisions. It will be a single elimination competition with the winners advancing until there are two finalists.

As host nation, the United States will be allowed four players in each of the men's and women's divisions. Apart from the United States, no more than two men and two women may be selected from each country.

The ITF will try to fill 20 of the berths in each of the men's and women's divisions with players nominated by national associations. Those players will be taken from the list of world rankings. The final eight spots in each of the men's and women's divisions will be chosen by the ITF from its 1983 world junior rankings.

VIEWING TIPS

All the top players have what is called a "big serve," meaning they can drive the ball over the net at a tremendous speed. Some men have hit the ball at speeds up to 150 miles an hour.

There's little time for a "return" by an opponent facing such a shot, so he or she stays alert and perhaps moves around a bit, anticipating where the ball might be hit. Some of the big servers commonly score an "ace," a point scored when the ball is driven past an opponent and there is no return.

Once the ball is "returned" the key items to watch for are the ground strokes; the forehand and backhand strokes. While most players are adept at both, one is sometimes weaker than the other.

Competitors try to play to the weakness of the opponent. Some players have countered exploitation of a weak backhand by gripping the racquet with two hands. This enables more power or strength for the return but has the disadvantage of limited reach.

The placing of shots to take advantage of an opponent's weakness is not restricted to power. Technical players often rely on "drop" or "lob" shots to score points, rattle their opponents and break their rhythm. A "drop" shot occurs when the ball is dropped just over the net with a soft touch of the racquet. This type of shot forces a player in the backcourt to charge the net in order to make the return. Many a player has raced up to the net and safely returned a "drop" shot only to see his or her opponent blast the ball back to the area that had been vacated. Some players prefer to "lob" the ball into the backcourt and force their opponents to run for the high, low velocity shot if they hope for a return. The "drop" and "lob" shots are important weapons in a tactical game. Endurance is obviously required when such tactics are used.

Power is more noticeable in the men's game, but in recent years, with the emergence of Martina Navratilova as the No. 1 player, who is Czechoslovakian born and now a U.S. citizen, power has also become an important part of the women's game.

TECHNICAL TERMS

Forehand — for a righthander, the stroke that takes place from the right side of the body. For most players, the forehand is an attacking weapon.

Backhand — for a righthander, the stroke that takes place from the left side of the body. Once considered a defensive stroke, the backhand has become an effective weapon for many players. The two-handed grip is common these days.

Deuce — a term used to say the score is tied at 40-all.

Advantage in — means the point has been won by the server after "deuce" has been reached.

Advantage out — means the server has lost the point after "deuce" has been reached.

Service fault — when the ball is incorrectly delivered or lands outside the court. It is also a fault if the server misses

the ball in his or her attempt to strike it. In the case of doubles play, a fault may be called if the ball strikes the server's partner on a serve. In the case of two consecutive faults, a server loses a point.

Let — if the properly-served ball hits the net before falling into an opponent's court, a "let" is called. The receiver is not required to play it and a new serve is taken. A "let" can also be called if the ball is served before an opponent is ready.

Chair umpire — officiates the match and usually sits in an elevated structure off to the side of the court.

Linesmen — declare if the ball stayed in play or landed beyond the court. There are 11 linesmen in a fully officiated match.

Rally — a series of shots returned across the net.

Volley — a shot hit before the ball touches the ground.

EQUIPMENT

Racquet — it must not be longer than 31 inches or more than 12 1/2 inches in width. The hitting surface consists of strings fastened to the frame and the hitting surface must not be more than 15 1/2-inches long and 11 1/2-inches wide.

Balls — are 2 1/2 to 2 5/8 inches in diameter and must weigh 2 1/16 ounces. They must meet bouncing requirements and be seamless. Yellow balls have come into play as they are easier for spectators to follow, although traditional white balls are still used on occasion.

Dress — women wear short dresses or tops with skirts and shorts. Men wear shirts and shorts. Both wear white rubber-soled shoes.

Court — is 78-feet long and 36-feet wide (used for doubles and mixed pairs). The singles court is marked inside the main court and is 27-feet wide but uses the full length of 78 feet. Markings designate serve areas and service lines. The courts can be made of synthetic material (such as asphalt) or grass, as in Wimbledon.

TOP CANADIANS

Canada will probably have only one representative in Los Angeles, Carling Bassett of Toronto, who hit the play-for-pay ranks in 1983 with great fanfare and promise. She also meets the age limitations.

CBC COMMENTATORS

BRIAN WILLIAMS

ERNIE AFAGANIS

BOB McDEVITT

JOHN WELLS

STEVE ARMITAGE

TED REYNOLDS

DON WITTMAN

BRIAN WILLIAMS

In 1982, Brian Williams was the recipient of the Foster Hewitt Award for excellence in sports broadcasting at the ACTRA Awards presentations. It was the second time he has won the coveted award.

Born in Winnipeg, Manitoba, Williams began his broadcasting career in Grand Rapids, Michigan, in 1968. From 1970 to 1973, he covered sports and news in private radio in Toronto and in 1974, joined CBC Toronto and the CBC network.

Williams' credits include baseball and horse racing coverage plus basketball coverage at the 1976 Olympics. In 1978, he was voted the outstanding sports commentator at the Commonwealth Games in Edmonton.

Williams is now one of the busier commentators on the CBC Sports' staff, hosting CBC Sportsweekend, Halftime, CBC's half-time CFL programme, World Cup Skiing, Canadian Grand Prix, and a host of other sports.

Williams may well establish himself as the premier sports commentator in the country this summer as he hosts CBC's planned 180 hours of coverage of the Summer Olympics from Los Angeles.

ERNIE AFAGANIS

There are few sportscasters in Canada who have been at the forefront of as many major sporting events as Ernie Afaganis.

A native of Lethbridge, Alberta, Afaganis joined CBC Edmonton in 1961 and was involved in the coverage of local, national and international sports events, including the Pan-Am Games in Winnipeg in 1967 and in Colombia in 1971. In 1975, he was coordinator of radio and television for the Canada Winter Games in Lethbridge and the following year was on-air host for CBC's internationally acclaimed coverage of the 1976 Summer Olympics from Montreal. He was host for CBC Television at the 1978 Commonwealth Games in Edmonton, the 1980 Winter Olympics at Lake Placid, New York, the 1982 Commonwealth Games in Brisbane, Australia, and the World University Games from Edmonton in 1983.

Afaganis' considerable experience will make him an invaluable commentator in Los Angeles in 1984.

STEVE ARMITAGE

Steve Armitage was born in High Wycombe, England in 1944 and came to Canada in 1953. He attended St. Mary's University in Halifax, where he received a bachelor of arts degree in political science and philosophy. His university football career led him into playing semi-professional ball.

Armitage began working for the CBC on a part-time basis in 1965, writing late-night sportscasts for radio and television in Halifax. His first on-camera experience as a commentator was during the Canada Games in Halifax in 1969. He joined CBC-TV Sports full-time in Halifax in 1970, and went to CBC British Columbia in 1974.

Armitage's television credits include Canadian Open Golf, Peter Jackson Classic, four Canada Games telecasts, the 1978 and 1982 Commonwealth Games, and Hockey Night in Canada. Armitage was praised for his work in 1982 on CBC's World Cup Soccer coverage and was the recipient of the Foster Hewitt Award for excellence in sports broadcasting in the spring of 1983.

BOB McDEVITT

Bob McDevitt is familiar to Canadian television viewers as co-host of Inside Baseball and as a commentator on CBC's Olympic coverage in Tokyo, Munich, Mexico and Montreal.

Born in Montreal, McDevitt attended Strathcona Academy and Montreal Catholic High before joining Canada's merchant marine to see the world. He began his broadcasting career at CHNO in Sudbury, Ontario in 1952. From there he went to CJQX, Quebec City and then to CJAD Montreal in 1954. He joined CBC Montreal as a sportscaster in 1961 and has since become one of Montreal's best-known broadcasting personalities.

McDevitt is an ex-Golden Glove middleweight boxer, an ace golfer, a bowler and a skier.

TED REYNOLDS

There are few Canadian broadcasters